Homebrewing

3rd Edition

by Marty Nachel

Homebrewing For Dummies®, 3rd Edition

Published by: **John Wiley & Sons, Inc.**, 111 River Street, Hoboken, NJ 07030-5774, www.wiley.com

For general information on our other products and services, please contact our Customer Care Department within the U.S. at 877-762-2974, outside the U.S. at 317-572-3993, or fax 317-572-4002. For technical support, please visit https://hub.wiley.com/community/support/dummies.

Wiley publishes in a variety of print and electronic formats and by print-on-demand. Some material included with standard print versions of this book may not be included in e-books or in print-on-demand. If this book refers to media such as a CD or DVD that is not included in the version you purchased, you may download this material at http://booksupport.wiley.com. For more information about Wiley products, visit www.wiley.com.

Library of Congress Control Number: 2022939032

ISBN 978-1-119-89127-7 (pbk); ISBN 978-1-119-89128-4 (ebk); ISBN 978-1-119-89129-1 (ebk)

SKY10034958_062422

Contents at a Glance

Table of Contents

Introduction

I'm just a humble homebrewer,
I've got no shiny copper.
I only brew five gallons a batch —
I just boil 'er up and hop 'er.

No foil labels, no fancy caps,
just plain glass bottle and stopper.
I pay no tax — just brew and relax,
then grab a beer and pop 'er!

Homebrewing is one of the most sublime hobbies. Like growing vegetables in your backyard garden or baking bread in your own kitchen, homebrewing enables you to recapture the hands-on rusticity of the olden days while producing something that's an absolute delight to consume. Just as nothing can substitute for layering a salad with tomatoes and cucumbers picked fresh from your own garden, nothing is as gratifying as sipping a fresh beer brewed on your own kitchen stove.

In addition to the personal enjoyment you can gain from swigging your own beer, you can't deny the deep sense of gratification that accompanies the kudos and congratulations of friends, family, and coworkers who equally enjoy your homebrewing efforts. Perhaps best of all is the widespread recognition that comes from winning awards — often quite valuable — in acknowledgment of your brewing prowess and expertise. This list of benefits is a just a glimmer of what homebrewing is like today.

The hobby hasn't always been this way. Modern homebrewing in the United States wasn't even a legal enterprise until 1979. Even after it became legal, homebrew still bore the disparaging mantle of *bathtub booze* and other such pejoratives, a residue of the illicit beer-making days during national prohibition.

Fortunately, we've come full circle. Homebrewers have been rightly credited with being the catalyst of the American brewing renaissance that started in the 1980's and hasn't abated since. The early homebrew pioneering spirits, longing for a beer more satisfying than the homogenous mass-market brands, were the ones who went on to open the first of the craft breweries that are so popular today. And as more of these craft-brewing operations open across the country and throughout the world, they expose more and more people to small-brewery quality and diversity. Inspired by the craft-brewing ethic and enthusiasm, many more people are now interested in brewing beer at home.

Following in footsteps far greater than my own, I began brewing my own beer in 1985. I didn't start homebrewing for lack of good beer, because plenty of good, locally available commercial beers were available. I chose to brew my own beer because I wanted to personally experience the magic of the beer-making process. After I started homebrewing, I quickly became hooked and realized only much later that as much as I was consuming the hobby of homebrewing, it was also consuming me.

Homebrewers tend to develop a love and enjoyment and respect for beer beyond its simple consumption. Homebrewers are ethereally connected to both the brewing past and the brewing future; they're champions of both a medieval art and an advanced science. Plus, the homebrewing community-at-large shares a common sense of purpose — of sharing information and ideas, of promoting education as part of the hobby, and of enriching and enlightening the general public by improving its collective perception of beer.

And despite anything you may have seen or heard or assumed on your own, facial hair isn't a prerequisite to being a good homebrewer. On the other hand, growing wild hair now and again is strongly encouraged among those who brew their own beer at home.

About This Book

I've written this book primarily with brewer wannabes in mind — those who have always stood on the sidelines wondering what it's like to play in the game. But unlike baseball, football, soccer, or any other team game of physical ability, homebrewing is more like a singles card game — one in which you can improve your skill through repetitive play (and at your own pace).

But this book isn't just a primer on the joy of playing Solitaire (if you'll excuse the analogy). This book tells you everything you need to know about this particular deck of cards, how to shuffle the deck, how to deal the cards, how to play various card games at different levels of difficulty, and finally, how to find and associate with others who share your interest.

Unlike other how-to books, *Homebrewing For Dummies*, 3rd Edition is arranged in such a way that you need not read it in order, cover to cover. Using the many cross-references provided within the text enables you to jump around to those sections that are of greatest interest to you. Please notice, however, that certain chapters deal with topics that depend on your having read some previous chapters for basic comprehension. But don't worry; where this sort of thing occurs, I make the point clear.

Whether you've ever made a homebrew — or even tasted one, for that matter — isn't important for you to read and appreciate this book. Even with so many different beers to make and so many different ways to make them, you should eventually be able to master them all after reading *Homebrewing For Dummies*, 3rd Edition. This book not only provides all the parameters of tried-and-true beer styles but also encourages you, the reader, to go off on your own brewing tangent. Be bold, be daring; invent a beer style all your own — just be ready and willing to share it with others.

Foolish Assumptions

I wrote this book with some thoughts about you in mind. Here's what I assume about you, my reader:

- You like beer.
- You want to brew your own beer at home.
- You weren't convinced brewing good beer at home was possible.
- You want to impress your friends and family with your new hobby.
- You've already brewed your own beer but want to make it even better.
- You're already a homebrewer, but you're looking for all the latest tips, trends, and recipes available.
- You view homebrewing as a first step to professional brewing and financial independence. (You're not the first person to think this!)

I use many additional conventions throughout this book, and I think I should explain them to you:

- **All recipes and text assume that the batch size is 5 gallons:** Unless I say otherwise, you can assume that all recipes create a 5-gallon batch of beer. The same goes for any other times that I discuss quantities or aspects of a batch of beer.

» **The text and recipes use U.S. measurements:** Every weight and liquid measurement is given in standard pounds, gallons, and ounces. See the Cheat Sheet at `www.dummies.com` for conversions.

» **All beer styles and beer-style parameters are based on the Beer Judge Certification Program Beer Style Guidelines:** This hierarchical listing of major beer-style classifications and substyles (which you can find on this book's Cheat Sheet at `www.dummies.com`) was established by the BJCP for recipe formulation and evaluation purposes.

Icons Used in This Book

In keeping with the traditional *For Dummies* style, this book uses icons — those little pictures in the margins — to serve as guideposts for various kinds of information. You can use them to pick out information customized to your needs.

TECHNICAL STUFF

Explains technical subjects that are important only if you're really getting into homebrewing (or you're a techno-head). Those who are neither of these can skip these sections altogether.

TIP

Shows pointers, suggestions, and recommendations that can make your homebrewing go more smoothly.

REMEMBER

Draws your attention to important information you should remember for future reference. Sometimes it flags material that I've already mentioned elsewhere but that you should read again (for good measure).

WARNING

Kinda self-explanatory. You might want to read these and take them seriously so you don't botch a batch.

Beyond the Book

This book's Cheat Sheet offers The Beer Judge Certification Program's list of the world's beer styles, a list of homebrewing abbreviations and slang, a table of common metric conversions for homebrewers, and a lengthy discussion of ingredients. You can get it simply by going to `www.dummies.com` and searching for *Homebrewing For Dummies Cheat Sheet.*

Where to Go from Here

Now that you have a quick overview of what to expect from this book, you can begin your trek through the world of homebrewing. Go ahead, flip through the book or begin with page 1 — it doesn't matter to me. All I ask is that you have fun with your hobby and never take yourself or your brew too seriously.

Still here? What are you waiting for?

1 First Things First

IN THIS PART . . .

Become acquainted with the homebrewing hobby and those who practice it.

Get a feel for the homebrewing timeline.

Prepare for that first brew day.

Familiarize yourself with the equipment needed to brew beer at home.

Clean and sanitize your home brewery to make sure your beer is as good as it can be.

» Do I have what it takes?

Chapter 1
Welcome to the Wonderful World of Wort

One vexing question for the homebrewer wannabe is "why go through the trouble of brewing beer at home when I can just buy it at the local store?"

Well, for starters, brewing beer at home is no trouble if you enjoy what you're doing, and with the help of this book, you can certainly enjoy homebrewing. Secondly, homebrewed beer can be every bit as good as — if not better than — a lot of commercial beer, with more flavor and character than most. In fact, avoiding mass-market beer was the original inspiration for homebrewing. Thirdly, homebrewing is a hobby that pays many dividends, from having your own house brand of beer to hanging colorful award ribbons on your wall to earning the undying admiration of your beer-drinking buddies. (***Warning:*** Admiration can be addictive.)

In this chapter, I give you an overview of the topics covered in detail in the rest of the book as well as a bit of the history of homebrewing and its recent surge in popularity.

Homebrewers Abound!

Becoming a homebrewer means you're in good company. According to the American Homebrewers Association (AHA) in Boulder, Colorado, an estimated 1.1 million homebrewers are brewing in the United States. That's a lot of brewers. And the hobby continues to expand every year. Recent estimates indicate that over 1,000 brick-and-mortar and online homebrew supply retailers and over 2,000 homebrewing clubs have popped up in response to homebrewing's growing popularity. Most of these clubs are small, but the national group (AHA) boasts 19,000 members. Homebrewing associations are growing worldwide, too.

The explosive growth in homebrewing has been closely mirrored by a tremendous increase in small, craft breweries in the U.S. — this is no coincidence. Since homebrewing became legal over 40 years ago, the interest in hand-crafted beer has blossomed, and over 9,000 brewpubs and craft breweries have opened in this same period of time. The growth in the American craft-brewing industry has been so dynamic that even European countries with long and respected brewing histories have had no choice but to sit up and take notice. Small, craft breweries have been opening up around the world.

In the more than 35 years that I've been involved in homebrewing, I've had the pleasure of meeting and speaking with hundreds of people who share a common interest in beer and homebrewing. Here are some of the reasons so many folks seem to enjoy brewing their own beer:

- To participate in the do-it-yourself homebrewing trend — what other hobby allows you to drink the fruits of your labor?
- To make beers comparable to hard-to-find craft beers and expensive classic brews from around the world.
- To share homebrewed beer with friends and family members (beware of mooches).

All the Right Stuff

New homebrewers are no different from other hobbyists; they're champing at the bit (or foaming at the mouth) to get started with their hobby. Although this unbridled enthusiasm is good, jumping headlong into the unknown isn't. You need to incorporate some degree of planning into your decision to homebrew. What kind of equipment do I need, and where can I find it? How much time do I need to dedicate to this whole process? What kind of ingredients do I need, and where can I buy them? What other preparations do I need to make? What do I do with the beer when I finish brewing? Can I take a homebrewer's deduction on the IRS 1040 long form? These are the questions you need to ask (and answer!) before you make the plunge. Conveniently, all the answers you need are right here in this book. (And no, the IRS doesn't give a homebrewer's tax deduction. Sorry.)

Gathering the equipment you need

Like having the right tools to do work around your house, having the right equipment for brewing your beer is essential.

Although the equipment needed at the beginner level is relatively inexpensive, you may want to try your hand at brewing beer without the cost commitment of buying the equipment first. If you happen to know of other homebrewers in your area, ask to participate in one of their brews so you can get a feel for the hobby, or search out local homebrew clubs for assistance.

If you're ready to commit to buying your own equipment, check out Chapter 2 for all the details on the equipment required to get started and pursue each level of brewing thereafter.

Tracing the homebrewing timeline

Homebrewing wannabes are understandably concerned with how much of a time commitment is necessary to brew beer at home. To someone not familiar with the fermentation processes, this takes a little extra explaining. First, you have the hands-*on* part of brewing: the actual cooking of the *wort* (unfermented beer; rhymes with *dirt*) on the stovetop, the *fermentation* (conversion of sugars to alcohol and CO_2 by yeast) and *aging* (maturation) processes, and then the bottling of the beer. What most people aren't aware of is the hands-*off* part of brewing — the stage when the brewer does nothing but wait patiently. This part not only constitutes the longest segment of the timeline, but it also represents a test of the brewer's patience and self-restraint.

At the beginner level, you need at least two or three hours on brewing day to properly sanitize the equipment, brew and cool the wort, *pitch* the yeast (add it to your wort), seal the fermenter, and clean up whatever mess you made. (Part 3 details the brewing day process.) You need to set aside the same amount of time on the day you bottle the beer. (Chapter 14 provides all you need to know about bottling.)

In between the brewing and bottling days, however, you face the little matter of fermentation. The yeast typically needs at least seven days to complete the fermentation cycle — sometimes more, depending on extenuating circumstances. You need do nothing more than wait patiently for the yeast to complete its task. Even after you've bottled your beer, you still need to wait patiently while your brew conditions in the bottles — two weeks is the recommended minimum length of this conditioning process.

At the beginner level, and if you brew on a Saturday, your brewing timeline may look something like the following:

1. Brew day (S). Ferment the beer Su-M-T-W-Th-F.
2. Bottle day (S). Condition the beer Su-M-T-W-Th-F-S-Su-M-T-W-Th-F.
3. Drink the beer!

As you begin to employ different ingredients, equipment, and processes in your beer-making repertoire, expect the timeline to expand. Secondary fermentation (a helpful extra aging step — see Chapter 11) adds another two weeks to the timeline, and advanced brewers, for example, may spend as many as eight to ten hours in a single day brewing their beer from grain (see Chapter 12).

Please note that homebrewing is a pursuit that requires a higher degree of dedication than, say, making TikTok videos, but the rewards are considerable (and tasty!) In addition to personal gratification, quality homebrew can inspire a certain respect from your fellow brewers, awe in non-brewers, and other intangibles that make all the effort worthwhile.

Adding ingredients galore!

Like various kinds of bread, all beer styles consist of the same basic ingredients. The difference is that the ingredients vary slightly in attributes and quantities required from one beer style to the next. Although wheat bread may look and taste different than rye bread, they're very much alike and made in very much the same way.

At the commercial level, brewing uses grain (mostly malted barley), hops, yeast, and water (see Chapters 4 through 7). Thanks to many stores and Internet sites that specialize in homebrewing supplies, homebrewers today have access to most of the same ingredients used by corporate brewhouses everywhere. Of course, these shops don't just provide the everyday ingredients for the average beer; different hop varieties and yeast strains from around the world are now available in the homebrewing market.

With the help of specially made products, such as malt syrup derived from grain (see Chapter 4), beginner homebrewers can easily produce beers that emulate those made commercially. Intermediate- and advanced-level homebrewers may even make their beer with the same grains used by their favorite commercial brewers.

Beyond the four basic building blocks of beer, dozens of other flavorings and additives can contribute different flavors and textures to your brew (see Chapter 8), and a number of other agents can affect the appearance of your brew (see Chapter 9).

TIP

Although thriftiness is a virtue, you need high-quality ingredients to produce high-quality beer — so loosen your grip on the purse strings when buying homebrew ingredients.

Not all of these ingredients are necessary to make great beer, but they exist for you, the brewer, to use if you're so inclined. In your house, you're the head brewer — you make the choices (but read about 'em in Parts 2 and 3 first).

WARNING

Like home cooking, homebrewing doesn't come with an automatic guarantee of quality. Certain responsibilities and expectations are squarely on the brewer to ensure that each batch of beer turns out right. Failure to heed simple rules and suggestions can result in a less-than-perfect brew and a waste of time, effort, and money.

Preparing wisely

Good homebrew starts with good preparation, and good preparation starts with a complete list of ingredients. Nothing is more aggravating than starting your brewing procedures only to find that you're missing a necessary ingredient. Before you head off to your homebrew supply shop or place an order on the Internet, consider all your needs. Occasionally, homebrewers fail to look beyond the beer recipe and forget something as simple — but essential — as bottle caps.

Another important preparation consideration is having the brewery in order — clearing your workspace of clutter and having all your equipment present and accounted for (see Chapter 2). Removing free-roaming pets to another part of the house is always a good idea.

Don't forget that your in-home brewery should be properly ventilated to allow for the escape of carbon monoxide (if using gas burners) as well as steam and moisture.

Sanitizing your equipment is also high on the preparation checklist (see Chapter 3); you never want your brew to come in contact with equipment that isn't properly clean and sanitized to protect against beer-ruining bacteria.

All done — now what?

So, say your beer is done and ready to drink — what next? Well, grab a bottle opener, a clean beer glass, and a seat, because it's time to revel in your success. While you're admiring the brew in your glass and savoring its flavor on your palate, consider how you can best commemorate your efforts:

- Invite a bunch of your closest (and thirstiest) buddies over to sample it.
- Give it away as gifts to close friends and family members deserving of your time and talent.
- Increase your good standing with bosses and other influential people by presenting them with a bottle of beer of your own making.
- Swap a couple of bottles with other homebrewers in your area.
- Submit some entries to homebrew competitions around the country. (See Chapter 29 to find out more about homebrew competitions.)

TIP

One of the most incredible awards is having your homebrew replicated and sold by a nationally distributed brand — kinda like your mom's chocolate chip cookies being made by Sara Lee. Several well-known microbrewers solicit homebrew entries to their own annual, sponsored competitions. The winners may receive a cash award and royalties or have their beer recipe reproduced as a one-time-only specialty beer and sold to the public. And don't overlook the added benefit of gaining insightful tips while brewing your beer side-by-side with a professional brewer!

Or you can do as I do when I'm particularly pleased with a batch of brew — hoard it, hide it, jealously guard it, and only take a bottle out to celebrate the most sublime accomplishments in life — like making another batch of great beer!

IN MEMORIAM

In 1985, a talented brewer by the name of Russell Schehrer won the coveted "Homebrewer of the Year" award at the National Homebrew Competition in Boulder, Colorado. Using that accomplishment as a springboard, Russell launched a short but brilliant career as a brewer and brewing consultant in the fledgling microbrewing industry.

I had the pleasure of meeting Russell briefly one summer afternoon many years ago. Amidst his busy brewing schedule, he took the time to show me around his brewhouse at Wynkoop Brewing Company in Denver. The impromptu tour included a visit to the lagering cellar downstairs, where he proudly proffered samples of his beers fresh from the fermenters. Once back at the bar, he casually chatted with me as I tasted my way through a complimentary flight of house brews.

Though our meeting was brief, it gave me a short insight into Russ's love of good beer and his dedication to his craft. And it was cause for me to mourn his sudden passing in 1996 at the age of 38. Russ's spirit and enthusiasm sparked both the homebrewing and craft brewing communities in the United States. There is now a "Russell Schehrer Award for Innovation in Craft Beer" given annually by the Brewers Association to a single individual who has shown dedication and service to the craft beer industry.

Another notable loss to the homebrewing community happened in late 2020 with the passing of homebrewing icon and legend Mike "Tasty" McDole. His rise to fame was like that of most others — winning numerous awards at homebrewing competitions. But Tasty set himself apart from the rest not just by making great beer, but by sharing it with anyone and everyone who wanted to try it. All seemed to agree that "tasty" was a concise way to describe his beer, and so the name stuck (Mike was also known for making "tasty" cookies, but that's a conversation for another time).

After winning the Sam Adams LongShot competition, Tasty went on to brew collaboration beers with several commercial breweries, including Russian River, 21st Amendment, and Heretic Brewing Company.

Throughout much of it, Tasty was burnishing his media credentials, too. He was co-host of "The Jamil Show" and "Can You Brew It?" and was also a regular on the "Sunday Show" on The Brewing Network (a multimedia resource for brewers and beer lovers).

And I'm left thinking that the song "*In Heaven There is no Beer*" is no longer true.

» Understanding the three levels of equipment and equipment prices

» Deciding what equipment you need and when

Chapter 2

Setting Up Your Beeraphernalia

Forget any preconceived notions you may have about shiny copper kettles and coils taking up your whole kitchen and huge wooden vats bubbling and churning in the cellar — those notions are the product of vivid imaginations and vintage Hollywood movies. Human civilization is well into the stainless-steel and plastic age, where everything is smaller, more durable, and lighter weight.

Every homebrewer is a first-time brewer at least once, which means that every homebrewer needs to start with at least the minimum amount of equipment. With its barest essentials, homebrewing requires three tools: a *brewpot* in which you boil the *wort* (the German term for beer before it's fermented), a container in which you ferment the beer (the *fermenter*), and bottles in which you package the beer.

If this list sounds overly simplistic, that's because it is. Actually, the proper brewpot needs to conform to specific acceptable parameters, the fermenter must be airtight and yet be able to vent carbon dioxide, and the bottles require bottle caps, which in turn require a bottle-capping device. And your list of needs has only begun.

You will also want a number of smaller (but no less important) items that all brewers need to have in their breweries. And as you may find out, brewers who continue to brew beer are likely to continue to buy or build additional time- and effort-saving equipment as they need it. This chapter discusses the necessary equipment at all levels of homebrewing because more advanced equipment is required to produce the more advanced beer styles found later in the book.

REMEMBER

Don't panic — just follow along at your own pace. You don't need to progress to levels you're not comfortable with. Although some brewers feel compelled to advance as rapidly as possible, others find their niche and stick with it. Above all else, homebrewing should be an enjoyable undertaking.

Sniffing Out Sources

The first step in your homebrewing expedition is to locate your local homebrew supply retailer — if one exists. If a simple Google search doesn't turn up a local supplier, I'm positive it will provide dozens of online alternatives. Take a few minutes to peruse the equipment and supplies — especially the ingredients. To the first-timer, the vast quantities of equipment and ingredient choices can be somewhat intimidating.

Homebrewing equipment varies, as shown in Figure 2-1, and any homebrew supplier worth its salt can get you just about anything you need or desire (for homebrewing, that is!)

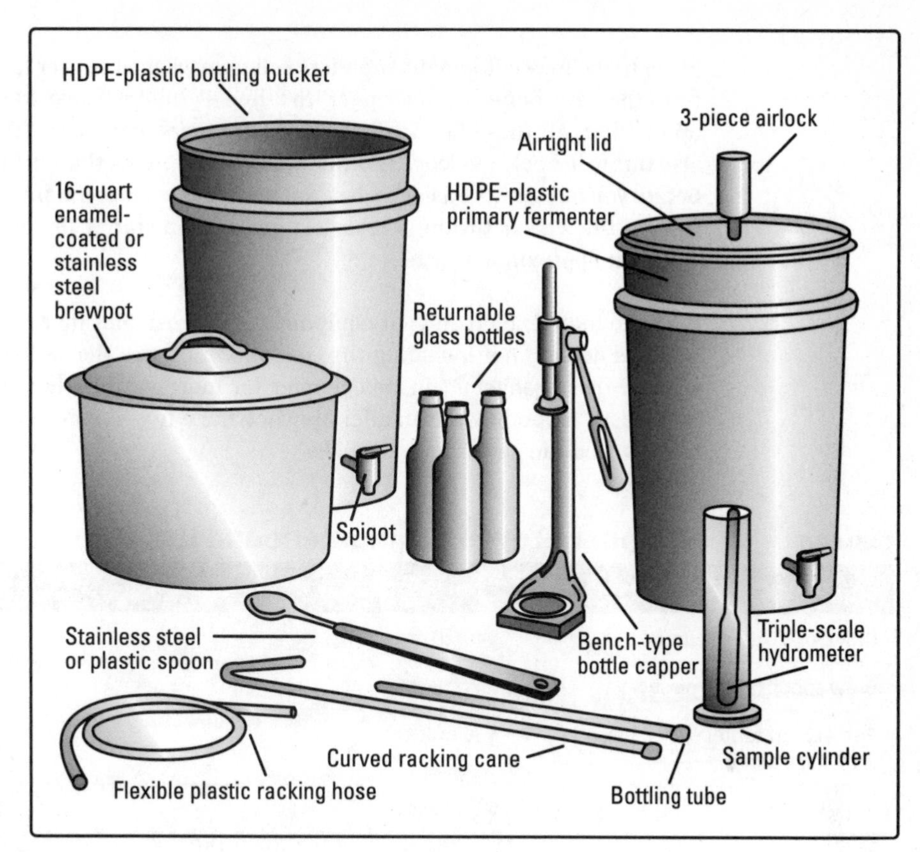

FIGURE 2-1: Many homebrew shops sell this basic equipment as a start-up kit.

Square One: Equipment for the Beginning Brewer

Square one generally denotes a starting point (although it's also been used to describe this author), and this section is no different: It serves as the starting point in your homebrewing career. Before you can embark on this career path, however, you need to buy the tools of the trade.

So much equipment, so little time . . .

For the benefit of beginning homebrewers, in this section I recommend and discuss only the minimal amount of equipment needed; however, I may mention additional convenient and time- and effort-saving pieces along the way. Thrift is also a consideration; I typically recommend cheaper alternatives over more expensive equipment and methods.

Many homebrew equipment suppliers sell prepackaged starter kits that can range from the bare-bones to the top-of-the-line — all-inclusive starter kits can run up to $200. All these kits include the basic equipment essentials, but some kits also throw in books, videos, or other unnecessary items that just inflate the price. Before you buy a kit, consider what you need and what you want to spend. To help you get the wheels turning, Table 2-1 gives you a starter list of necessary items and their approximate costs.

If you go high-end on all your equipment, your cost adds up to well over a couple hundred dollars, not including the cost of bottles (see the section "What do I do with all these gadgets?" in this chapter for more information about bottles and their cost). If you buy the smaller brewpot and a two-handed capper to cut some corners, you can save about 25 bucks.

TABLE 2-1 **Beginner Brewing Equipment and Its Cost**

Equipment	Approximate Cost
Brewpot, 16 qt. minimum	$40/20 qt.
Brew spoon (HDPE plastic)	$4 or less
Primary fermenter (HDPE plastic) with spigot, lid	$20 or less
Airlock	$2 or less
Drilled rubber stopper for airlock	$2 or less
3 to 4 feet of food-grade plastic hose, ½ inch in diameter	$3
Bottling or "priming" bucket (HDPE plastic) with spigot	$15 or less
Bottles (must be the reusable type that don't use twist-off caps)	$30–$40 for one batch of beer (5 gallons); the exact number of bottles depends on their size: 12 oz., 16 oz., 22 oz., or 1 qt.
Bottle rinser	$15
Bottle brush	$4
Bottling tube (HDPE plastic) with spring valve	$4 or less
Bottle capper	$40 (bench-type) or $16 (two-handed)
Hydrometer (triple scale) with cylinder	$13 ($5 or less for the cylinder)

What do I do with all these gadgets?

Okay, you've read the list in Table 2-1 and made your own list of what equipment you need. You're ready to go shopping, right? Not so fast. You probably want to understand a little bit about what it is you're buying. The following list gives you some insights into what all these gadgets do so you can be a more informed consumer.

- **Brewpot:** Chances are you already have a large pot of some sort in your kitchen, but if your brewpot is made of enamel-coated metal, make sure it's not chipped where it may come in contact with your beer. Your brewpot also needs to have a minimum 16-quart capacity, but I highly recommend you go ahead and upgrade to the 20- quart pot listed in Table 2-1.

  TIP

  The more of your wort you boil, the better for your finished beer. So, when it comes to brewpots, the bigger the better.

- **Brew spoon:** Regardless of how well equipped your kitchen is, every homebrewer needs to have a spoon dedicated for brewing beer and nothing else. A brew spoon needs to be stainless steel or HDPE (food-grade) plastic, and it needs to have a long handle — 18 inches or more. Avoid wooden spoons because they can't be kept thoroughly sanitized (and they can splinter).
- **Primary fermenter:** The *primary fermenter* is where you pour the cooled wort shortly after you're done brewing. You must be able to seal this vessel airtight for the duration of the fermentation. A primary fermenter needs to have a minimum capacity of 7 gallons and an airtight lid with a hole in it (to accommodate an airlock with an attached rubber stopper). These specially made plastic fermenters come with removable plastic spigots positioned near the bottom for easy use.

  TECHNICAL STUFF

  The kinds of plastics used in homebrewing are of the same quality and standards as those plastics used in the food industry. In fact, another name for *HDPE (high-density polyethylene)* is *food-grade plastic*. Unlike lesser grades of plastic, HDPE restricts gaseous transfer through the plastic (though not completely).

- **Airlock:** An *airlock* is an inexpensive (but incredibly simple and efficient) tool that allows the carbon dioxide gases to escape from the fermenter during fermentation without compromising the antiseptic environment within. Filled halfway with water, this setup lets gas escape without allowing any air (and, therefore, germs) into the fermenter. A similar contraption, called a *bubbler,* is a two-chambered device that works on the same principle. The difference is that you can easily clean and sanitize the inside of an airlock (unlike the totally enclosed bubbler). Both mechanisms work equally well otherwise, but the airlock, shown in Figure 2-2, is my first choice.

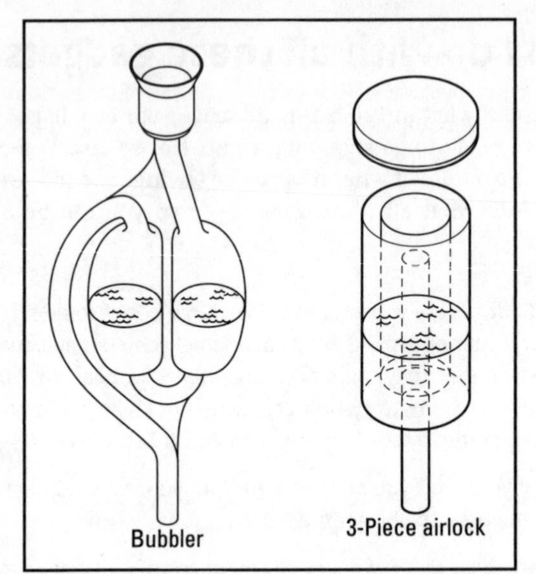

FIGURE 2-2: An airlock allows carbon dioxide to escape from the fermenter.

- **Drilled rubber stopper:** You need a rubber stopper to fit over the stem of the airlock or bubbler to act as a wedge when you insert the airlock into the hole in the fermenter lid. These drilled stoppers come in numbered sizes (for example, a #3 stopper). Be sure you buy a stopper that fits the opening in your fermenter lid. (Your homebrew equipment supplier can determine what you need.)
- **Plastic hose:** Flexible plastic hosing is a multifunctional piece of equipment you use to transfer your beer from vessel to vessel or from vessel to bottle. It's an important part of your equipment package and one that you need to always keep clean and undamaged. You want to have 3 to 5 feet of food-grade hosing.
- **Bottling bucket:** The *bottling bucket* is a vessel you need on bottling day. It doesn't require a lid, but it's considerably more efficient if you buy a bucket with a removable spigot at the bottom. The bottling bucket is also called a *priming vessel* because you prime your fermented beer with corn sugar just prior to bottling. (I discuss the priming process in detail in Chapter 14.)
- **Glass bottles:** Your bottles must be the thick, heavy, returnable kind. Don't use any bottle with a threaded (twist-off) opening — a bottle cap doesn't seal properly across the threads. You need enough bottles to hold 5 gallons of beer: 54 12-ounce bottles, 40 16-ounce bottles, or any combination of bottles that adds up to 640 ounces. You can buy brand-new bottles from a homebrew supply shop, but you can get used bottles much more cheaply from commercial breweries.

TIP

Find out whether a local liquor store sells any beer in returnable bottles (not the cheap recyclable kind). If it does, buy a couple of cases, drink the beer, and voilà! You have 48 bottles (not to mention a swollen bladder and a nasty headache).

Another alternative, albeit an initially more expensive one, is to buy the self-sealing *swing-top* bottles. See the sidebar "Swingtime" in Chapter 14 for more information.

- **Bottling tube:** A *bottling tube* is a hard plastic tube that's about a foot long and comes with a spring-loaded valve at the tip. You attach the bottling tube to the plastic hosing (which you then attach to the spigot on the bottling bucket) and insert the tube in the bottles when filling them. Should you decide to start canning your beer (see Chapter 15), this item could then be called a *canning tube*.
- **Bottle brush:** A *bottle brush* is another inexpensive but important piece of equipment. You need this soft-bristle brush to properly scrub the inside of the bottles prior to filling.
- **Bottle rinser:** A *bottle rinser* is a curved plastic or brass apparatus that you attach to a faucet. It works as an added convenience for rinsing bottles. This device isn't an absolute necessity, but for the money it's a good investment.

TIP

If you buy a bottle rinser, take note of which faucet in your home you plan to use. Utility faucets usually have larger hose threads and others, such as bathroom and kitchen faucets, have fine threads where an adapter may be needed. Make sure the bottle rinser and any adapters have a rubber washer (gasket) in place.

- **Bottle capper:** You need a *bottle capper* to affix new bottle caps to the filled bottles. These come in all shapes, sizes, and costs.

  Most cappers work equally well, but I suggest that you choose a bench-type capper, like the one shown in Figure 2-3, over the two-handed style. A *bench capper* is free-standing and can be attached to a work surface (permanently, if you like), which leaves one hand free to hold the bottle steady.

- **Triple-scale hydrometer:** A *hydrometer* is a fragile glass measuring device used to calculate the density of your beer as well as the amount of alcohol that the yeast has produced in your homebrew. *Triple scale* refers to the three different measuring scales within the hydrometer (see the sidebar "Of liquid density and hydrometers . . ." in this chapter).

TIP

Some people argue that a hydrometer isn't a necessary piece of equipment at the beginner level. I disagree. A hydrometer isn't very expensive, it's easy to use, and anyone who wants to progress in the world of homebrewing needs to learn how to use one. Therefore, I recommend adding a hydrometer to your initial shopping list — and be sure to buy a plastic cylinder to go with it.

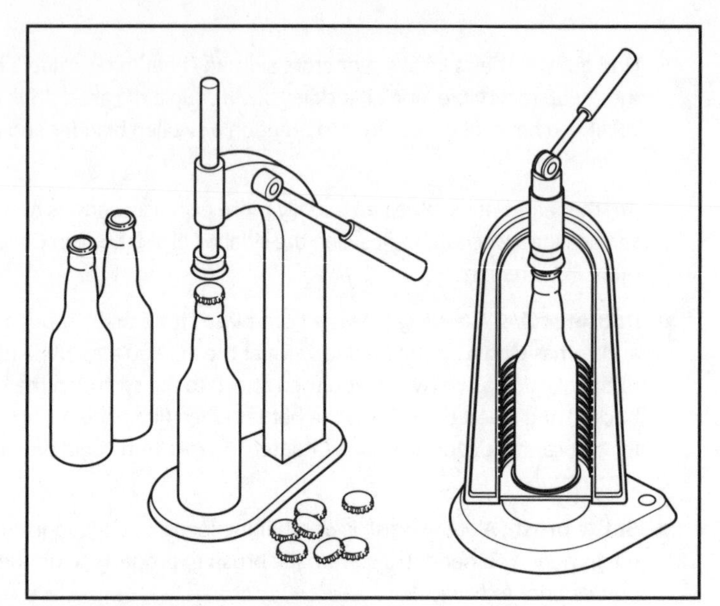

FIGURE 2-3: You can attach a bench-type bottle capper to a work surface for easy use.

OF LIQUID DENSITY AND HYDROMETERS

TECHNICAL STUFF

A hydrometer is a long, cylindrical, narrow glass device designed to measure liquid density. It's weighted at the bottom and has a numeric scale or scales inside for measuring purposes. With the weighted end submerged in the liquid, the calibrated stem projects out of the liquid; the density of the liquid determines the height of this projection.

A triple-scale hydrometer features three separate scales. Two of them — the *specific gravity scale* and the *Balling scale* — measure *liquid density* (the density of liquids in relation to the density of water), but the third measures potential alcohol. Ordinary water has a specific gravity of 1.000 at 60 degrees Fahrenheit. (For comparison's sake, at the same temperature, gasoline has a specific gravity around 0.66, whole milk is about 1.028, and mercury is 13.600!)

The Balling scale performs the exact same function as the specific gravity scale, except that it reads in different incremental numbers called *degrees Plato*. A homebrew with a specific gravity of 1.048 has a density of 12.5 degrees Plato. (The difference between these two measurement scales is similar to the difference between the Fahrenheit and Celsius temperature scales; homebrewers seem to prefer the specific gravity scale.)

So, what's the point? Measuring the density of your brew accomplishes two goals: It tells you when your brew is done fermenting (and thus, when it's time to bottle your beer), and it allows you to calculate the alcohol potential of your brew. Of course, potential alcohol and actual alcohol are two different things, which is why you need to take two different hydrometer readings. Taking a hydrometer reading before you ferment the wort gives you the *original gravity;* it tells you the *alcohol potential.* Taking a second hydrometer reading after fermentation is over gives you the *final gravity* (also called *terminal gravity)* and a *final alcohol potential.* Subtracting the F.G. (final gravity) from the O.G. (original gravity) on one scale and the final alcohol potential from the initial alcohol potential on the other scale tells you, in mathematical terms, how much of the sugar your yeast ate and how much alcohol is in your brew.

When yeasts eat sugar they produce alcohol, so any decrease in gravity results in a reciprocal increase in alcohol.

A few things to remember:

- Although a hydrometer is a very reliable method of measuring specific gravities and figuring alcohol potentials, the readings skew if the liquid temperature is not near 60 degrees Fahrenheit at reading time. Hot wort readings are lower than they should be and cold bottling readings are higher than they should be due to the temperature-sensitive nature of liquid density. Therefore, always measure at 60 degrees Fahrenheit (or use a *temperature correction scale* — ask your homebrew retailer for details).
- Alcohol potential readings are measured in *alcohol by volume* (ABV), not *alcohol by weight* (ABW) (see Chapter 6).
- Surface tension in liquids causes something called a *meniscus effect.* The tendency of liquids to cling to other surfaces creates a meniscus. The *meniscus* is the concave appearance of the beer between the wall of the cylinder and the exterior of the hydrometer. Be sure to sight your reading at the lowest point of the meniscus.
- A hydrometer, like the one shown in the figure, can also call attention to possible fermentation problems. Average healthy yeasts consume at least 65 percent of available sugars (usually more); if the final gravity reading of your beer is

(continued)

(continued)

not 35 percent or less of the original gravity, a lot of sugar may still be in the beer (see Chapter 10 for details on taking hydrometer readings).

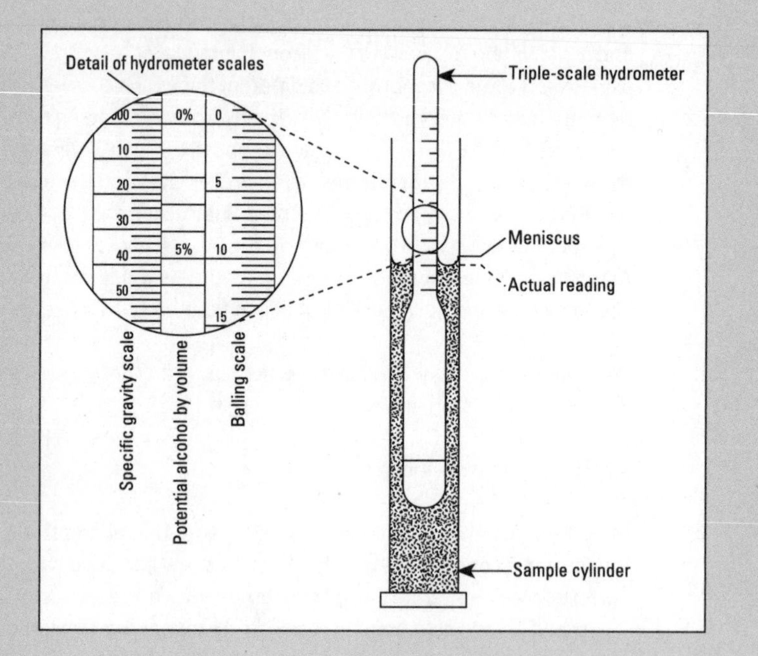

Square Two: Equipment for the Intermediate Brewer

Okay, you've mastered homebrewing techniques at the novice level and you're looking for a bigger challenge. Well, you've come to the right place. This section is for the budding homebrewer who intends to get more personally involved in the brewing processes. A more hands-on approach to anything calls for more specialized equipment (a car owner intending to do her own vehicle maintenance can't get far without the right tools). A lot of different procedures await you at the intermediate level of homebrewing, each with its own degree of difficulty (see Chapter 11).

Now what do I need?

The list of equipment in Table 2-2 is based on the additional needs of the homebrewer who endeavors to try all the procedures outlined in Chapter 11. Those brewers who aren't compelled to try all the intermediate brewing procedures need to pick and choose the items that best suit their needs and levels of confidence. Figure 2-4 shows a couple of the more important items you need.

TABLE 2-2

Intermediate Equipment and Its Cost

Equipment	Approximate Cost
Glass carboy (5 gallon)	$43 or less
Another airlock	$2 or less
Rubber stopper for carboy (drilled)	$2 or less
Carboy brush	$5 or less
Racking tube or cane	$3
8-inch plastic funnel	$10 or less
Kitchen strainer	$10 or less
Sparge bags	$5 (reusable nylon)
	$.50 (throw-away)
Lab immersion thermometer (or similar)	$8
Grain mill	$125 and up
Kitchen or postal scale	$20–$30

FIGURE 2-4: A glass carboy and a hand-cranked grain mill are important additions that you may want to make to your home brewery.

What do these gizmos even do?

New challenges in homebrewing often call for new equipment. Before you take off on this new adventure, take a gander at the following list so you know exactly what you need and why you need it.

- **Glass carboy:** *Carboys* are the large cylindrical jugs that water delivery companies used for years until they switched to the plastic carboys used today. Because these plastic carboys are typically used for water and aren't really appropriate for homebrewing use, you need to purchase a glass carboy from your local homebrew supply store. The principal use for a glass carboy in homebrewing is as a secondary fermenter, where you age and mature your beer.

  TIP

  Carboys may come in 3- to 15-gallon capacities, but the 5-gallon size best matches the typical batch of homebrew; therefore, it's probably the best choice for homebrewing purposes.

- **Rubber stopper:** If you intend to use the carboy as a fermenter, you need another drilled rubber stopper to fit the carboy's neck (usually a #6 or #7 stopper). As with the plastic primary fermenter, the carboy needs to be sealed with an airlock while the beer inside is aging.
- **Airlock:** You may not actually need another airlock in the brewery, but you may find you like to have a spare one around — besides, it costs less than a couple of bucks!

  TIP

  Having a second airlock allows you to brew two batches in quick succession. While one batch is aging in the carboy, another can be fermenting in the primary fermenter.

- **Carboy brush:** If you want to continue to use the carboy as a fermenter, you need a carboy brush. This heavy-duty, soft-bristle brush is specially designed to reach every curve and corner of the carboy during cleaning.
- **Racking tube:** *Racking* is the act of transferring beer from one vessel to another, or into bottles (or cans), while leaving yeast sediment and particulate matter behind. Because carboys don't offer the convenience of a spigot, you need a hard-plastic, curved racking tube — also called a *cane* — to siphon the beer out.
- **Funnel:** Because the opening of the carboy is so small, a good funnel is a handy thing to have around. I recommend one with an opening at least 8 inches in diameter.
- **Kitchen strainer:** With the addition of loose grain, hops, and other ingredients to your brewpot, a strainer with a handle becomes a necessary piece of equipment. Food-grade steel mesh is better than plastic; don't settle for a

strainer with a diameter of less than 10 inches or one without a strong handle. You may have to go to a culinary specialty store to find the right one.

- **Sparge bags:** Regardless of whether you have a strainer, *sparge bags* are effective for steeping grain or keeping whole-leaf hops under control in the brewpot. You can buy reusable nylon bags with drawstrings, or you can buy the inexpensive throw-away kind.
- **Lab immersion thermometer:** Because temperature control becomes more and more important in brewing at the intermediate level, you probably want to have an immersion thermometer in your brewery. A lab-quality immersion thermometer is capable of temperature readings above the boiling point (212 degrees Fahrenheit or100 degrees Celsius at sea level) and as low as 40 degrees Fahrenheit (or 4.4 degrees Celsius).
- **Grain mill:** A *grain mill* is one of the more expensive items you need. You use the grain mill to crack the grain prior to brewing with it. You can buy pre-cracked grain, but many homebrew stores don't crack it properly (and precracked grain can also go stale more quickly). The mill-less homebrewer can find inventive ways to crack the grain, such as putting it into a large sealable plastic bag and rolling it with a rolling pin or baseball bat.

  WARNING

  Whatever you do, don't use a coffee grinder to do your grain milling. If you do, your grain ends up looking like sawdust — and how it looks is just the beginning of your problems. Grinding your grain too finely causes your beer to have an unpleasant, bitter, astringent taste.
- **Kitchen or postal scale:** After you start to brew beer according to specific recipes, you may find that you need many ingredients in small quantities. A good kitchen or postal scale is vital to getting these quantities just right because it can measure fractions of ounces.

Square Three: Equipment for the Advanced Brewer

Some homebrewers become so completely engrossed and absorbed in their hobby that their craving for homebrewing information is only surpassed by their need to take full control of the brewing processes they perform. Welcome to the world of advanced homebrewing (also known as homebrewing geekdom).

What separates this level of homebrewing from the intermediate level (besides this mania) is that you produce wort from grain only — just like the commercial brewers make beer. To do so, you must master the process known as *mashing.*

Mashing is the method of producing your wort from raw grain instead of using malt syrup. (See Chapter 12 for more on mashing.) And even though the learning curve is pretty steep, mashing allows you to make cheaper and potentially more-flavorful beer.

I need even more stuff?

As you progress even farther up the homebrewing evolutionary ladder, you need to obtain the proper equipment for your brewing needs. Table 2-3 shows you the additional items that are necessary to perform the brewing procedures outlined in the advanced brewing chapter (Chapter 12). You may have already purchased some of these items for the intermediate level of brewing, which means you're ahead of the game. If you kept your wallet close to your hip at the beginner and intermediate levels, here's where the cost is gonna catch up to you.

In addition to these brewery-specific items, you need a set of ordinary measuring spoons for some of the testing techniques.

TABLE 2-3 Advanced Equipment and Its Cost

Equipment	Approximate Price
Large-volume brewpot (7+ gallons)	$115 or more /32 qt.
12–20 qt. brewpot (to mash in)	$0 (you should already have one at this brewing level)
Lauter tun	$20
3–8 qt. stock pot (for holding sparge water)	$0 (you should already have one at this brewing level)
Immersion wort chiller	$60 or more
pH papers	$4
Lab immersion thermometer	$8
Grain mill (if not using preground malt)	$125 and up
Kitchen or postal scale	$20–$30
Gypsum (calcium sulfate)	$2 or less
Calcium carbonate (food-grade chalk)	$2 or less
Calcium chloride	$2 or less

Note: *These items are absolutely necessary for all-grain brewing (making your beer from nothing but grain), but not necessarily for partial-mash brewing (making your beer primarily from extract but adding more fermentable ingredients by also using grain).*

What else could I possibly need another doodad for?

Okay, you've handled all the intermediate homebrewing procedures with ease. Now you really want to brew beer like the pros, but you need the equipment that helps you do that. Study this list (and double-check the balances on your credit cards).

Check out Chapter 30 to find out how to make many of these items inexpensively. Chapter 12 discusses many of these items and processes in greater depth.

- **Large-volume brewpot:** Because all-grain brewing requires you to boil the entire volume of beer, you need a brewpot that is large enough to hold 7 gallons or more of wort (which eventually boils down to 5 gallons) with room to spare at the top. Purchased new, this item can be a major expense. Check local garage sales and thrift stores. You can also find cheaper, large-volume ceramic-lined pots from other equipment sources (or simply make the brewpot yourself by following the directions in Chapter 30).
- **Mashing brewpot (12–20 quarts):** If you already have a smaller brewpot left from your beginner days, that's all you need here.
- **Lauter tun:** A *lauter tun* is a fairly simple device that allows you to drain the wort away from the grain after the mashing process. It basically acts as a large-volume strainer or colander. See Chapter 30 for instructions on building your own lauter tun.
- **Stock pot (4–8 quarts):** You use this pot to heat water for sparging purposes. *Sparging* is pouring hot water through the bed of grain in your lauter tun to recapture all the malt sugars still contained within it. You can use any household pot capable of holding this volume of water.
- **Immersion wort chiller:** An *immersion wort chiller* is basically a coil of ⅜- to ½-inch copper tubing with a fitting on one end that connects to a water source. As the coil is immersed in the hot wort, cold water flowing through the tubing removes the heat by thermal conductivity. The hot water flowing out the opposite end can be recaptured and used for various purposes. Check out Chapter 30 for information on building an immersion wort chiller.
- **pH papers:** These disposable test papers are absolutely necessary for the mashing processes described in the advanced brewing chapter. pH papers measure the acidity and alkalinity of your water. Simply dip the test strip into your wort for about one minute and then compare the strip to the color comparison chart. (See Figure 2-5.)

TIP

Always work in good lighting when testing pH.

For a handy alternative, consider investing in a pH meter. See Chapter 31 for more details.

- **Lab immersion thermometer:** An important piece of equipment at the intermediate level, this thermometer is absolutely necessary for the mashing procedures in all-grain brewing.
- **Grain mill:** Unless you want to continue to rely on other people to grind your grain for you (and often charge you for the service) or whack an enormous amount of grain yourself with a rolling pin, you want to invest in a good grain mill. Don't say I didn't warn you.
- **Kitchen or postal scale:** A good scale is absolutely necessary at this brewing level. You may opt to buy a scale at a culinary specialty store. Check out Table 2-2 for pricing information.

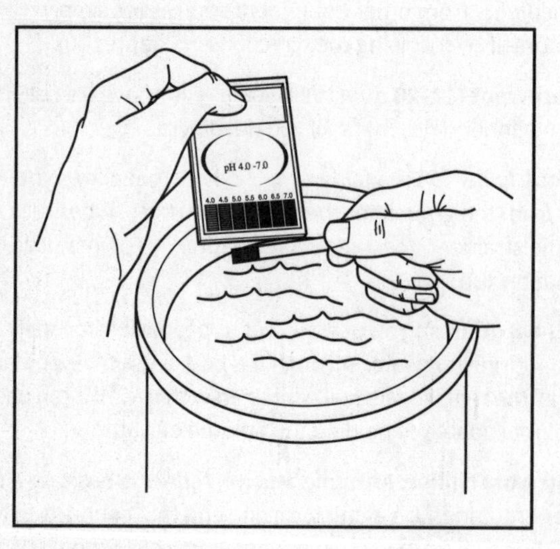

FIGURE 2-5: Testing pH is an important part of the advanced brewing process.

- **Gypsum:** Along with calcium carbonate and calcium chloride, you may need gypsum to adjust the pH of your water. You can use gypsum to simulate the gypsum-laden water of Burton-on-Trent, but it only lowers pH when mashed with grain. For more information on the unique brewing water of Burton-on-Trent, see Chapter 7.
- **Calcium carbonate:** Calcium carbonate raises pH. You can also use it to simulate the water sources of classic stouts and porters.
- **Calcium chloride:** You can use calcium chloride in place of gypsum to lower pH without increasing the sulfate level in the water. It also works in place of

salt (sodium chloride) to add chlorides without increasing the sodium content of the water.

- **Lactic acid:** This is another handy tool in your toolbox for adjusting the pH of your brewing water, and it's also readily available through your favorite homebrew supplier.

With the addition of all these new and larger pieces of equipment to your collection, your kitchen is likely to become a lot more cluttered on brewing day. And in order to get a large-volume brewpot up to a rolling boil, you're also probably going to want increased burner output and heating capacity.

For these reasons (and others), many advanced brewers have moved their brewing operations into their basements, garages, and utility rooms (and some of their spouses have moved to new addresses). Although this expansion idea has merit, never overlook the safety considerations of such a move — have you ever tried to explain homebrewing procedures to an insurance claims adjuster?

CHILLIN' OUT

Because the advanced level of homebrewing involves *full-wort boils* (boiling the entire batch of wort at once), it's imperative that you're able to cool 5 gallons of wort down quickly — cold water baths in your kitchen sink just don't cut it anymore.

Although the immersion-type wort chiller listed in Table 2-3 is a dandy (and highly recommended) piece of equipment, the gadget-freak homebrew geek can find another, more efficient wort-chilling device. It's called a *counter-flow wort chiller*, and it's more like the chillers commercial breweries use. At the homebrewing level, a counter-flow chiller consists of a copper tube (much like the immersion-type wort chiller) inserted into a rubber hose. Whereas the hot wort runs through the copper tubing in one direction, cold water runs through the hose in the other direction. This process cools the wort very rapidly while allowing the brewer to recapture the hot water flowing out the end of the hose for future use.

Yet another alternative to cooling your wort is what's called a *plate chiller*. This works in pretty much the same way as a counter-flow wort chiller, but this handy-dandy little contraption is incredibly effective at reducing the temperature of your wort in a short span of time. Consider what your time is worth, though — these suckers aren't cheap. The average brand-name plate chiller will set you back about a hundred bucks or more. And don't forget — just like any other piece of equipment in your home brewery, your plate chiller needs to be sanitized before every use. This can be accomplished with brewery-friendly chemicals (see Chapter 3) or by running very hot water through it.

» Keeping those beer-swilling fungi and bacteria at bay

» Determining the best cleaning agents for your equipment

» Cleaning and sanitizing your equipment

Chapter 3
Creating Your Own Department of Sanitation

So you have all your brewing equipment, and now you're ready to brew, right? Not so fast, rookie.

Anyone who intends to become a proficient brewer of good beer must properly clean and sanitize all brewing equipment first. You can find out about sanitation techniques in several different ways. You can read about sanitizing, ask other brewers sanitation questions, and experiment with sanitizers on your own. Or — I guarantee — you can find out about them by accident. Contaminating a batch of beer out of carelessness is a painful lesson to endure. The only fate worse than throwing out 5 gallons of bad beer is drinking 5 gallons of bad beer (hiccup) — especially after you've spent your time and effort bottling it all. In this chapter, I explore the different levels of cleanliness required by brewing and give you information on the products and practices that can help you meet those standards. I also discuss the nasty little vermin these practices help you fight.

No Dirty Words: Sanitation Lingo

Scrupulously clean brewing equipment and a pristine brewing environment are the keys to making good beer. And by clean, I don't mean just soap-and-water clean. In homebrewing, serious sanitation is necessary.

Take a closer look at a few important words used in this chapter. *Clean,* as it pertains to homebrewing, means that you've removed all dust, dirt, scum, stains, and other visible contaminants from your brewing equipment and bottles to the best of your ability. After the visible contaminants are history, you need to *sanitize* your equipment and bottles; sanitation is the elimination of invisible contaminants (bacteria and other microorganisms) that can ruin your brew. Clean requires a little elbow grease; sanitized requires chemicals.

Never assume that clean equipment is sanitized, and never assume sanitized equipment is clean. For the good of your beer, practice good cleaning and sanitizing techniques — in that order.

A third and equally important word is *sterilize.* Sterilization is another method of germ-killing accomplished with very high temperatures (over 200 degrees Fahrenheit). Boiling your wort for at least an hour is an effective way of sterilizing the ingredients in your beer. After your wort cools, however, air-borne, water-borne, and human-borne germs can easily recontaminate it. For this reason, clean and sanitized equipment is imperative. From the boiling point forward, you need to treat your wort like a person without an immune system — safeguarded from the bacterial world.

Battling Bacteria (and Fungi)

Nothing is more important to your production of clean, drinkable, and enjoyable beer than utilizing proper sanitizing procedures prior to your brewing. You must sanitize or sterilize anything and everything that will come into contact with your beer at any time.

"What's the big deal?" you may ask. Well, millions of hungry *microbes* just love to make meals of freshly brewed beer. These microbes are in your home, on your body, and even in the air you breathe (cough, wheeze). Bacteria and fungi are the forms of microbes that you need to be wary of — they're both opportunistic, and if you let them have their way with your brew, they do so (almost always with negative results). With very few exceptions (meaning specific beer styles), beer that bacteria contaminated smells and tastes awful.

NO PATHOS FOR PATHOGENS

Because freshly brewed beer is warm and sweet, it's the perfect breeding ground for microbiological opportunists. However, none of the bacteria that grow in beer are even remotely as harmful as the bacteria found in raw eggs, fish, or uncooked meat that cause people to become deathly ill. The germs that breed in beer are just free-loading little buggers that make your beer taste bad. Beer germs won't kill you, but throwing out a batch of brew just may.

TECHNICAL STUFF

Ironically, certain bacteria and fungi work for the betterment of beer, but only under strict control. Because the classification *fungi* consists of mold spores and wild yeast, beer yeast actually falls into the fungus category. However, beer yeasts are of the friendly, laboratory-controlled variety. A couple of strains of bacteria also show up in beer (intentionally), but mostly in specific Belgian specialty beers that are still intentionally inoculated with beer-friendly bacteria.

Fungi and bacteria thrive in very warm temperatures — up to 120 degrees Fahrenheit. The activity of these microbes does tend to decrease as the temperature drops, which is why cooling down your hot wort as quickly as possible is imperative (as further described in Chapter 10). The cooler, the better.

TIP

So, how can you get rid of these little beer-ruining pests? Well, in truth, you can't really get rid of them completely; the idea is to keep them away from your beer (or at least minimize their effect). I provide the following helpful tips to assist you in deterring these foes:

- Keep your brewery (kitchen, laundry room, basement, or wherever you make your beer) as clean and dust-free as possible. Another to consider — when grinding grain, be sure to do it somewhere other than in the brewery. Grain ducts can contain spoilage microbes.
- Quarantine all furry, four-legged family pets in another part of the house while you brew or bottle your beer.
- Consider every cough and sneeze a threat to your beer.
- Finally, treat your equipment well. Clean and sanitize it properly prior to brewing, rinse it well, and dry it off after every use and before storing it away. Keep your equipment stored in a dust- and mildew-free location if at all possible. You may even want to go as far as sealing all your equipment in large-capacity garbage bags between brewing sessions.

Soaps for Suds: Cleansers and Sanitizers

The variety of chemicals that you can use to clean and sanitize your homebrewing equipment includes iodine-based products, chlorine-based products, *caustics* (which can burn your skin), ammonia, and a couple of environmentally safe cleansers that contain oxygen-based *percarbonates*. The following bits of information are some pros and cons to the use of these various chemicals:

- **Ammonia** is good for cleaning bottles in a dilution of 1 cup of ammonia to 5 gallons of water — if you can stand the pungent odor. If you use ammonia for sanitizing, be sure to give your equipment a thorough hot-water rinse. Also, make sure to avoid prolonged exposure to ammonia fumes, and wear gloves if you have sensitive skin. Goggles are also a good idea.
- **Chlorine** is an ingredient in simple household bleach, which is very effective and cost-efficient for sanitizing homebrewing equipment. One ounce of bleach per gallon of water is sufficient, which makes a gallon of generic bleach an incredibly good deal. Be sure to buy unscented bleach and to rinse all equipment thoroughly with hot water. An exception: Chlorine bleach can corrode stainless steel brewing equipment, so avoid using bleach for these items if you can.

  WARNING

  Never mix ammonia with chlorine bleach; this combination releases toxic chlorine gas.
- **Iodine-based sanitizers** are popular in the medical field and the restaurant and commercial brewing industries as a disinfectant. You can apply iodine's disinfectant properties to homebrewing, but note that it stains plastics as well as human skin. Although iodine-based products may vary in strength, the typical dilution ratio is 1 ounce of iodine per 5 gallons of water. Iodine-based products are also FDA-approved as no-rinse sanitizers.
- **Lye** is a caustic that you want to use only to remove the most stubborn stains and obstinate organic material from bottles or glass carboys. Technically, caustics are cleansers and not sanitizers. However, most small concentrations of caustic material dissolve and kill almost any bacteria and organic buildup. If you use lye, make sure that you always wear protective gear, such as goggles and rubber gloves.
- **Percarbonates** accomplish their cleaning activity with oxygen molecules; they produce oxygen bubbles and help to loosen soils. Because of this unique cleaning method, sanitizers that work with percarbonates, such as One Step, don't require rinsing.

- **Sodium metabisulphite** is another food-grade sanitizer that doesn't require rinsing. A 4-ounce-to-1-gallon dilution is a standard mixture, but at about $2 per 4 ounces, a 5-gallon solution runs you ten bucks!
- **TSP** (trisodium phosphate) is a safe and effective nonsudsing powdered cleanser good for cleaning beer bottles, glass carboys, and even glasses used for beer drinking. TSP is not a sanitizer, however, and thorough rinsing is imperative. Also, because TSP is a skin and eye irritant, always wear protective gear when you use this cleanser.

Several brand-name sanitizers, including B-T-F Iodophor, Star San, Saniclean, One Step, PBW (Powdered Brewery Wash) and B-Brite, along with generic sodium metabisulphite, are available through homebrew supply stores. TSP, ammonia, and chlorine bleach can be purchased at your local grocery and/or hardware stores. The capacity of these products to sanitize homebrewing equipment is directly proportionate to the way in which you use them; in other words, if you don't follow instructions, don't blame the manufacturer for a blown batch of beer.

TIP

Dilution rates and contact time are important variables to consider when cleaning and sanitizing. Read all product instructions before using.

For my money, ordinary unscented household bleach is still the best bet in a pinch for cleaning out dirty glass carboys.

Cleaning Up Your Act: Equipment Cleaning Practices

The most effective methods of sanitizing involve soaking rather than intensive scrubbing. For this purpose, the best place to handle sanitizing procedures is a utility basin or large-capacity sink. (A bathtub can do in a pinch, but bathtubs often harbor tons of bacteria, soap residues, and, occasionally, small children. Remove all these potential contaminants prior to use — especially the wee ones.) Remember that chlorine can wreak havoc on stainless steel; if you're sanitizing with bleach, make sure your bleach and basin are compatible.

WARNING

Never use any abrasives or materials that can scratch your plastic or metal equipment, because pits and scratches are excellent hiding places for those wily bacteria. Using a very soft sponge that you've devoted to cleaning only homebrew equipment is a good idea.

Okay, so now that you're ready to begin sanitizing, follow these instructions:

1. **Place the items you want to sanitize in the plugged utility basin and begin drawing cold water into the basin.**

   Because chlorine is volatile, don't use hot water with bleach; the heat of the water causes the chlorine gas to leave the water much more quickly.

   If you're sanitizing the fermenter, carboy, or bottling bucket, you need to fill only those items rather than the whole basin or sink. You can place smaller items in the sanitizing solution within these larger items. However, for bottles, you need to fill the entire sink.

2. **As the water runs, add cleansing/sanitizing chemicals according to package directions, or pour in 1 ounce of unscented household bleach per gallon of water.**
3. **Completely immerse all the items you want to sanitize in the sanitizing solution.**

   Don't forget to include the fermenter lid, which you have to force into the fermenter sideways. Always allow 30 minutes for all bottles and equipment to soak.

4. **After 30 minutes, remove your equipment and thoroughly rinse the various pieces in hot water.**
5. **Sanitize the spigots on the fermenter and bottling bucket by draining the sanitizing solution through each spigot.**
6. **Allow everything to air dry.**

TIP

   The fermenter lid, placed upside down on a clean surface, is a good place to dry the smaller sanitized items.

WARNING

In spite of all your hard work, you may still occasionally end up with a batch of contaminated beer — how and by what you may never know. That's why attention to detail is so important.

Bottle Cleanliness Is a Virtue

When you're absolutely sure that your brew is bottle-ready (you can verify this decision with a hydrometer reading — see Chapter 2), you need to clean and sanitize your bottles. You can clean your bottles pretty much at your convenience if you store them properly, but sanitizing your bottles too far ahead of time may lead to bacterial recontamination.

TIP

Using a dishwasher with a dry cycle is a convenient way of cleaning bottles (be sure you load the bottles into the dishwasher upside down). This practice does *not* relieve you from your bottle-sanitizing duties.

To sanitize your bottles, follow these steps:

1. **Fill the entire basin or sink with water and sanitizer (per package instructions).**

   Of course, exactly how much water you need to add depends on the capacity of the utility basin or sink — and don't forget to adjust the volume of sanitizing chemical to the volume of water (I give you some guidelines in the "Soaps for Suds" section, but always read the label on your particular sanitizer). You need enough water to immerse at least 54 12-ounce bottles. Again, add cleansing/sanitizing chemicals according to package directions, or pour in the proper amount of unscented household bleach (1 ounce per gallon of water).

2. **As you immerse the bottles, make sure the sanitizing solution fills each one, with no pockets of air left in them.**
3. **Allow the bottles to soak for 30 minutes (or according to the sanitizer's package directions).**
4. **After 30 minutes, affix the bottle rinser to the faucet (you may have to use an adapter) and turn on the hot water.**

   Don't worry about water spraying everywhere; the bottle rinser is designed to hold back the water pressure until you slip a bottle over the opening and apply downward pressure.

5. **Clean the bottles one by one with the bottle brush while the sanitizing solution is still in them.**
6. **Drain the sanitizing solution from each bottle, rinse each bottle twice with the bottle rinser, and allow the bottles to air-dry.**

TIP

   One stumble into several dozen free-standing bottles can make for a doozy of a breakable mess. Put your cleaned bottles back into 6-pack holders or cardboard cases to prevent accidental catastrophes.

Don't forget that you also need to sanitize your bottle caps before using them. Boil them for 10 minutes in a small pot of water on your stove top. If you're using the oxygen-barrier type of bottle cap, however, you should soak them in a percarbonate or iodine-based solution for the same amount of time. Boiling this type of cap reduces its ability to absorb oxygen.

REMEMBER

Sanitizing cans is just as important as sanitizing bottles. If you plan to can your homebrew, you can find the directions for sanitizing your cans and equipment in Chapter 15.

2

It's in There: The Nuts and Bolts of Beer

IN THIS PART . . .

Learn about the malts and malts extract that form the foundation on which to build your brews.

Discover the wonderful world of hops, without which your beer would be pretty boring.

Delve into a little microbiology via yeasts and other microbes responsible for fermenting your beer.

Consider the importance of the water you use to brew your beer; it constitutes up to 95 percent of it.

Ponder the possibilities presented by all the adjuncts and flavorings you can use in your beer.

Investigate the optional additives and preservatives available to improve your brew.

- Malting and mashing
- Distinguishing between base grains, adjunct grains, and specialty grains
- Extracting malt
- Comparing and contrasting malt extracts

Chapter 4
Malt: A Tale of Two Sources (Grain and Extract)

The word *malt* generally refers to the natural maltose sugars derived from certain grains (mainly barley) that eventually become beer. At the commercial brewing level, as well as the advanced homebrewing level, brewers produce beer through procedures that create and capture the malt sugars from the grain. At the beginner and intermediate levels of homebrewing, however, a commercially produced malt syrup that homebrewers can easily use to make beer at home eliminates the need for these procedures.

In this chapter, I look at the different types of grains used in brewing as well as the processes the grain undergoes to become brew-ready. I also explore the shortcuts available in the form of malt extract and compare and contrast its two forms: dry and liquid.

Going with Grain

Of the four main ingredients used to make beer (barley, hops, yeast, and water), barley — really, grain in general — makes the biggest contribution. It's responsible for giving beer its color, its underlying flavor, its sweetness, its body, its head of foam, and its *mouthfeel* (or the textural qualities of beer on your palate and in your throat — *viscosity*, or thickness; carbonation; alcohol warmth; and so on). Grains also contribute the natural maltose sugars that feed the yeast, which in turn converts the sugars into alcohol and carbon dioxide during fermentation.

For as long as humans have been making beer, they've experimented with all different kinds of *cereal grains* for beermaking purposes. Wherever grains grew uncultivated, the indigenous peoples made a beer-like beverage from them: wheat in Mesopotamia, barley in Egypt, millet in Africa, rice in Asia, and corn in the Americas.

Cereal grains are the same ones that are puffed, popped, pulverized, and poured into the colorful boxes of breakfast cereal that line your grocer's shelves: corn flakes, Rice Krispies, Wheat Chex, oatmeal. Name any cereal grain, and you can bet someone has tried to put it in beer (don't get me started with Fruity Pebbles!). One grain that isn't very popular at the breakfast table is the one that works best for making beer: barley. (It works pretty well in soup, too.)

Barley grows in two major strains: *6-row* barley and *2-row* barley. These names refer to the number of rows of barley kernels visible when you look down from the top of the stalk. 2-row barley is generally used to make ales, and 6-row barley is generally used to make lagers (but these aren't hard-and-fast rules).

Malting

Before you can brew with barley, it must undergo a process known as *malting*. The malting process, simply put, simulates the grain's natural germination cycle. (Who says it's not nice to fool Mother Nature?) Under closely monitored conditions, malting companies wet the barley kernels and allow them to sprout. As the seedlings begin sprouting, the starchy insides of the kernels (or *endosperm*) begin to change. This modification causes the hard, starchy endosperm to begin to break down into natural malt sugars (*maltose*) that brewers later liquefy, during the mashing process. (See the "Mashing" section in this chapter for details on this process.) One of the most important features of this process is the production of the enzymes brewers later use in the mashing process. In addition, the maltose sugars that form during the process, along with proteins and dextrins, help contribute to the aforementioned color, flavor, sweetness, body, mouthfeel, and foam in the finished beer.

Only after the barley has undergone the malting process does it become *malt*, or *barleymalt*.

Malted barley is an incredibly complete and convenient package, seemingly designed exclusively for brewing beer. Each grain kernel contains *carbohydrates* (which eventually convert to sugar), *enzymes* (which do the actual converting), *proteins* (which provide yeast nutrition, mouthfeel, and head stability), and a *husk* (which, when multiplied by thousands, acts as the perfect natural filter bed through which you can drain the unfermented beer).

TECHNICAL STUFF

Very few commercial brewers — usually only the huge beer factories — do their own malting. Professional malting companies (also called *maltsters*) malt most of the grain for the brewing industry (including smaller commercial brewers and homebrew supply shops).

It should be noted that other grains such as wheat and rye, and even sorghum, may also be malted.

Mashing

In order to make beer from the malted grain, the starch within the kernels of malt must be made soluble. This liquefying process takes place during the mashing procedures in a vessel called a *mash tun*. The mashing process is where the natural enzymes found in grain break down the grain's starches; hot water then dissolves the starches so they leech out of the cracked grain. After you've rinsed all the malt sugars from the grain, you transfer the syrupy-sweet malt tea, called *wort*, over to the brew kettle, where you boil it. (For more on mashing, see Chapter 12.)

Homebrewers who make their beer with nothing but malt extract can avoid the mashing process altogether.

Wort (rhymes with dirt) is the German word for unfermented beer. Some brewers also call wort *green beer* (and not just on St. Patrick's Day).

Mixing it up with other grains

Although barley is the best base grain for brewing, it's by no means your only option. You can enhance the flavor of barleymalt in beer with specialty grains or substitute the barley with adjunct grains. The following list details the characteristics of these different types of grains:

- **Base malted grain** is the main source of fermentable sugars and the body and flavor of the beer. Base grain must undergo modification during malting; make sure it's fully mashed before brewing with it. Most commercial beer recipes and many all-grain homebrew recipes call for more than one type of base grain.
- **Specialty grains** allow the brewer to add all kinds of colors, flavors, and textures to beer, therefore providing a variety of visual, aromatic, and taste enhancements. Also, specialty grains may contribute dextrins and head-retaining and body-building proteins (the beer's body, not yours). These grains create complexity in beer (and perplexity in the beer critic). Most specialty grains don't require mashing because they don't add significant amounts of fermentable sugars to the wort. Simply put, without the use of specialty grains, very few distinctive beer styles would exist.

  In a 5-gallon batch, which typically starts with about 10 pounds of grain, you don't need much specialty grain to lend a noticeable effect. Depending on the grain type, quantities of as little as ¼ of a pound are detectable in the finished beer.
- **Adjunct grains** are unmalted cereal grains that still add fermentable sugars to the wort (as well as some underlying flavor). Adjunct grains, such as corn and rice, are popular for fiscal reasons; they're used in place of the more expensive barleymalt. They're also used to reduce flavor and make lighter-bodied beers.

TECHNICAL STUFF

  Corn and rice aren't malted like barley, so brewers must cook them in a cereal cooker to gelatinize the starchy interior of the grain in order for the brewer to extract their sugars. *Gelatinization* is a softening of the hard grain kernel. Although corn and rice aren't popular with homebrewers, those who do use these grains must also gelatinize them by cooking them on the stove-top before adding them to the mash.

A few specialty grain types aren't malted but still undergo mashing procedures (because throwing these unmalted specialty grains in with the rest of the malted grains in the mash tun is the only logical time and place to add them to the beer). These unmalted specialty grains include roasted barley, raw wheat, and raw oats, among others, and are used for flavoring and texture purposes, not for adding fermentable sugars. Intermediate and advanced homebrewers can easily add uniqueness to their brews by simply adding specialty grains to their mashing vessel.

TO ADD-JUNK OR NOT TO ADD-JUNK?

Although enhancing a beer's malt character with specialty grain is perfectly acceptable, many purists (this author included) shy away from substituting barleymalt with adjunct grain. One way to enhance the barley character of a beer is by adding wheat or rye to the recipe, which gives the beer a distinctively different flavor and enhanced mouthfeel The most obvious examples of brewers substituting barley with adjuncts occur at the big corporate brewhouses, where they replace the rich malt character of barley with lighter and cheaper adjunct grains like corn and rice (much to the delight of millions of oblivious beer drinkers).

Manipulating grain: Kilning and milling

In addition to these grains, you can also manipulate malted barley in a variety of ways to create unique specialty malts. *Kilning*, or roasting the grain to various degrees, is one way of achieving this variety. Depending on the degree of roasting, specialty grains imbue beer with a broad palette of earth-toned colors, and their flavor contributions range from caramelly to chocolatey to roasty to smoky. *Milling* is the process of cracking the grain husk to allow access to the natural sugars contained within the kernel (also called cracking).

TIP

Don't mill highly kilned grains such as roasted barley and black malt. Because they're quite brittle, they have a tendency to crumble during the milling process, creating a fine, dark grain powder that adds harshness to your beer.

Homebrew recipes usually call out specialty grains by the pound or in increments of a pound. In the absence of a kitchen or postal scale, you can measure specialty grains with relative accuracy by using a measuring cup.

For conversion purposes, 1 cup of milled grain equals approximately 1/4 pound, ergo, 4 cups equal 1 pound.

Enjoying the Ease of Extracts

Fortunately for homebrewers (particularly novices), they can make beer much more easily, without having to deal with grains. (It sounds too good to be true, doesn't it?) The same companies that malt the raw grain for the brewing industry have also figured out a way to make a product that homebrewers can rehydrate to reproduce the wort you get by mashing malted grain. These companies market the product as *malt extract*, and it's been nothing less than a boon to the homebrewing industry (some professional brewers use it, too).

Malt extract (also called *malt syrup*) is a premade, premeasured beer concentrate. Malt extract starts out as wort produced from grain that is then dehydrated to the point that it contains as little as 20 percent water content. Basically, all you need to do is add malt extract to water and boil it. I may be oversimplifying the process just a tad, but all-inclusive malt extract kits are just about that easy. The hardest part of the brewing process is often deciding which kit to buy. (I give plenty of extract-based beer recipes in Part 5.) For more on brewing with a kit, take a look at Chapters 10 and 17.

These concentrated malt extracts usually come premeasured (in pounds or kilograms) in cans or heavy-duty plastic bags. The typical can of malt extract weighs 3.3 or 6.6 pounds, and these extracts are available in most of the recognized beer styles. Malt extract can imbue your homebrew with all the malt flavor, sweetness, body, and mouthfeel you'd get if you made it from grain.

TIP

For full body and flavor, use two 3.3-pound cans to make one full batch of beer (5 gallons), or no less than 1 pound of extract per gallon of water (1 pound of extract per gallon of water results in a beer with a specific gravity of 1.040; 6.6 pounds in a 5-gallon batch results in a specific gravity of 1.052).

TECHNICAL STUFF

The rather odd (by U.S. standards) measure of 3.3 pounds was set by the British, who pioneered the malt-extract-producing industry. The majority of kits initially sold in the U.S. were from the U.K., where 3.3 pounds is 1.5 kilograms (the standard can size).

Kits are all-inclusive setups that include a *prehopped* malt extract (an extract that already has the hop bitterness added to it) and a packet of yeast to match the style of beer listed on the can's exterior. These kits come in a variety of colors and flavors and are clearly labeled according to the style of beer they produce. I recommend these kits for all first-time homebrewers. Be aware, however, that not all extracts are the same quality. Cheaper malt extracts often add sugar (read the labels). For better-tasting brews, pay a little extra and buy top-quality *all-malt* extracts — you'll be glad you did.

Also, don't follow any directions provided with cans of extract that recommend adding sugar to the brew. Just follow the brewing guidelines in Chapter 10.

Graduating to other malty methods

Although homebrew kits specify the particular beer styles they're ideal for, they can also be somewhat confining in this respect. Homebrewers who rely on the kit-maker to reproduce true beer styles may decide at some point to take more personal control of the situation. Graduating into the realm of extract brewing without a kit requires the brewer to separately buy and add whatever ingredients don't come with the can of extract: The hops, yeast, and whatever specialty grains the recipe calls for. (I cover the details on how to work with these various ingredients in Chapter 11.)

LOVIBONDS TO LOVE AND SRMs, EBCs, AND HCUs 4 U 2 C

All of the various maltsters who malt the grain for the American brewing industry produce it in much the same way. One of the industry standards they follow is the production of kilned grains according to a color scale called the *Lovibond scale.* Actually, the Lovibond method of color measurement can be applied to wort, malt extract, and beer as well, but these qualities all trace their roots back to the malt-house.

Because you can more easily *see* differences in color depth than *describe* them accurately, the Lovibond scale designates a specific number to each specific color depth. Each of the specialty grains on the upcoming list has its own degree on the Lovibond scale (though Lovibond can be abbreviated as L, most packages and recipes just use the number without the *L*). Here are those numbers, including some base malts for comparison:

- Pale Lager 1.6
- Pale Ale 1.8
- Vienna 3
- Munich (light) 10
- Munich (dark) 20
- Crystal 20–120
- Chocolate 350
- Black Patent 500+
- Roasted barley 500+

A more updated color scale for beer is the American standard of color measurement — the *SRM* (Standard Reference Method) scale. It closely approximates the older Lovibond scale, with the main difference being that the SRM scale is much more accurate because it relies on a *spectrophotometer* (an instrument used to measure the absorbance of light — and no, you don't need to buy one) to do the measuring. The Lovibond scale, on the other hand, relies on the human eye to discern color depths compared to tinted glass filters.

When a homebrewer has enough confidence to take this leap on his own, he's maltriculated (okay, graduated) to the intermediate level of homebrewing.

I always encourage intermediate homebrewers to start with the palest base extract available because they're the most neutral-tasting and allow the most flexibility. You can always add dark color and additional flavor to a beer by using specialty grains.

Comparing liquid versus dry malt extract

Malt extract comes in two distinct forms. One is *liquid,* which is quite thick and viscous, and the other is *dry,* which is a rather sticky powder. These two forms share similarities that far outnumber their differences. Actually, the main distinction between liquid and dry extracts is that dry malt extract (*DME* in homebrewer lingo) has been spray-dried to remove up to 99 percent of its moisture content.

Convenience is also a benefit of working with DME: Though it can get sticky if it contacts water, steam, or humid air, it's nowhere near as messy as liquid extract. You can effortlessly and accurately measure DME with little cleanup required. The storage factor can also come into play. Just like bread, liquid extract can grow mold when exposed to air, so you need to use opened cans as soon as possible. DME, because of its minuscule moisture content, can simply be refrigerated in self-sealing plastic bags. Dry extract is also a great convenience to those who practice the yeast-propagating techniques I discuss in Chapters 6 and 12.

TIP

Unopened cans of liquid extract have a fairly long shelf-life. They may be usable for up to two to four years, but as with most consumables, the fresher they are, the better for your beer (and don't even think of using malt extract from a can that's bulging at the seams). Six to eight months is the generally accepted window of freshness. Dry malt extract has a much longer shelf-life; if you keep it sealed and refrigerated, DME can last almost indefinitely.

I need to point out that, for all its usefulness, DME has its disadvantages. It's not packaged according to any particular style; it's just sold in light, amber, dark, and wheat variations. You also pay for its convenience; because of the extra processing required to produce it, DME is more expensive than liquid extract. Of course, you're also getting more bang for your buck (because of the lower water content in DME), which brings up another good point: Because of the difference in water content, using dry extract in place of liquid extract affects your gravity readings in a side-by-side, pound-for-pound comparison. This difference adds up to about one specific gravity degree per pound, with the DME having a greater yield than liquid extract. Woo-hoo!

THICK AS A BRIX

Malt extract manufacturers use heat and/or vacuum power to remove moisture from the wort, which concentrates the wort into an extract. How much water they remove determines the extract's *viscosity,* and the percentage of remaining solids determines the *brix.* The brix scale provides a number that correlates to the amount of sugar (solids) found in a 100-pound sample. Most malt extracts range between 70 and 80 brix.

From an economic standpoint, it makes more sense to buy the most concentrated extract available — those with the highest brix rating. To make this point clearer, 3½ pounds of 80 brix extract contain as much fermentable sugar as 4 pounds of 70 brix extract. Unfortunately, not all malt extract manufacturers disclose this information on the product labels, so you may have to ask your retailer.

Also, be aware that extracts with high brix ratings may be unsuitable for making pale beers because the extra heat needed to concentrate the wort usually results in darker and more caramelly malt extracts.

IN THIS CHAPTER

» Understanding hops' contributions to beer

» Discovering where hops come from

» Using hops for bittering, flavoring, and aromatizing

» Making hop substitutions

Chapter 5
Hop Heaven

If malts represent the sugar in beer (as I discuss in Chapter 4), hops surely represent the spice. As a matter of fact, you use hops in beer in much the same way that you use spices in cooking. The divine mission of hops is to accent the flavor of beer and, most importantly, contrast the sweetness of the malt. This spiciness isn't all hops have to contribute, however.

There are three primary contributions of hops to beer:

- Aroma
- Flavor
- Bitterness (through alpha acids)

Additionally, there are two secondary contributions of hops to beer:

- Extended shelf life (through beta acids)
- Improved head retention

In this chapter, I discuss the plant origins of hops and the various ways these plants become the products you see on the shelves at the homebrew shop. I also look at the world's hop-growing regions and explain how to decipher hopping instructions in brewing recipes. Finally, I give you some tips on keeping your hops fresh (and what you can expect if you don't).

Seeing the Hop Flower Up Close

For the uninitiated, the hop cones used in the brewing process grow on vines that may reach upwards of 25 feet on commercial hop farms. Hop plants are hardy perennial plants that are quite prolific under ideal conditions, and each may produce up to 2 pounds of dried hop cones per season. Figure 5-1 shows you what hops look like.

FIGURE 5-1: Hops are vining plants with conelike flowers.

TECHNICAL STUFF

Humulus lupulus (also known as *hops*) is one of a small number of species distantly related to the *cannabis* plant; hemp, the nettle, and the elm are also distant cousins to cannabis.

Closer inspection of a mature hop cone, shown in Figure 5-2, reveals that it's mostly vegetative material (leaves and stems and whatnot), but at the base of each little leaf is a cluster of minute yellow sacs about the size of pinheads. These sacs are the waxy *lupulin glands* that contain the bitter acids, resins, and essential oils that contribute bittering, flavoring, and aromatic qualities to beer. Only when boiled extensively do these tiny glands erupt and deliver their precious contents.

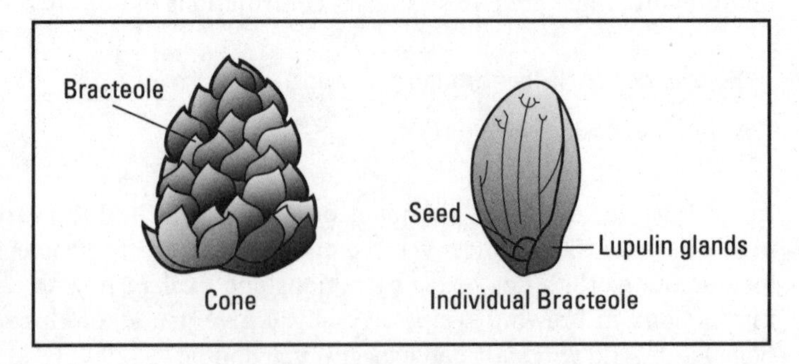

FIGURE 5-2: A close-up of the hop cone reveals the lupulin glands.

The various methods of processing and packaging hops have made delivering hop character to your homebrew easier; you can choose between whole leaf hops, hop pellets, hop extracts, and cryo hops.

Isomerization takes place when the hops' lupulin glands dissolve and release their acids and resins into the wort. Through boiling, the alpha acids are converted to soluble iso-alpha acids, which are the main source of hop bitterness. Complete isomerization in boiling wort may take up to an hour.

Traditionally speaking, brewers handpicked hops from the bine and air-dried them in bulk before tossing them whole into the brewkettle. Today, however, hops are processed and sold in four different forms, which I describe in the following list.

- **Whole-leaf hops:** As they did in the old days, farmers pick, dry, and bale the hops exactly as they come off the bine. A downside is that whole-leaf hops rarely come in oxygen-free packaging, leading to oxidation and staleness (which you can delay if you store your hops properly in dark, cool, and dry conditions).
- **Pellets:** Hop processors create pellets by pulverizing hop flowers and compacting them into small pellets about the size of a pencil eraser. Ounce-for-ounce, these pellets take up only a quarter of the space of whole leaf hops, but the process that pulverizes the hops also ruptures the hop lupulin glands. On the plus side, the ruptured lupulin glands allow the acids and resins to isomerize more quickly. Also, compressed hop pellets make packing and storing more efficient, and the hop is rendered more stable. To guard against oxidation, the best way to package pelletized hops is in nitrogen or in oxygen-barrier bags. If packaged and stored properly, pellets deteriorate at only one-tenth the rate of whole hops (see the "Freshness is fundamental" section in this chapter for more information).

  Hop pellets are often referred to as *T-90 hops* or *T-45 hops*. The numbers simply tell you what fraction of the original dried hops material makes it into the pellet.

- **Hop extract:** Just as with malt extract, you can make your job easier by buying a highly concentrated liquid product that keeps the important components and characteristics of hops intact. Although you typically find these extracts in the large breweries, some extracts are available to homebrewers (particularly the hop oils).

  You can find three basic prepackaged hop extract products. One is a concentrated bittering and flavoring agent that you can easily isomerize. The second is Late Hop Essence, which adds spicy and floral hop flavors to the beer, and the third (commonly known as *hop oil*) is strictly for aroma adjustments in post-fermentation beer.

Initially, processors used steam distillation and chemical extraction to capture these hop products, but the steaming process negatively affected their flavor and brewers became concerned about residual chemicals left in the product. More recently, a newer CO_2 extraction process extracts oils and alpha acids with none of the previous problems.

Whether you use extracts, essences, or oils, you add them in small amounts (usually measured in increments of teaspoons). These seemingly small amounts can have a big effect on the finished product, because the human senses can perceive quantities in *parts per million.* Therefore, a 2-ounce bottle of hop oil is sufficient to treat 30 gallons of beer (six batches of homebrew)!

- **Cryo hops:** This is a relatively new hop product that allows brewers to get the same level of bittering, flavor, and aroma in their beer with just a fraction of the vegetal matter included in traditional pellet or whole cone hops. Cryogenic (a deep-freezing process that uses liquid nitrogen) processes allow the lupulin found in whole hop cones to be extracted with minimal oxidation and packaged in powdered or pelletized forms. The result is an intensified hop character in the finished beer without the vegetal off-flavors.

DRY HOPPING

Dry hopping is adding hops (in any form) to the beer after primary fermentation for an added touch of hop aroma. Hop pellets are good for dry hopping, but cryo hops are even better because of their reduced vegetal matter.

You find two schools of thought as to whether you can dry hop without contaminating your beer. One side says the hops are unboiled and may potentially contaminate your brew; the other side (the one I agree with) says the alcohol in the fermented beer is antiseptic enough to keep any bacteria at bay.

If you want to dry hop your beer, you should do so during secondary fermentation (see Chapter 11 for more info on secondary fermentation). In any case, whatever you put into the secondary fermenter needs to be strained out of the brew on bottling day. The best way to avoid sucking up hops or anything else from your secondary fermenter is to attach a *sanitized* plastic or stainless steel scrubber that you would ordinarily use for washing dishes to the end of your racking cane.

Hopping with Variety

More than 200 recognized hop varieties now exist, and most of them grow in one of the seven well-known hop growing regions throughout the world (see Table 5-1). Many of these varieties bear names that hint at their origins.

TABLE 5-1 **Major Hop Zones**

Hop Growing Region	Regional Hop Variety
Hallertau District, northern Bavaria, Germany	Hallertauer
Zatec, Bohemia, Czech Republic	Saaz
Victoria, Australia	Pride of Ringwood
County Kent, England	East Kent Goldings
Pacific Northwest, United States (Idaho, Oregon, Washington)	Mount Hood
British Columbia, Canada	Olympic
New Zealand	Motueka

Outside of the regions listed in Table 5-1, hops also grow in parts of Belgium, France, Poland, Slovenia, and my backyard, but these regions aren't nearly as distinguished as those shown in the table.

Regardless of their place of origin, the vast majority of cultivated hop varieties are *hybrids* of original wild varieties, crossbred to capitalize on specific genetic qualities such as high yields and resistance to disease. An amazing amount of effort has gone into such hop cultivation, especially considering that you use hops rather sparingly in the brewing process (only a few ounces are needed for a 5-gallon batch of homebrew).

You may be asking yourself, "So if I use hops in such a minimal fashion, why do so many regions grow so many varieties?" Well, the answer is quite simple. Each hop variety offers different nuances in bittering intensity, flavor, and aroma. The differences between them are often so subtle that even the most experienced brewers and beer judges are hard-pressed to recognize their individual attributes in a given beer — especially when you consider that brewers often use blends of different hops in a single batch of beer.

Each hop variety is more or less bitter (like lovers scorned). But instead of measuring hop bitterness in the number of forlorn letters sent and pleading phone calls made, brewers use a scientific scale to determine hops' *percent alpha acid content*. Alpha acid content is the component within the lupulin gland that correlates to bitterness, and brewers are very aware of these percentages when they formulate recipes so that they can estimate the hops' bittering potential in the beer. They also acquaint themselves with each hop variety's unique flavoring and aromatic properties so they know how and when to use them. See the "Bittering potential is important too" section in this chapter for more information.

- Hops that are used for their bittering potential are *bittering hops* or *kettle hops*.
- Hops that are used for flavoring (but not necessarily bittering) are *flavoring hops* or *late-kettle hops*.
- Hops that are used for their aromatic contributions are *aroma hops* or *finishing hops*.
- Hops that are held in school gymnasiums are *sock hops*.

Hey, this ain't rocket science.

How and when you use the hops determines the effect that they have on the finished brew. The longer you boil the hops, the more bitterness dissolves into the wort (up to a point). Boiling hops for five minutes to a half an hour imbues the beer with far less bitterness than the hops could potentially add, but you get some hop flavor. Adding hops very late in the boil and boiling them for less than five minutes provides the beer with aromatics and little else.

Many homebrew recipes tell you not only which hop varieties to use and in what quantities but also how long to boil them to get bittering, flavoring, or aromatizing characteristics from them. In a homebrew recipe (including the recipes in this book), you may see something like the following instruction: 1.5 oz. Galena (60 mins.), 1 oz. Kent Goldings (15 mins.), and 0.5 Cascade (5 mins.). This notation tells you that you want to boil an ounce and a half of Galena hops for 1 hour (for bittering), add an ounce of Kent Goldings hops in the last 15 minutes of the boil (for flavoring), and add just a half-ounce of Cascade hops in the last 5 minutes of the boil (for aroma).

TIP

You don't want to boil aroma hops for more than 5 to 10 minutes because the aromatic oils are very volatile and vaporize fairly quickly. The longer you boil these hops, the more their aroma diminishes.

TECHNICAL STUFF

First wort hopping is yet another method of imbuing your beer with hop flavor. Unfortunately, this method, which requires the brewer to add hops to the brew during the sparging/lautering phase of mashing, is only useful to brewers who produce their beer entirely from grain (see Chapter 12 for more information).

NOBLE HOPS: BREWING ROYALTY

Noble hops are distinguished old-world varieties, most of which have been cultivated for centuries. They have relatively low alpha acid contents but are popular for their aromatic and flavoring characteristics. Among the noble varieties are Hallertauer, Hersbrucker, Spalt, and Tettnanger in Germany; Saaz from Bohemia in the Czech Republic; and Styrian from the former Yugoslavia.

European noble varieties are typically more expensive than the same varieties grown in North America, so many homebrew supply shops and catalogs may not feature them (but commercial beer labels often boast of their use).

Selecting the Best Hops

Homemakers who want everything they cook or bake to come out tasting just right tend to fuss about the finer details of their recipes. Having the right ingredients isn't enough — they have to be fresh, too.

And so it is with beer. It's important to use the right hops for your brew — especially if you are duplicating a recipe, but it's even more important to use the freshest hops you can. If you use old or stale hops, you could be brewing up a recipe for disaster.

Freshness is fundamental

The freshness of hops is vital to the outcome of the beer. And, of course, in order for them to stay fresh, you need to store your hops properly. This means that you need to keep them packed in nitrogen- or oxygen-barrier bags and refrigerated (or, preferably, frozen) for long-term storage. But first things first: You must know how to identify the fresh hops from the stale hops.

The first indicator of a hop's freshness is its color. Fresh hops that are whole leaf form usually have a light (almost lime) green color; fresh pelletized hops are typically a darker shade of green (a few hop varieties, such as Goldings, have a yellowish cast) and may have a shiny exterior due to the dried hop resins. Hops that look brown, dried out, and curled are probably pretty old; if the tiny lupulin glands are orange instead of yellow, the hops are *oxidized* (stale) — get rid of 'em.

Check hops for aroma, too. Fresh hops have a fresh and piquant aroma that you may describe as piney, earthy, woody, floral, spicy, herbal, citrusy — there's even tropical fruit. Any hops that have a pungent odor reminiscent of Parmesan or Romano cheese or unlaundered gym socks are likely to be old and oxidized — throw them away. Any off flavors and aromas evident before you use the hops will surely manifest in your beer.

Hop varieties are also graded according to their *stability,* which refers to how well they keep in storage. The freshness scale assigns a rating (very good, good, fair, or poor) based on the percentage of the hop bitterness that remains after a six-month storage period at 70 degrees Fahrenheit (21 degrees Celsius). Unless you buy your hops in large quantities, however, you don't really need to concern yourself with their stability. Just make sure that you buy them fresh, store them right, and use them soon.

Bittering potential is important too

After freshness, bittering potential is the next most important consideration in your choice of hops. At harvest time, farmers measure hops for their alpha acid content. You express the alpha acid content as a percentage of the acid's weight relative to the weight of the whole hop flower. For example, the 2006 Northdown crop from the U.K. has an alpha acid content of 7 percent, which means that 1 pound of these hops contains 0.070 pounds of bittering acids. This information appears on hop packaging as 7.0 AAU, which means *alpha acid units.*

Each hop variety has a different acid content than another, and brewers need to take this discrepancy into consideration. Alpha acid contents also vary slightly from one growing season to the next, depending on the elements, and from one place of origin to another. In this way, hops are to brewers what varietal grapes are to winemakers.

Rumor has it brewers in the post-war Soviet Union resorted to bittering their beer with ox bile when hop shipments became impossible to obtain. To your health, Komrade!

Utilizing the utilization factor

Homebrewers need to be aware of the *utilization factor,* particularly when brewing high-gravity beers. Utilization refers to the amount of bitterness (alpha acid) extracted from the hops during the boiling phase. Both boiling time and beer gravity (density) affect utilization.

The longer you boil the hops, the more bitterness you extract from the lupulin glands and dissolve into the wort. This rule is only true up to a point, however; by the time you boil your hops for 90 minutes, all available bitterness should be extracted.

Higher-gravity worts use hops less efficiently; the density of the wort keeps the alpha acids from easily dissolving into the liquid. This tendency is especially apparent in wort gravities of 1.050 and higher. Most recipes already take this utilization factor into account, but if you're taking a low-gravity recipe (1.050 or lower) and increasing its malt content, you need to calculate the *gravity adjustment* (GA) factor when figuring the appropriate hop increase in order to keep your beer flavor in balance.

Or you could just rely on one of the many homebrewer phone apps out there that do all the calculations for you (see Chapter 31 for more info).

TIP

Don't worry, the following is a sample formula that can help you find the GA when necessary: GA= wort gravity – 1.050, ÷ 0.2. For example, if your wort gravity is 1.070, your calculation should look something like this: GA= 1.070 – 1.050 = .020; .020 ÷ 0.2 = 0.10. This means you have to use 10 percent more hops to achieve the same amount of bittering in a beer with a 1.070 gravity as a beer with a 1.050 gravity. See — still not rocket science.

Calculating AAUs

Many homebrew recipes call for a certain hop variety by name or require a certain number of alpha acid units (*AAUs*). These suggested varieties aren't always available to all homebrewers, so you may have to make hop substitutions by figuring AAUs. This equation is simple, assuming you or your supplier knows the alpha acid content of the hops that you plan to use.

Here's how you can plug in the numbers: Say that a recipe calls for 3 ounces of Northern Brewer hops with 7.5 percent alpha acid; this means that the recipe requires 22.5 AAUs (3 ounces × 7.5 percent alpha acid). To achieve bittering purposes only, you should be able to use 2 ounces of Chinook hops (for example) with an alpha acid content of 11.25 percent (2 ounces × 11.25 = 22.5 AAUs).

Note: I say "for bittering purposes only" because Chinook hops and Northern Brewer hops differ in taste.

Be sure to consider your recipe batch size; 22.5 AAUs called for in a 10-gallon batch would be twice as bitter if used in a 5-gallon batch!

Despite being an imperfect science, calculating AAUs is much easier for homebrewers to deal with than IBUs (International Bitterness Units). The difference is that AAUs measure how much alpha acid a recipe calls for; IBUs actually measure bitterness in beer.

TECHNICAL STUFF

The formula for figuring IBUs in beer is rather complex. A Bitterness Unit is equal to 1 milligram of isomerized alpha acid in 1 liter of beer (okay, maybe this really *is* rocket science).

One more system for figuring bittering units in homebrew recipes is *homebrew bitterness units*, or *HBUs*. The HBU system is virtually identical to the AAU system. You calculate HBUs by multiplying the alpha acid percentage of a given hop by the number of ounces of that hop the recipe requires. For example, if a recipe calls for a total of 24 HBUs, you need 3 ounces of hops with 8 percent alpha acid, or 6 ounces of hops with 4 percent alpha acid (or any other ounce/percentage combination whose product is 24).

The lists in Table 5-2 provide the most popular beer styles and their recommended approximate HBU levels.

TABLE 5-2

HBUs by Beer Styles

Ales	HBU	Lagers	HBU
Altbier	10–20	Bock	8–12
Barley wine	15–40	Pilsener	8–13
Kölsch	8–15	Doppelbock	10–15
English brown ale	5–10	Munich Dunkel	7–11
American brown ale	10–20	Münchner-Style Helles	7–13
Pale ale	10–17	Dortmunder/European-Style Export	8–12
India pale ale	13–20	Rauchbier	7–10
Porter	8–12	Vienna/Märzenbier	8–12
Classic Irish-style dry stout	8–15		
Sweet stout	5–10		
Stout (imperial)	15–40		
Berliner Weisse	2–3		
Weizen/Weissbier	4–7		

Taking Note of Top Hops

There isn't a more exciting segment of the global brewing industry than the hop-growing industry, and thankfully, this enthusiasm works its way down to the homebrewing community as well.

The North American hop-growing industry has developed a reputation for its experimentation with new and experimental hop varieties. Of course, North American homebrewers are quick to take note and follow suit. But this is not to say that hop growers around the world are not participating fully; new hop cultivars from Down Under (Australia and New Zealand) are among the world's hottest hops at this time.

Table 5-3 shows a list of the top ten most popular hops among homebrewers over the past several years, as well as a list of ten new and experimental hops to watch in the future.

TABLE 5-3 **Popular and Up-and-Coming Styles of Hops**

Popular Hops	Hops to Watch
Citra	Nectaron
Cascade	Strata
Mosaic	Talus
Amarillo	Cashmere
Simcoe	Rakau
Centennial	Riwaka
Magnum	Zythos
Galaxy	Loral
El Dorado	Waimea
Saaz	BRU-1

IN THIS CHAPTER

» Understanding the basics of yeast

» Exploring fermentation

» Propagating yeast

» Figuring alcohol content

Chapter 6
Yeast and Fermentation

Yeast is one of the four primary ingredients in beer (the other three are grain, hops, and water). Although yeast is an ingredient that the average beer consumer rarely contemplates, brewers often consider it the most important ingredient. As a matter of fact, yeast can have a greater influence and effect on the finished beer than any other single ingredient.

Brewers categorize and classify beer styles by the type of yeast used to ferment them; therefore, they choose a yeast according to the style of beer they want to make. In this chapter, I discuss the nuts and bolts of yeast and its role in fermentation, as well as give you the lowdown on the myriad of options you have when choosing a yeast for your brew. I also provide some tips on figuring alcohol content and deliver a bit of bad news for those of you hoping to brew a nonalcoholic batch.

There's a Fungus among Us

Yeast is a member of the fungus family. It's a living single-celled organism and one of the simplest forms of life. Because it has cell-splitting capabilities, it's also *self-reproducing.* Yeast is the one ingredient responsible for carrying out the fermentation process in brewing.

YEAST GENUS AND GENIUS

For all the biology fans out there, here's the scoop on yeast. You can classify beer yeast into two categories, or species, of the genus *Saccharomyces*: *Saccharomyces cerevisiae* and *Saccharomyces pastorianus* (occasionally referred to as *S. carlsbergensis*), in deference to Louis Pasteur, who participated in the isolation and identification of this strain of yeast.

Bread yeast is also a part of this genus, but that's just a crummy factoid.

- *Saccharomyces cerevisiae* (*S. cerevisiae*) is commonly known as *ale yeast* and contains many substrains. It's a *top-fermenting* strain, meaning it floats on the top of the beer. Virtually all ale yeast works best in fairly warm temperatures (60 to 70 degrees Fahrenheit).
- *Saccharomyces pastorianus* (*S. pastorianus*) is a *bottom-fermenting* strain (meaning it sinks to the bottom of the fermentation vessel at the end of fermentation) and is better known as *lager yeast*. Brewers developed lager yeast to ferment beer in cooler temperatures, and it works best between 38 and 50 degrees Fahrenheit. This strain is sometimes referred to as *S. carlsbergensis*, for the Danish brewery where brewers isolated and developed it in 1883.

Fermentation, simply put, is the natural conversion of sugar to alcohol. Yeast has a voracious appetite for sweet liquids. And, in exchange for a good, sweet meal, yeast produces equal amounts of ethanol (ethyl alcohol) and carbon dioxide. Yes, the alcohol in your beer is similar to that which is added to gasoline, except car ethanol is made from corn (yikes, adjunct gas!)

Yeast not only ferments beer, but it also ferments wine and any other naturally alcoholic beverage. Because yeast produces carbon dioxide, it's also what causes bread dough to rise.

The temperature at which beer ferments can have a great effect on the finished product. The top-fermenting ale yeast strains can complete their gluttonous feast in as little as three days. This quick, warm fermentation has a tendency to give the resulting beer a rich and complex aroma and flavor profile. As a direct result of the marriage of yeast type and temperature, ales tend to be fruity and estery. *Estery* is a word used to describe a beer that possesses aromas reminiscent of flowers or fruits. Some yeast strains generate more esters than others.

Lager yeast actually developed a gradual genetic acclimation to its surroundings over hundreds of years. But because the cool temperatures at which lager yeast feeds result in sluggishness, lager yeast needs lengthier fermentation periods to complete its job. On the up side, however, the benefit of such long and labored fermentation is the absence of fruitiness and buttery character found in ales. Lagers are therefore cleaner, smoother beers.

The word *lager* comes from the German *lagern*, which means *to store.* Because summertime fermentations often resulted in sour beer, brewers knew better than to brew beyond late spring. To keep up their stores of beer, Bavarian brewers began brewing bigger-bodied beers in March and storing them in Alpine caves throughout the warm summer months. Over time, the yeast actually performed better under these cool conditions.

The Magic of Fermentation

Fermentation is, indeed, magical and mystical. A simple yeast cell consumes sugar (in liquefied form) and in turn excretes alcohol and carbon dioxide in addition to hundreds of flavor compounds. As part of the growth process, a single cell reproduces by cloning itself — splitting into two separate cells. Multiply this chain of events by billions and trillions, and you have fermentation.

It's cyclical

Before yeast can begin eating and multiplying, it must do its aerobics — taking in as much of the oxygen from the wort as possible. Similar to oxygen-breathing life forms, yeast needs oxygen to complete its metabolic processes. After the yeast cells scavenge all or most of the oxygen in the wort, they remain in suspension (float around in the liquid) for maximum contact with the liquid sugars. After the yeast consumes most of the sugars, it begins to *flocculate,* or clump together and fall out of suspension. At this point, the yeast has lost energy and is preparing for a state of dormancy.

You can clearly separate the fermentation cycle into three phases:

- **Yeast growth phase:** This is the initial phase when the yeast cells absorb the oxygen in the wort in preparation for their feast.
- **Fermentation:** This is the main event — the yeasts are devouring the sugars in the wort and producing alcohol and CO_2. Dividing yeast cells double the total number of yeast cells in the wort every day.
- **Sedimentation:** This is the anticlimactic close of the fermentation cycle; with the wort now devoid of oxygen and short on fermentable sugar, the yeast begins to flocculate and settle to the bottom of the fermenter.

Peak fermentation is known as *high kraeusen* (pronounced *kroy*-zen). High kraeusen usually occurs between days three and five of fermentation, assuming that the yeast got off to a good start.

Factoring in fermentation variables

How well fermentation takes place and how long it lasts depends on many variables, including temperature, the amount of oxygen in the wort, the amount of yeast *pitched* (added), the *viability* (health) of the yeast pitched, and the amount of available fermentable sugars in the wort.

- **Fermentation temperature,** of course, should be within the recommended ranges of the yeast according to species. Ale yeast works best in temperatures between 60 and 70 degrees Fahrenheit. Lager yeast performs best when temperatures are between 38 and 50 degrees Fahrenheit.

  Fermentation temperatures that are too low slow down the fermentation or even stop it cold. Extreme temperatures on the high end cause an increase in fermentation activity and an increased risk of unpleasant aromas and flavors. High fermentation temperatures (above 75 degrees Fahrenheit) often result in off flavors and production of an alcohol other than ethyl alcohol.

- **Proper oxygen levels in wort** enable the yeast to grow. You need to properly aerate your wort prior to pitching the yeast. You can aerate by sloshing the cooled wort around in the fermenter or with an oxygenating device called a *beer stone* (see Chapter 31 for more information on beer stones).

- **The amount of yeast pitched** is important primarily because of lag time. *Lag time* is the length of time between the pitching of yeast into the wort and the time that active fermentation begins to take place (for healthy fermentations, lag time shouldn't exceed 24 hours). Lag time is affected by the *pitching rate* (the number of cells added to the wort).

  If the yeast volume is slow to multiply to desired quantities, any mutant yeast cells or bacteria present can easily take over and ruin a batch of beer. You can avoid this problem by pitching the proper amount of yeast (overpitching is always better than underpitching). I recommend 1 cup of *yeast slurry* (a high concentration of yeast cells in solution) per 5-gallon batch. See the section "Propagating yeast" in this chapter to find out more about how to increase your yeast quantities.

  WARNING

  One bacterial cell per 1,000 yeast cells constitutes a serious contamination and may result in a blown batch of beer.

- **Yeast viability** is rarely a problem with fresh yeast products purchased new. Viability comes into question when you use an old, out-of-date yeast product or attempt to revive old, tired yeast from the bottom of a bottle-conditioned commercial beer (such as a well-aged Belgian Trappist Ale).

- **The amount of available fermentable sugars** has a direct effect on the quality and length of fermentation. The more food you give the yeast cells, the longer they continue to eat — up to a point. At around 8 or 9 percent alcohol, fermentation becomes self-destructive to yeast. In that concentration of alcohol, most beer yeast can no longer continue fermenting; it falls into a stupor and eventually quits working. Reminds me of some people I know.

When brewers set out to create a beer with an alcohol content greater than 8 or 9 percent, they bring in more alcohol-tolerant yeast strains equal to the challenge.

Liquid yeast versus dry yeast: A foamenting debate

You've decided on a yeast type, so now you're ready to brew, right? Not so fast — you still have to choose what *form* of that yeast you're going to use. Yeast for the homebrewer comes in both a dry form and a liquid form. Because of its convenience, I highly recommend dry yeast at the beginner level. Dry yeast comes in granular form in small foil packets. You simply tear these packets and sprinkle the yeast across the top of your beer.

It's fair to say that liquid yeast comes in greater stylistic variety than dry yeast, but dry yeast producers have made great strides in recent years, introducing many new style-specific yeast strains. I still encourage you to progress to liquid yeast cultures as soon as you're comfortable with the handling procedures outlined in this chapter.

How dry I am . . .

The small packets (or do you say *sachets?*) of dried yeast that come with malt extract kits are sufficient to ferment a 5-gallon batch of homebrew. Dry yeast is freeze-dried, so it should last a long time (but refrigerate all yeast to maintain optimum freshness). And best of all, it's the cheapest option.

TIP

For the best results with dry yeast, always rehydrate the dormant cells by pouring them into a cup of warm water (as I explain in Chapter 10). This gentle wake-up call prepares the yeast for the upcoming fermentation. Be sure to sanitize the vessel in which you rehydrate the yeast.

In the early days of homebrewing, dry yeasts weren't entirely sterile; mutant yeast and bacteria sometimes mingled with the good yeast in the packets. You could only hope that the good yeast cells far outnumbered the bad. Also, dry yeast often consumed a greater percentage of available sugar in the wort, which resulted in lower terminal gravities and drier beers (it's almost as if they were drinking up for lost time). Now I'm happy to report that these problems are largely a thing of the past. And whereas in the past dried yeast was available only in relatively generic packets simply labeled "Ale" or "Lager" with no further classification, today you can find a much greater selection of beer-style-specific dried yeast strains.

But even with the greater variety of dry yeast strains today, the incredible diversity of liquid yeast strains available still makes it the obvious choice for making many more beer styles. Check out Table 6-1 for some pros and cons of using dry yeast.

TABLE 6-1 **Dry Yeast Qualities**

Dry Yeast Positives	Dry Yeast Negatives
Less expensive	More limited with regards to beer style
Easily stored	May create drier beers (depends on brand)
Easy to use	Packets not always freshness-dated
Always ready to use	
Easier to pitch amount necessary	

Liquid assets

Brewing supply companies produce pure liquid yeast cultures in a sterile environment; these come with limited guarantees for good brewing results. Luckily, they culture the yeast according to individual beer styles. A small handful of companies are now producing sterile liquid yeast cultures for both the homebrewing and commercial brewing industries. Many of these cultures were obtained from their traditional sources, such as Trappist abbey breweries and prestigious brewing institutes in Europe. Check out Table 6-2 for a comparison of the positives and negatives of using liquid yeast cultures.

To give you an idea of the wide range of individual yeast strains available, White Labs (one of the original and best-known producers of liquid yeast cultures) produces 27 different ale cultures, 15 different lager cultures, 19 different Belgian ale and wheat style cultures, and 9 different Brett and bacteria cultures.

SMACK PACKS

You may come across Activator packs (typically referred to as *smack packs*), or liquid yeast cultures sold in foil packets. These packets contain both a small amount of pure yeast culture and a smaller, sealed plastic packet filled with a small amount of sterile liquid medium and malt nutrient. This packaging keeps the yeast from feeding until you're ready.

The responsibility of feeding the nutrient mixture to the yeast is yours. While holding the foil pouch firmly on a flat surface with one hand, locate the inner packet and pop it with the heel of the other hand. The little packet is pretty squirmy, so popping it may take a couple of tries. After the inner packet has burst, shake the foil pouch briskly to fully mix the yeast and nutrient.

The packet may take between three and five hours to expand. Allow the pouch to plump up before you pitch the yeast into your wort. Always read and follow the directions printed on the back of these foil packets.

TABLE 6-2 Liquid Yeast Qualities

Liquid Yeast Positives	Liquid Yeast Negatives
Pure yeast strains	More expensive than dry yeast
Wide variety of styles	May have to propagate yeast in advance
True to style profiles	May have to propagate before pitching into high gravity brews

Propagating yeast

Whether you prefer to work with vials or foil pouches, you may find that they don't provide you with the proper volume of yeast for pitching into a 5- or 10- or 15-gallon batch (depending on your beer's original gravity). Both types require you to *propagate* (increase by natural reproduction) the yeast by feeding it more sugar and nutrient in a separate container.

By adding more fermentable sugar in liquid form, you're encouraging your yeast to eat heartily, be fruitful, and multiply. Eventually, over the span of a few days, you'll have the proper volume of yeast to pitch into a 5-gallon batch of beer.

REMEMBER

These procedures apply to liquid cultures only, not freeze-dried yeast.

TECHNICAL STUFF

High-gravity worts (those with gravities of 1.056 or higher) have a greater need for yeast. For every gravity increase of 0.008 above 1.048, double the yeast volume.

Propagating can take place in any glass vessel that you can seal with a rubber stopper, such as a mason jar, an old wine carafe, or an expensive glass flask. The bottom line is that you must thoroughly sanitize the propagating container and seal it with an airlock, just as you would any other fermentation vessel.

TIP

You can create the perfect sterile holding tank with a large 22-ounce or quart-size beer bottle. The small rubber stopper that fits the hole in the primary fermenter lid will also fit the bottle's opening.

Here's how to put your sterile holding tank to good use:

1. **Sanitize your bottle as you would any other piece of homebrewing equipment, along with a rubber stopper and an airlock.**

   (See Chapter 3 for more about sanitizing.)

2. **Mix ½ cup of pale dry malt extract with 2 cups of filtered water and boil.**
3. **When the extract and water mixture has cooled, pour the wort into the bottle, add the yeast culture, and give it a good shake to introduce some oxygen into the wort.**

   If you use a funnel, make sure it's sanitized, too!

4. **Seal the bottle with the stopper and airlock.**

Lager yeast tends to reproduce more slowly than ale yeast, even at proper temperatures. Therefore, higher pitching rates are necessary in order to achieve the same concentration of yeast cells in the fermenting beer. The general rule is to pitch double the amount of lager yeast, or 2 cups of yeast slurry per 5-gallon batch.

You need to maintain a fairly high temperature (75 degrees Fahrenheit) for the first 24 hours of the incubation period to encourage rapid yeast growth. The best time to pitch the yeast into your wort is while you can see visible, active fermentation taking place; definitely pitch the yeast before it sediments out of suspension. For batches of beer larger than 5 gallons or with gravities greater than 1.056, you can easily increase the yeast volume by propagating your culture a second or third time, using the same procedures outlined above.

TIP

You can skip step #2 and the need to produce fresh wort for your yeast starter. Homebrew suppliers now sell canned wort specifically for this purpose.

WARNING

Every time you transfer the yeast to a new vessel, you increase the risk of contamination. Always practice immaculate sanitation when it comes to yeast handling.

Yeast energizers and nutrients

As if all the different yeast choices discussed earlier in this chapter weren't enough, you can also find energizers and nutrients for beer yeast. These vitamins and minerals are dietary supplements for yeast, designed to accelerate cell growth.

AND THEN THERE'S KVEIK

One particular yeast that's been turning the homebrewing industry on its ear is called *Kveik* (pronounced *kvike*). This beast of a yeast comes from a long farmhouse brewing tradition on the west coast of Norway, and it's taking the U.S. by storm.

Kveik yeast is not considered "normal" beer yeast (it's a genetically different strain of saccharomyces), and even though it is considered an ale yeast, it is being used to produce lagers due to its clean fermentation. It's also an extremely resilient yeast, being able to ferment in excess of 100 F. and as low as 50 F. (also at significantly higher alcohol concentrations).

At higher temperature, Kveik yeast can complete its fermentation cycle in as little as 48 hours (it's little wonder that the Norwegian word Kveik comes from the same root as the English word "quick".)

Another big attraction for using Kveik yeast is its production of tropical fruit flavors that complement and accentuate similar flavors from many new hop varieties — especially those from Australia and New Zealand.

And it also has its own substrains, known as Espe, Voss, and Hornindal. You can also find proprietary substrains of these yeasts being propagated by some of the bigger yeast labs.

So, let's recap the benefits of using Kveik yeast:

- Fermentation temperature control is less of an issue
- Rapid fermentation/short fermentation cycle
- Lower risk of off-flavors
- Unique flavor profiles

These products, which you can easily obtain through your regular homebrew supplier, are fairly inexpensive (but not always necessary). You only need to use energizers and nutrients for high-gravity worts (those over 1.056) or fermentable beverages with less than 60 percent malt content, such as Cider or Mead, because your malt and (to a lesser extent) brewing water contain most of the essential nutrients necessary for yeast nutrition.

Yeast Sources

To get you started, here's a brief list of the largest and most popular yeast brands, producers, and suppliers.

Liquid Yeast	Dried Yeast
Wyeast	Lallemand
White Labs	Fermentis
Omega	Danstar
Imperial	Mangrove Jack

Considering Alcohol Content

You can brew beer at home without caring one whit about its alcohol content, but I think you'd be in a very small minority. All the homebrewers I know are very interested in knowing how much alcohol is in their brew, whether it's on the high side or the low side. And they also make a concerted effort to target specific alcohol levels in their beer.

The same can be said for millions of non-homebrewers who simply want to know how much alcohol they're consuming when they drink commercially made beers. This section helps you understand how alcohol levels in beer are measured and how that information is expressed to the consumer.

ABV versus ABW

You can express alcohol content in beer in two ways. Both are scientifically accurate, but one can be somewhat misleading when compared to the other. What I'm talking about here is the measurement of *alcohol by volume* and *alcohol by weight.*

The more common method of listing alcohol content in beer is by actual percentage of volume, which is the law in the U.K. and Europe. In the U.S., some corporate brewers list the alcohol by weight. Darn Yankees gotta be different.

TIP

Hydrometers used by homebrewers always register alcohol by volume, and they say so right on the paper insert (see Chapter 2 for information on hydrometers).

By standard measure, a pint of water weighs 1 pound (actually a fraction of an ounce more). A pint of alcohol, on the other hand, weighs only .79 pounds. Because alcohol weighs less than water (and beer, and most other liquids), the weight of alcohol appears to be lower in weight comparisons. Rather deceptive, don't you think?

To make the point clearer, imagine the container of beer as a carton of ten masonry bricks. If you take out one brick and fill the open space with a foam block of equal size, the foam block still takes up 10 percent of the space in the carton, but it weighs considerably less than the brick it replaced.

So, a beer with an alcohol content of 3.2 percent by weight actually contains 4.05 percent by volume; a beer that is 4 percent alcohol by weight actually contains 5 percent by volume. To figure it out yourself, convert an ABW reading to an ABV by multiplying the ABW by 1.25. To convert an ABV reading to ABW, multiply the ABV by 0.79. Are you having fun yet?

Just remember that figures for weight are *lower* than figures for volume.

N/A (nonalcoholic) beer is n/a (not achievable)

Brewers who want to produce a nonalcoholic brew at home are going to be sorely disappointed. In order to make a beer without alcohol, you need a lot of money to pay for the equipment or a lot of extra steps that are hardly worth the time or effort.

As illustrated in this chapter, yeast is one of the four primary ingredients in beer. It's not only the catalyst for fermentation, but it also adds all kinds of aromas and flavors to beer and is a major influence on the beer's texture and mouthfeel. Therefore, just not adding yeast to the beer is not a viable solution to making nonalcoholic beer. Unfermented beer is very thick, sweet, uncarbonated, and not at all thirst-quenching.

Commercial brewers are able to produce nonalcoholic beers in a number of ways, all of which require equipment and technology far beyond the resources of homebrewers. All things considered, it's a lot cheaper and easier to buy nonalcoholic beer at your local store.

» **Examining the elements that affect water**

» **Debating the use of bottled water**

Chapter 7
On the Water Front

Water is just one of the four primary ingredients used to make beer, but considering that it constitutes up to 95 percent of a beer's total ingredient profile, water can certainly have a tremendous influence on the finished product. Fortunately, today's brewers can alter and adjust the chemical and mineral make-up of a given water source to suit their brewing needs.

The various minerals and salts found in water used for brewing can accentuate beer flavors or contribute undesirable flavor components. In many cases, water chemistry is key in the flavor profile of a classic beer style.

Having said that, however, most of you will never apply the information in this chapter to your brewing habits. Why? Because in spite of the somewhat ominous statement made above, you can still make good beer with average tap water. Thousands of homebrewers are proving it every day. A very general rule says, "If your water tastes good, so will your beer." A caveat is important here, though: This general rule pertains solely to extract-based homebrews.

The importance of certain aspects of water composition — namely *pH balance* (see the "pHundamentals of pH balance" section in this chapter) — becomes much more important when homebrewers begin mashing their own grains. And water chemical and mineral profiles are really only important to the small percentage of homebrewers who are determined to imitate the water found in famous brewing cities around the world.

H_2OH: Understanding How Water Chemistry Affects Your Homebrew

At the homebrewing level, water is perhaps the most overlooked ingredient in the beer recipe, and understandably so. The subject of water chemistry can get pretty complicated, and the majority of homebrewers just don't want to immerse themselves in something so deep. Although water purity is genuinely important for making good beer, your need for concern ranges from not-all-that-important at the beginner homebrewing level (see extract brewing in Chapter 10) to immensely important at the advanced homebrewing level (see all-grain brewing in Chapter 12). This assumes, of course, that your current water source is perfectly drinkable.

REMEMBER

At any skill level, make sure that you keep the following things in mind:

- If your water is from a private underground well, it may be high in iron and other minerals that may affect your beer's taste.
- If your water is softened, it may be high in sodium.
- If your water is supplied by a municipal water department, it may have a high chlorine content. Other than chlorine, the *filtering* (the primary method of removing elements and impurities from water) performed at municipal water sources usually produces water that is sufficiently pure for brewing.

High iron, sodium, and chlorine contents in your brewing water are not desirable. If these chemicals and minerals are present in your brewing water, you may want to consider buying bottled water for your brewing needs.

TIP

If you're interested in finding out the chemical profile of your municipal water, call your local public works department and request an analysis of their water — this information is usually provided free-of-charge. However, if you use a private water source, such as a well, you may have to hire an independent company to perform a water analysis for you. In addition to comparing your water analysis to that of famous brewing cities in Europe (see the nearby sidebar), you can be the first on your block to have one!

WATER WORLD

Compare your water analysis with the water profiles of some of Europe's great brewing cities.

	Burton	Munich	London	Dortmund	Plzen
Calcium	294	75	50	225	7
Carbonate	200	180	160	180	15
Chloride	36	60	60	60	5
Magnesium	24	18	20	40	2
Sodium	24	2	100	60	2
Sulfate	800	120	80	120	5

Something Is in the Water

What is it about crystal-clear water that's so inviting — to drink, to swim in, to brew with? Ah, but this subject matter is murkier than it seems. And as a homebrewer, you can't dilute the reality that even crystal-clear water harbors things you need to know about. In the following section I plumb the depths of these topics. My advice to you is to pay attention and just go with the flow.

pHundamentals of pH balance

pH is an abbreviation for *potential of hydrogen* or *power of hydrogen,* depending on whom you ask. *pH balance* refers to the acidity and alkalinity level in various liquids; you measure this balance on a 14-point pH scale. A rating of 1–6 on this scale is *acidic,* and a rating of 8–14 is *alkaline.* A pH of 7 is *neutral,* or *balanced.*

For beginners, the pH balance in brewing water is, for the most part, irrelevant. When brewers progress to mashing procedures, however, monitoring pH levels in mashing water is absolutely critical. At the more advanced levels of homebrewing, you may need to add either gypsum or calcium carbonate to the water to achieve the desired pH level when a given water source is either acidic or alkaline. (See the "Mineral ions" section in this chapter for information on the effects of gypsum and calcium carbonate on brewing water.) For pH measuring and adjustment procedures, see Chapter 12.

TIP

Speaking in very general terms, brewers prefer slightly acidic water over alkaline water; a pH level of 5.5 is usually ideal. Slightly alkaline water is acceptable for brewing dark beers, however, because dark grain's acidity strikes a natural balance with the alkaline profile of the water.

Antibacterial agents

Chlorine — the one element municipal water treatment stations add to water — is something that beginner brewers need to be particularly aware of. Chlorine is added to water as an antibacterial agent. Even in minute dilutions (measured in parts per million), chlorine kills bacteria, and it can kill your beer, too — in terms of flavor, that is. Don't worry about the fluoride added to some municipal water supplies; as far as I know, it has no negative effect on the beer.

WARNING

Chlorinated water used for brewing may create *chlorophenols* in your beer. Chlorophenols are unpleasant-smelling and -tasting compounds that are reminiscent of burnt plastic and cheap vinyl furniture. (How's that for mental imagery?) You can avoid this problem in a few different ways, depending on the time, money, and energy you have to spend.

- Buy and attach a carbon filter to the faucet you draw your brewing water from. Carbon filters are very effective at removing chlorine. On the down side, this method can be expensive.
- Buy bottled water from a bottled water delivery company or by the gallon at your local supermarket. This method can save you time (especially if you get your water delivered to your door), but it also can prove inconvenient if you have to drag jugs of water home from the store. (See the following section for more information about buying bottled water.)
- Preboil all the water you need for your beer. Boiling causes the chlorine to melt into a gas and float up and out of the water, evaporating in the steam. This method is effective, but it can be a time- and energy-consuming practice, and it only works if the municipal water source uses chlorine. Some municipalities use *chloroamines*, which are more stable in water and are not driven off by boiling. Check with your municipal water source to clarify which your source is using.
- Buy a bunch of hydrogen and oxygen atoms, some molecule glue, and start your own water factory. This method can land you in a padded room.

TIP

Not all water sources get the chlorine treatment. Some rural water supplies are contaminated with *enterobacteria* (otherwise known as *wort spoilers*). Consider having a water analysis company determine whether your water is contaminated with this foe. If there are enterobacteria in your water, keep your water heater set at 160 degrees Fahrenheit or higher and, for sanitizing purposes, rinse your equipment with hot water only.

Hard facts, fluid concepts

Many people have a tendency to see water as being merely soft or hard, but water chemistry is just not that simple. Soft water is very low in mineral content, and hard water has a very high mineral content. What *is* pretty simple, though, is the generalization that soft water is preferable to hard water because adding minerals to the water (if needed) is a lot easier than removing them.

TECHNICAL STUFF

Of course, if you have hard water, you must determine whether you have *temporary hardness* or *permanent hardness.* Temporary hardness refers to the presence of soluble bicarbonates of calcium and magnesium that *precipitate* out when you boil the water. Precipitation occurs when mineral ions are attracted to one another, bond together, and then fall out of solution as sediment (see the section "Mineral ions" later in this chapter). Permanent hardness refers to water hardness after you've boiled the water and all the nonprecipitating minerals are still there. Your water can be temporarily hard, permanently hard, or both at once — prior to boiling, that is.

Mineral ions

In simple terms, *mineral ions* are components of mineral salts that dissolve in water. And because ions have either a positive or negative charge, they're electrically attracted to the ingredients used to make beer (malt, hops, and so on). The effects of these mineral ions can range from enhancing protein coagulation (which helps to clarify beer) to accentuating the flavor of the malt.

Some mineral salts — namely calcium carbonate and magnesium carbonate — are responsible for leaving the telltale white scale on the sides of pots of boiling water.

At least seven principal ions exert a substantial influence on the beer-making process. The following list provides a brief description of these ions and their influences (the term ppm means *parts per millions*):

- **Calcium:** Lowers pH and assists enzyme action during mashing.
- **Carbonate:** Halts enzyme action and promotes harsh flavor derived from hops.
- **Chloride:** At high levels (250+ ppm) may enhance the sweetness of beer.

- **Bicarbonate:** Halts enzyme action and promotes harsh flavor derived from hops.
- **Magnesium:** Lowers pH and is an important yeast nutrient at 10 to 20 ppm.
- **Sodium:** Has no chemical effect and may impart roundness (fill out beer flavor). At too high a concentration, sodium can also give a salty flavor.
- **Sulfate:** Has no chemical effect and may impart harsh dryness when used with sodium.

Yet brewers sometimes use other mineral salts to adjust the pH level of their mashing water (see the "pHundamentals of pH balance" section in this chapter) or increase the ion profile of their brewing water. These include

- **Calcium carbonate:** More commonly known as *chalk,* calcium carbonate raises pH; 1 teaspoon in 5 gallons of liquid adds 60 ppm of carbonate and 36 ppm of calcium.
- **Calcium sulfate:** More commonly known as *gypsum,* calcium sulfate lowers pH; 1 teaspoon in 5 gallons of water adds 140 ppm of sulfate and 60 ppm of calcium.
- **Magnesium sulfate:** More commonly known as *Epsom salt,* magnesium sulfate lowers pH; 1 teaspoon in 5 gallons of water adds 100 ppm of sulfate and 25 ppm of magnesium.
- **Sodium chloride:** More commonly known as *table salt,* sodium chloride has no effect on pH; 1 teaspoon in 5 gallons of water adds 170 ppm of chloride and 110 ppm of sodium.

Trace metals

Also considered secondary ions, trace metals don't have a significant impact on beer flavor unless they're present in large quantities; then these trace metals can ruin a brew altogether. Copper, iron, lead, manganese, and zinc are some trace metals that may be found in a natural water source.

Although most of these trace metals are generally undesirable in brewing water, a few are actually beneficial in very small amounts. Manganese, copper, and zinc, for example, are valuable nutrients for yeast-cell development. Iron, on the other hand, can have an extremely detrimental effect on beer flavor, and lead can be toxic to yeast (not to mention humans) in high quantities. You can remove all of these metals from the water by filtration or distillation, or you can simply adjust their concentrations by diluting with filtered or distilled water.

WETTING YOUR APPETITE

No doubt, you've heard ads for beer that tout "from the land of sky-blue waters" or "brewed with pure, Rocky Mountain spring water." Breweries like to boast about the purity of the water that they use to brew their beer.

Some of the classic world styles of beer became classics because of the water used to make the beer. The famed Pilsner beers of Bohemia, such as Pilsner Urquell, are considered premier examples. These crisp, hoppy Lagers are made with extremely soft water that the brewers pump from the aquifers below the brewery. By contrast, the legendary British ales of Burton-on-Trent, such as Bass Ale, are made with particularly hard water. Considering these examples (among others), it's obvious that water can play a big role in beer flavor.

But any water, regardless of its source, can be manipulated to match the profile of another source. For example, brewers wanting to emulate the beers from Burton-on-Trent simply add certain minerals called *Burton salts* to the brewing water in a process known as *Burtonizing.*

Buying Brew-Friendly Bottled Water

WARNING

If you choose to buy your water, you may be tempted to buy *distilled* water because it's the purest form available. But distilled water is also completely devoid of some of the important natural elements beneficial to beer.

Distilled water

Distilled water is made by boiling water, recapturing the steam, and cooling it back down to liquid form. This steam distillation method leaves all natural elements, chemicals, and impurities behind. Distilled water is relatively inexpensive and widely available.

TIP

I try to strike a compromise. I like to use about two to two-and-a-half gallons of municipal water straight from the kitchen faucet for the boiling in the brew kettle (most, if not all, of the chlorine is gassed out). Then, to cool and dilute the wort in the fermenter (just prior to pitching the yeast), I use up to three gallons of store-bought distilled water that I've refrigerated. See Chapter 10 for more details on these processes.

Reverse osmosis water

Another good option is using reverse osmosis (RO) water for brewing. This is a filtration process that de-mineralizes water by causing it to flow under pressure through a semi-permeable membrane. The osmotic membrane is permeable by water molecules but not by dissolved ions, inorganic solids, and other contaminants.

RO systems are typically made up of between three and five stages of filtration. In addition to the membrane, there are also pre-filters and postfilters depending on whether water passes through them before or after it passes through the membrane. The sediment filter removes particles like dirt, dust, and rust; the carbon filter reduces volatile organic compounds like chlorine and other contaminants that give water a bad taste or odor. Finally, the membrane removes up to 98 percent of total dissolved solids in the water. (See Figure 7-1.)

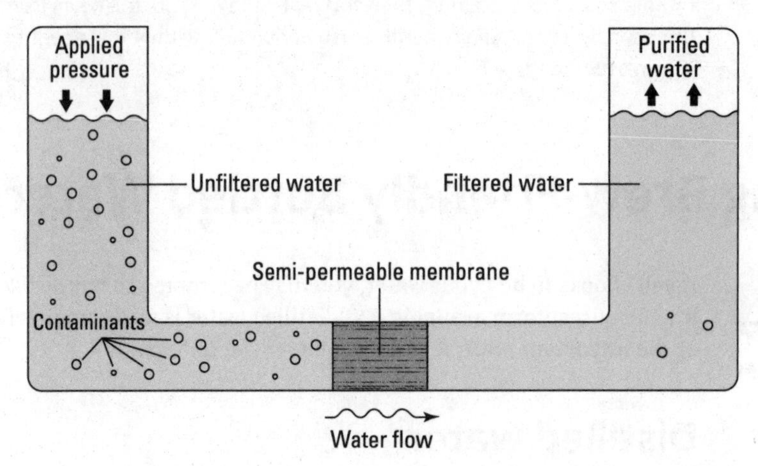

FIGURE 7-1: How reverse osmosis filters work.

WARNING

Because RO water doesn't contain enough minerals, it can actually leech minerals from the body if it's being consumed as drinking water. This means that some of the vitamins and minerals being consumed in your food will be urinated away. Fewer minerals consumed and more minerals being excreted can cause serious negative side effects and possible health problems.

Although using distilled water is better than using basic tap water, reverse osmosis water is considered the superior choice. And although the water distillation process is difficult to perform at home, RO filtration is easy if you have an RO system installed in your home.

IN THIS CHAPTER

» Adding to your brew with adjuncts

» Savoring flavorings

» Spicing up your beer with herbs and spices

Chapter 8
Adjuncts and Flavorings

Anyone paying even the slightest bit of attention to the current beer market knows that brewers are now putting a lot of unusual ingredients into their beers — ingredients that may make the beer purist choke on her Old Frothy. Fruits, herbs, sugars, spices, breakfast cereals, and who knows what else show up in commercial beers almost as frequently as bubbles.

This trend hasn't always been the case, though experimentation is far from the cutting edge. Beer makers through the ages have used some odd ingredients in their beers from time to time. But homebrewers, with their innate desire to experiment and push the limits, just seem to take the concept to another level.

These unusual ingredients, whatever they may be, aren't limited to the role of flavorings, although flavoring is often their primary purpose. Brewers also utilize a variety of *adjunct* ingredients (any fermentable ingredients other than malted grains) to jack up alcohol levels, to thin out or fill out a beer's mouthfeel, or even to enhance the beer's foaminess. Adjuncts aren't the same as *adjunct grains* (cereal grains such as rice and corn used to make beer in general), which I discuss in Chapter 4. For the purposes of this chapter, the adjuncts I focus on are nongrain sugars that you can use in smaller portions to add certain flavors or fermentable ingredients to the beer-making process.

REMEMBER

Keep in mind that the line between adjuncts and flavorings is often blurry (along with everything else after a few tasty homebrews). Adjuncts are used with the express intent of contributing fermentable sugars, but they can also add flavor; flavorings are used with the express intent of adding flavors, but they may also add fermentable sugars.

You won't find any hard-and-fast rules about how to use adjuncts and flavorings in your brews — you're limited only by your own imagination. Given the vast amount of experimentation in the world of homebrew, though, some adjuncts and flavorings just go better with certain beer styles than others (like smoke character in Porter, for example). In this chapter, I give you the lowdown on adjuncts and flavorings and how to use them. I also explore the rising popularity of using sugar, fruits, herbs, and spices in homebrewing.

Adjuncts: Sugar, Sugar. . . Aw, Honey, Honey

Adjunct sugars are often called *kettle adjuncts* because you add them directly to the wort in the brew kettle instead of treating them in a separate vessel like adjunct grain. These kettle adjuncts are available in many different forms. Some are sweeter than others, and some ferment more easily than others. The following list describes some of these sugars:

- **Fructose:** Found in fruits and, to a lesser extent, malted grain. The sweetening power of fructose is more than 1½ times that of refined white sugar (which is also known as *sucrose*, or table sugar).
- **Dextrose:** Also a refined white sugar derived from *hydrolyzed* cornstarch (starch that has reacted with water and changed into glucose). Dextrose is highly fermentable and popular for priming (see Chapter 14 for more about dextrose and priming). Another name for this is *corn sugar*.
- **Glucose:** Derived from starch (on a molecular level, glucose and dextrose are identical) and many fruits. Glucose (and dextrose) has about 70 percent of the sweetening power of ordinary table sugar.
- **Sucrose:** A compound of one molecule each of glucose and fructose; sucrose is found in sugar cane, sugar beets, sorghum, and malted grain. Table sugar is about 99.5 percent sucrose.
- **Lactose:** Found in milk. Beer yeast can't ferment lactose, so whatever lactose you add to your beer will remain there. Lactose is common in infant formula and various confections — not to mention sweet stout — and has about 40 percent of the sweetening power of sucrose.

Most often, you find these sugars in processed form (such as refined white sugar), but you can also use some of them in their natural form, as is the case with honey and pure maple syrups. Again, the primary objective in using adjunct sugars is to add fermentable ingredients to the beer (which results in increased alcohol levels), and the secondary objective is to imbue the beer with unique flavor. The following is a list of optional adjuncts that contain various sugars:

- **Honey:** Honey is made from the nectar of flowers and processed with enzymes secreted by the honeybee. The two main ingredients in honey are glucose and fructose, with traces of sucrose and maltose — say that three times fast! Honey is highly fermentable and can add delicate sweetness and aroma to your brew, depending on the type of honey you choose. The quality and flavor of honey can vary greatly from one variety to the next (literally thousands of varieties are on the market), but light honeys, such as alfalfa and clover, work well in beer because their flavor is less aggressive. Because it's so fully fermentable, using honey also results in thinner-bodied beers. For this same reason, using honey also results in more alcohol per pound of honey added to the beer (compared to the same quantity of malt extract). Check out Chapter 20 for more information about honey.
- **Rice syrup or corn syrup:** Both rice and corn syrup are very neutral in flavor. Using high percentages of these processed syrups (relative to the rest of the ingredients) results in pale-colored, lighter-bodied, lighter-flavored beers, such as North American Light Lagers. These syrups are also effective in raising alcohol levels in dark beers without appreciably affecting the beers' flavor profiles. ***Note:*** Use only brewer's grade rice or corn syrup. Both of these syrups are highly fermentable and result in higher alcohol levels per pound of syrup added (compared to the same quantity of malt extract). Also note that rice syrup is available in a powdered form known as *rice syrup solids*.
- **Sorghum syrup:** Pure white sorghum syrup is especially handy for creating low-gluten or gluten-free beers (see Chapter 23 for more information on gluten-free brewing), but you can also use this syrup like rice or corn syrup for making lighter-bodied and -colored brews.
- **Maple syrup:** Natural maple syrup is mostly sucrose with some *invert sugar* (a mixture of certain forms of glucose and fructose. See the sidebar "Making invert sugar syrup" for more information.) The more natural the syrup, the better (pure maple syrup must weigh no less than 11 pounds per gallon). Depending on the quality, which is based on the percentage of maple sugar in the syrup, maple flavor may be very assertive in the beer. Maple syrup, depending on the sugar content, is about 65 percent fermentable, which means the yeast eats about 65 percent of whatever amount you add to your beer.
- **Brown sugar:** Brown sugar is derived from unrefined or partially refined sugar (cane or beet), and flavored with molasses. It's usually available in light and dark brown choices. The darker brown the sugar, the more residual flavor it leaves in the beer.

» **Molasses:** Molasses syrup is produced during the refining of white sugar from sorghum or from the juice of sun-ripened cane. Be sure to buy unsulfured molasses (sulfur fumes used in the sugar-making process are retained in molasses and must be commercially extracted). Usually, molasses is available in three colors/flavors — light, dark, and blackstrap — based on its degree of caramelization and concentration.

TECHNICAL STUFF

Light molasses results from the first boiling of the cane, and dark molasses is the product of a second boiling. Blackstrap molasses, produced from a third boiling, is a waste product in the sugar industry, but it's great for stouts and other dark beers.

» **Treacle:** Often incorrectly defined as molasses in the King's English, treacle is a brown-colored syrup also known as *refiner's syrup.* Although it's derived in much the same way as molasses, it often comes clarified and decolorized, so it's not as dark and aggressive in flavor as molasses. Treacle isn't an equal substitute for molasses, but it still makes an interesting adjunct sugar for beer-making purposes.

» **Belgian candi sugar:** Chunky, caramelized sugar in crystals and granular form are popular in Belgian strong ales and Trappist beer varieties; they usually come in golden to dark amber varieties. Candi sugar enhances a beer's flavor and alcohol levels. More recently, candi syrup has become available to homebrewers. Pound for pound, the syrup gives more color and caramelized flavor than the sugar crystals. Belgian candi sugar is a good source of sucrose.

» **Turbinado sugar:** Also known as raw sugar, turbinado sugar is a partially refined, coarse, beige-colored crystal that still contains some of the molasses from the original sugar. Depending on the source, turbinado sugar may contain impurities. Homebrewers who can get their hands on this stuff like to experiment with it in high-gravity ales such as English old ales or barley wines. Check your local ethnic grocery store for turbinado sugar. It's also another good source of sucrose.

» **Demarara sugar:** Demarara sugar is very close in character to turbinado sugar but with a darker color and more pronounced molasses flavor. Readily fermentable, it's excellent for dark ales.

You should add these naturally occurring sugars sparingly to your brew, and they shouldn't constitute a large percentage of the total fermentable ingredients in your recipe. One pound or less per 5-gallon batch is a typical amount. Make sure you stay away from using refined white sugars (sugar made from cane or beets) in brewing. White sugars used in quantities of more than 20 percent of total fermentable ingredients result in a noticeable cidery smell and taste. Also, white sugars are so highly fermentable that your beer will have a measurable increase in alcohol while suffering a measurable decrease in body and mouthfeel. Dextrose (corn sugar) is the only granular white sugar that you should use for priming beer at bottling time (see Chapter 14 to find out more about dextrose and bottling).

MAKING INVERT SUGAR SYRUP

A handful of beer styles — primarily those from England and Belgium — regularly use added sugar in their recipes. Because using large amounts of refined sugar can create a cidery tang in beer, brewers can safely make and use invert sugar to reduce the sugar's acidic effect on their beer's flavor. Here's how:

Ingredients:

- 8 pounds of white cane/beet sugar
- 2 pints of water
- 1 tablespoon (or 3 teaspoons) of citric acid

Directions:

1. Mix all ingredients in a large pot and heat to boiling (the mixture will foam and then turn a clear, golden color).
2. Cool and then dilute in water to reach a total volume of 1 gallon.

One pint of this liquid invert sugar equals 1 pound of granular sugar.

Add too much of this sugar to your beer, and you can still get a cidery taste. I recommend that invert syrup make up less than 20 percent of your total fermentable ingredients.

Dextrose is also the primary choice of fermentable sugar when making hard seltzers (see Chapter 22).

Flavoring Your Brew with Flavorings

Beyond adding adjunct sugars to your brew, an unlimited number of flavorings exist that you can add to beer. Some may contain sugars that result in added gravity and alcohol, but I cover most of those flavorings in previous sections in this chapter. In this section, I focus on those ingredients that are primarily used to add unique flavors to beer.

The goal when using these flavorings is to complement the underlying beer flavor, not to create a whole new one. Whenever possible, make sure you add these ingredients directly to the brewpot to take advantage of the disinfecting action of the boiling wort and to meld the flavors into the brew. (I note the exceptions to this "add to the brewpot" rule in the section "Herbs and Spice and everything nice".)

Funky flavorings: The exotic and the esoteric

The following is a list of flavorings that are commonly used in the homebrewing world:

- **Chocolate:** Beer made with chocolate is an *esoteric* (old-but-not-out-of-date) brew that brewers made only occasionally (most brewers create chocolate character in their beers by using chocolate malt, which has nothing to do with the cacao bean). But for those who want the real chocolate experience in their beer, there is a great option: cacao nibs. *Cacao nibs* (also referred to as *cocoa nibs*) are the key ingredient in chocolate; they are crushed seeds from the cacao plant. Although they're not technically chocolate themselves, they have a wonderful cocoa aroma to them, and will provide a very subdued cocoa-like flavor to any beer. You can add them directly to your brewpot or you can put them in your secondary fermenter.

  Cocoa powder is also an option, but it comes with a caution. High levels of cocoa powder usage can create a chalky character in beer that leaves an unpleasant mouthfeel in the finish. Cocoa powder can also contain more than 20 percent fat, which, if overused, could leave an oil slick on the surface of your beer and impact head retention. Adding a judicious level of cocoa powder directly to the brewpot is the most common method.

  Gives a whole new meaning to the term chocoholic, doesn't it?

- **Spruce essence:** Spruce beer was an early American favorite. Using the new spring growth (the needles) of the spruce tree was the old-fashioned method. Today, you can buy spruce essence through your homebrew supplier, but this stuff is pretty potent. Two to five teaspoons give your beer a refreshing spruce taste. Pretend you're a patriot and spruce up your favorite ale.
- **Licorice:** Drinkers often experience a licorice flavor in dark beers even when it hasn't been specifically added to the brew. Brewers who like this flavor can add all they want to their own beer by using unsweetened brewer's licorice sticks, which you can find at your homebrew supply shop. But be careful not to overuse licorice — a little goes a long way. One or two inches are sufficient for a 5-gallon batch. Licorice is especially good for porters, stouts, and Schwarzbiers.

- **Fruit flavorings:** Some fruit flavorings are available without added sugar. You use these liquid flavorings in the same way you use fruit juices or extracts, except that unsweetened fruit flavorings don't require fermentation time. Doses depend on the fruit, the brand, your personal taste, and so on. Fruit flavorings are much easier to work with than real fruit; they're widely available and never out of season. To preserve as much fruit character as possible, some producers even suggest adding the flavoring to the beer at bottling time. These flavorings work well in virtually all beer styles, but the darker the beer, the more flavoring you need to compete with the flavors of the underlying beer. (Also see the sidebar, "Fruit pursuit.")
- **Oak chips/oak extract:** Brewers wanting to emulate the oaky character of traditional India pale ales or their favorite oak-aged Belgian beers can try using oak chips. Because oak adds tannin to beer, you never want to boil the chips. (*Tannin* is derived from organic compounds such as cereal grain husks, oak bark, grape skins, and the rinds of shelled nuts. Tannin is a sharp, astringent [bitter] flavor; if you've ever accidentally eaten some of the red rind found inside a pecan, you know how unpleasant tasting tannin can be.) The best way to use oak chips is to steam them for 15 minutes (to sanitize them) before adding them to the secondary fermenter. You can find oak chips in regular and toasted form (hold the butter). Oak flavor is also available in extract form. For more information on barrel aging and wood aging beer, see Chapter 25.
- **Lactose:** Lactose powder has a very limited use in the homebrewing world from a flavoring perspective— it's primarily used to add sweetness and body to beer without the risk of cidery flavors or higher alcohol levels. Beer yeast can't ferment lactose, so the lactose retains virtually all of its sweetness. Lactose is a prerequisite for making London-style sweet stout (also called cream stout or milk stout for obvious reasons). Six to twelve ounces per 5-gallon batch gets the job done.

  Peanut butter: Yeah, you read that right. The creamy, peanut-flavored spread that was a big part of your childhood is now following you into adulthood. But it's not actual peanut butter that goes into the beer (there's way too much oil in peanut butter); it's a powder made from peanut butter with most of the oil pressed out of it. You can also opt for peanut butter flavor extracts. Either of these can be easily found on the Internet.
- **Smoke:** Rauchbier (smoked beer) is another esoteric brew. Fans of German Rauchbier — and even some Scottish ales — can emulate their favorite smoky brews by adding wood-smoked or peat-smoked malts to their grist. Keep in mind that a little goes a long way.

  TIP

  You can buy these malts at homebrew supply shops or create them at home on a barbecue grill or smoker (see Chapter 30 for more information on creating your own smoked malts). It is suggested to not use liquid smoke extracts, as these can impart off-flavors when used in beer.

- **Vanilla:** Homebrewers can choose between working with pure vanilla extract and using the purist's vanilla bean, though the latter is more common in beer making. Commercial brewers seem to have added vanilla flavor to just about any beer style you can think of — not all with great results.
- **Orange peel:** Due to the popularity of Belgian witbier, dried orange peel is available at most good homebrew supply stores. Choose between sweet orange or bitter (Curaçao) orange variety. A couple of ounces per 5-gallon batch are a typical amount.
- **Fruit liqueurs:** Certain fruit liqueurs can be used for flavoring beer, but because they contain large amounts of refined sugar, they're best as priming agents (see Chapter 14 to read more about priming with liqueurs). Do I need to remind you not to use cream liqueurs?

FRUIT PURSUIT

In addition to the fruit flavorings discussed above, there are other more authentic — and difficult — ways to add fruit character to your beer. The first, of course, is using actual fruit. One issue is making sure the fruit you're using isn't introducing bacteria to your brew (the fruit will need to be sanitized before adding it to the beer). Another issue is that some fruits, when boiled (to sanitize) causes the pectin to "set" (*pectin* is a natural jelling agent that helps solidify fruit jams). Lastly, fruits decompose throughout the fermentation and aging processes, so they leave a gunky mess behind in your beer.

Enter fruit puree. You can choose to puree your fruits on your own at home — and you'll still need to sanitize it before adding it to your brew in the last few minutes of the boil. Or you can buy some of the many brands and flavors of high-grade fruit puree products already available to homebrewers. Commercially produced purees can be added either to your brewpot or your primary fermenter.

Whether you choose to use real fruit or fruit puree, remember that you'll not only be flavoring your beer, you'll be adding more fermentable sugars (in the form of fructose), so you'll need to make sure that your beer is fully fermented before proceeding with bottling or canning procedures. Failure to do so may result in exploding bottles or popping cans.

Herbs and spice and everything nice

At some point in your blossoming brewing career, you're likely to grow the same wild hair that every other homebrewer has grown. One day you'll be contemplating your next brew over an odoriferous plate of Italian food when out of nowhere it'll hit you: — "Hmmm, I wonder what garlic beer tastes like?" You may laugh, but somebody actually made a garlic beer (unfortunately for those of us who tasted it). In fact, in the world of homebrew, you're hard-pressed to find a stone left unturned.

Herb and spice beer is one of the categories that really challenges the conventional ideas of beer, although what seemed alien a half a dozen years ago is now reaching the mainstream. Coriander, nutmeg, ginger, cloves — you name it. And cinnamon, which once seemed passé, has made a big comeback and can be found in profusion in the craft beer market.

Your spice rack at home presents an (almost) unlimited variety of choices for your next brew, but don't make the same mistake many brewers before you have made. Just because you like the taste of cumin and lemongrass doesn't mean adding such a combination to your brew makes a great beer. Before forging ahead, you need to reflect a bit on your idea. Try to imagine the taste of the beer you have in mind. Is it something you want to drink two cases of? If so, move cautiously, remembering that using too little of an ingredient is better than using too much.

TIP

Give your beer flavoring idea a taste test: Try brewing a little "tea" of the herb or spice you have in mind and strain it into a commercial beer similar to the style you intend to make. You may also want to jot down your tasting notes to help fine-tune your final recipe.

You can introduce herbs and spices two ways in the beermaking process:

- **Add them directly to the brewpot.**
- **Put them in the secondary fermenter.** (See Chapter 11 for more on secondary fermentation.)

If you go the brewpot route, wait until the last 15 minutes of the boil. Allowing certain herbs or spices (such as cinnamon bark) to boil in the wort for long periods of time can sometimes create an astringency or harshness similar to the result of boiling grain.

If you hold out until the secondary fermentation stage, you need to sanitize the ingredients. Hold the bleach — this is a job for distilled alcohol. Whatever consumable spirits (whisky, vodka, gin, and so on) you may have in your home can get the job done. Allow the herb or spice of choice to soak in ½ cup of whatever booze you choose for about a week prior to putting the herb or spice in the secondary fermenter; what you do with the spiced liquor is your business. Actually, dumping the entire herb/spice liquor concoction into the secondary fermenter is okay, too.

TIP

To make the ingredient-soaking process easier, try fashioning a small filter or pouch out of an unused coffee filter or fresh tea bag you've emptied of its contents; close with a twist-tie or string.

REMEMBER

Fresh and whole herbs and spices are better than those that are old, stale, chopped, or powdered.

Spices

A wide variety of spices are available for you to use to enhance the flavor of your brews. The following is a short list of some of the most popular spices in the homebrewing world — the tried-and-true choices:

- **Allspice:** Allspice is one of the more interesting spices to use; within the single small berry is a natural mixture of flavors reminiscent of cinnamon, clove, nutmeg, and juniper berries. Brewers often use allspice in seasonal pumpkin beers.
- **Anise:** The star anise variety is most common. This spice gives beer a subtle licorice undertone.
- **Cardamom:** The plump seeds of the cardamom family appear in culinary applications as diverse as coffee flavoring, barbecue sauces, and curry powder. Used judiciously, cardamom lends beer a unique and subtle spicy flavor.
- **Caraway:** You rarely use this seed on its own, but it's a natural complementary flavoring for anyone attempting to make a flavorful rye beer.
- **Cinnamon:** Cinnamon seems to be the go-to spice for pastries and other confections. Cinnamon works well in big-bodied beers made for wintertime consumption. Make sure you use cinnamon bark rather than powder because you can easily remove the sticks from the brew; cinnamon powder (unless filtered out) remains in the beer and may create a harsh flavor and an unpleasant lingering mouthfeel.
- **Cloves:** Clove-like aromas and tastes occur naturally in some beer styles — most notably the Bavarian Weizenbiers and some Belgian ales. Homebrewers can introduce this clove character by using whole cloves — in small quantities. Many people perceive cloves to have a strong *phenolic* or medicinal character.

- **Coriander:** Coriander is the seed of the same plant from which cilantro is derived. The lemony coriander is a key ingredient in a traditional Belgian witbier, but it also works well in many beer styles.
- **Gingerroot:** The flavor of raw gingerroot (also known as just *ginger*) is intense and spicy-hot or sharp in anything but small quantities or dilutions. The actual flavor — most closely associated with ginger ale (soda) — actually works quite well in beer and Mead. The key is to use grated gingerroot rather than ginger powder. Use gingerly; 1 ounce in a 5-gallon batch of beer is plenty noticeable.

  The original ginger ale really was ale. The concoction was a standard beer in colonial America because the colonists used ginger and other spices in the absence of hops to offset the malty sweetness of beer.
- **Juniper berries:** Because juniper berries are used to make gin, you can use them to give your brew the same aroma and flavor as gin — if you happen to like gin.
- **Vanilla bean:** Although high-quality vanilla extract is easier to work with, the oil of the vanilla bean can also lend a pleasant mouthfeel to your brew while it gives a rich aroma and flavor. For best results, use *macerated* (crushed) vanilla beans during secondary fermentation only.

Herbs

The following herbs are also worth trying in your homebrew:

- **Sweet gale:** This herb is an aromatic seasoning that many Belgian brewers use to add a lightly sweet flavor. Use sparingly.
- **Heather tips:** Dried heather tips were popular in Scotland to balance malty sweetness before the advent of hop usage. You can find a heather ale currently available in the United States by the brand name Fraoch.
- **Mint:** Mint isn't normally high on the list of brewing herbs, but I can personally attest that it can work in certain beer styles if handled properly — a mint stout stands out in my memory. You're probably familiar with peppermint and spearmint, but some lesser-known mint varieties, such as apple mint, are less assertive and equally refreshing.

REMEMBER

Many other popular cooking herbs can also successfully flavor beer; basil, oregano, and rosemary come to mind. Be bold, be brave, be intrepid, and be ready to drink two cases of whatever it is you dream up!

IN THIS CHAPTER

» Exploring additives and preservatives

» Using clarifying agents

» Working with acidifying agents

Chapter 9
Making Your Brew Bionic: Additives, Preservatives, Finings, and Clarifiers

Welcome to the chapter that concentrates on all the nonessential minor ingredients sometimes found in beer. The various elements discussed in this chapter have little or nothing to do with beer flavor and aren't absolutely necessary for making good beer. However, you can use all of the elements defined here to *polish* your homebrew (in other words, to manipulate your beer in various ways that may affect the quality and perception of the finished product).

It's important to note the distinction between quality and the perception of quality. *Quality* is an objective term; homebrew is either well made or it isn't. *Perception of quality,* on the other hand, is subjective. The clarifying agents outlined in this chapter, for example, help you produce crystal-clear beer. Most drinkers *perceive* transparent beer as being better than cloudy or hazy beer, but in fact, a beer's clarity has little bearing on its quality. A perfectly clear beer isn't necessarily well made, and a cloudy beer may be incredibly well made. And New England IPAs are something altogether different.

To Add and Preserve

You can use a wide variety of other ingredients to affect the outcome of your finished beer. These optional ingredients fall loosely into the additives and preservatives category. *Additives*, generally speaking, affect the interactions among the basic ingredients (malt, hops, yeast, and water) — how they behave throughout the mashing, boiling, cooling, and fermentation phases of homebrewing. *Preservatives*, generally speaking, preserve the character of the beer you create. None of these products are absolutely necessary for making good beer, but they can be helpful. The following list provides some of these options:

- **Burton salts:** *Burton salts* is a generic name for a blend of natural minerals that emulates the brewing water in the English brewing city of Burton-on-Trent. Burton salts increase the hardness of brewing water (see Chapter 7 for more information on water hardness) and also help prevent chill haze.
- **Foam control:** *Foam control* inhibits the formation of foam during primary fermentation, which means that your brew hangs on to the head-forming compounds during the brewing process. Thus, the addition of foam control results in denser heads when you pour the finished beer for consumption. You can add foam control to the wort at the same time that you add the yeast. One teaspoon per 5-gallon batch is all you need.
- **Heading compound:** This compound improves head retention in the finished beer and increases foam stability. One teaspoon dissolved in a half cup of water is sufficient for a 5-gallon batch. This compound is available in both liquid and powdered form; the liquid form is more expensive, but it's also easier to work with than the powdered form. The average homebrew shouldn't need the assistance of artificial heading compounds unless it has a very, very low original gravity or a very low malt content.

REMEMBER

The difference between foam control and heading compound is that foam control suppresses natural foaming during fermentation and preserves it for pouring; the heading compound artificially increases foaming in the beer.

The most popular heading compound is *polypropylene glycol alginate,* which is derived from seaweed.

- **Maltodextrin:** Dextrins are the (beer) body-building components of malted grain; the more dextrins in the beer, the fuller the mouthfeel. Maltodextrin powder is a convenient shortcut to creating body and mouthfeel in low-gravity beers.
- **Yeast energizer:** As the name suggests, this additive energizes old and tired yeast and is helpful for reviving stuck or slow fermentations. Dissolve a teaspoon of energizer in a cup of boiling water, cool, and add directly to the fermenter. To avoid having to open a sealed fermenter, try anticipating the need for yeast energizer (such as in beers with original gravities over 1.056) and add the energizer directly to the brewpot in the last 10 minutes of the boil (or to the secondary fermenter as you rack the beer over to it). See Chapter 6 for more information on yeast energizers.
- **Yeast nutrient:** Typically, this type of product consists of di-ammonium phosphate and nitrogen. This yeast fertilizer provides the yeast with a balanced diet and is perfect for yeast starters and low-malt-content worts. It's also particularly useful when making hard seltzers. You can find more on yeast nutrient in Chapter 6 and more on hard seltzers in Chapter 22.

A Little Clarification, Please

Regardless of whether you work with malt extracts or grains, whole hops or pellets, dry yeast or liquid cultures, a number of organic compounds are floating around in your brew: proteins, starches, oils, resins, yeast cells basically, particulate matter of all shapes and sizes. Given time, most of this stuff eventually settles out of your beer naturally. Time, however, isn't a friend to beer. This urgency is why brewers often resort to the use of *clarifying agents* to impel this floating matter to clump up and fall to the bottom of the fermenter. All clarifying agents can be considered preservatives since they remove organic particles from the beer that might otherwise cause your beer to eventually develop off flavors and aromas.

Generally speaking, what little particulate matter remains suspended in your brew doesn't initially affect the taste or aroma of your beer in an adverse way; it mostly affects the visual presentation. Whether you want a clear beer for competition purposes or for personal preference, clarifying agents can help clear up your beer.

Note: Beer filtration is an expensive option that's open to you nonetheless; I discuss this procedure in Chapter 31.

Some of the clarifying agents in the following list are organic or mineral in composition and have been used for eons (not to be confused with mineral ions). A couple of these agents, such as Irish moss and isinglass, are called *finings.* Finings do the same job as the other clarifiers — the rest are just technologically advanced products of our modern era.

- **Bentonite:** *Bentonite* is a nonorganic material combined with a form of powdered clay. Bentonite is more closely associated with winemaking, but it also works well in beer. Just mix this material with water (according to package directions) and add to the secondary fermenter a week prior to bottling.
- **Gelatin:** Gelatin is derived from collagen in pork and cattle skin and bones. It's a colorless, tasteless, and odorless water-soluble protein that attracts negatively charged proteins and yeast. Gelatin works best when you rehydrate it, pour it into cool beer, and give it 5 to 7 days to accomplish its task after primary fermentation is complete.

  Use 1 teaspoon per 5-gallon batch of beer. Dissolve the gelatin in 1 cup of cool water and slowly heat over a low flame for about 15 minutes; do *not* let it boil. Add the mixture to the fermenter immediately after it has cooled.
- **Irish moss:** Also known as *carrageenan* (and *copper finings* in the U.K.), Irish moss is actually a form of brown seaweed. Because this substance is a *kettle-coagulant* (meaning it works in the brew kettle), you want to add it to the brew during the boil. Doing so causes a lot of the protein in the wort to coagulate as it cools. Irish moss comes in flaked and powdered form.

  Because Irish moss requires a rehydration period in order to be effective, add ½ tablespoon of it to the wort in the last 15 minutes of the boil (this amount is sufficient for a 5-gallon batch).
- **Isinglass:** Derived from the swim bladders of sturgeons, isinglass is perhaps the most unusual of the fining family of clarifiers; however, it's also highly effective. *Isinglass* (also known as *white finings*) attracts negatively charged proteins and yeast, causing them to settle out of the beer. You use isinglass in the same way you use gelatin, but isinglass may be a little harder to dissolve in water (follow package instructions). This naturally gelatinous substance comes in powdered form, and 1 teaspoon of this powder treats a 5-gallon batch.

  TECHNICAL STUFF

  Because isinglass finings have a charge opposite that of the other finings, you can use them in combination with some of the other finings or clarifiers to improve beer clarification. By contrast, if you use two similarly charged finings simultaneously, they interfere with each other's activity and actually impede beer clarification.
- **Polyvinylpolypyrrolidone (PVPP):** *PVPP* is actually made up of minute beads of plastic that are statically charged, which allows them to attract particulate matter to themselves like electrostatic glue. Rehydrate the PVPP in tap water (that has been boiled) for about an hour before stirring it gently into the finished beer in the last few days of secondary fermentation. Another positive

quality of PVPP is that it's very effective at combating chill haze. Use ¼ ounce per 5-gallon batch.

You don't need to be concerned about having powdered plastic in your brew. The largest consumer of PVPP is the pharmaceutical industry, which uses it to produce capsule-type drugs.

- **Silica gel:** *Silica gel* is a hard, granulated form of hydrated silica that works by absorption. Each particle is a hollow silica honeycomb with pores just large enough to let haze-forming proteins in. As each particle adsorbs the protein, the particle falls out of solution and forms a firm sediment on the bottom of the fermentation vessel.

  Silica gel is a lot like PVPP without the rehydration; stir silica gel into the secondary fermenter a few days before bottling or kegging. Use ½ ounce per 5-gallon batch of beer.

- **Sparkolloid:** Sparkolloid is a brand-name blend of polysaccharides and diatomaceous earth. It's popular in the winemaking industry, but you can also adapt it to the clarification of beer. Heat 1 gram of Sparkolloid per gallon of beer in water and then add it (hot or cooled) to your beer as you transfer the brew from the primary fermenter to the secondary fermenter.
- **Super Kleer KC Finings:** *KC finings* are an excellent all-purpose two-stage fining agent that contains kieselsol and chitosan (derived from shellfish). The fining process works by creating both strong positive and negative charges in the beer which allow for larger yeast clumping and faster clearing. Add to secondary fermenter for clarifying within 12 to 48 hours.
- **Tannic Acid:** Derived from oak, tannic acid is a great clarifier that stabilizes the beer as well. It reacts with proteins (but not polyphenols). It can be added multiple times throughout the brewing process, but correct dosing is important because too much can give your beer a tannic taste — use according to package directions.
- **Whirlfloc:** A blend of Irish moss and purified carrageenan that helps precipitate haze-causing proteins and beta glucans. Add one tablet (per 5 gallons of brew) in the last 15 minutes of the boil.

The Acid Test

Brewers can introduce a number of different acids to beer at various stages in the brewing process; each acid has its own purpose (additive, preservative, or clarifier), and they should all be readily available at well-stocked homebrew stores.

Please note that the discussion here about various acids is not about souring beer (see Chapter 25).

The following is a list of those acids and general descriptions of how they can aid you in the beer-making process. Exactly how you use these acids depends on your needs (always follow package directions). For questions regarding pH balance, see Chapter 7.

- **Ascorbic:** *Ascorbic acid* is an antioxidant, which qualifies it as a preservative. Ascorbic acid protects beer from the off aromas and tastes associated with oxidation. This acid is also known as vitamin C. Use ½ teaspoon per 5-gallon batch (overuse lends a citrus flavor to your beer). Add to beer at bottling time.
- **Citric:** *Citric acid* protects against haze, increases the acidity of brewing water by lowering the pH, and aids in the fermentation process. You can also find it premixed in a product called Acid Blend, which is a convenient mix of citric, malic, and tartaric acids.
- **Lactic:** *Lactic acid* is a mild acid used to *acidify* (lower the pH of) the mash or sparge water. (See Chapter 12 for more on mashing and sparging.) Lactic acid gives Berliner Weisse beer its characteristic tartness. When you use lactic acid, add 1 teaspoon per 5-gallon batch just prior to bottling.
- **Malic:** *Malic acid* increases the tartness in beer. Like citric acid, you can find malic acid premixed in Acid Blend.
- **Phosphoric:** You can use *phosphoric acid* in weak dilutions (approximately 1 part phosphoric acid per 10 parts water) to acidify mash water.
- **Tartaric:** *Tartaric acid* increases the tartness in beer and is also an ingredient in Acid Blend.

3 Ready, Set, Brew!

IN THIS PART . . .

Get a quick start on your homebrewing hobby by checking out beginner brewing.

Graduate to a more hands-on approach to making your own beer with intermediate brewing.

Start making "all-grain" beer with advanced brewing techniques and say goodbye to recipe kits and malt extracts.

Kick your homebrewing into high gear with high-tech brewing; you'll be mere steps from brewing like a professional.

» Brewing step by step

» Reading hydrometers

Chapter 10
Beginner Brewing Directions

My philosophy is that beginning brewers have to start somewhere (profound, huh?), and that somewhere needs to be with an all-inclusive homebrewing kit. A *kit* is simply a package you buy from a homebrew supply store that includes all the ingredients (pre-hopped malt extract and a packet of yeast) that you need to brew a particular style of beer. The kits I'm referring to here are ingredient kits only (as discussed in Chapter 4), mind you; they don't include any equipment.

But brewing beer from a kit also has a possible downside, depending on your perspective. At the beginner homebrewing level, you the brewer have little personal control over most of the beer-making process. (Practicing proper sanitation is the glaring exception to this rule — see Chapter 3.) When you use a kit, much of the thinking and the work have been done for you. (I like to compare homebrewing at the beginner level to making soup from a can. Cold, fizzy soup. Darn tasty soup.) Don't get me wrong — this extra guidance is good for those of you just starting out in the world of homebrewing who want to work with a net the first few times through the process.

And so, in exchange for its simplicity, brewing at the novice level has its limitations. Making brewing easy means keeping it simple, and keeping it simple means not using unusual ingredients or lengthy procedures. Because you're relying on the malt extract producer to provide all the ingredients in one tidy kit, many of the world beer styles can't be faithfully duplicated at the beginner level of homebrewing. Instead, what you find at the beginner level in Chapter 17 are time- and effort-saving hints and shortcuts for making a beer that comes reasonably close to the intended beer style.

The two biggest pluses to brewing at this level are the speed at which you can produce beer and the rapid rate at which you can conquer the learning curve associated with it. The more quickly and cheaply you can produce beer, the more you can make. The more you make, the more efficient you become and, presumably, the more you comprehend about the nuts-and-bolts of brewing. You can master several aspects of homebrewing (sanitation, racking, observing fermentation, and bottling) at the beginner level. Thus, another simple rule at the beginner level: The more you brew, the better your beer gets. It's a delicious circle.

Gathering the Tools You Need

Before you start the brewing process, make sure you have all your homebrewing equipment (see Chapter 2), you've properly sanitized it (see Chapter 3), and it's in place and ready to use. Here's a quick equipment checklist for you:

- **Airlock**
- **Brewpot with lid**
- **Brew spoon**
- **Coffee cup or small bowl** (for proofing the yeast)
- **Fermentation bucket with lid**
- **Rubber stopper** (to attach to the airlock, if needed)
- **Hydrometer** (the hydrometer cylinder isn't necessary at this time)

Now you just need a couple of simple household items to complete the ensemble. Gather together a long-handled spoon or rubber spatula (for scraping the gooey malt extract from the cans), hot pads (to hold onto hot pots and pans), and a small saucepan (to heat up the cans or bags of extract). Speaking of which, be sure to have your homebrew kits on hand — your beer will be awfully watery-tasting without them!

I recommend either two 3.3-pound cans of pre-hopped malt extract (plus yeast), or one 6.6-pound can. A six-pound bag of malt extract would suffice. This is the appropriate amount for the average 5-gallon batch of beer. The style of beer or brand of malt extract is your choice.

Brewing Your First Batch

Enough of the preliminary stuff. Here's where the rubber meets the road — it's time to get brewing! This section walks you through the step-by-step process of brewing at home. Just follow along and you can make great beer in no time.

The following numbered list covers 24 steps that walk you all the way through the brewing process. Twenty-four steps may sound pretty intense, but I assure you they're easy, quick, and painless steps (unless you consider turning on a burner to be exhausting work). Besides, when you're done, you've brewed your first beer!

1. **Fill your brewpot about ⅔ full with clean tap water or bottled water and then place it on the largest burner of your stove.**

   Use bottled water if your home's water source is loaded with chlorine, iron, or high concentrations of other trace metals. (See Chapter 7 to find out more about the importance of good water.)

   The exact volume of water isn't terribly important during this step, because you add cold water to the fermenter later to bring the total to 5 gallons.

2. **Set the burner on medium-high.**
3. **If working with canned extract, remove the plastic lids from the kits and set the yeast packets aside. If working with bags, skip to warming them in the saucepot for a couple minutes (step 6).**
4. **Strip the paper labels off the two cans of extract and place the cans in a smaller pot or saucepan filled halfway with tap water. Place the pot or saucepan on another burner near the brewpot.**

   The water's purity isn't important here because you don't use this water in the beer.

5. **Set the second burner on medium.**
6. **Using hot pads, flip the cans in the warming water every couple of minutes.**

7. **As the water in the brewpot begins to boil, turn off the burner under the smaller pot (containing the cans), remove the cans from the water, and remove the lids from the cans.**
8. **Using a long-handled spoon or rubber spatula, scrape as much of the warmed extract as possible from the cans into the water in the brewpot. If working with bags, just snip a big corner off the top and pour into the brewpot.**
9. **Immediately stir the extract/water solution and continue to stir until the extract completely dissolves in the water.**

   This malt extract/water mixture is now officially called *wort.*

WARNING

   If you don't stir the wort immediately, you risk scorching the extract on the bottom of the brewpot.

10. **Top off the brewpot with more clean tap or bottled water, keeping your water level a reasonable distance — about 2 inches — from the top of the pot to avoid boilovers.**
11. **Bring the wort to a boil (turn up the burner if necessary).**
12. **Boil the wort for about an hour, stirring the pot every couple of minutes to avoid scorching and boilovers.**

WARNING

   Never put the lid on the brewpot during the boiling phase! Stove-top boilovers occur regularly when a brewpot's lid is on. Boilovers aren't only a sticky, gooey mess, but they're also a waste of good beer!

13. **Turn off the burner and place the lid on the brewpot.**
14. **Put a stopper in the nearest sink drain, put the covered brewpot in the sink, and fill the sink with very cold water.**

   Fill the sink completely (or up to the liquid level in the brewpot if the sink is deeper than the brewpot).

15. **After 5 minutes, drain the sink and refill it with very cold water — repeat as many times as you need until the brewpot is cool to the touch. You can add a bunch of ice to the water in the sink to help speed up the cooling process.**
16. **While the brewpot is cooling in the sink, draw at least 6 ounces of lukewarm tap water into a sanitized cup or bowl.**
17. **Open the yeast packets and pour the dried yeast into the cup or bowl of water.**

   Called *proofing,* this process is a gentle but effective way to wake up the dormant yeast and ready it for the fermentation to follow.

18. **When the brewpot is relatively cool to the touch, remove the brewpot lid and carefully pour the wort into the fermentation bucket.**

    Make sure the spigot is closed!

19. **Top off the fermenter to the 5-gallon mark with cold, clean water, pouring it vigorously into the bucket.**

    This splashing not only mixes the wort with the additional water, it also aerates the wort well.

    The yeast needs oxygen in order to get off to a good healthy start in the fermentation phase. Because boiled water is virtually devoid of oxygen, you need to put some oxygen back in by aerating the wort. Failure to aerate may result in sluggish and sometimes incomplete fermentations.

20. **Take a hydrometer reading.**

    See the section "Brewing day reading" in this chapter for specific information about this process.

21. **After you take the hydrometer reading and remove the hydrometer, pour the hydrated yeast from the cup or bowl into the fermenter and give it a good brisk stir with your sanitized brew spoon.**
22. **Cover the fermenter with its lid and thoroughly seal it.**
23. **Put the fermenter in a cool, dark location, such as a basement, a crawl space, or an interior closet.**

    WARNING

    Don't put the fermenter in direct sunlight or where there's a daily fluctuation in temperatures, such as your garage. This temperature fluctuation can mess with your beer's fermentation cycle.

24. **After the fermenter is in a good place, fill the airlock halfway with water and replace the cap; attach the rubber stopper and position it snugly in the fermenter lid.**

    Check to make sure that the fermenter and airlock are sealed airtight by pushing down gently on the fermenter lid. This gentle pressure causes the float piece in the airlock to rise; if it doesn't, you have a breach in the seal. Recheck the lid and airlock for leaks.

    Fermentation should begin within the first 24 hours and last anywhere from 7 to 10 days. This wait can be nerve-wracking for first-timers, but patience is rewarded with great beer.

How quickly the beer begins to ferment and how long the fermentation lasts depends on the amount of yeast, the health of the yeast, the temperature at which the beer is fermenting, and whether the wort was properly aerated. Healthy yeast, mild temperatures (65 to 70 degrees Fahrenheit), and an abundance of oxygen in the wort make for a good, quick ferment. Old, dormant yeast, cold temperatures, and under-oxygenated wort cause fermentations to start slowly, go on interminably, or even quit altogether.

After your beer has been in the fermenter for about a week or so, check the bubbling action in the airlock. If visible fermentation is still taking place (as evidenced by the escaping bubbles), continue to check the bubbling on a daily basis. When the float piece within the airlock appears to be still and the time between bubbles is a minute or more, your beer is ready for bottling. Before you begin the bottling procedures, however, you need to take a second gravity reading to make sure that the fermentation is complete (see the section "Prebottling reading" later in this chapter for specifics on how to do this).

WARNING

Bottling beer before it's done fermenting may result in exploding bottles. Chapter 14 gives you the lowdown on this nasty mishap and how to avoid it.

Taking Hydrometer Readings

I cover the purpose of a hydrometer and how to use one in homebrewing extensively in Chapter 2. The following information shows you specifically how to take hydrometer readings on brewing and bottling days. If you have any lingering questions on this subject, please check out Chapter 2.

Brewing day reading

You want to take the first hydrometer reading on brewing day (see Step 20 in the "Brewing Your First Batch" section of this chapter). To take a good reading, do the following:

1. **Lower the sanitized hydrometer directly into the cooled and diluted wort inside the fermenter.**

   TIP

   As you lower the hydrometer into the wort in the fermenter, give the hydrometer a quick spin with your thumb and index finger; this movement dislodges any bubbles clinging to the hydrometer that may cause you to get an incorrect reading.

2. **Record the numbers at the liquid surface on the hydrometer scales.**

   You need this information on bottling day to decide whether fermentation is complete and to figure out the alcohol content in your beer. The gravity of your malt extract and water mixture will determine the numbers you'll see on the scales. Typically, 6 or so pounds of malt extract diluted in 5 gallons of water appear on the hydrometer's O.G. scale as 1.048, and the alcohol potential (as noted on the hydrometer's alcohol potential scale) is around 6 percent.

Prebottling reading

When you think your beer is ready for bottling (based on the bubbling action in the airlock), it's time to take another hydrometer reading. When compared to the first (brewing day) reading, this reading helps you decide whether your beer is actually ready to be bottled.

1. **With your hydrometer test cylinder in hand, take a sample of beer from the spigot of the fermenter.**

   Be sure to fill the cylinder to within 1 inch of the opening, leaving room for liquid displacement of the immersed hydrometer.

2. **Immerse the hydrometer in the beer, record the numbers at the liquid surface of the hydrometer, and compare with those numbers recorded on brewing day.**

   Remember that the average healthy yeast consumes at least 75 percent of the available sugars in the wort. If the final gravity reading on your fermented beer isn't 25 percent or less of the original gravity, too much maltose sugar may be left in your beer.

Here's a sample equation: If your beer has an original gravity of 1.048, subtract 1 so that you have 0.048; then multiply .048 by 0.35, which results in 0.017. Now add the 1 back in. If the final gravity of your beer is higher than 1.017, you want to delay bottling a few more days.

CALCULATING ALCOHOL CONTENT PERCENTAGE

TECHNICAL STUFF

Shown here is a sample equation to help you figure out how much alcohol has been produced in your beer during fermentation. If you find this all a bit confusing, I suggest you check out the sidebar "Of liquid density and hydrometers" in Chapter 2.

Here's a sample figuring for your first batch of beer. If you use about 6 pounds of liquid malt extract for your brew, your original gravity (or *O.G.* in homebrew lingo) is in the neighborhood of 1.048. If your yeast is good and hungry, your final gravity *(F.G.)* a week or so later (after fermentation) will be about 1.012. Because a *ten-forty eight* (also acceptable homebrewer lingo for the 1.048 gravity) represents an alcohol potential of 6 percent, and a *ten-twelve* (the 1.012 gravity) represents an alcohol potential of 2 percent, the yeast produced 4 percent alcohol in your brew. (Subtract the final alcohol potential from the original alcohol potential to derive the alcohol content percentage.)

» Amping up your ingredients

» Conditioning your hair, er, I mean your beer

Chapter 11
Intermediate Brewing Directions

This chapter picks up where Chapter 10 leaves off, encouraging you, the budding homebrewer, to get more personally involved in the brewing processes and become less dependent on the malt extract producer. This increased involvement means that you choose and add a variety of ingredients to create your brew, as well as perform other, more involved brewing procedures.

Before attempting any procedures outlined in this chapter, I strongly recommend that you first read the beginner brewing directions in Chapter 10. If you already have, well . . . then read on!

Taking Control of Your Beer

The basic differences between beginner and intermediate homebrewing can be easily — but not completely — summed up in a few lines. Intermediate brewers can

» **Use specialty grains (to add more color and flavor in your beer).**

» **Choose and add hops (as opposed to using hopped extract).**

» **Use liquid yeast cultures (instead of freeze-dried yeast).**

» **Perform secondary fermentation procedures.**

The combination of ingredient changes and new procedures can make a world of difference in the quality of your homebrew. And you don't even have to apply these changes all at once.

TIP

Try to make your ingredient changes one at a time in successive batches of beer. This staggered experimentation allows you to appreciate how each process makes an incremental improvement in your beer.

Beer, as I discuss in Part 2, basically consists of four simple ingredients: malt (or barley), hops, yeast, and water. Brewers can use various combinations of these ingredients to produce a vast array of beer styles. But regardless of how many variations of these basic beer-making ingredients you use, you can scientifically dissect all beer styles into three simple variables: color, bitterness, and gravity. These variables are defined by the ingredients that go into the brewpot: The *color* is defined by the grain (or malt extract), the *bitterness* by the hops, and the *gravity* by the grain- or malt-extract-to-water ratio. A fourth variable, responsible for defining the Ale, Lager, or Mixed-Style classifications, is the *yeast strain* used to ferment the beer.

REMEMBER

If you haven't already found a source of good brewing water, by all means, do so now. (See Chapter 7 to find out more about how to choose your water.)

Fooling Around with Ingredients

Your first step away from being a novice brewer is to take effective but simple measures toward improving your beer. The first of these measures has to do with adding more and better ingredients. (The second deals with conditioning your brew differently. See the section "Conditioning for Better Beer" in this chapter for more information.)

WARNING

Whenever you buy homebrewing ingredients, make sure you store them properly if you aren't going to use them immediately. You need to refrigerate all grains, hops, and yeast packets (freeze the hops if you plan to store them long-term). Never allow any of your ingredients to lie around in a warm environment or in direct sunlight, even if they ask you nicely. Think of beer ingredients as food products and think of how most food products decay over time — especially in warmer environments.

Grain and strain

Specialty grains are typically those that are *kilned* (roasted) to various degrees of roastedness after they're *malted* (see Chapter 4 for more on malting) — and some aren't malted at all (specialty malts come already malted and kilned, so you don't need to concern yourself with these processes). Such grains don't substitute for malt extract; they improve it by adding a variety of visual, aromatic, and taste enhancements as well as head-retaining and body-building proteins and dextrins (see Chapter 4 for more information on the function of specialty grains in beer making).

You can add all kinds of colors, flavors, and textures to your beer by adding specialty grains to the brewpot — but don't add them directly! Specialty grains, like all other grains in the brewing business, are never boiled; you should *steep* them at subboiling temperatures (160 to 170 degrees Fahrenheit) just long enough for them to yield their goods. Twenty minutes to a half hour is sufficient.

Boiling grain can lead to a number of problems in your beer, not the least of which is the harsh, astringent, tannin-like taste and mouthfeel that can ruin a whole batch of beer.

I suggest you crack your specialty grain, steep it in a separate pot, and then strain it into the wort in the brewpot. Or, steep it in the brewpot before you add the extract. And make sure you use a grain bag that acts like a big tea bag to allow the hot water to leech all the colors and flavors out of the grain.

With the exception of the most highly roasted grains, you always want to crack, or *mill*, your specialty grains prior to the steeping procedures to maximize the flavoring potential of the grain. You have the added choice of buying the grain already cracked or cracking it yourself at home. For the sake of freshness, you really want to crack your own grain. If you choose not to buy a grain mill, you can still find inventive ways to mill your grain. Try putting the grain into a self-sealing plastic bag and using a rolling pin to crush it (even a baseball bat can do the job). The idea is just to crack the hard outer grain husk, not to mill the grain into flour — don't even think about using your coffee grinder to do this job.

As an intermediate brewer with the ability to add color and flavor to your beer by using specialty grains, you no longer need to buy amber or dark extracts to make amber or dark beers. In fact, after you're comfortable using specialty grains, you're better off deriving these colors and flavors from grain anyway; the taste difference is appreciable.

Another great characteristic of specialty grains is that you don't need to add a whole lot of them in order to influence the flavor of your beer. The amount of specialty grains that most malt extract-based recipes call for rarely exceeds 2 pounds.

More often than not, at least half of the total amount of specialty grain consists of *crystal malt* (also called *caramel malt*) — often considered an extract brewer's best friend. Crystal malt is kind of an all-purpose specialty grain because it can add color, mouthfeel, mild sweetness, and caramelly grain flavor to beer all at once.

Hop to it

You can continue to exert your beery autonomy by making your own choices in hop varieties and adding them as you see fit. Remember that about 200 different hop varieties grow around the world, and new or experimental cultivars pop up regularly. Each hop variety offers different nuances in flavors, aromas, and bittering intensity (see Chapter 5 for more on hops).

TIP

The typical 5-gallon batch of medium gravity beer (1.040 to 1.050) rarely requires more than 3 or 4 ounces of hops to achieve the desired bittering, flavoring, and aromatic profile. Of course, this estimation depends on the type of hops you use (and their corresponding alpha acid contents) as well as the style of the beer you intend to make.

You can add hops to the brewpot at any time; brewers typically add hops at one-hour, half-hour, and quarter-hour increments (homebrew recipes typically specify which increments to use). What you want to get out of the hops determines when you want to introduce them into the boil. Adding smaller quantities at various intervals imbues your beer with a more complex aromatic, flavoring, and bittering profile than if you add a whole bunch all at once. The following are very general guidelines for hop usage:

- You want to boil bittering hops for at least 60 minutes.
- You want to boil flavoring hops for 10 to 30 minutes.
- You want to add finishing (aromatic) hops in the last 5 minutes of the boil — or even just after you've turned off the heat.

Regardless of whether the hops are pellets or whole leaves, you have the choice of dropping them into the kettle loosely or putting them into a disposable or reusable hop bag. If you choose to throw the hops loosely into the kettle, you need to strain the wort on its way into the fermenter. A hop bag, on the other hand, works in much the same way as a tea bag: It allows the hops to steep in the boiling wort without requiring you to strain them later. Just use a strainer, tongs, or your brew spoon to remove the hop bag at the end of the boil and toss its contents on the compost pile.

WARNING

Hops and house pets can be a fatal combination. If certain dogs ingest discarded hops, they may develop a condition called *malignant hyperthermia*, which manifests itself as heavy panting and a rapid heartbeat. Keep Fido — and all pets, for that matter — away from your hop supply (new or used.)

Check out Chapter 5 for more information about hops.

Yeasty beasties

Yeast is another one of the ingredients that you can change and improve, and it's also the fourth variable in the beer-making process (after gravity, color, and bitterness). Yeast is largely responsible for how the finished beer turns out. The time, effort, and high-quality ingredients you put into your brew are all for naught if your yeast ruins everything.

TIP

Liquid yeast cultures may not come with guarantees of purity, but they can measurably increase the quality of your beer. And you can't dispute that the stylistic variety that's available in liquid yeast cultures is lacking in the world of dry yeast — though things are definitely improving on that front.

WARNING

A small downside to using liquid yeast products that aren't ready-to-pitch is that you may need several days to increase the yeast quantity to the proper pitching rate. So if you use liquid yeast, you may need to plan your brewing itinerary in advance (if you plan to brew on Saturday, you better start preparing your yeast by Thursday). Always read and follow the directions on the liquid yeast products you purchase. (See Chapter 6 for more information on liquid yeast cultures and their preparation.)

Conditioning for Better Beer

As I mention earlier in this chapter, using different ingredients is only one way that intermediate homebrewers set themselves apart from the beginners. The other way is by using different methods of conditioning.

Conditioning means allowing your beer additional time to mature, mellow, clarify, and carbonate.

Secondary fermentation

Secondary or *two-stage fermentation* is all about conditioning your beer. When you brewed at the beginner level, you put the fresh wort in the primary fermenter, let the yeast do its thing, and then you bottled the beer. The beer had about two weeks to condition in the bottle before you started sucking it down. You did the right thing (within the limitations of your equipment and expertise), but now you can do more.

At the beginner level, taking the freshly fermented beer out of the primary fermenter was necessary not just because the initial fermentation was over, but also because all those little yeasties, fresh from a gluttonous feast, were about to start decomposing. That's right, enzymes in the sugar-starved yeast begin to break down the yeast cells. This is called yeast *autolysis.* Autolysis can impart a sulfury, rubbery stench and flavor to your beer. So leaving your fresh, young beer sitting on that bulging layer of self-destructing yeast dregs is akin to allowing your child to wallow with pigs in the mud — and you don't want to smell either one of them when they're done. Racking your beer over to a secondary fermentation vessel effectively leaves most of the sedimented yeast and other organic matter behind.

So if bottling the beer after one week worked before, why can't it now? It still can, but now that you're introducing more ingredients into the brewpot, the added flavors and textures in your beer need more time to blend together. By allowing the beer to undergo a secondary fermentation, you promote a mellowing process that makes a noticeable improvement in your beer.

Having shared this information about racking your beer over to a secondary fermenter, now I'm obligated to tell you that there is another school of thought on this topic that suggests secondary fermentation is not only unnecessary but also potentially harmful to your beer if you succeed in aerating or contaminating it. Yep. Every time you transfer your beer, there is the increased risk of exposure to air and bacterial contaminants along the way.

If you find yourself sitting on the fence on this issue, perhaps go without secondary fermentation if your beer is a simple ale. On the other hand, if it's a lager, or if you want to dry hop or add flavorings, and so on, then read the next section closely.

Considering the advantages of secondary fermentation

Allowing your beer to age in a secondary fermenter before you bottle it also reduces *yeast bite*, the harsh flavor and mouthfeel associated with having excessive yeast sediment in the bottle.

Because the yeast has eaten most of the consumable sugars in the wort during primary fermentation, secondary fermentation yields very little yeast activity and rarely produces a measurable amount of alcohol. This second fermentation period is just an opportunity for all the beer's ingredients to acclimate to one another and establish a good, friendly (and tasty) relationship.

The secondary fermenter represents a world of new possibilities for your brew. You can add many different additives and flavorings to the secondary fermenter that may have a huge effect on the finished beer. (See Chapters 8 and 9 for ideas on what to add at the secondary fermentation stage.)

The two-stage aspect of secondary fermentation also allows you to perform some real beer-improving feats:

- **Dry hop:** You can impart more hop aroma to your beer by simply adding ¼ ounce to 2 ounces of hops (in pellet or whole-leaf form) to the secondary fermenter and then draining your beer over them. You can do the same thing with spices, too. Chapter 5 has more information on this process.
- **Make true Lagers:** In order to make genuine Lager beers, you must age the beer in the secondary fermenter for at least a few weeks at very cold temperatures (32 to 40 degrees Fahrenheit) for proper flavor development. (Check out Chapter 26 for ideas on how to set up a lagering cellar.)
- **Clarify your brew:** You can add various clarifying agents to the secondary fermenter to speed up the process of clarification. Typical finings and clarifiers include isinglass, gelatin, Sparkalloid, and PVPP. Chapter 9 gives you more information about finings and clarifiers.

One final vote in support of secondary fermentation: By using this procedure, you can not only quit worrying about unfinished primary fermentations (and exploding bottles), but you can also actually cut the primary ferment short by a day or two if that helps you rack the beer over to the secondary fermenter at a more convenient time. This shortcut is possible *only* after the peak fermentation activity subsides (usually by the fifth or sixth day of a normal, healthy fermentation).

Jumping into secondary fermentation

Secondary fermentation always needs to take place in either glass or stainless steel vessels. A 5-gallon glass carboy is the most popular secondary fermentation vessel, though a few homebrewers prefer to age their beer in stainless steel soda kegs. However, I don't recommend secondary fermentation in plastic vessels. Even the food-grade plastics used to make homebrewing equipment are penetrable by certain gasses (such as oxygen) over an extended period of time.

TIP

PROPAGATION PREPARATION

In anticipation of future brews, consider maximizing your time and consolidating your efforts on behalf of imminent yeast propagations. In plain English, that means instead of making one small batch of sterile wort for propagating yeast for a single batch of beer, try to make a lot of wort and divide it into several bottles. You can store these bottles of sterile wort for long periods of time to be used for future yeast propagations.

Start with a half-dozen or so cleaned and sanitized bottles (you choose the size — larger is better) with an appropriate number of sanitized bottle caps. Prepare a medium gravity wort (1.040–1.050) by using pale malt extract — enough to fill all your bottles two-thirds full. Boil and cool the wort, pour it into the bottles using a sanitized funnel, and cap the bottles.

In order to ensure that the wort is completely sterile, you must boil the capped bottles (this is a crude form of pasteurization). To do so, place the bottles in a deep pot and fill the pot with tap water so that the water in the pot rises to the liquid level inside the bottles. Place the pot on the stove and bring the water to a boil; turn off the heat immediately (be very careful during this process; bottles have been known to burst!). To avoid any possibility of thermal shock, allow the bottles to cool down with the water in the pot — this may take a while, so be patient. After the bottles have cooled, dry them and store them in the refrigerator. When you need to propagate your next liquid yeast culture, you have good, sterile wort ready and waiting.

Or, if you don't want to go DIY on this, you can just buy cans of premade sterile wort through your favorite homebrew supplier.

WARNING

Remember that no phase of homebrewing is exempt from cleaning and sanitizing. When you add another fermentation phase, you must disinfect all the equipment that goes along with it. In addition to the use of a good sanitizing agent, you want to use a carboy brush to make sure you scrub the entire inner surface of the carboy. Rinse the carboy well with hot water and allow it to air-dry. Be sure to have an appropriately sized, sanitized rubber stopper to seal the carboy, as well as an airlock. Don't forget to sanitize all other equipment, especially the plastic hosing, before you use it. If necessary, review the sanitation methods I discuss in Chapter 3.

If you decide to use additives or flavorings and they're liquids (or can be dissolved in water), you can simply pour them into the carboy prior to adding the beer (which takes care of mixing). If your additive or flavoring is bulky or leafy, you want to place it in a hop bag or some kind of filter for easy removal. This bag saves you some work, because you have to strain whatever you put into the secondary fermenter out of the brew on bottling day.

Speaking of bottling, the procedure is delayed another week or two while the beer is mellowing in the carboy. A secondary fermentation isn't really worth the effort unless you allow it to last at least one week. Two to three weeks is the norm, and a month or more may be needed for Barley Wines, Imperial Stouts, and other complex and high-gravity beers and Meads.

Before transferring your beer from the primary fermenter to the secondary fermenter, you want to be sure that the initial, vigorous fermentation (also called *high kraeusen*) is complete. You can do this check simply by watching the bubbles in the airlock; if they appear at half-minute or longer intervals, you can proceed with the following racking procedures.

1. **Place your primary fermenter on a table or sturdy work surface and position the empty carboy on the floor directly below the fermenter.**
2. **Connect one end of the plastic hose to the spigot on the primary fermenter and put the other end inside the carboy.**

   Be sure that you space the two vessels so that the dangling plastic hose reaches the bottom of the carboy — this practice prevents aerating the beer as you drain it. You may want to prop the carboy up on beer bottle cases, a step stool, or large books (basically, anything that can withstand the weight of a carboy full of beer).

   If you invest in a carbon dioxide kegging system, you can fill your carboy with CO_2 (because it's heavier than air) before you rack the beer into it. This practice helps limit oxidation of the beer. Just let the CO_2 flow into the carboy at 1 to 2 *psi* (pounds per square inch). (See Chapter 16 for more about kegging.)
3. **Fill the carboy with beer to within an inch or two of the opening.**

   In some cases, you may have to stop the flow of beer before it finishes draining out of the primary fermenter; in other cases, you may have to top the carboy off with clean water that you've boiled and cooled down. What little water you may need to add doesn't affect the beer's gravity.

TIP

   Speaking of gravity, you don't need to take a hydrometer reading when you rack the beer from the primary to the secondary fermenter, but if you do you can get an idea of how your brew is progressing and how long you need to consider leaving it in the carboy. Getting a beer sample from the hose into the hydrometer test cylinder can be tricky and may lead to a big mess if you're not careful. The key is to control the flow of beer with the spigot on the primary fermenter. Just remember to practice good sanitation and avoid aerating your beer.
4. **Place the appropriate rubber stopper in the neck of the carboy, fill your airlock halfway with water, and place it in the hole in the rubber stopper.**

5. **Store the filled carboy in a cool, dark place for a couple of weeks.**
6. **Padlock the door to the room where you've stashed the carboy and position a sentinel at the threshold. You're just 14 days away from some of the best beer you've ever tasted.**

TIP

MASTERING THE ART OF SIPHONING

The use of a glass carboy in homebrewing requires you to practice your siphoning techniques, because glass carboys don't come equipped with spigots. To perform such siphoning, you need a curved racking tube (or *cane*) and your plastic hosing. (I discuss racking tubes and other necessary equipment in Chapter 2.)

The most effective siphoning occurs when the opening of the siphon hose is lower than the bottom of the vessel you're siphoning the beer out of (the lower the better). If you keep large air bubbles out of the siphon hose, you also increase the siphoning efficiency; air bubbles can actually slow or stop liquid flow. They can also oxidize the beer.

You can use a handful of ways to start a siphon, but not all of them are appropriate for homebrewing. For speed and simplicity, sucking on one end of the siphon hose sure gets a flow going, but it also opens the door to all kinds of contamination possibilities. Some brewers feel that a good gargle and rinse with whiskey or vodka prior to sucking on the hose is a good temporary cure for this problem. Personally, I think it's in bad taste (and so was that pun).

A better idea is to add a false end to the siphon hose that can be removed as soon as the beer begins flowing. A stiff straw, a piece of copper tubing, or a short piece of small-diameter hosing can be fitted snugly inside the siphon hose. After starting the flow of beer by sucking the false end, you can remove it and allow the flow to continue. One brewer I know uses the cylindrical part of a turkey baster to accomplish this. With the baster's bulb off and the thin end held tightly inside the siphon hose, one good inhale and the beer is flowing. (And no fouled beer!)

Another, more widely accepted practice is to fill the plastic hosing with water just prior to fitting it onto the racking tube. After you connect the tube and hose (with the tube resting in the carboy), just drop the open end of the hose into the bottling bucket and the beer automatically starts to flow. This method may take a few tries before you get the system down. But what are a few beer stains on the floor in pursuit of a healthy libation?

If all of these methods of starting a siphon seem difficult, then maybe you just want to cut to the chase and invest in something called an *autosiphon*. This handy contraption allows you to very quickly and easily get a siphon going with just a little pump action. Check it out.

When you're ready to bottle your well-conditioned brew you'll have no choice but to use siphoning procedures to drain the carboy, because glass carboys don't have spigots for convenience. Lucky for you, I've provided all the helpful information you need in the "Mastering the art of siphoning" sidebar.

Tertiary fermentation

Tertiary or *three-stage fermentation* is really no different from two-stage fermentation in its objective and procedure. Brewers don't typically need to rack a beer over to a third fermentation vessel, but it may be useful under certain conditions:

- If, after a prolonged secondary fermentation, you have a considerable build-up of yeast sedimentation on the bottom of the carboy, tertiary fermentation can help you avoid the yeast autolysis problem mentioned earlier in this chapter. This situation is only likely to happen in very high-gravity barley wines, Russian imperial stouts, or other similar beer styles. (Part 4 gives you some insight on beer-style descriptions and parameters.)

INTERMEDIATE HOMEBREWING BASICS AT A GLANCE

This flowchart shows you, in a nutshell, the steps you need to take to brew at the intermediate level. Enjoy!

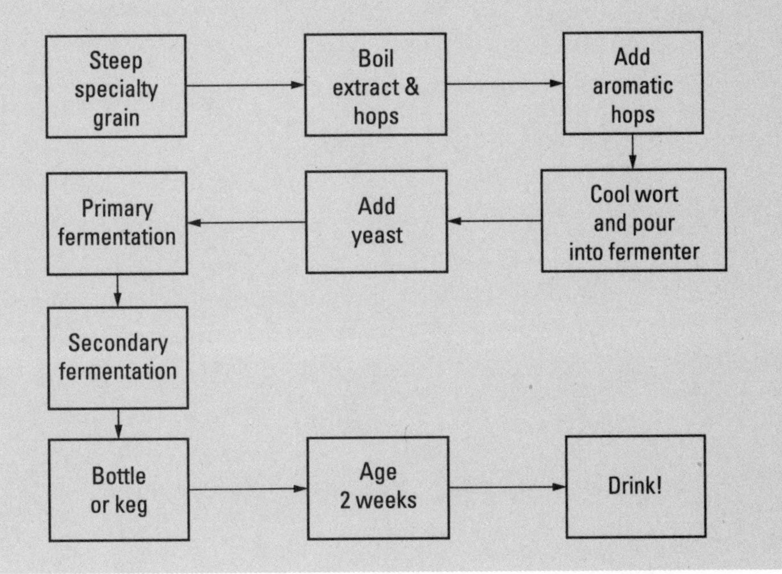

» If your beer has been sitting on real fruit in the secondary fermenter, you may consider a brief tertiary fermentation. Racking the beer off the decomposing fruit before you bottle it may go a long way toward melding the fruit flavors into the beer as well as reducing the pectin haze that the fruit often creates. (*Pectin* is a carbohydrate that occurs naturally in ripe fruit. Because of its thickening properties, it can solidify to a gel that, diluted in your beer, can create a hazy appearance — called *pectin haze* — in the beer.)

WARNING

Keep in mind that every time you handle your brew, you increase the odds of aeration and contamination. Always practice good beer handling and sanitation techniques.

» Comparing partial and full mashing

» Starting from scratch with all-grain brewing

» Increasing batch size

» Harvesting yeast

Chapter 12 Advanced Brewing Directions

You've made it — you're now at the advanced stage of the homebrewing process! You're pumped, you're psyched — you're ready to take the ultimate step in homebrewing. The first and biggest step between the intermediate and advanced levels of homebrewing takes you from relying on prepared extracts to making beer from scratch out of grain. The process integral to this step is *mashing* — and, no, the process has nothing to do with boiling spuds.

After you master the mashing procedures that I outline in this chapter, you've pretty much joined the ranks of the professional brewers. And even though you're still making beer in relatively small amounts, you are, for the most part, unlimited as to where your talent, knowledge, and ability can take you.

REMEMBER

Many homebrewers have gone on to new careers in the brewing industry; some have even opened up their own craft breweries and brewpubs.

After mastering the science of producing beer from grain, many advanced brewers (in their never-ending quest to achieve bigger and better brews) concentrate on the bigger picture (and pitcher). Five gallons of beer is no longer worth the time and effort of brewing for these guys; 10 and 15 gallons a crack — now that's brewing! You may want to consider these possibilities for yourself (check out Chapter 13 for some inspiration).

As I discuss in Chapter 11, after you graduate to another level of homebrewing you must acquaint yourself with new procedures and new equipment — see the section about advanced homebrewing equipment in Chapter 2.

In the first part of this chapter, I mention general brewing procedures. I cover exactly how to perform these procedures later in this chapter. Also, be aware that your comprehension of this chapter relies on knowledge you gain by reading the two preceding chapters — make sure that you check them out first.

Yes, We Have No Potatoes: Mashing Procedures

Put your potato peeler away; the kind of mashing I'm talking about is the process by which you manipulate your grain to create and capture the natural grain sugars that feed the yeast during fermentation. At the beginner and intermediate levels of homebrewing, you can cut corners by buying commercially made malt extract (concentrated wort). By using mashing procedures, however, you make your own wort directly from grain.

How is *mashing* different from *steeping* specialty grains? As I discuss in Chapter 11, you steep specialty grains primarily for coloring and flavoring your beer, not for their contribution of fermentable sugars (which you get by mashing). In the absence of malt extract, you need base grains to produce the malt sugars that feed the yeast during fermentation. (As the name implies, *base grain* is the foundation on which the beer is built.) The production of these sugars from the grains takes place during the mashing procedures.

The mashing process utilizes the naturally occurring enzymes in pale malts to convert the starch in the grain kernels to sugars. These malt sugars then become food for the yeast during fermentation.

TECHNICAL STUFF

What do these enzymes actually do? Well, you can think of a starch molecule as a bunch of sugar molecules arranged like beads on a string. These enzymes cut the bonds (or strings) between the sugar molecules (the beads). This process, called *conversion*, frees up the sugars so that the yeast can utilize them. Conversion occurs when enzymatic action in the mash tun or vessel converts the starches in grain to soluble sugars that the yeast can consume.

Three important variables

You should consider the following three important variables in mashing:

- **Temperature:** In terms of the mashing temperature's effect on the finished beer, higher temperatures (153° to 158° Fahrenheit) create a less fermentable wort, and, conversely, lower temperatures (148° to 153° Fahrenheit) produce a more fermentable wort. This knowledge enables you to exercise more control over the flavor and mouthfeel of the finished beer. A more fermentable wort results in more alcohol and less body in the beer. A less fermentable wort results in less alcohol but more body and mouthfeel.

TECHNICAL STUFF

  If you really must know, high mashing temperatures promote the action of *alpha-amylase,* which produces less fermentable sugars than does the *beta-amylase* promoted by lower mashing temperatures. Both alpha- and beta-amylase are already present in malted grain.

- **pH:** As I discuss in Chapter 7, *pH* is the measurement of the acidity or the alkalinity of the mash. The pH of the mash needs to be between 5.0 and 5.5 for the enzymes to work best. (I cover exactly how to adjust the pH in the section "Easing into Mashing with a Partial Mash" later in this chapter.)
- **Time:** Time is the last variable; you must give the enzymes sufficient time to work. Theoretically, 10 to 20 minutes is sufficient, but you generally want to give yourself some leeway — 60 to 90 minutes — to ensure complete conversion.

Don't worry — you don't need to know how the mashing process works for it to work predictably every time. Just make sure that the temperature, pH, and time are in order. After all, you don't need to know the workings of internal-combustion engines just to drive a car!

Gimme some water: Simplified water treatment for mashing

I'm going to let you in on something: I'm making assumptions about you at this point. I'm assuming that you've already brewed a few batches of beer and you have a supply of good, clean, chlorine-free water with which to brew. Fair enough? Now if you're going to start all-grain brewing (mashing), you need to take a few more water variables into account:

- **The hardness of your brewing water:** By *hardness,* I mean the amount of minerals dissolved in the water. If you have a difficult time creating a lather with soap, you can probably safely say that your water is hard (or that you need to find better soap).

Hard water isn't necessarily a bad thing. Brewers specifically use hard waters to create certain beer styles, such as pale ales, Dortmunder exports, and some dark beers. Excessive hardness, however, can be detrimental to your brew.

TIP

One easy way to remove temporary hardness is to boil the water for 30 to 60 minutes and let it cool. (Boiling also offers the benefit of removing chlorine.) After it cools and settles, siphon the water off of any precipitated sediment. This process generally removes chalky (calcium carbonate) hardness. See Chapter 7 for more information on water hardness.

- **The pH of your mash water:** To prepare mash correctly, you need a mash water pH of 5.7 to 6.3 (lower for pale beers and higher for dark beers) because the acidity level of the mash will automatically increase when the *grist* (grain) is added to the wort. How much it increases depends on how much dark grain is added; dark grain is naturally more acidic. Check the pH of your water — if it's higher than 6.5, you need to add gypsum and boil as you would to decrease temporary hardness (which I describe in the preceding Tip paragraph). Because you may use any one of so many different types of water, this process is not a cure-all, but it tends to work well in practice for most types of water. Check out Chapter 7 for more on manipulating water pH with additives.

REMEMBER

Remember that the pH level is what's most important for mashing procedures to work correctly — the mash must be between 5.0 and 5.5 pH. The actual mineral content is important, but not as important as the pH.

- **The temperature of the mash:** After mixing crushed malt with water, you can generally expect a 10-degree Fahrenheit or so drop in temperature. This change means that, for a mash temperature of 150° to 158° Fahrenheit, your mash water must be 160° to 168° Fahrenheit. (Coincidentally, this temperature range is the ideal *sparge* or rinse water temperature.)

And then there were three: Mashing types

You have three basic types of mashing procedures. All three procedures are in use in the commercial brewing industry, and you can use any of them at the home-brewing level. The following list describes these procedures:

- **Infusion:** This procedure is the most basic form of mashing (and also the easiest). You just mix the crushed malt with water and stabilize the temperature at 150° to 158° Fahrenheit. You then measure and adjust the pH to 5.0 to 5.5 and hold the mixture at that temperature level for 60 to 90 minutes. Infusion mashing requires that you use *fully modified* (or pale ale) malts. This mashing method is primarily found in use in Great Britain and most American craft breweries for making ales. (See the Infusion Mashing Procedure Flow Chart in Figure 12-1.)

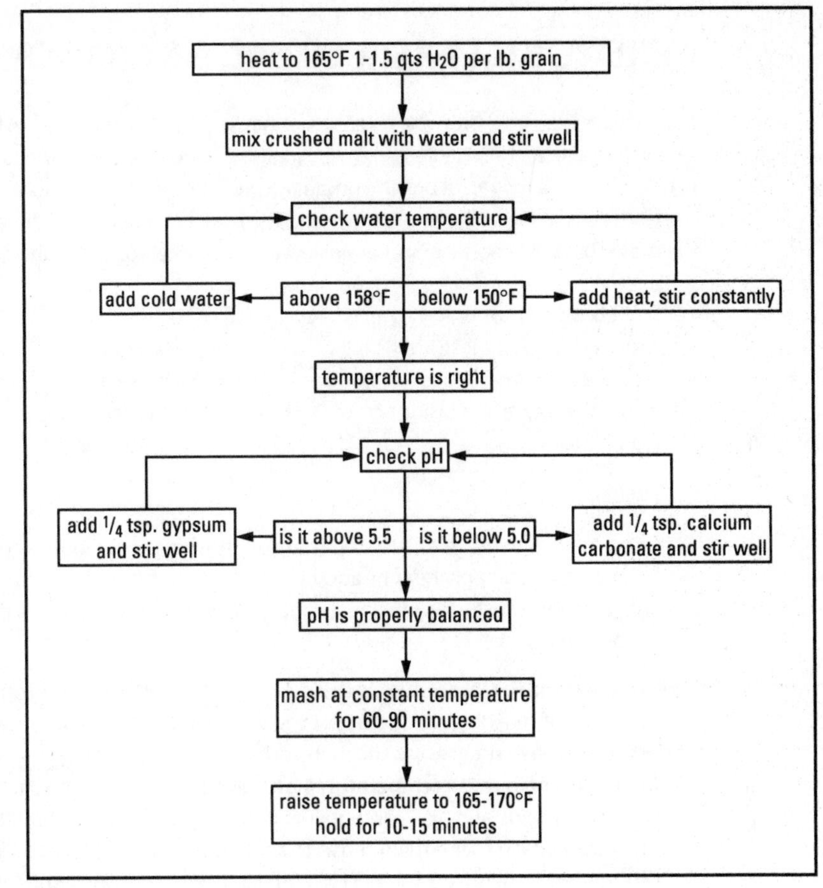

FIGURE 12-1: Just follow the arrows for a perfect infusion-mashing procedure.

REMEMBER

The *modification* of the grain mentioned in the preceding paragraph occurs at the malting stage (see Chapter 4 for more on malting). You can purchase your grain according to your desired level of modification — for example, 2-row English pale malts are typically more highly modified than others (see Chapter 4).

- **Step infusion (or multistep infusion):** This mashing method is like infusion mashing but gives you even more control over the process. Mix the water and crushed malt as you do in regular infusion mashing, adjust the temperature to 122° to 131° Fahrenheit, and hold at that temperature for 15 to 30 minutes; you then boost the temperature to the starch conversion range (150° to 158° Fahrenheit). This process is a *protein rest.* Providing a protein rest enables other enzymes present to break down large proteins in the malt to smaller proteins. These smaller proteins contribute to body and head retention. Generally, a protein rest is necessary only for less-modified malts, such as lager malts.

CEREAL KILLERS: CEREAL GRAIN MASHING

Many major industrial breweries, such as Anheuser-Busch, Coors, and Miller, use raw (unmalted) cereal grains to lighten the flavor, body, and color of their beers — typically, light lagers. They first must boil the unmalted grain (as with a decoction mash) to make the grains' starch available to the enzymes. The brewers then return the boiled grains to the mash for conversion. Adjunct grains may include rice, corn, rye, and oats.

For homebrewing purposes, however, buying "flaked" adjunct grains is much easier and less time-consuming; these grains are pregelatinized (precooked) (see Chapter 4 for more on these grains). In this form, you can simply mash them with the rest of your base and specialty grains, using one of the three methods mentioned in this chapter.

The main advantage to the step-infusion mashing technique is control. Generally, you apply heat or add boiling water to bring the mash through the temperature rests. By judiciously applying heat, you can control temperatures more precisely.

- **Decoction:** This procedure is the most complicated and time-consuming method of mashing. The basic procedure is similar to that of a step mash in that the mash progresses through various temperature ranges. You take the mash through these temperatures by pulling off the thickest part of the mash — grains and all — and boiling it in a separate vessel. You then return this thick mash to the main mash to bring the entire mixture to the next temperature rest. You can perform up to three decoctions and temperature rests.

  The main advantage to decoction mashing is that the boiling helps to impart a rich, malty character to certain beer styles, such as bocks, Märzens, and Weizens.

  Very few homebrewers use the decoction method of mashing, because decoction mashing requires extra time, effort, and expertise. Unless you're trying to make truly authentic versions of these three beer styles, this method is usually not worthwhile. For these reasons, I don't cover decoction mashing any further in this book.

The mash-out

After you have completed conversion in your mash, you need to finalize the mashing process by doing a mash-*out*. Regardless of which mashing method you use, raise the mash temperature to 160° to 170° Fahrenheit for about 15 minutes after starch conversion is complete. (If water pH and temperature are right, complete conversion should occur after 60 minutes.) You want to do so for the following two reasons:

- When you rinse the sugars from the grains, the thick and syrupy wort flows faster at these high temperatures. (See the "Lautering" and "Sparging" sections in this chapter.)
- These temperatures also destroy the enzymes in the mash after the enzymes accomplish their task. This enzyme destruction preserves the degree of fermentability of the wort, which you purposely set with your mashing temperatures.

Lautering

Now for the question that you've been dying to ask: "After I create all these liquefied sugars, how do I separate them from the grains?" Transfer the mash into a *lauter tun*, a vessel with some sort of strainer or *false bottom* arrangement and a tap for draining the wort away from the grain. (See Chapter 2 for more information about lauter tuns.)

After transferring the mash to the lauter tun, carefully draw off the sweet, syrupy liquid called *first runnings*. First runnings have a very high specific gravity because they have a high concentration of sugars. *Second runnings* (the residual wort rinsed from the grain during sparging) have a rather low gravity because they're heavily diluted by the sparge water. First and second runnings together achieve a more moderate starting gravity for your beer when you combine, boil, and reduce them in the brewpot. (See the sidebar "Parti-gyle brewing" later in this chapter.)

Unfortunately, these first runnings contain a lot of solid matter (grain husks, finely ground malt, and so on). To make a stable beer, you must eliminate most of this solid matter. How do you achieve this task? Just draw off the first runnings and *recirculate* them, or pour them back over the top of the grain in the lauter tun. Recirculation relies on the grain husks to filter, and thus clarify, the wort. Recirculate the wort through your grain bed only until the wort begins to run clear. After you clarify the runoff this way, you can drain it into the brewpot and rinse (or *sparge*) the grains.

WARNING

Excessive recirculation of the first runnings may result in wort oxidation and other off flavors that show up in the finished beer. Chapter 25 gives you tips to combat such troubles.

Sparging

Sparging is rinsing the grain bed with hot water. Why do you need to sparge? Because the grain bed still retains a lot of liquid sugar after you collect the first runnings. You therefore need to percolate treated water (pH of 5.0 to 5.5, temperature of 165° to 170° Fahrenheit) through the grain bed. (I address the topic of water pH in Chapter 7.) You then collect the second runnings just as you do the first runnings (but you don't need to recirculate them).

Sparging is an important part of the mashing procedure because the process enables you to maximize the grain yield by capturing most of the fermentable sugars from the grain. (You get the most wort for your money.) You need to be aware, however, that oversparging can negatively affect your brew's taste; see Chapter 27 for troubleshooting advice. When the sparge water you're pouring through the grain bed begins to run clear, you need to stop sparging. (Two quarts of water per pound of grain in the recipe is the general rule.)

Truth be told, you can skip the sparging process altogether, but that would be like throwing money out the window; there's still a lot of fermentable sugar in the grain bed that you'd be leaving behind. Also consider that without diluting your first runnings, your wort will have a much higher finishing gravity.

It's in the bag

There is yet another option to avoid sparging procedures while saving time in your brew day; it's known as *brew-in-a-bag* (or *BIAB*).

By using a durable food safe fabric filter that's placed inside your brewpot, the mashing and boiling process is simplified through the use of just one vessel and one burner for the entire process.

The BIAB process allows you to mash your grain in your brewpot and remove it all relatively simply and quickly. The best part is that this process allows you to forego the sparging procedures.

Two things you need to know about the BIAB process:

- The bag full of spent grain will not only be heavy, but also very hot when it's removed from the brewpot. The only safe and smart way to remove it is by using an overhead hoist-and-pulley system. Come-along cable pullers or inexpensive manual boat trailer winches can be easily found at your local home improvement store or online. Slowly hoist the bag from the kettle to allow for an even flow with minimal splashing (and resulting potential oxidation).

PARTI-GYLE BREWING

Due to the nature of first- and second-run wort, you can quite conceivably create two different brews from the same initial mash by utilizing *parti-gyle brewing.* A recipe with a very high grain-to-water ratio can conceivably produce a high-gravity first-run wort (such as a barley wine or old ale) and still provide enough residual sugar in the second runnings for a low-gravity beer (such as a mild or a bitter). To avoid any dilution of the first-run wort and to minimize dilution of the second-run wort, don't increase the beer volume of either brew to full batch size (5 gallons or otherwise) — leave them as two smaller partial batches. Parti-gyle brewing methods obviously require two separate fermentation vessels as well.

The general rule says that the first third of the wort contains half the sugars. Because a 50/50 split of the wort would leave the second-run wort too weak, I recommend that you shoot for a 30/70 split.

- » You'll still need to carefully squeeze most of the remaining hot wort out of the grain while it's in the bag dangling over your brewpot. Insulated rubber gloves are highly recommended for this. Again, try to squeeze the grain in a way that minimizes splashing.

Easing into Mashing with a Partial Mash

The concept of partial mashing is to substitute some — but not all — of the malt extract with pale malt to provide the fermentable material. You generally continue to use specialty grains (crystal malt, roasted malts, and so on) in the same quantities as you do in extract-based recipes (which appear in Chapter 10).

Why do a partial mash rather than an all-grain batch (which I discuss in the next section)? Partial mashing is a great way to familiarize yourself with the mashing procedures for the following reasons:

- » The smaller quantities of grain and water are easier to handle.
- » You don't need a large brewpot. (The brewpot left over from your beginner homebrewing days is fine.)
- » You don't need a lauter tun. (A kitchen colander or strainer is sufficient.)
- » The entire process is less time-consuming and is generally easier if your beer is not completely dependent on the mashing process.

To perform the following partial-mash procedures, here's what you need:

- A bottling bucket or similar bucket (to hold wort).
- An 8- to 20-quart pot (in which to mash) — your brewpot is sufficient for this purpose. Larger is better.
- A strainer or colander.
- A 2- to 10-quart stock pot (for holding sparge water). Larger is better.
- Some pH papers (you should always have plenty on hand because you may need to check the wort several times) or a pH meter.
- A set of teaspoons.
- Gypsum (calcium sulfate). You should always have at least a teaspoon on hand, but you may end up not needing any at all.
- Calcium carbonate (food-grade chalk). You should keep at least a teaspoon of this on hand as well, but you may not need any at all.
- A lab immersion thermometer.
- A grain mill (if you aren't using preground malt).
- A postal or kitchen scale (to weigh the malt).
- Pale malt base grain. (For a beginner's mash, 2-row pale ale malt is preferable because it's fully modified and thus easier to work with.)
- Other specialty grains as specified in your ale recipe.

Here's a step-by-step run-through of a partial mash:

1. **Add 1⅓ quarts of treated water per pound of grain (based on the recipe you're using) to your brewpot.**

   See the nearby sidebar "Adjusting pH levels" to prepare your water.

2. **Heat your water to 160° to 168° Fahrenheit.**

   This range is the *strike* temperature.

3. **Add your crushed malt to the water and mix well.**

REMEMBER

   A reminder about the correct crushing of your grain: As you crush the malt, don't grind it too finely — this only creates problems later. Just try to crack the husk of the malt to expose the white, starchy interior. (This step may take some careful adjustment of the mill to get it just right.) Try to keep as much of the husk intact as possible.

4. **Check the temperature of the mash (holding the thermometer in the center of the mash for a more accurate reading).**

TIP

Thermometers generally need about 10 to 20 seconds to register correctly.

The temperature should now be 150 to 158 Fahrenheit.

5. **If the temperature is too low, apply heat while stirring constantly; if the temperature is too high, add small amounts of cold water to bring the temperature lower than 158° Fahrenheit.**

TIP

Watch for wort scorching, and don't exceed 158° Fahrenheit; higher temperatures destroy the enzymes. If you do overshoot 158°, add small quantities of cold water to bring the temperature back down as quickly as possible.

6. **After the temperature stabilizes, use a teaspoon to draw up some of the liquid that's on top of the grains and then let the liquid cool to room temperature so that you can check the pH.**

7. Following the instructions provided with the pH papers, dip the paper into the mash sample contained in the teaspoon, read the pH, and record the level in your notes (or simply use your pH meter).

Discard all used strips and wort samples.

Is the pH between 5.0 and 5.5? If so, you're home free!

8. **If the pH level and temperature are correct, cover the mash and hold the temperature at 150° to 158° Fahrenheit for 60 minutes.**

Remember, if the pH level is *not* between 5.0 and 5.5, you *must* adjust it to this range. The enzymes need this pH range to work correctly and produce a well-made beer.

TIP

Check the temperature of the mash every 20 minutes. You may need to adjust the temperature back into the 150 to 158 degree Fahrenheit range by heating and stirring constantly.

During the last 45 minutes of the mash, you need to start preparing your sparge water.

9. **In a separate pot, heat two quarts of water per pound of grain (as called for in your recipe) to 160° to 170° Fahrenheit.**

You use this water to rinse the grains. If you're using water with a pH level higher than 7.0, you need to lower the pH to between 5.7 and 6.5. (Check the pH after every mineral addition.)

TIP

ADJUSTING pH LEVELS

How can you adjust the pH? If the pH is too high, add half a teaspoon of gypsum and stir well. Check the pH again, as I describe in Steps 6 and 7 of the nearby list. Repeat these steps until the pH level is between 5.0 and 5.5. At any rate, don't add more than 2 teaspoons of gypsum to the mash. Natural materials in the malt resist changes in pH, so adding larger amounts of minerals doesn't really change the pH. What if the pH level is lower than 5.0? You simply add calcium carbonate in the same way that you add gypsum if the mash pH level is too high. (But never add more than 2 teaspoons of any mineral; if you are unable to reach a desired pH level by using 2 teaspoons of mineral additive, you're just wasting money while negatively affecting the taste of your beer.)

10. **After starch conversion (after 60 minutes), raise the temperature of the mash to 160° to 170° Fahrenheit and hold for 10 to 15 minutes.**

    This stage is the *mash-out.* After the mash-out, you need to strain out the liquid (wort) and rinse the grains. This process is *lautering and sparging.*

11. **Pour or ladle the mash into the strainer suspended over your bottling bucket and let the sweet wort drain out of the grains.**

    This process may take a few minutes.

    REMEMBER

    Don't squeeze or press the grains to hasten the draining of the wort. Just let gravity do the work naturally.

12. **Next, put the strainer full of grain over your brewpot and recirculate the cloudy wort in your bottling bucket back through the grains in the strainer.**

    The grain filters out most of the minute solid particles in the wort.

    Now it's time to sparge.

13. **Pour the hot (165° to 170° Fahrenheit) sparge water over the grains to rinse away the sugars trapped in the grain.**

14. **After you pour out all the sparge water, let the grains that are still in the strainer drain for 5 to 10 minutes into the brewpot.**

You're done! Just add the malt extract to the brewpot and brew as you normally would an all-extract batch (see Chapter 10). Now you deserve a beer!

FIRST WORT HOPPING

First wort hopping (FWH) is an old yet recently rediscovered process for adding hop character to your brew. At the beginning of the sparging process, you add hops to the brew kettle where you collect the first runnings. The idea is that the hops steep in the collecting wort (which usually runs out of the lauter tun at temperatures ranging from 150° to 170° Fahrenheit, depending on your setup) for the duration of the sparge; this steeping produces a complexity of hop bitterness and aroma that you can't get by using any other method.

One study among professional brewers determined that using FWH resulted in a more refined hop aroma, a more uniform bitterness (no harshness), and a more harmonious beer overall (compared to an identical beer produced without FWH).

Your best bet is to use only low alpha finishing hops for FWH and to use at least 30 percent of the total amount of hops used in the boil. This FWH addition should therefore be taken from the hops intended for finishing additions. How's that for an odd reversal of hop additions?

Going All Out with All-Grain Brewing

Are you ready to brew beer from scratch? This procedure is the ultimate in control for a brewer. All-grain brewing gives you complete control over the entire malt flavor and source of fermentable material for your beer — something not possible if you use malt extracts.

The main difference between partial mashing and all-grain brewing is size — more grains, more water, bigger brewpot, and so on are all necessary in all-grain brewing. I describe the three pieces of equipment you need to go from partial mashing to all-grain brewing in the following list:

- **A large brewpot:** This item needs to be at least 7 gallons in capacity because you're collecting the entire volume of wort. Boiling the entire batch volume is a *full wort boil* (6 to 7 gallons of wort boil down to the typical 5-gallon batch size).
- **A wort chiller:** Because you're boiling 6 to 7 gallons of wort, you really need an effective way to chill the wort to pitching temperature (approximately 70° Fahrenheit) within 30 to 45 minutes. Cold-water baths in the sink just don't cut it anymore.

» **A lauter tun:** This item is really a big, glorified strainer. Generally, this vessel can hold up to 20 pounds of mash (crushed grain and water). It has a false bottom with holes or slots that enable you to drain the sweet wort from the grain.

TIP

Check out Chapter 30 for money-saving tips on how to make your own equipment.

Other than these changes in size and equipment, the mashing, runoff, and sparging procedures are just about the same.

Note: If you haven't done any partial mashing yet, refer first to the section "Easing into Mashing with a Partial Mash" earlier in this chapter for terms and concepts (you have to walk before you can run). In this section, I discuss in detail only the differences between the two processes.

Here's a step-by-step run-through of an all-grain infusion mash; just follow these steps:

1. **Heat 1⅓ quarts of treated water for every pound of grain in the recipe to 160° to 170° Fahrenheit.**

   See the section "Gimme some water: Simplified water treatment for mashing" earlier in this chapter for details.

2. **Mix in crushed malt and stir well.**

   This process is *mashing in* (sometimes called the *dough-in*).

3. **Check the temperature (150° to 158° Fahrenheit) and the pH (5.0 to 5.5) of the mash and adjust as necessary to reach these levels.**

4. **Hold the mash at this temperature for 60 to 90 minutes to achieve total starch conversion.**

   You may need to reheat mash to keep it in the correct temperature range.

5. **In the meantime, prepare 2 quarts of treated sparge water per pound of grain.**

   See Step 9 in the "Easing into Mashing with a Partial Mash" section for instructions on treating sparge water.

6. **After starch conversion, raise the temperature of the mash to 160° to 170° Fahrenheit and hold for 10 to 15 minutes.**

   This step is the mash-out.

7. **Carefully ladle or pour the mash into your lauter tun.**

8. **Into a saucepan, very slowly draw off 1 or 2 quarts of the wort from the spigot or hose at the bottom of the lauter tun and then take the sweet wort (first runnings) and pour (or *recirculate*) it over the top of the grain bed.**

   Continue until few or no solid particles appear in the runoff. This task may take 1 or 2 gallons of wort to accomplish.

   TIP

   Try to keep splashing and frothing of the wort to a minimum. You can do so by always using a piece of hose connected to the spigot on your lauter tun. Never let the wort just waterfall into the saucepan as you recirculate or sparge, because doing so can cause aeration of the wort, which can result in off flavors and aromas (and a beer that goes stale more quickly).

9. **After the first runnings clear up, start letting the wort drain slowly into your brewpot.**

   This process should take 10 to 15 minutes. Use a long length of plastic hose to let the wort drain gently into the bottom of the brewpot — and make sure you avoid aerating the wort.

   WARNING

   If the wort runs off too fast, the grains may compact down on themselves. If that happens, you get what's called a *stuck runoff,* which is one huge pain in the mash! You can't drain any more wort from the mash. The only solution is to stir the entire mash and start the runoff again.

10. **Carefully watch the level of the wort above the grains and, after the level is about ½ inch above the top of the grain bed, begin to add your sparge water, which should be 160 to 170° Fahrenheit.**

    To add the sparge water, pour about 2 to 4 quarts at a time periodically over the grain. (Don't overfill the lauter tun.)

11. **Continue to add the sparge water and run off the resulting wort over the course of the next 45 to 60 minutes.**

    Slower is better in this process.

    Always keep some sparge water above the top of the grain bed. Don't let the grain bed run dry! After you use all the sparge water, you then — and *only* then — let the grain bed run dry.

    If you run off and sparge too fast, not only can you get a stuck runoff, but you may not extract enough sugar from the grains, which can result in lower-than-expected original gravities.

12. **After you've added all the sparge water, just let all the liquid in the lauter tun drain into the brewpot and then close the tap and clean out the grain in the lauter tun.**

You should collect 6 to 7 gallons of wort. The grain left in the lauter tun makes great garden mulch or hog slop.

REMEMBER

At this point, you may want to consider first wort hopping procedures (see the "First Wort Hopping" sidebar)

WARNING

Carefully put the brewpot on the stove or heating element— remember that you have 6 to 7 gallons of hot wort in there. This amount of wort weighs more than 50 pounds.

13. **Bring the wort up to a boil and boil for 60 to 90 minutes to reduce the volume of the wort to 5 to 5½ gallons; add hops and other ingredients per the recipe.**

TIP

You may need to experiment with the actual boil time to boil off just the right amount of water to get 5 to 5½ gallons of wort. This variation occurs because everyone's stove or heating apparatus is different.

14. **Fifteen minutes before the end of the boil, put your rinsed immersion wort chiller into the brewpot and bring the wort back up to a boil.**

This step effectively sterilizes the chiller (see Figure 12-2). (If you're using a counter-flow-type wort chiller, don't immerse it in the wort.) See Chapter 2 for more information on wort chillers.

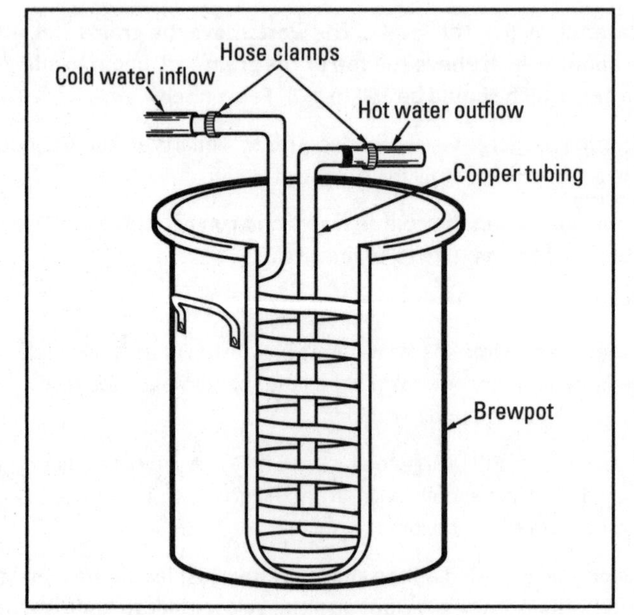

FIGURE 12-2: An immersion wort chiller, shown here in a brewpot, works like a reverse radiator.

TIP

DO'S AND DON'TS FOR ALL-GRAIN BREWING

Brewing can get pretty hectic with all that equipment sitting around and ingredients everywhere. The following list may help make your brewing experience go a bit more smoothly. ***Note:*** A fitting complement to reading this list may be to have a cold one from your last batch before beginning this batch.

The following list describes a few things you need to do:

- Sanitize and sterilize everything that comes in contact with your beer!
- Treat the mash for the correct mash pH.
- Grind the malt correctly.
- Stir the mash well.
- Use a wort chiller.
- Use ready-to-pitch liquid yeast cultures or high-quality dried yeast.
- Aerate the cooled wort well.
- Use secondary fermentation techniques.

The following list describes several things *not* to do:

- Allow the beer to become contaminated.
- Overgrind the malt.
- Boil the grain.
- Mash or sparge with alkaline water.
- Oversparge the grain.
- Add too many minerals to your mash.
- Scorch the mash.
- Aerate hot wort.
- Pitch yeast into hot wort.
- Aerate fermented wort.
- Let the fermented beer sit on the yeast too long.
- Get too serious — it's still a hobby!

15. **Add 1 teaspoon of Irish Moss to the wort.**

    This clarifying agent helps clear the finished wort. (See Chapter 9 for more on clarifiers.)

16. **Finish boiling the wort and, after the boiling is done, hook up the wort chiller to your sink and cover the brewpot.**

17. **Run cold water through the chiller to cool the wort to lower than 80° Fahrenheit.**

    You're probably going to need to move your hot and heavy brewpot to a location nearer your faucet and sink — do so carefully.

    The preferred method is to chill your wort to the same approximate temperature as your yeast culture — typically, room temperature.

WARNING

    The water exiting the wort chiller is *very hot* (180° Fahrenheit and hotter)! Be very careful, because this water can easily scald you.

18. **Siphon or pour the cooled wort into a sanitized fermenter.**

    As you do so, try to introduce as much air into the cooled wort as possible to aerate it for the necessary yeast growth. You can do so by pouring the wort vigorously into the fermenter and by rapidly stirring the wort with your brewing spoon.

19. **Pitch your yeast (just pour it into the wort) and attach the airlock (just like with any other type of brew).**

20. **Have a beer.**

Congratulations! You're now an all-grain brewer.

Increasing Your Batch Size

Many homebrewers, after mastering the mashing techniques of all-grain brewing, find themselves in need of yet another challenge. Of course, in addition to experiencing the thrill and satisfaction of achieving a formidable goal, most homebrewers are also primarily interested in serving a common need — making more beer!

That the mashing procedures I outline in this chapter require more knowledge, effort, and, perhaps most important, time than other brewing procedures do is obvious. Because of time considerations, many all-grain brewers try to maximize their brewing sessions by brewing a greater volume of beer at one time. All things considered, this practice makes perfectly good sense.

Formulating the recipes for these increased batch sizes is no big deal. Increases in ingredients correspond to increases in the number of gallons you want to brew — the ratios don't change. To brew larger volumes of beer, however, you need equipment capable of handling those larger volumes: a bigger brewpot, a bigger lauter tun, and a larger fermenter (or more fermenters). Other considerations include a burner or heating element capable of bringing larger volumes of liquid to a boil (and adequate venting of such equipment), greater volumes of yeast slurry for fermenting bigger batches of beer, and lots of available bottles or kegs for packaging and storing your bodacious brews.

At this point in the brewery expansion, the kitchen becomes, for most people, obsolete. Handy and inventive brewers like to move their operations into a large laundry room, the basement, or a garage. Be sure to check out Chapter 13 for ideas about large-scale, semi-commercial brewing systems.

And on goes the argument about whether a beer geek really *is* committed or really *should be.*

Harvest Time: Reusing Your Yeast

After brewers progress to greater levels of brewery output, as I mention in the preceding section, yeast again becomes an issue. Because larger batches of beer require greater volumes of yeast slurry to achieve correct pitching rates, you must factor cost and effort into the brewing requirements.

Buying more packages or test tubes of sterile yeast culture for each batch that you brew may be an intelligent option but certainly isn't frugal. Yeast propagation is a smart option but may require multistep propagation procedures to achieve the desired pitching rates.

At this time, you may want to consider the possibilities of collecting yeast from a healthy fermentation to repitch in your subsequent brews. After primary fermentation is complete, *harvesting* the yeast from the fermenter is a simple matter. Here's all you need to do:

1. **Prepare a sanitary jar with stopper and airlock per the starter culture instructions in Chapters 11 and 26.**

   You use this vessel for collecting and storing the yeast.

2. **Drain the fermented beer from your primary fermenter into a bottling bucket, carboy, keg, or whatever you normally use.**

3. **Remove the siphon tube and put the cover back on the primary fermenter.**
4. **Sanitize a ladle or spoon and dig yeast off the bottom of the fermenter; then pour the yeast into the jar and seal it with the airlock.**

   Try to collect 4 to 8 ounces of yeast slurry/sediment.
5. **Put the jar in the refrigerator if you're not planning on using it right away.**

   You may store the yeast this way for a week or two, maximum.
6. **To reuse the yeast after refrigeration, take the jar out of the fridge and let it warm to room temperature.**
7. **Swirl the slurry and pitch it into the cooled wort of your next batch.**

TIP

Before reusing the yeast, taste a sample of the brew you took it from. (Hydrometer reading samples are great for this task.) If the beer tastes contaminated, the yeast slurry is also contaminated. Reusing the yeast from an imperfect batch of beer makes no sense. I don't recommend reusing yeast more than two or three times either, but let your taste of the subsequent beer be your guide and don't ever become lax on the rules of sanitation.

» Brewing systems that will blow your mind -and maybe your budget

» Brewing systems that will cause you to reconsider your career path

Chapter 13

High-Tech Brewing

If you thought the previous chapter was advanced, you ain't seen nothing yet! Some of the brewing systems I'm about to introduce you to will bring you to within a few steps of being a commercial brewer. Well, minus a federal brewer's license, a tax I.D., a property inspection, state and local brewing permit . . .

Thankfully, you still don't need any of this official paperwork to brew beer at home, but given the direction homebrewing is going, could governmental involvement and oversight be far behind? I'd like to say I'm kidding, but!

To say that the hobby has grown in leaps and bounds (and hops!) in the past decade is an understatement. One of the ways it's been growing is in the volume of beer that can be produced by the average brew system designed for at-home use. Whereas in the previous chapters a 5-gallon batch is standard and a 10-gallon batch is the exception, it seems like 10-gallon batches are becoming the standard and a 1-barrel batch is easily within the realm of possibility.

There are even automated brew systems that can produce anywhere from between 2.5 to 30 gallons. They're also being manufactured with either electric heating elements or gas jets. You can get them with multiple vessels or you can go the single kettle, all-in-one route. The choices are almost endless.

Some of these systems are not much bigger than a bread maker, thus they are more kitchen-friendly. But most of these systems are considerably larger and would be more at home in a basement, a large laundry room or the garage (and I know some guys who have actually constructed "brew sheds" in their back yards!)

Is it Bigger Than a Breadbox?

First among the complete all-grain brewing systems are the smaller, sleeker, more-plastic-than-metal units that can perch on your kitchen countertop. These include:

- **BeerMKR ($549):** This countertop beer maker with a one-gallon capacity has been dubbed the "Keurig of Beer". Not sure how the folks at Keurig feel about that comparison — or the folks at BeerMKR, for that matter, but the comparison is obvious.

  This compact unit allows you to brew and ferment your all-grain beer right there on the kitchen counter next to the toaster oven. The carbonating and serving part take place in a separate, smaller unit that is placed in your refrigerator. And notifications about the status of your beer can be sent to your phone — how cool is that?

  It seems that for all the investment in time and money that go into each brew, though, that the end result would be greater than just a single gallon of beer. I'm getting parched just thinking about that.

  Beer Trivia: The creators of this product appeared on the TV show Shark Tank back in 2020 (Season 12, Episode 23). They received an offer from investor Kevin O'Leary, but ultimately turned it down.

- **BrewArt BeerDroid ($499):** The BeerDroid is also compact enough to operate on your countertop or a small, sturdy table and the brewing processes can be controlled via Wi-Fi. Each batch will produce 10 liters of beer or just over 2.6 gallons.

  Each beer is made with a pre-packaged kit called a BrewPrint, which means you're kinda locked into buying your ingredients from the BrewArt company. These kits are malt extract based rather than grain based (I cover this distinction in Chapter 12).

  In order to dispense your beer, you must also invest in the companion unit called the BeerFlo. This tabletop draught system costs as much as the BeerDroid itself, totaling almost $1,000 for both. But if you don't have the time and you do have the disposable income . . .

- **Brewie+:** The Brewie is a fully-automated all grain brewing machine that allows you to brew with minimal time investment. Updated heating elements bring your water to mashing temperature and wort to boil faster, significantly decreasing the overall brewing process time.

  This unit is designed to produce up to 5 gallons of wort without any supervision. The process is simple, just add the ingredients and start the recipe program. You'll have chilled wort ready for fermentation when the process is complete. There is even a cleaning cycle you can run after you've pumped the wort into your sanitized fermenter!

Now the bad news: The original manufacturer was forced to close down production, so these units are becoming harder and harder to find. Unfortunately, this also means that they are no longer covered by a manufacturer's warranty. But there is a dedicated community of Brewie enthusiasts that banded together to provide open-source software updates, bug fixes, and general support to any and all Brewie owners. Check out `rebrewie.org` to see what the community has put together and how they've breathed new life into an awesome brewing system.

Out of the Kitchen and Into the Garage

So, having covered the R2-D2s and BB-8s of the homebrewing world, let's move on to the real beer automatons. Let's start with a trio of seemingly similar units, from lowest price to highest. All of these tend to be tall and cylindrical, fairly compact, electrically heated and are considered all-in-one systems.

- **Brewer's Edge Mash and Boil ($249 to $360):** This entry level brew system is kind of stripped down for economy's sake, which is what helps make brewing with it so affordable. With a capacity of 16 lbs. of grain and 7.5 gallons of water you can still make a wide variety of beefed-up brews.

  This sleek all-electric unit plugs into any 110V GFI (ground fault interrupter) household outlet, and its adjustable thermostat (switchable from Fahrenheit to Centigrade) and internal sparging basket lets you mash and boil in the same vessel. It also features a delayed start timer so you can program the Mash and Boil to begin heating up the water before you come home from work or before you get up in the morning. All of these features are viewable on an LCD display.

  The lesser model is sold without a pump; the greater model comes with a fully integrated pump, which makes liquid transfers effortless. Some do-it-yourselfers just buy a separate pump and hosing and work it into the system on their own.

- **KegLand DigiMash ($280):** The DigiMash from KegLand is one of the most affordable brewing systems of its kind and it's a great value all around. It includes the 9-gallon DigiBoil electric kettle and the stainless-steel mashing accessory pack.

The electric kettle has dual heating elements; one is 1,000 watts and the second is 500 watts that combine for 1500W of power. You can choose to use them one-at-a-time or both, depending on your brewing process; everything you need to mash and boil all in one unit. And it has a digital controller to boot!

This unit is also available with an optional recirculation pump kit, which will add about another $100 to the bottom line.

- **KegLand BrewZilla ($400 to $430):** Even if you don't like the product, you gotta love the name! Actually, BrewZilla is the new name for the brew system formerly known as RoboBrew.

  Essentially, BrewZilla is a fancier DigiMash. But there are two key differences worth noting: BrewZilla features programmable mash steps, as well as a delayed start (your mashing water is heated ahead of time giving you a jumpstart on your brew day). The other major difference between the two systems is that the BrewZilla also features a built-in pump for recirculating the wort. This is "set-and-forget" brewing at its best.

  You can buy this system with either a 110V capacity or 220V capacity. You can also supersize your system by increasing the brew volume from 35 liters/9.25 gallons up to 65 liters/17.1 gallons with 220V capacity; that'll cost you about $650 for the pleasure.

- **Grainfather:** Now we're wandering into upper echelon territory of automated brew systems. Grainfather is widely regarded as one of the best and most reliable all-in-one brewing systems for at-home use. All three of the models listed below share many basic features, so I'm going to focus on those areas in which they differ.

  - *Model AG608:* Capacity: 46 liters / 12 gallons; Heating element: electrical 220V; Digitally controlled, programmable (no BlueTooth); Price: $499
  - *Model AG605:* Capacity: 30 liters / 8 gallons; Heating element: electrical 110V; Programmable, manual or app; BlueTooth connectivity; $899
  - *Model AG606:* Capacity: 70 liters / 18.5 gallons; Heating element: electrical service 220V; Wireless control, app; LCD Controller (magnetically mounted); Price: $1998

Bigger Is Betterer?

As good as the previous all-in-one brew systems are -and they are unquestionably good — many homebrewers still prefer to brew like their professional counterparts — that is, with a multiple vessel brew house. The problem is, though, that when you start adding vessels and equipment, your brewery footprint expands rather quickly. The more equipment you have, the more space you need to house it. And keep in mind that while some grow vertically and some grow laterally, they ALL grow monetarily!

Now that we've cleared the air on that issue, let's get down to the goods. The handful of brew systems listed below are perennially on rabid homebrewers' wish lists. Like many units in the previous category, most of these share a lot of commonalities, so I'm going to focus instead on their greatest qualities.

Oh, and you're also going to see the acronyms RIMS and HERMS mentioned a bit in this part. To understand what they're all about, check out the "A Primer on RIMS and HERMS" sidebar at the end of this chapter.

- **BrewBuilt BrewSculptures:** First, a quick explanation of the name — BrewBuilt is a division created by online homebrew supply store, MoreBeer!, that focuses specifically on the research and development and manufacturing of high-quality brewing products; BrewSculptures is what they call their finished creations (and they all have that funny little "TM" next to their name).

  Their finished creations include a few different models, including:

- **BrewBuilt Tippy Dump Digital BrewSculpture V4:** Configured vertically, this unit relies on gravity to aid in moving liquid from one vessel to another.

  Beer Trivia: Before electricity and other modern technological advancements, all commercial breweries relied on gravity to move liquid within the brewery throughout the brewing process. Many old brew houses were built three and four stories high in order to accomplish this.

  As its name suggests, this unit's claim to fame is the tipping mash tun that allows for easy dumping of the spent grain when you're done with that part of the process. Another intelligent innovation is the mash tun being situated right over the hot liquor tank, thus conserving heat and energy. HERMS-type coil recirculation. The heavy-duty frame on which this all sits is castered for easy movement.

  Other features include:

  - Capacity: choice of 10 or 20 gallons (the 30-gal. "XL" can also be special ordered)
  - Heating element: gas burners, propane or natural gas (see Technical Info below)
  - Touch screen control panel (optional)
  - Price: $6,395 to $6,595

TECHNICAL STUFF

Though some homebrewer do-it-yourselfers can probably handle it, it's highly recommended that natural gas sculptures be installed by a professional plumber.

- **BrewBuilt Low Rider Digital BrewSculpture V4:** The name of this unit gives a clue to what makes it special: easy accessibility. The Low Rider is a single tier brew system that allows you to look into and interact with every kettle without the need for a step or a ladder. On the flip side of this benefit is that you lose the gravity feature, so this unit has two pumps for moving liquid around. It has a HERMS-type coil recirculation.
  - Capacity: choice of 10 or 20 gallons
  - Heating element: gas burners, propane or natural gas
  - 7-inch touch screen control panel, standard
  - Programmable mash steps
  - Price: $6,495 to $6,795
- **BrewBuilt Low Rider Digital Electric BrewSculpture V4:** At first glance, you'd think this system is basically the previous system with electrical heat instead of gas heat. Well, you're partly right. It's pretty much everything you see in the Low Rider V4 above, but it's also available in large, extra-large and *"Honey, we're gonna need a bigger house!"* size.
  - Capacity: choice of large, 10-gallons, extra-large, 20-gallons and XXL, 1 barrel (50-gallon mash tun)
  - Heating element: electrical service. Large and XL models require a GFCI 30-amp / 220V circuit to power the heating elements and a single 115V circuit for the pumps and control panel. The XXL model requires two GFCI 30-amp / 220V circuits and a single 115V.
  - 7-inch touch screen control panel, standard
  - Programmable mash steps
  - Price: $6,495 to $8,495
- **Blichmann Engineering:** Considered by some to be the Rolls-Royce of homebrewing systems, Blichmann Engineering's turnkey Pilot brew systems feature just about everything you need to start brewing and are tailored made for designing and perfecting batches. This is why some larger commercial craft brewers use Blichmann systems as a testing platform for new and experimental beers.

These are horizontal systems that include kettles, heaters, controls, pumps, a chiller, all the hoses and fittings you need, and a sturdy stainless steel brew table as well.

And Blichmann continues to introduce a wide range of options in their Pilot systems.

- They can be either gas or electric
- They can be from 5-gallon to 1-barrel capacities
- Two or three vessel options are available
- They can be set up for either HERMS or RIMS

A peek at the window sticker says 10-gallon electric or gas RIMS Pilot systems start from $5,499. But as you see from the options above, these systems can be built *a-la-carte*, with each option adding another line item to the bottom-line total.

So, for any homebrewer who wants to satisfy the urge to feel like a professional brewer without jumping through governmental hoops, earning income or paying excise taxes, high-tech brew-at-home systems are the way to go.

A Primer on RIMS and HERMS

Many all-grain beer system manufacturers make two different types of recirculating systems, both of which get the job done efficiently. But the RIMS and HERMS systems are different for a reason.

To start with, RIMS is an acronym for *recirculating infusion mash system*, and HERMS is the acronym for *heat-exchanged recirculating mash system*. These were created for those who are brewing greater volumes of beer at one time. After your brew system reaches the 10-gallon plateau, it becomes both difficult and somewhat dangerous to move around pots of liquid that weigh more than 100 pounds.

It's at this point that many brewers invest in a pump to aid in transferring wort — and that same pump can also be employed to recirculate wort through the mash. Recirculating helps to accomplish two things: It gives you better control of your mash temperature by reducing "hot spots" in the grain bed; it also aids in clarifying your wort (the grain bed itself acts as a natural filter).

Both systems use a recirculation pump to control the temperature of the mash; they vary only in how they heat the wort. And because both systems employ a heat source, there's no need for the mash tun to be jacketed (wearing the latest insulated brewhouse couture).

In a RIMS system, the heat pump runs continuously, recirculating the wort from the bottom of the mash tun up to the top. The wort flows through a pipe that is warmed by a heating element that can be alternately turned on or off as needed to maintain a constant mash temperature; this on–off cycling is commonly controlled by a thermostat and temperature probe.

The wort is also recirculated bottom-to-top in a HERMS system, but the pipe through which the wort flows passes through a heat exchanger or a coil that is immersed in hot water in the hot liquor tank. Instead of turning the heat source off and on, it's the pump that is thermostatically controlled to maintain the proper temperature.

TECHNICAL STUFF

Hot liquor tank is the industry term for "vessel where water is heated up." It has nothing to do with liquor, oddly enough.

So, RIMS or HERMS: which is better? The choice of one system over the other is mostly personal preference. For single-infusion mashes, HERMS uses less energy and has fewer parts. But for brewers who prefer to do step mashes, RIMS is probably the better choice. When everything is said and done, both will have accomplished the same goals.

4 Packaging Your Brew

IN THIS PART . . .

Figure out what to do with your beer after it's done fermenting and aging.

Learn the quickest and easiest way to store your beer in bottles.

Consider the option of canning your beer.

Weigh the pros and cons of kegging your beer.

Take note of all the possibilities of owning a kegging system.

» Bottling wisdom

» Putting the bubbles in your brew

» Priming procedures

» Choosing your caps

Chapter 14
Bottling Your Brew

Bottling homebrew isn't a difficult procedure, but brewers often deride it as one that's tedious at worst and boring at best. But for thousands of people who brew their beer at home, bottling represents the only option for packaging their finished brew.

The key to breaking the tedium is to get your system down to a science — and to drink a brew while you're bottling one. (Kind of like whistling while you work, except that you're sucking brew and not blowing air.) The more you go through the bottling steps, the more familiar they become, and then you can begin to anticipate your next move. Having all the necessary equipment sanitized and ready to go before you begin any of the bottling procedures is especially handy.

Picking Out Bottles

Using good, sound, safe bottles is an important part of the bottling process. Your beer may start out as a world-class brew, but if the bottles aren't worthy, you can end up with leakers, exploders, and sticky messes. When you're buying bottles, don't skimp.

Bottles come in all sizes and shapes, but before I delve into the various choices, I want to give you a few very important suggestions. Your homebrew bottles

- **Should be the thick, returnable type (no cheap throwaways).** The thick, returnable-type bottles — if you can still find them — can withstand repeated uses; cheap, twist-off throwaways mean thin glass and easy breakage.
- **Should be made of colored glass (the darker the better).** Light damages beer; tinted glass protects against light damage.
- **Shouldn't have a twist-off opening.** Bottle caps can't seal across the threads on twist-off bottles.
- **Should be of uniform size.** Although uniform bottles aren't a requirement, having all your beer in bottles of the same size and shape makes capping and storing much easier.

Even within these parameters, you still have a fairly wide choice in usable bottles; however, availability may become an issue. You can easily purchase brand-new 12- and 22-ounce bottles through homebrew supply shops, but the cost is sometimes prohibitive — if not for the bottles themselves, for the cost of having them shipped across the country if you don't have a local supplier.

TIP

Check with your local craft brewers (if you have any); you may be able to buy bottles directly from them.

The American brewing industry continues to package beer — albeit in limited markets — in a variety of 7-, 12-, 16-, and 22-ounce and quart-size returnable bottles; check with your local beer retailer. A few European brewers package their export beer in reusable bottles; the popular 17-ounce Weizenbier bottles are a good option.

Using larger bottles is a way to expedite the bottling process as well as free you from its drudgery. The more beer the bottles can hold, the fewer bottles you need. For instance, to bottle an entire 5-gallon batch of beer in 7-ounce nip bottles, you need to clean, fill, and cap more than 90 of them. If you use 22-ounce bottles, on the other hand, you need only 30 of them.

Homebrewers should also be aware that homebrewing competitions place strict limitations on the size and color of bottles allowed in competition. For more information on homebrew competitions, check out Chapter 29.

Ready, Set, Bottle!

Before you start any bottling procedures, take a hydrometer reading of the beer in the fermenter to verify that fermentation is sufficiently complete. Just steal a little beer out of the spigot to fill the hydrometer cylinder to within an inch of the top (but no more). (See Chapter 2 for complete directions on taking hydrometer readings.)

TIP

After you take your hydrometer reading, *don't* pour the beer from the cylinder back in with the rest of the beer — if you do so, you risk contaminating your beer. But don't throw the sample down the sink, either. It may be uncarbonated, but it's still good beer — drink it! You may be surprised to find out how good it already tastes.

After you've made certain that the beer is done fermenting, retrieved the bottling equipment, and quarantined the family pets, you're ready to start the bottling process. As always, setup starts with sanitizing all the necessary equipment, which includes the following:

- **A bottling bucket**
- **A racking cane** (if bottling from a vessel without an attached spigot, such as a glass carboy)
- **A plastic hose**
- **A bottling tube** (with spring-action or gravity-pressure valve)
- **Bottles** (enough to hold 640 ounces of beer)
- **Bottle caps** (enough to cap all your bottles, plus some extras — just in case); see "Crowning Achievements" later in this chapter for more on caps

You need to sanitize all of these items before bottling, so you also need a sanitizing agent; for more information on sanitizing and sanitizing agents, see Chapter 3. You also need the following:

- **A bottle brush**
- **A bottle rinser**
- **A bottle capper**
- **Two small saucepans**
- **Dextrose (corn sugar) for priming — ¾ cup;** see "A Primer on Priming" later in this chapter
- **A beer to drink**

Now, here are the steps for the bottling brigade:

1. **Fill your utility tub or other designated sanitizing basin with enough cold water to cover your submerged bottles, first adding bleach or another sanitizing agent to the water according to the package directions.**
2. **Submerge as many bottles as you need to contain your full batch of 5 gallons of beer.**

REMEMBER

Make sure your bottles are scum-free before dunking them in the sanitizing solution. Any bottle with dried or living crud in the bottom needs to be scrubbed separately with a cleanser such as trisodium phosphate (TSP) before you sanitize it.

TIP

You can fill and submerge the bottles in less than half the time if you place a drinking straw in the bottles; the straw enables the air within the bottle to escape through the straw instead of slowly bubbling through the opening (your bottling tube with the valve detached suffices here).

3. **Allow your bottles to soak for at least half an hour (or the time necessary according to package directions).**
4. **Crack open your bottle of beer.**
5. **While the bottles soak, dissolve ¾ cup of dextrose in a pint or so of water in one of the saucepans, cover the solution, and place it on a burner over low heat.**
6. **Put your bottle caps into your other saucepan, fill the pan with enough water to cover all the caps, and place the pan on another burner over low heat.**

TIP

Put enough bottle caps for as many bottles as you have soaking plus a few extra; having too many sterilized caps ready for bottling is better than not having enough.

7. **Allow both pans to come to a boil, remove them from the heat, and allow them to cool.**
8. **After the bottles soak for half an hour, connect the bottle rinser to the faucet over the sanitizing tub.**
9. **With one hand over the opening (so that you don't get squirted), turn on the hot water.**

   After the initial spray, the bottle washer holds back the water pressure until a bottle is lowered over the stem and pushed down.

10. **Start cleaning the bottles one-by-one with the bottle brush, and then drain the sanitizer, rinse your bottles with the bottle rinser, and allow them to air dry.**

    Continue this step until all bottles are clean.

TIP

Visually check each bottle for cleanliness rather than just assume that they're all clean.

WARNING

Four dozen free-standing bottles make one heck of a messy and breakable domino effect. Always put your cleaned bottles back into six-pack holders or cardboard cases to avoid an aggravating and easily avoidable accident.

11. **Take a sip of beer.**
12. **Drain the utility tub of the bottle-cleaning water.**
13. **Place the bottling bucket in the tub and fill it with water and the sanitizing agent of your choice.**
14. **Place the bottling hose, bottling tube, and hydrometer cylinder into the bottling bucket and allow them to soak for half an hour (or according to sanitizing agent directions).**
15. **While the bottling equipment soaks, retrieve the still-covered fermenter from its resting place and place it on a sturdy table, counter, or work surface about 3 or 4 feet off the ground.**

    At this point, you need to set up your bottling station, making sure that you have the priming sugar mixture (still in the saucepan), bottle caps, bottle capper, bottles, and hydrometer with cylinder on hand.

    If you're bottling your brew directly from the primary fermenter, you want to have already taken a hydrometer reading to confirm completion of fermentation. If you're bottling from your secondary fermenter (glass carboy), incomplete fermentation isn't a concern, and you can take a hydrometer reading (to determine final gravity and alcohol content) as the beer drains into the bottling bucket.

16. **After half an hour, drain the sanitizing solution from the bottling bucket through the spigot on the bottom and, after the bucket is empty, thoroughly rinse the remaining pieces of equipment (hose, bottling tube), along with the bottles and caps, and bring them to your bottling station.**
17. **Take a sip of beer.**
18. **Place the bottling bucket on the floor directly below the fermenter and connect the plastic hosing to the spigot on the fermenter, allowing the other end of the hosing to hang inside the bottling bucket.**

    If you're initiating the bottling procedures from your glass carboy, you can't rely on the convenience of a spigot to drain out the beer. You need to use your racking cane and siphon the brew. Chapter 11 explains siphoning procedures in more detail.

19. **Pour the dextrose and water mixture into the bottling bucket.**

The dissolved corn sugar mixes with the beer as the beer drains from the fermenter into the bottling bucket. After you've bottled the beer, this sugar becomes another source of food for the few yeast cells still remaining in the liquid. As the yeast consumes the sugar, it produces the beer's carbonation within the bottle. Eventually, the yeast again falls dormant and creates a thin layer of sediment on the bottom of each bottle.

If, by chance, you bottle a batch of beer that isn't fully fermented or you somehow add too much dextrose at bottling time, you may find out first-hand what a mess exploding bottles can make. Excess sugar (whether added corn sugar or leftover maltose from an unfinished fermentation) overfeeds the yeast in an enclosed bottle. With nowhere for the pressure to go, the glass gives before the bottle cap. Kaboom! Mess! Do not overprime. (Use no more than ¾ cup of dextrose in 5 gallons of beer.) See the "A Primer on Priming" section in this chapter for more advice on priming.

20. **Open the spigot on the fermenter and allow all the beer to run into the bottling bucket.**

Don't try to salvage every last drop from the fermenter by tilting it as the beer drains down the spigot. The spigot is purposely positioned about an inch above the bottom of the fermenter so that all the spent yeast and miscellaneous fallout remains behind.

21. **After the last of the beer drains, close the spigot, remove the hose, and rinse it.**

Avoid splashing or aerating your beer as you bottle it. Any oxidation that the beer picks up now can be tasted later. Yuck.

22. **Carefully place the bottling bucket up where the fermenter was, connect the rinsed hose to the spigot on the bottling bucket, and attach the bottling tube to the other end of the hose.**

23. **Arrange all your bottles on the floor directly below the bottling bucket (keeping them all in cardboard carriers or cases to avoid potential breakage and spillage).**

24. **Open the spigot on the bottling bucket and begin to fill all the bottles.**

Gently push the bottling tube down on the bottom of each bottle to start the flow of beer. The bottle may take a short while to fill, but the process always seems to accelerate as the beer nears the top. Usually, a bit of foam rushes to the top of the bottle; don't worry! As soon as you withdraw the bottling tube, the liquid level in the bottle falls.

25. **Remove the tube from each bottle after foam or liquid reaches the top of the bottle.**

Figure 14-1 shows you how full you want your bottles to be.

TECHNICAL STUFF

After you remove the bottling tube from the bottle, the level of the beer falls to about an inch or so below the opening. Homebrewers have differing opinions as to how much airspace (or *ullage*) is necessary. Some say the smaller the airspace, the less oxidation that can occur. Others claim that if you don't have correct ullage, the beer can't carbonate properly. Rather than jump into the fray, I say if it looks like the space in bottles of beer from commercial breweries, go with it!

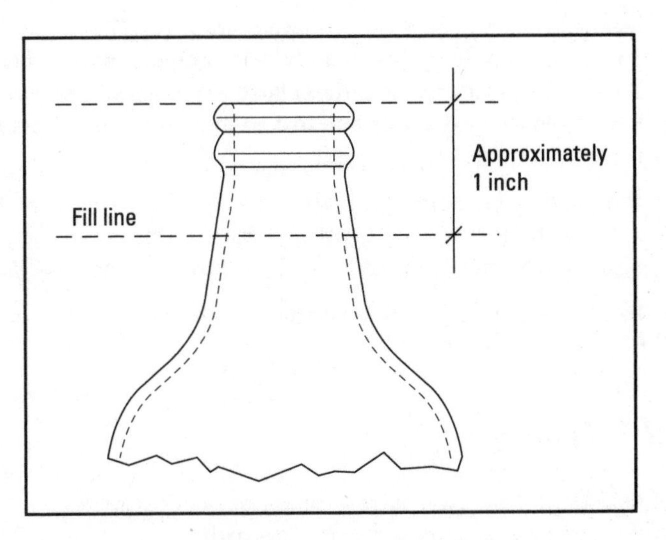

FIGURE 14-1: Correct bottle fill level.

26. **After you completely drain the bottling bucket, close the spigot, remove the hose, toss it inside the bottling bucket, and set everything aside to be cleaned after all the bottling procedures are complete.**

27. **Place all the bottles on your tabletop or work surface; place a cap on each bottle, position your bottles in the capper (one at a time), and pull down on the capper handle or levers slowly and evenly.**

You may want to do this task as soon as each bottle is full as insurance against everything that can go wrong when full bottles of your precious brew are sitting around open.

TIP

Both bench- or two-handle-style cappers come with small magnets in the capper head designed to hold and align the cap as you start crimping. I don't trust the magnet to hold the caps in alignment and prefer to seat them on the bottles by hand.

Occasionally, a cap may crimp incorrectly. If you suspect that a cap didn't seal right, tilt the bottle sideways and check for leakage. If you find you have a leaker, yank the cap and replace it. (You boiled extras — right?)

28. **Your homebrew needs to undergo a two-week conditioning phase, so store your liquid lucre in a cool, dark location (such as the same place that you kept the fermenter).**

This phase is where the remaining yeast cells chow down on the dextrose and carbonate your beer.

REMEMBER

Putting your brew in the fridge isn't a good idea — at least for the first two weeks — because the very cold temperatures stunt the yeast's carbonating activity.

29. **You must thoroughly rinse your brewing equipment in hot water and store it in a place that's relatively dust- and mildew-free. You may even want to go that extra step and seal all your equipment inside a large-capacity garbage bag.**

TIP

This step may be the most important one of all, not so much for the brew just made but for the next one. Consider this step an insurance policy on your next batch of beer. Boring but worthwhile, like most insurance policies.

30. **Finish drinking your beer (if you haven't already).**

SWINGTIME

If you're looking to save a few bucks on bottle-capping equipment and a little time on bottling procedures, you may want to consider packaging your brew in the swing-top bottles known as *Grolsch bottles.* These bottles aren't only unique in style, they also provide you the advantage of not needing to commit to drinking a full bottle at one sitting because they're self-sealing.

You do face some negatives with swing-top bottles, however. Unless you know someone who drinks a lot of Grolsch (or similarly packaged products) and wants to part with the empty bottles, the cost for two cases of these bottles can be considerable. This type of bottle also requires a little more attention at sanitation time. You need to remove the rubber gasket and clean the plastic (or ceramic) top thoroughly. Be aware that the gaskets can wear out and occasionally need to be replaced after repeated uses.

Finally, for those of you who want to send your homebrew to competitions, stay away from bottling your beer in swing-top bottles; these bottles aren't accepted at major competitions in the U.S.

After two weeks pass, check to see whether the bottles have clarified (the yeasty cloudiness has settled out). Chill a bottle or two for taste-testing. Like any commercial beer, you need to decant homebrew before drinking, not only to release the carbonation and the beer's aromatics but also to pour a clear beer. Drinking homebrew out of the bottle stirs up the sediment, creating a hazy beer. (See Chapter 26 for more information on proper decanting practices.)

Tanks a Lot! Bottling Kegged Beer

If you invest in a CO_2 system for kegging your beer, you may appreciate the ways you can use a CO_2 system for certain bottling applications, too. To get the lowdown on CO_2 kegging systems for homebrewing, check out Chapter 16.

For all its convenience and time- and effort-saving simplicity, kegging homebrew does have some limitations. What happens if you want to take a sample of your beer over to a friend's home on poker night? What happens if you want to send a beer out to a homebrew competition in another state? You probably don't want to lug your kegging system over to your buddy's house, and having your kegged beer evaluated at faraway competitions is out of the question. Or is it?

Carbon-aid: Sharing kegged beer in plastic bottles

TIP

One enterprising company has created a simple little device called the *Carba-Cap*. This little thingamajig is designed like a ball-lock fitting on a soda keg, and it's threaded so that you it can screw it onto plastic soda bottles. You can dispense some of your kegged beer into a plastic soda bottle, seal the bottle with the Carba-Cap, and pressurize the soda bottle to maintain the carbonation in the beer. Of course, you have to remove the Carba-Cap each time you want to pour beer from the bottle.

These caps are available in plastic (costs about $7) and stainless steel (costs about $12). Currently, the Carba-Cap is available only in the ball-lock style. Owners of kegs with pin-lock fittings are out of luck, at least for the time being.

A couple of things to keep in mind when using the Carba-Cap: Carbonated beer in a pressurized plastic bottle isn't the ideal situation, nor should it be. Homebrew isn't meant to be stored in soda bottles for long periods of time. The Carba-Cap bottling method simply enables you to dispense and transport smaller quantities of beer from your keg. And because you use the Carba-Cap with plastic bottles, close attention to gas pressure is important; 40 psi is the maximum recommended pressure for standard plastic soda bottles.

One last caveat: Soda bottles — pressurized or not — are never accepted at homebrew competitions.

TIP

The Carba-Cap also enables you to carbonate water, juice or any other beverage in your home for a spritzy, refreshing drink.

Counterintelligence: Flowing from keg to bottle for competition

If you want to send samples of your kegged beer to far-flung homebrew competitions, you can bottle your kegged beer in one of two ways:

- Fill your bottles by using your kegging system's beverage dispensing hose.
- Fill your bottles by using a *counterpressure bottle filler,* hooked up to your kegging system.

The first method is suspect because the beer not only loses carbonation during the transfer but also risks picking up oxidation or contamination along the way. The second method is far more sound and proper for a competition-worthy beer.

A *counterpressure bottle filler* is an apparatus that first backfills the bottle with CO2, thus purging the bottle of air, and then maintains pressure within the bottle while the beer is flowing in through the filler tube. Counterpressure bottle filling eliminates both the loss of carbonation and the threat of oxidation and contamination. A typical counterpressure bottle filler setup includes a gas line, a beer line, a filler tube, and shutoff valves. Figure 14-2 shows how to use a counterpressure filler. For more detail, refer to package directions.

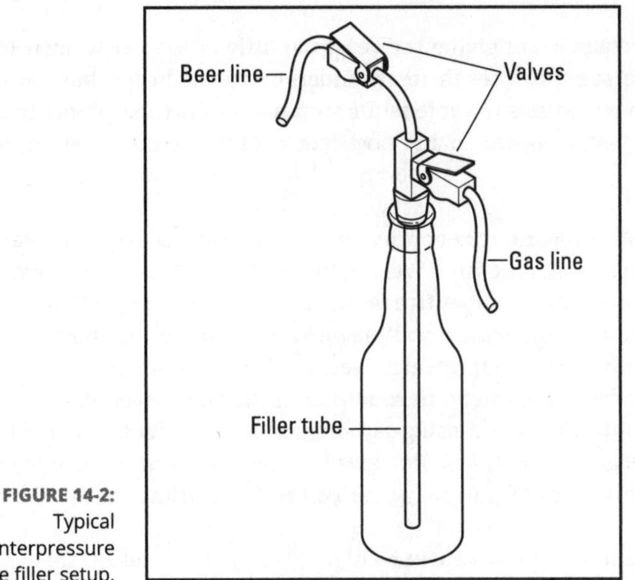

FIGURE 14-2: Typical counterpressure bottle filler setup.

A Primer on Priming

As you may know, yeast is responsible for producing the natural carbonation in beer and other fermentable beverages (see Chapter 6 for more on yeast and fermentation). And, because carbon dioxide escapes from the fermenter, you may be wondering how you can put the carbonation back into your beer. The answer is a simple little trick called priming.

Priming means adding more fermentable sugar to the beer just prior to bottling it. The small number of yeast cells that remain in the solution when you bottle your brew gladly see to it that they eat the sugars you add and thus provide the desired carbonation within the bottle. Of course, this process doesn't happen overnight. You need to allow another one to two weeks before your beer is properly carbonated and ready to drink.

Getting ready to prime

When you choose a priming sugar for beer, you need to consider two things: the *quantity* and the *fermentability* of the priming ingredient you're going to use. The first factor is dependent on the second factor.

As I mention earlier, the idea of priming is to put more fermentable sugar into the beer so that the yeast can create the needed carbonation within the bottle. But consider the consequences of giving the yeast too little or too much sugar to eat: Too little priming sugar can result in an under-carbonated beer, but too much sugar may cause your bottles to explode! Don't panic — I discuss proper priming quantities in the "Deciding which and how much primer to use" section in this chapter.

Two important points regarding beer priming: First, not all beer styles contain the same level of carbonation. A Berliner Weisse, for example, is far more effervescent than, say, a Scotch ale. At a competitive level, you may want to take this discrepancy into consideration; otherwise, you may just want to use the standard measure of priming sugar detailed in the next section. The second important point is that high-gravity beers you intend to condition in the bottle over longer periods of time are likely to build up increasing carbonation levels as they age. If you plan on storing a particularly big barley wine away for several months, you may want to cut back on the amount of priming sugar you add at bottling time.

TIP

Another consideration for those who brew high-gravity beers and age them a long time: If your beer has been aging for a month or longer, what yeast is left in it is probably old and fatigued. With your yeast's declining viability in mind, you probably want to add some fresh yeast to the beer along with the priming agent at bottling time. Using generic dry yeast is perfectly acceptable here.

Deciding which and how much primer to use

Different sugar sources (refined sugar, honey, molasses, and so on) have different levels of fermentability, which means that the more fermentable sugar a priming mixture has, the less of the mixture you need. Conversely, you need more of a priming mixture with less fermentable sugar. You can potentially use any one of the adjunct sugars mentioned in Chapter 8 for priming purposes. Note that because you use them in such small quantities, priming sugars have virtually no effect on the beer's taste.

TIP

To keep the priming process simple, I recommend using dextrose (corn sugar). Dextrose is highly fermentable, widely available, easy to work with, and inexpensive.

TIP

Regardless of what form of priming sugar you use to prime your beer, always dissolve and dilute it in boiling water first, and allow the priming mixture to cool before adding it to the beer. The amount of water used to boil the sugar in is of little concern — 1 or 2 cups are typical.

In the average 5-gallon batch of beer, 3/4 of a cup (*not* 3/4 of a pound!) of dextrose is the maximum recommended amount for priming. Using more than this may result in exploding bottles but is more likely to result in over-carbonated beer and *gushers* — bottles that act like miniature volcanoes when your buddies pry the caps off. Hmmm, sounds like a good prank, come to think of it.

Exploring alternative primers

Although dextrose (corn sugar) is the cheapest and most convenient priming agent available to homebrewers, you do have other options when you're ready to carbonate your beer. Read on . . .

Dry malt extract: The purists' choice

Brewing purists may cringe at the thought of adding a refined white sugar to homebrew, so they often use a more-unadulterated alternative. *Dry malt extract*, or DME, is a second choice for priming beer. But, as I point out in Chapter 4, DME is only about 70 percent fermentable. Therefore, you need to use more DME than dextrose (which is about 99 percent fermentable). If you take the purists' route, make sure you increase your priming volume to 1 1/4 cups of dry malt extract per 5-gallon batch of beer.

Not only do you need to use more DME than dextrose, but you also need to allow more time for the carbonation within the bottle to build up. Yeast can consume and convert the simple dextrose sugars into carbon dioxide much more quickly than it can the more complex maltose sugars found in malt extract.

Fruit liqueurs: The exotic choice

As a really progressive homebrewer, yet another priming ingredient exists that not only carbonates your beer but also imbues it with various fruit flavors: fruit liqueurs. Most liqueurs are a great alternative priming agent for the following reasons:

- **Liqueurs contain a fair amount of sugar.** One 750 milliliter bottle contains just about enough sugar to prime a 5-gallon batch of beer. Because the actual sugar content of any liqueur depends on the company that made it (although it more likely has too little sugar than too much), you may want to add another ounce or two of dextrose to be sure.
- **Fruit liqueurs are available in a variety of flavors.** My local liquor store stocks cherry, blueberry, blackberry, peach, strawberry, raspberry, orange, and even black currant liqueur.

TIP

FOR KEGGERS ONLY

If you intend to keg your beer, you may choose to prime before you keg it or not to prime it at all. The use of kegs and compressed carbon dioxide gas cylinders allows you to carbonate beer without the use of priming sugars (see Chapter 16 for more about the kegging process).

If you choose to prime your kegged beer, you can afford to be a little more relaxed about overpriming than if you bottled your beer — kegs come with pressure relief valves to vent excessive pressure. No exploding kegs!

- **Fruit syrups used in liqueurs are usually of high quality.** Fruit liqueurs offer rich and consistent fruit flavor and aroma.
- **Liqueurs are already antiseptic.** Because they contain alcohol contents of up to 40 percent, no further treatment is necessary before adding them to your beer. (Don't worry about the added alcohol; the total content in your beer isn't likely to rise more than 1 or 2 percent, at most.)

REMEMBER

Use only translucent liqueurs — never cream liqueurs. Cream liqueurs add an unappealing milky haze to your beer (yech!).

Crowning Achievements

Although I typically refer to bottle caps, keep in mind that many brewers call caps *crowns.* Caps or crowns — whatever you call them, they're one of the most useful but inexpensive tools available to you, the homebrewer.

By and large, a bottle cap is a bottle cap is a bottle cap. They're plentiful, inexpensive, come in a limited variety of colors, and are usually sold by the batch (60 pieces — includes extras) or by the gross (144 pieces). Bottle caps are metal on the outside with a plastic seal on the inside. That plastic gasket is what makes one kind of bottle cap special (see the "Rare air" sidebar in this chapter). You need to sanitize all bottle caps before using them. To do so, simply boil them in water or soak them in your sanitizing agent of choice.

RARE AIR

Oxycap is a brand of bottle cap that has an inner seal that actually absorbs oxygen within the sealed bottle. These feature a special scavenger liner that absorbs oxygen molecules trapped in the headspace during bottling and prevent further oxygen absorption, thus keeping beer flavors fresher longer.

These caps are moisture-activated (which means you need to store the caps in a humidity-free location). Unlike all other plain bottle caps, you should never boil or soak these special caps prior to using them.

These oxygen-absorbing caps are especially important to homebrewers who create high-gravity beers with long shelf-lives; oxy-liner caps guard against the oxidation (absorption of oxygen by the beer) that usually affects aging beers. Instead of oxygen being absorbed by your beer, it's absorbed by the cap. These caps generally cost about 50 percent more than regular caps, but considering the bottom line, they're worth it.

Shortly after the oxygen-absorbing caps were introduced to the homebrewing market, skeptical and inquisitive members of a homebrew club staged an unscientific experiment using these caps. They bottled a batch of hoppy pale ale using both the Pure Seal cap and regular bottle caps. Labeled simply beer "A" and beer "B," other club members then evaluated the aroma and taste of both beers and commented on their freshness levels. By a notable margin, club members preferred the beer capped with the newfangled crowns.

Because bottle caps are expendable (you use them once and then discard them), such a one-time-use piece of equipment is actually more like an ingredient — you need to replenish it for each batch of beer you brew and bottle. And because you may choose to bottle your beer in self-sealing, swing-top bottles, you may have no need for bottle caps at all (you find more on swing-top bottles in the "Swing-time" sidebar earlier in this chapter).

IN THIS CHAPTER

» Why canning is better than bottling

» Choosing the right can

» Sealing your beer inside the can

» Submitting canned homebrew to competitions

Chapter 15

Doing the Can-Can: Canning Your Beer

Way back in 2002, the Oskar Blues Brewery in Lyons, Colorado, did the unthinkable; they had the audacity to start packaging their flagship Dale's Pale Ale in aluminum cans. At the time, canned beer of any kind was looked down upon with the same scorn reserved for Old BudMill type beers. Canned beer was considered cheap, of questionable quality, and, folks who hadn't updated their opinions since the 1940's still believed that beer in cans tasted like the cans themselves!

Even stalwart brewer Samuel Adams, which boastfully claimed in its 2005 Beer Drinker's Bill of Rights that "*Beer shall be offered in bottles, not cans, so that no brew is jeopardized with the taste of metal*" had to admit canning craft beer was a revolutionary move. Oopsie.

TECHNICAL STUFF

For decades modern beer cans have had a thin polymer lining on the inside, which means the beer never comes in contact with the aluminum. There is an asterisk, however — acidic beers can slowly eat away at that lining, which is why certain beers in cans should not be cellared long-term.

Ultimately, Oskar Blues' bold move proved to be a smart one, as the majority of craft brewers have made the conversion to canning their beer from bottling it — or at least they do a combination of both. And the reasons for canning beer rather than bottling it are as simple as they are smart.

In no particular order, cans:

- Are more environmentally friendly
- Are less fragile (unbreakable)
- Are 100% impervious to light (light is a well-known "beer destroyer")
- Are easier to sanitize than bottles
- Are easier to stack and store than bottles
- Weigh less than bottles
- Are quicker to chill than bottles
- Have that "cool factor" when handing out to friends

As to the first two points, cans make much more sense than bottles when going backpacking, camping, to the beach, or when imbibing poolside.

As to the third point, beers that are exposed to light — especially sunlight — will get "lightstruck" (that's "skunky" to lay people — see Chapter 28), which is not a particularly pleasant aroma in your homebrew. Furthermore, cans are also better at keeping your beer from getting oxidized, but only if you seal them properly. I cover these processes later in this chapter.

Points four through six are valid reasons for homebrewers to consider when packaging and storing their brew. Point number seven is important when it's time to start consuming.

Finally, and, let's be honest — there's nothing cooler than handing out chilled cans of your brew to your bros!

Kicking the Can Down the Road

So now that I've sold you on the idea of canning your beer, allow me to caution you about the downside: it ain't cheap.

If you're operating on a beer budget, you may have to simply read and dream your way through this chapter. But if you scored big time on that Bitcoin transaction or you're confident of the support you'll get on GoFundMe, then dream big!

In order to get an idea of your estimated cash outlay, you'll need to figure in the one-time fixed cost of the canning apparatus; then you'll need to consider the recurring per-can cost. Unlike bottles, cans are a one-use only vessel; there's no re-using them. I'll talk more about specific cans a bit later in this chapter.

In order to proceed with any canning plans, the first order of business is to shop around for the contraption that will be doing all (most) of the work — and that's called a *seamer*. It's called this because that's really all it does — it crimps the seam between the body of the can and the lid.

To start with, you'll find that there are manual crank seamers and there are electric seamers, each with price tags that reflect how much work they do and how much work you do. Manual crank seamers fetch anywhere from $450 at the low end to about double that at the high end. Electric seamers start around the low $1,000's and can easily go up to over $2,000. It all depends on what bells and whistles they come with and what their canning capacity is. More on that later . . .

TIP

If purchasing a seamer is too cost-prohibitive, here are two creative ways to reduce or avoid that high cost:

- If you are a member of a homebrew club, consider splitting the cost among the whole membership; thus every club member will get their turn to use the club-owned equipment.
- Check with your local commercial mobile canning company to see what their minimum quantity of beer is (some charge based on the quantity of beer, some charge on the quantity of cases of beer).

Next, you'll probably notice that there are a surprising number of different sizes and types of cans and lids. And material widths and diameters. And pricing. It can get a bit confusing, actually.

The vast majority of cans in the commercial market are 12-oz and 16-oz, but there are alternatives to these. You may encounter cans referred to as "stubby", "slim" and "sleek"; this mostly has to do with their width.

In terms of liquid content, the most common can sizes are:

- 8.4 oz., called a Nip (short for Nippersink)
- 16-oz., logically called a Pint
- 19.2-oz., called a Stovepipe
- 24-oz., alternately referred to as Tall Boy, Man Can or Silo
- 32-oz., Crowler

Why 19.2-oz? Becauseit equates to 568.26 milliliters, the equivalent of an Imperial Pint.

And the "crowler"? This is a 32-oz can that is often sold to-go at craft breweries. This is an option open to homebrewers, too, depending on which seamer they have.

TIP

A "crowler" is a made-up word based on the original take-home beer vessel, the "growler". The difference is that a growler is made of glass and holds 64-oz, while the crowler is a can that holds half that amount of beer.

Not all can lids are made the same, either. The most common lid is the stay-tab type, which is found on most beers, soda-pops and energy drinks. More recently, though, another type of lid has joined in the fun; it's called a "full aperture" lid (also known as a wide mouth). This lid, once removed, leaves the can end wide open for your beer guzzling pleasure. But be careful to dispose of the removed lid properly as the edges could be sharp.

TIP

Note that beer can lids are officially referred to as *ends*.

While shopping around for your seamer, be sure to note which sizes and shapes of cans it can accommodate. Most of the higher-end seamers come with adapters that allow them to accommodate different can sizes. Also inquire about buying cans and lids directly through your seamer retailer, or you can always just find a separate source. It's all a matter of cost and convenience.

Ever heard of "economy of scale"? It's pretty simple: the greater the quantity of an item purchased, the lower the per-piece price. This is never truer than when it comes to aluminum cans. At the commercial level, breweries buy entire truckloads of cans in order to fetch the best price per can. Keeping this simple economic principal in mind, you might want to plan your beer canning needs ahead of time to buy in greater bulk, or maybe even share the costs of a larger buy with other homebrewers in your area.

Also, while shopping for your cans, note that some sellers quote can and lid prices together, while some price and sell them separately — buyer beware.

A Canning We Will Go . . .

Following is an overview of the actual canning process. Before getting to that point, however, there are a couple of things to consider.

First, your beer will need to be carbonated before consuming it, right? So, will you be batch priming your brew in the can in the same way that is detailed in "Bottling Your Brew" (Chapter 14)? Or will you be force-carbonating your brew ahead of time? For this you'll need the kegging equipment outlined in Chapter 16.

While batch priming is far less expensive than buying all the kegging equipment, it leaves one major thing to be desired. When priming a beer, the carbonating process takes place inside the bottle or can after it's been sealed. Ideally, however, the beer should already be carbonated when you go to can it. The foaming that is caused by the turbulence of beer going into the can acts as a CO_2 barrier that helps to keep oxygen from coming into contact with your beer, which keeps oxidation at bay after the can has been sealed.

TECHNICAL STUFF

Oxidation is a form of staling. Just as bread goes stale, so does beer; how quickly or how badly it stales has to do with how much oxygen comes in contact with your brew.

Using a "beer gun" to fill your cans (see Chapter 14) gives you double protection from oxidation as the gun allows you to lay down a protective blanket of CO_2 in the can before you even start transferring beer into it. This technique is called *purging*.

It Seams Simple Enough

Let's take a look at the process of canning beer using one of the least expensive seamers out there; keep in mind "least expensive" is code for more labor-intensive. This seamer operates with a combination of manual lever-pulling and electric motor spinning.

The process should start with having all of the necessary items present and accounted for before getting started. This includes:

- Your seamer
- The beer to be canned
- All siphoning and beer transfer equipment (sanitized) if the beer is batch primed
- A "beer gun" and all the associated CO_2 equipment if the beer is pre-carbonated
- Enough beer cans to contain all the beer

» Enough lids to seal each can

» A bucket of sanitizing solution made with Star San food-grade sanitizer (for more on Star San, see Chapter 3)

» A spray bottle with a light sanitizing solution. This is not entirely necessary, but it helps to clean up the beer mess on various surfaces

» Clean rags to wipe up spray and spills

When you have all necessary items, follow these steps to begin canning:

1. **Dump all the can lids into the bucket of sanitizing solution. Grab one-at-a-time, as needed.**
2. **Dunk an empty can in the sanitizing solution and swish it around for a couple of seconds. Briefly drip dry.**
3. **Fill the can with beer. If this is beer that has been batch primed, it will be very flat as you siphon it into the can; try to fill as high as possible to avoid leaving air space within the can. If the beer is pre-carbonated, fill the can as high as you can with a little protective layer of foam on the top.**

   TECHNICAL STUFF

   If working with a beer gun, the purging pressure should be about 10-30 PSI; the beer filling pressure should be 3-5 PSI.

4. **Place a sanitized lid on top of the can.**
5. **Carefully place the filled can on top of the seamer pedestal. By turning the manual lever, you raise the can into the can seaming machinery.**
6. **Start the motor, which starts the can spinning.**
7. **Push the seaming lever for a couple of seconds, then pull it forward a couple of seconds to complete the two-part seaming operation.**
8. **Turn the motor off.**
9. **Lower the pedestal and remove the filled can of beer.**
10. **Take a sip of beer.**
11. **Repeat until done.**

TIP

While it might be tempting to fill all the cans first, and then seal them all, second, it's highly recommended that you complete them one-at-a-time. This avoids unnecessary oxidation and a potential domino effect of spilled beer.

To get an idea of what it's like to work with a fully automatic seamer, you'd follow all of the steps above minus number seven. That would be done for you, courtesy of your monetary investment in an upscale canning device.

While the typical aluminum can weighs less than half an ounce, its thin walls can withstand the more than 90 pounds of pressure per square inch that is exerted by the carbon dioxide level in canned beer.

Canned Beer and Homebrew Competitions

So now let's address the all-important question: Is canned homebrew allowed in BJCP sanctioned competitions?

Because of the growing number of homebrewers who can their beer rather than bottle it, it naturally follows that more cans are likely to be submitted to homebrew competitions. As to whether or not that's permissible, the official BJCP stance is this: "*The BJCP doesn't care what the entry medium is; that's entirely up to the Competition Organizer.*"

In other words, the decision is left to local competition organizers as long as their decision does not violate BJCP Sanctioned Competition Rules (these rules can be found on the BJCP website: www.bjcp.org).

There is a potential issue at stake, however. Homebrews in competition are always evaluated blindly; this means the judges have no idea who made the brews they are tasting. If only one entry is submitted in a can and all the rest are in bottles, anonymity is in question and judges' objectivity potentially goes out the window.

As more and more cans are submitted into competition, this becomes less and less an issue, but it simultaneously creates a new one. Unlike bottles, cans cannot be recapped between first and second judging rounds (as is currently done with bottles).

The typical BJCP sanctioned competition requires two bottles per entry; the first one is used for first round judging as well as mini-Best-of-Show judging. The second bottle is reserved for Best-of-Show judging, assuming an entry makes it to that level. Canned beer moving on from first round judging to mini-Best-of-Show would be at a disadvantage.

So why not just make it standard for homebrewers who can their beer to submit three cans per entry? No can do, as that opens up a Pandora's Box of concerns over canned beer entries getting an unfair advantage over bottled beer entries. And competition organizers don't want to add to entry sorting time and storage space by accepting three cans or bottles for each entry.

The term "can of worms" comes to mind.

» Kegging your beer

» Dispensing your brew

Chapter 16
Kegging: Bottling's Big Brother

As I mention in Chapter 14, homebrewers seem to universally agree that bottling is the worst part of homebrewing. The cleaning, storing, sanitizing, and capping of bottles is very tedious and time-consuming. If you can't stand bottling, kegging your brew is a viable option if you have a little disposable income.

In this chapter, I give you some advice on how to make decisions that answer the questions you face when you decide to keg your own beer: "What type of keg do I need (and what equipment goes along with it)?"; "How do I sanitize it properly?"; and "How do I tap it like a pro?" (See Chapter 14 for information about how to bottle your kegged beer when you want to transport small amounts.)

Roll Out the Barrel: Buying Your Kegging Equipment

Buying kegging equipment isn't easy; that's why I'm here — to simplify your decision. The system I recommend for homebrewers is a 5-gallon soda keg system, because it's easier to clean, fill, handle, and obtain than commercial beer kegs. Using commercial beer kegs requires special tools and equipment, and they're almost impossible to clean properly without more expensive equipment, not to mention their typical size is 15.5 gallons!

REMEMBER

Any kegging system, even on the homebrewing level, is going to require somewhat costly specialized equipment, such as a CO_2 tank with regulators and hoses. These items can take a bite out of your wallet even if you buy them used. On the positive side, a CO_2 setup is multifunctional; you can use it for filtering and force-carbonating your beer, among other things (see Chapter 31 and the "Making bubbles: Carbonating procedures" section in this chapter).

Here's what you need for the kegging procedures outlined in this chapter:

- **One or more stainless steel soda kegs:** A new keg can cost as much as $100, although a used one may be as little as $40. Whatever route you choose, be sure your kegs seal properly and hold pressure.

  TIP

  Soda keg fittings come in two types — *ball lock* or *pin lock* — and either type is acceptable. These names relate to the configuration of the valve connection that allows pressurized gas to flow into (but not out of) the valve until you depress it (kind of like the valve on a bicycle or car tire). Pin lock configuration tends to be a bit more expensive.

- **A pressurized carbon dioxide tank:** This tank will run you $75 (used) to $150 (new), and it costs another $20 to $25 each time you refill it.
- **A carbon dioxide tank regulator (preferably a dual gauge):** This item isn't cheap either — it sets you back $75 to $90.

  TIP

  Tank regulators are available in single gauge and dual gauge types. The single gauge only tells you the pressure of the gas flowing through the gas line; the dual gauge is better because it tells you the line pressure as well as the gas pressure remaining in the tank.

- **Appropriate quick-disconnect fittings (for ball or pin lock):** Get one fitting for the gas inflow and one for the liquid outflow. They're reasonably priced at $6 to $8 each.
- **A carbon dioxide hose line (gas inflow line):** It's not a bad deal at about $1 per foot.
- **A beer dispenser line with a tap faucet (liquid outflow line):** This is another item with a fairly cheap price: $5 to $10.
- **A sanitizing agent:** I recommend Iodophor (an iodine-based sanitizer), which costs $2 to $10 depending on the container size. Star San is another effective no-rinse sanitizer.

WARNING

Although ordinary household bleach is fine for sanitizing most other homebrew equipment, stainless steel is an exception. Chlorine can actually eat away the surface of stainless steel at high concentrations or over an extended period of time, especially at low pH levels. If you must use bleach out of desperation, use only 1 ounce per 5 gallons and limit contact time with the keg to 30 minutes. Consider yourself warned.

- **A screwdriver and adjustable wrench:** You may have these items lying around your house.
- **A carboy brush or similar cleaning brush:** Again, you may already have an appropriate brush.

Figure 16-1 shows you what your soda keg system looks like when you're all set up and ready to keg.

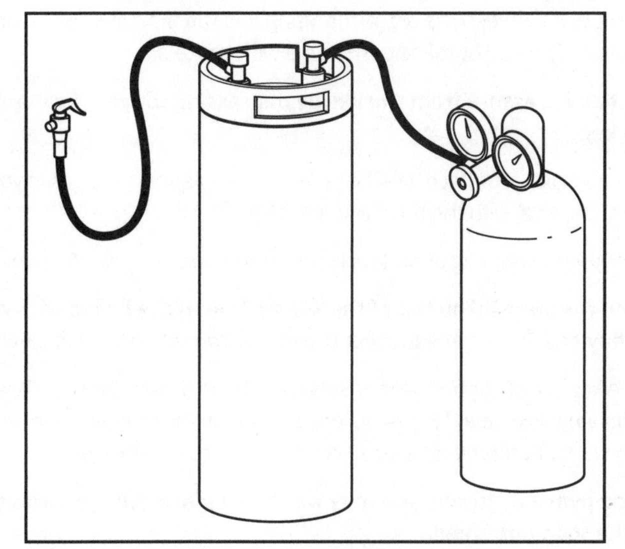

FIGURE 16-1: The typical soda keg setup for homebrewers, including a 5-gallon keg, CO_2 tank, dual CO_2 gauges, and dispensing hoses and fittings.

Getting Your Keg Up and Flowing

After you've made your decisions and your purchases, the first thing you want to do is thoroughly clean and sanitize your kegging equipment. I cover the information on how to do this in the following section. When you have a beer ready to keg, all you need to do is follow the easy directions I provide a bit later in this chapter.

Clean 'em out and fill 'em up: Sanitizing and racking procedures

When it comes to storing your beer in kegs, the cleaning and sanitizing of your equipment is important (just as it is with any other aspect of homebrewing). Unlike bottles, however, kegs pose a slightly different problem: Because kegs have many parts, it's more difficult to make sure that all the parts are equally clean and sanitized. This means you need to disassemble your keg in preparation for the cleaning and sanitizing procedures. After you've properly disinfected and reassembled it, filling it with your brew is a snap. The following steps walk you through sanitizing your keg.

1. **After obtaining all the necessary system parts, hook up the regulator to the CO_2 cylinder.**

   Make sure you use the gasket that comes with the regulator. This gasket must be in place between the regulator fitting and the CO_2 tank to prevent gas leakage. (Too bad humans don't come with gaskets.)

2. **Vent any pressure from the keg by depressing the relief valve on top of the keg.**

   If your keg doesn't have a relief valve, you can depress the gas in valve (at the top of the keg) with the tip of a screwdriver.

   WARNING

   Always vent your keg of pressure before you open or disassemble it.

3. **Open the large lid on top of the keg and clean the inside with water and a carboy brush. Visually inspect the inside to make sure it's clean.**

   TIP

   If the keg is dirty or has beer or soda residue in it, you can clean it with some *trisodium phosphate* (TSP) — never use ordinary household soap. Rinse well with water. Remember that TSP is a cleanser, not a sanitizer.

4. **If you own a used keg, you may want to replace the five gaskets to get rid of the soda pop smell.**

   Alternatively, you can remove the gaskets and soak them in ethyl or grain alcohol (be sure you rinse the alcohol away very thoroughly). See Figure 16-2 for the locations of the gaskets you may need to clean or replace. If it's a new keg, proceed to Step 5; if you're dealing with used gaskets, the following checklist can help you find and clean them:

   - The first gasket is easy to find — it's around the lid. Remove it, clean the lid thoroughly, and replace the gasket.
   - Another two gaskets are around the outside of the tank plugs (the in/out fittings). Carefully remove these gaskets and either clean or replace them. Make sure to refit the plugs onto your keg.

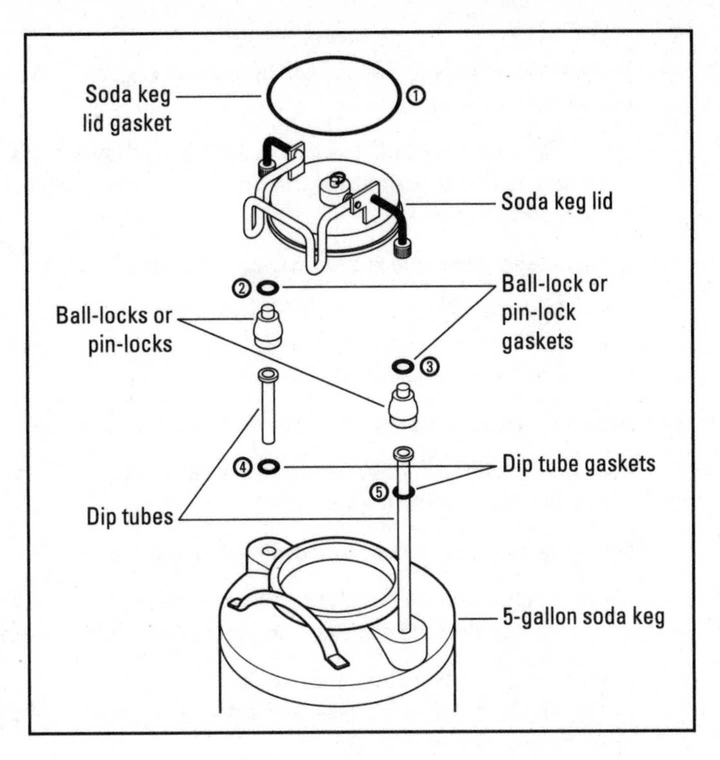

FIGURE 16-2: Locations of the five rubber gaskets on a typical soda keg.

- The last two gaskets are hidden on the dip tubes; you can find them by using an adjustable wrench to loosen and remove the tank plugs one at a time (don't strip the plugs). Be careful not to lose any of the small pieces (including the gaskets) inside the tank plugs.

  Removing these plugs one at a time is important because the tank plugs aren't interchangeable — each is a different size and/or shape. Be sure not to mix up the dip tubes (found under the tank plugs) either. The fluid out tube is as long as the tank is deep, and the gas in tube is about ½ inch long.

- Thoroughly clean the tank plugs (inside and out) of any soda pop syrup or beer residue with a small brush and warm water (four out of five brewers recommend using an old toothbrush).
- Remove the dip tubes by pushing them up from the inside with your hands (don't use pliers because they can damage the tubes).
- Now you can remove the two gaskets around the dip tubes and clean or replace them.
- Clean the inside and outsides of the two dip tubes (don't mix them up). Reassemble the keg and apply 10 *psi (pounds per square inch)* of carbon dioxide to see whether it still holds pressure. If the keg doesn't hold pressure, check to make sure you reassembled the keg properly and tightened all the fittings.

You want to disassemble and clean the keg on a regularly scheduled basis — every third brew or so.

5. **After the keg is clean, fill it with 1 to 2 ounces of Iodophor sanitizer (or according to the directions for the sanitizer of your choice) in 5 gallons of cool water to sanitize it.**

   Leave the sanitizer in the keg for at least 15 minutes.

TIP

   Don't forget to depress the out valve to allow Iodophor to flow up into the long dip tube. You should also turn the keg upside down or on its side for 15 minutes so that you sanitize the top, too.

6. **After at least 15 minutes, drain the solution from the keg.**

   Pour some of the sanitizing solution in a bucket so that you can soak the lid in it while you rinse and fill the keg.

7. **Rinse the inside of the keg and drain all excess water.**

   Be sure you run some water through the out dip tube: Put the lid on the keg, apply CO_2 pressure, and dispense the water as if you're tapping a beer.

WARNING

   If there is any question about the cleanliness of your water, I suggest pre-boiling it before using it to rinse your kegs — or buy gallons of cheap bottled water for this purpose.

8. **Rinse and replace the keg lid. Pressurize the keg to 10 psi and release the CO_2.**

   This step purges air from the keg.

9. **Sanitize your siphon hose and siphon the finished beer into the keg through its lid hole.**

   If you're keeping track of your beer's gravity and alcohol content, this is the time to take another hydrometer reading with your sanitized hydrometer cylinder. (See Chapter 2 for more information on taking hydrometer readings.)

10. **Rinse the sanitized lid and then seal the keg.**

    Don't forget to properly seat the gasket.

11. **Apply 10 psi to the keg and vent.**

    Repeat this step five times to ensure that the atmosphere inside the keg is almost pure CO_2.

REMEMBER

    If the kegs aren't kept under 5 to 10 pounds of pressure, the gaskets may not seal completely. Be sure your keg is always under pressure while you're storing beer in it.

Making bubbles: Carbonating procedures

Okay, so you've filled the keg. Now how do you carbonate it? This section describes the method in minute detail.

Force carbonating is exactly what it sounds like — you're forcing CO_2 into the beer by pressurizing the keg to a certain psi level (see Figure 16-3).

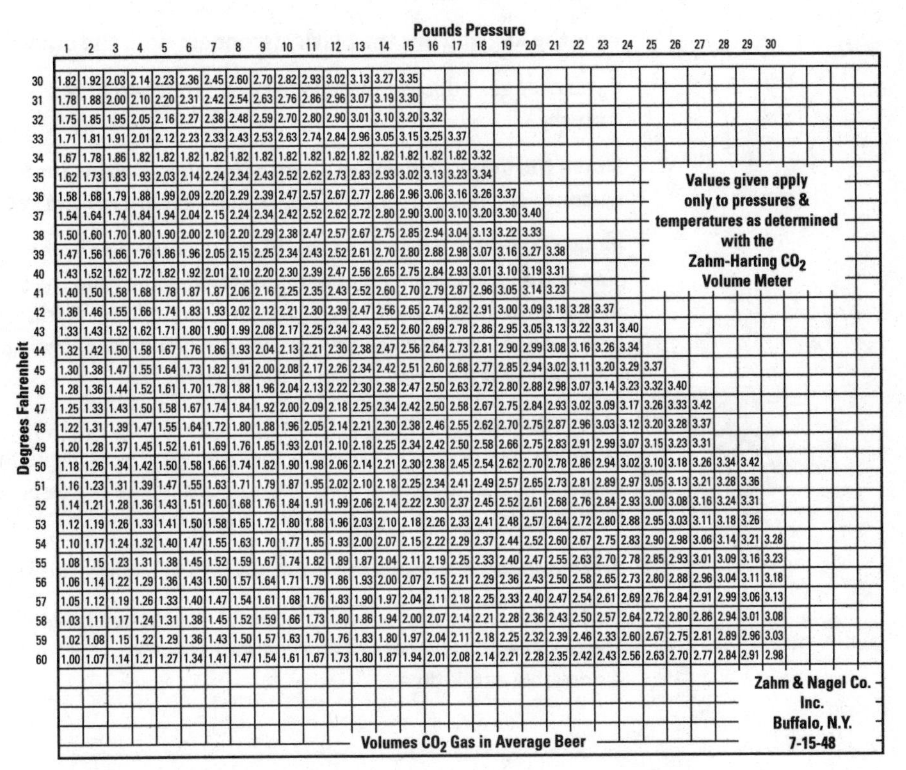

Pounds Pressure

Degrees Fahrenheit	1	2	3	4	5	6	7	8	9	10	11	12	13	14	15	16	17	18	19	20	21	22	23	24	25	26	27	28	29	30
30	1.82	1.92	2.03	2.14	2.23	2.36	2.45	2.60	2.70	2.82	2.93	3.02	3.13	3.27	3.35															
31	1.78	1.88	2.00	2.10	2.20	2.31	2.42	2.54	2.63	2.76	2.86	2.96	3.07	3.19	3.30															
32	1.75	1.85	1.95	2.05	2.16	2.27	2.38	2.48	2.59	2.70	2.80	2.90	3.01	3.10	3.20	3.32														
33	1.71	1.81	1.91	2.01	2.12	2.23	2.33	2.43	2.53	2.63	2.74	2.84	2.96	3.05	3.15	3.25	3.37													
34	1.67	1.78	1.86	1.82	1.82	1.82	1.82	1.82	1.82	1.82	1.82	1.82	1.82	1.82	1.82	1.82	1.82	3.32												
35	1.62	1.73	1.83	1.93	2.03	2.14	2.24	2.34	2.43	2.52	2.62	2.73	2.83	2.93	3.02	3.13	3.23	3.34												
36	1.58	1.68	1.79	1.88	1.99	2.09	2.20	2.29	2.39	2.47	2.57	2.67	2.77	2.86	2.96	3.06	3.16	3.26	3.37											
37	1.54	1.64	1.74	1.84	1.94	2.04	2.15	2.24	2.34	2.42	2.52	2.62	2.72	2.80	2.90	3.00	3.10	3.20	3.30	3.40										
38	1.50	1.60	1.70	1.80	1.90	2.00	2.10	2.20	2.29	2.38	2.47	2.57	2.67	2.75	2.85	2.94	3.04	3.13	3.22	3.33										
39	1.47	1.56	1.66	1.76	1.86	1.96	2.05	2.15	2.25	2.34	2.43	2.52	2.61	2.70	2.80	2.88	2.98	3.07	3.16	3.27	3.38									
40	1.43	1.52	1.62	1.72	1.82	1.92	2.01	2.10	2.20	2.30	2.39	2.47	2.56	2.65	2.75	2.84	2.93	3.01	3.10	3.19	3.31									
41	1.40	1.50	1.58	1.68	1.78	1.87	1.87	2.06	2.16	2.25	2.35	2.43	2.52	2.60	2.70	2.79	2.87	2.96	3.05	3.14	3.23									
42	1.36	1.46	1.55	1.66	1.74	1.83	1.93	2.02	2.12	2.21	2.30	2.39	2.47	2.56	2.65	2.74	2.82	2.91	3.00	3.09	3.18	3.28	3.37							
43	1.33	1.43	1.52	1.62	1.71	1.80	1.90	1.99	2.08	2.17	2.25	2.34	2.43	2.52	2.60	2.69	2.78	2.86	2.95	3.05	3.13	3.22	3.31	3.40						
44	1.32	1.42	1.50	1.58	1.67	1.76	1.86	1.93	2.04	2.13	2.21	2.30	2.38	2.47	2.56	2.64	2.73	2.81	2.90	2.99	3.08	3.16	3.26	3.34						
45	1.30	1.38	1.47	1.55	1.64	1.73	1.82	1.91	2.00	2.08	2.17	2.26	2.34	2.42	2.51	2.60	2.68	2.77	2.85	2.94	3.02	3.11	3.20	3.29	3.37					
46	1.28	1.36	1.44	1.52	1.61	1.70	1.78	1.88	1.96	2.04	2.13	2.22	2.30	2.38	2.47	2.50	2.63	2.72	2.80	2.88	2.98	3.07	3.14	3.23	3.32	3.40				
47	1.25	1.33	1.43	1.50	1.58	1.67	1.74	1.84	1.92	2.00	2.09	2.18	2.25	2.34	2.42	2.50	2.58	2.67	2.75	2.84	2.93	3.02	3.09	3.17	3.26	3.33	3.42			
48	1.22	1.31	1.39	1.47	1.55	1.64	1.72	1.80	1.88	1.96	2.05	2.14	2.21	2.30	2.38	2.46	2.55	2.62	2.70	2.75	2.87	2.96	3.03	3.12	3.20	3.28	3.37			
49	1.20	1.28	1.37	1.45	1.52	1.61	1.69	1.76	1.85	1.93	2.01	2.10	2.18	2.25	2.34	2.42	2.50	2.58	2.66	2.75	2.83	2.91	2.99	3.07	3.15	3.23	3.31			
50	1.18	1.26	1.34	1.42	1.50	1.58	1.66	1.74	1.82	1.90	1.98	2.06	2.14	2.21	2.30	2.38	2.45	2.54	2.62	2.70	2.78	2.86	2.94	3.02	3.10	3.18	3.26	3.34	3.42	
51	1.16	1.23	1.31	1.39	1.47	1.55	1.63	1.71	1.79	1.87	1.95	2.02	2.10	2.18	2.25	2.34	2.41	2.49	2.57	2.65	2.73	2.81	2.89	2.97	3.05	3.13	3.21	3.28	3.36	
52	1.14	1.21	1.28	1.36	1.43	1.51	1.60	1.68	1.76	1.84	1.91	1.99	2.06	2.14	2.22	2.30	2.37	2.45	2.52	2.61	2.68	2.76	2.84	2.93	3.00	3.08	3.16	3.24	3.31	
53	1.12	1.19	1.26	1.33	1.41	1.50	1.58	1.65	1.72	1.80	1.88	1.96	2.03	2.10	2.18	2.26	2.33	2.41	2.48	2.57	2.64	2.72	2.80	2.88	2.95	3.03	3.11	3.18	3.26	
54	1.10	1.17	1.24	1.32	1.40	1.47	1.55	1.63	1.70	1.77	1.85	1.93	2.00	2.07	2.15	2.22	2.29	2.37	2.44	2.52	2.60	2.67	2.75	2.83	2.90	2.98	3.06	3.14	3.21	3.28
55	1.08	1.15	1.23	1.31	1.38	1.45	1.52	1.59	1.67	1.74	1.82	1.89	1.87	2.04	2.11	2.19	2.25	2.33	2.40	2.47	2.55	2.63	2.70	2.78	2.85	2.93	3.01	3.09	3.16	3.23
56	1.06	1.14	1.22	1.29	1.36	1.43	1.50	1.57	1.64	1.71	1.79	1.86	1.93	2.00	2.07	2.15	2.21	2.29	2.36	2.43	2.50	2.58	2.65	2.73	2.80	2.88	2.96	3.04	3.11	3.18
57	1.05	1.12	1.19	1.26	1.33	1.40	1.47	1.54	1.61	1.68	1.76	1.83	1.90	1.97	2.04	2.11	2.18	2.25	2.33	2.40	2.47	2.54	2.61	2.69	2.76	2.84	2.91	2.99	3.06	3.13
58	1.03	1.11	1.17	1.24	1.31	1.38	1.45	1.52	1.59	1.66	1.73	1.80	1.86	1.94	2.00	2.07	2.14	2.21	2.28	2.36	2.43	2.50	2.57	2.64	2.72	2.80	2.86	2.94	3.01	3.08
59	1.02	1.08	1.15	1.22	1.29	1.36	1.43	1.50	1.57	1.63	1.70	1.76	1.83	1.80	1.97	2.04	2.11	2.18	2.25	2.32	2.39	2.46	2.33	2.60	2.67	2.75	2.81	2.89	2.96	3.03
60	1.00	1.07	1.14	1.21	1.27	1.34	1.41	1.47	1.54	1.61	1.67	1.73	1.80	1.87	1.94	2.01	2.08	2.14	2.21	2.28	2.35	2.42	2.43	2.56	2.63	2.70	2.77	2.84	2.91	2.98

FIGURE 16-3: Use this gas volume table to determine the right psi for your keg of beer.

The advantage of force-carbonating is that the beer has little sediment (especially if you allowed the beer to age in a carboy for two to three weeks). The beer is also ready to drink in a day or two. The following steps show you how to force-carbonate your brew:

1. **Chill your beer to 60° Fahrenheit or cooler and take the precise temperature of the beer.**

   (Check out Chapter 31 for the lowdown on stick-on type thermometers.)

2. **Next, hook up the CO_2 line to the "CO_2 in" plug on the keg.**

3. **Find the temperature of your beer at the left of the gas volume table in Figure 16-3 and then follow the top row of the table to the right to find the volumes of CO_2 to which you want to carbonate your beer. Follow the column that you choose down to the pressure (psi) indicated.**

   Check out the nearby "Pump up the volume" sidebar for more on volume.

4. **Open the CO_2 tank and set your regulator to the pressure you got from the gas volume table.**
5. **Vent the keg and put the black disconnect onto the out valve of the keg.**

   If you hear gas bubbling through the beer, congratulations: You did this step correctly.

6. **Shake the keg to force the CO_2 into the beer. Do this for 5 minutes, disconnect the CO_2 from the keg, and then shut off the gas.**

   Repeat Steps 5 and 6 as often as you can over the next 24 hours or so. Make sure you always keep the temperature-to-pressure ratio the same. If the temperature or the pressure changes, the amount of CO_2 dissolved into the beer changes. When you can't hear any gas going into the solution, you know your beer is at the desired level of carbonation.

WARNING

   Always disconnect the gas line from the keg before you shut off the CO_2 tank valve. Without pressure in the line, the beer may back up into the regulator. Remember that CO_2 is a pressurized gas; observe all necessary safety precautions. Consult your gas supplier for further information.

7. **After your beer reaches the desired CO_2 level, allow the keg to settle for a couple of hours before dispensing.**

   The CO_2 needs a few days to thoroughly dissolve into the beer, but your brew is drinkable at this time.

PUMP UP THE VOLUME

How much is a *volume?* Two volumes of CO_2 are the equivalent of two 5-gallon containers' worth of CO_2 compressed into a single 5-gallon container (the average beer has 2.4 to 2.7 volumes of CO_2).

How many volumes of CO_2 do you need to put into your beer? The answer depends greatly on the particular beer style, but here are some general guidelines to follow: British-style Ales = 1.75 to 2.5 volumes, American and European Lagers = 2.25 to 2.75 volumes, and highly carbonated beers (Weizen, Fruit beers, and Belgian Ales) = 2.75 to 3.25 volumes. Clearly, force-carbonating gives you much more control over your beer's carbonation than simple priming techniques.

Enjoying Your Brew: Tapping and Lapping Procedures

Here you go — your beer is kegged and ready to drink; all you need to do is grab your favorite beer glass and plop into your easy chair. Actually, you have to hook up the keg and start the flow of CO_2 first, but homebrew enjoyment doesn't get much easier than this.

After the beer is carbonated:

1. **Open the gas cylinder and set the regulator to 5 to 8 psi.**
2. **Vent the keg and hook up the gas and the dispense lines.**
3. **Tap and enjoy.**

Always tap your beer with the tap head wide open (depress the valve completely). Opening the tap only halfway causes foaming. Also, if the beer still foams too much (even when the tap head is wide open), turn the dispensing pressure down a pound or two by adjusting the line pressure on the gas gauge.

When you're done dispensing beer for the day, repressurize the keg to the original carbonating pressure (if you force-carbonated) or to 10 psi (if you primed it) to maintain the proper CO_2 level in the beer.

5

BJCP Beer Style Guidelines and Homebrew Recipes

IN THIS PART . . .

Kickstart your homebrewing hobby by making your beer the simplest way possible: Follow the recommendations in the beginner section.

Start personalizing your beer by adding new ingredients and techniques, courtesy of the intermediate recipe section.

Go all-grain and make tasty lagers found in the advanced recipe section.

Learn more about each beer style presented with the included BJCP Beer Style Guidelines.

on the chapter) beer styles

» Brewing these beers on your own (with kits/recipes, depending)

» Making the brewing process easier with tips and suggestions

Chapter 17

Beginner Suggestions and BJCP Beer Style Guidelines

This chapter doesn't provide "recipes" in the traditional sense of the word; rather, it shares suggestions for tweaking your kit beers to improve on them. You see, at the beginner level of homebrewing, it's so much more convenient to start by using pre-packaged kits sold through homebrew supply outlets. The downside is that your creativity is a bit stifled with these. That's the purpose of the suggestions provided in this chapter; to help you make small but significant improvements on otherwise simple beer kits.

You'll likely notice that all of the beer styles in this chapter are ales, for the simple fact that lagers are more difficult to produce at home. (However, you'll find plenty of lagers in Chapter 19, where I discuss advanced recipes).

Ales, by traditional definition, are beers fermented with top-fermenting yeast at warm (ambient) temperatures for relatively short periods of time. Ales are primarily associated with England and Ireland, but you can find them in a wide variety of styles in most brewing nations such as Australia, Belgium, Canada, and the

United States. Technically, California common (formerly known as steam beer) is a hybrid style; it's fermented with lager yeast, but at warmer temperatures.

Throughout the remainder of this chapter (and the next two, for that matter), wherever you see a beer style heading, it will always be accompanied by number or a number-and-letter designation. These are the beer style category designations as laid out by the BJCP. But rather than list the beer styles in order of their alpha-numeric category designations, I chose to go old-school and just list the beer styles alphabetically.

American Amber Ale (19-a)

Amber-colored ales are similar to pale ales in terms of the brewing process; their basic difference is in their color. The grains you use to impart the deeper hue in amber ales tend to give the beer a toasty character and a more complex malt palate. Amber ales are most often malt-accented, but they can also have an assertive hop character.

Flavor profile: Similar to American pale ale, but because of the addition of toasted grain or crystal malts, the amber ales are likely to be slightly darker and have a more pronounced toasty and malty aroma and flavor. Noticeable to assertive hop flavor and aroma aren't unusual. Medium-bodied.

OG/FG:	1.045–1.060/1.010–1.015
ABV:	4.5–6.2
IBUs:	25–40+
SRM:	10–17

Commercial examples: Boont Amber Ale, California; North Coast Red Seal Ale, California

Beginner suggestions: You can use either pale extract or amber-hopped extract — both finish within the generous color range for this style. If you choose the pale extract, try getting a little kettle caramelization by vigorously boiling the wort an extra half hour or more. Try adding 1 ounce of Cascade hops to the wort with 10 minutes left in the boil.

American Brown Ale (19-c)

As Americans are often inclined to do, American brewers have taken a foreign beer style and adapted it to local tastes. The American rendition of brown ale maintains similar color and gravity profiles but is dry rather than sweet and has far more hop character in the aroma and flavor.

Flavor profile: Medium to dark brown. Unlike English brown ales, American browns have a relatively high degree of hop bitterness, flavor, and aroma. Medium maltiness with chocolate accents along with caramel and nutty flavors and low diacetyl. Medium-bodied.

OG/FG:	1.045–1.060/1.010–1.016
ABV:	4.3–6.2
IBUs:	20–30
SRM:	18–35

Commercial examples: Brooklyn Brown Ale, New York; Avery Brewing Ellie's Brown Ale, Colorado

Beginner suggestion: Choose your hopped brown ale kit from among a number of brands that produce them. Try adding an extra dose of hop character by adding 1 ounce of your favorite American hops to the brewpot in the last 10 minutes of the boil.

American Porter (20-a)

American porter is a cousin of stout. This beer is very dark — typically opaque. It often takes on a reddish appearance in the presence of light. Dark-grain aromas dominate the nose. American porter is medium- to full-bodied with an alcohol content that ranges between 5 and 7 percent. The most noticeable characteristic is the dark-grain flavors derived from the chocolate malt or black malts in the grist. Hop bitterness combined with mild grain astringency balance the sweetness of the crystal malt.

Flavor profile: Opaque black. Fruity esters are okay. Hop flavor and aroma are non-existent to medium. No roast barley character — just the sharp bitterness of black malt with a hint of burnt charcoal-like flavor. Medium to full bodied and malty sweet with low diacetyl in the background. Hop bitterness is medium to high.

OG/FG:	1.050-1.070/1.012-1.018
ABV:	4.8–6.5
IBUs:	25–50
SRM:	22–40

Commercial examples: Great Lakes Edmund Fitzgerald Porter, Ohio; Anchor Porter, California

Beginner suggestions: Try producing the color and flavor in your porter by using specialty grains (dark caramel, chocolate malt, and black malt) rather than buying a dark malt extract — the result is more satisfying. Stir an ounce or two of blackstrap molasses into the brewpot for added complexity.

Baltic Porter (9-c)

English-style porter was traditionally brewed in countries bordering the Baltic Sea, but that style was greatly influenced by Russian imperial stouts. Thus, a Baltic porter may also be referred to as an imperial porter.

A Baltic porter often has the malt flavors reminiscent of an English brown porter and the restrained roast of a Schwarzbier with a higher OG and alcohol content than either. It's a very complex beer with multilayered flavors. Silky smoothness in the mouthfeel is a hallmark of the style.

Flavor profile: Baltic porter offers a rich, malty sweetness with a complex blend of deep malt, dried fruit esters, alcohol, and a prominent yet smooth, roasted flavor that stops short of burnt. It's mouth-filling and very smooth; it starts sweet, but darker malt flavors quickly dominate and persist through finish. The malt character can have a caramel, toffee, nutty, molasses, and/or licorice complexity, and you may taste a hint of roast coffee or licorice in the finish. Medium-low to medium bitterness from malt and hops just to provide balance.

OG/FG:	1.060–1.090/1.016–1.024
ABV:	6.5–9.5
IBUs:	20–40
SRM:	17–30

Commercial examples: Sinebrychoff Porter, Finland; Zywiec Porter, Poland.

Beginner suggestions: In order to achieve the minimum OG, you'd need to start with at least 8 pounds of dark malt extract. Try producing the color and flavor in your porter by using specialty grains (dark caramel, chocolate malt and de-bittered black malt) rather than buying a dark malt extract — the result is more satisfying. Toss an inch of brewer's licorice and/or a couple of ounces of blackstrap molasses into the brewpot for added complexity.

Best Bitter (11-b)

The history of this style of beer is rather hazy (but not the beer itself) because it probably developed over a long period of time and was influenced by a number of factors. To begin with, the pale malt needed to brew pale ale was developed only as recently as the 1700s — most of the barley malt used prior to this time was a brown malt (because of the kilning procedures) that resulted in darker beers. Secondly, hop character is very important to the English-style pale ale that drinkers recognize today, but hops were not in widespread use in England until the mid-16th century. Furthermore, the English people made a clear distinction between un-hopped ale and any beer made with hops; the latter were called *bitters*.

There does seem to be a bit of confusion when it comes to British bitters and British pale ales. In Britain, the family of bitters (ordinary, best, and strong) are usually draught-only beers, served by handpump or by gravity pour from a cask. This leaves them rather low in carbonation and soft on the palate. Pale ales, the style from which bitters emerged, are almost exclusively a bottled product, initially brewed for export only (but are now found on draught also). Pale ales tend to contain more alcohol and have much higher carbonation levels, as well as hop bitterness.

The parameters of the style are fairly loose, allowing for a generous range of color and a fair fluctuation in gravities. Two things are certain about pale ales: They exhibit fruity esters in the nose and a big hop presence in both the flavor and the aroma. In fact, hops are the key to developing a good pale ale. The classic English pale ale should use a hop from England known as Kent Goldings, but other aromatic varieties are perfectly acceptable. Pale ales are often *dry-hopped*, which is a method of imbuing the beer with a fresh hop aroma (without the bitterness) by adding hops directly to the beer while it's in the aging tank or barrel instead of during the boiling process. See Chapters 5 and 11 for more information on dry-hopping.

Flavor profile: Golden to deep amber. Lots of fruity esters can be expected. High hop bitterness, flavor, and aroma dominate low to medium maltiness. Toastiness and low levels of diacetyl are okay. Medium-bodied.

OG/FG:	1.040–1.048/1.008–1.012
ABV:	3.8–4.6
IBUs:	25–40
SRM:	8–16

Commercial examples: Fuller's London Pride, England; Timothy Taylor Landlord, England

Beginner suggestions: Start with 5 to 6 of pale hopped extract and steep between 1 and 1.5 pounds of 40-L crystal malt; strain into the wort. In the last 10 minutes of the boil, toss in between 0.5 and 1 ounce of a traditional English hop (Fuggles, Kent Goldings) for additional hop character. Prime with a lower dose of corn sugar (½ cup) to reduce carbonation levels.

Belgian Blond Ale (25-a)

This moderate-strength golden ale is a relatively new beer style — for a Belgian. It was created to appeal to drinkers of German or Czech pilsner beers. Its malty-sweet flavor gains complexity from the subtle fruity spiciness that comes as a result of the Belgian yeast strains used to ferment this beer.

Belgian blonds are similar in flavor to Belgian tripels, though they do not finish as dry or contain as much alcohol.

Flavor profile: Smooth and light grainy-sweet malt flavor, accented by fruity, phenolic spiciness. Occasional citric character of orange or lemon is experienced.

OG/FG:	1.062–1.075/1.008–1.018
ABV:	6.0–7.5%
IBUs:	15–30
SRM:	4–6

Commercial examples: Leffe Blonde, Belgium; LaTrappe Blond, Belgium

Beginner suggestions: Start with 6 to 7 lbs. of the palest malt extract you can find. Be sure to ferment with a quality Belgian style yeast.

California Common (19-b)

This beer style is one of the few that is indigenous to the United States. It was created in California during the Gold Rush era, and it was originally known as *steam beer*. When the Anchor Brewing Company in San Francisco trademarked the name, the style then became known as California common beer. (Steam beer got its name from the hissing of the barrels during fermentation; the carbonation sounded like steam as it escaped the vessels.)

This moderately malty but well-hopped beer is traditionally fermented with lager yeast, but at warm or ambient temperatures, which may give it light fruity esters.

Flavor profile: Malty with pronounced hop bitterness. Toastiness and a caramelly flavor are common in this beer. Finish is dryish with firm bitterness. Medium-bodied.

OG/FG:	1.048–1.054/1.011–1.014
ABV:	4.5–5.5%
IBUs:	30–45
SRM:	9–14

Commercial examples: Anchor Steam, California; Southern Tier 2X Steam, New York

Beginner suggestions: Start with 6 pounds of amber hopped malt extract. Add 1 ounce of American hops (Cascade, Centennial) in the last 10 minutes of the boil. Be sure to ferment with a non-German strain of lager yeast.

English Barley Wine (17-d)

The term *barley wine* sounds more like something you make from grapes, and yet its name mentions a grain. What's up with that? Well, the name implies a beverage made from barley but that has the strength and character of wine; you soon see that the name is apropos.

Barley wine is a classic English style of old ale. With its huge body, almost-overwhelming malty flavor, and the kick of a mule, barley wine isn't for the weak-kneed. These complex and alcoholic brews pack a one-two punch of flavor and strength because of the high level of fermentable sugars, or *gravity*. Barley wine has more than twice the strength of a European pilsner. The resulting alcohol content is around 8.5 to 12 percent by volume. Needless to say, these potent potables aren't intended for summer consumption. In fact, brewers usually produce barley wine in limited quantities, often earmarked for holiday celebrations. And because of its alcoholic strength and high terminal gravities, you can store barley wine for future consumption.

The color range for barley wine is forgiving, usually starting out around copper and working its way into the deep ambers. The nose is pungent — an olfactory cornucopia of fruits and malt aromas, ethanol, and hop bouquet. Correctly balancing the bold, malty character of this style requires copious amounts of hop bittering, further intimidating the novice beer drinker. The finish is always long, complex, and warming in the throat.

Flavor profile: Copper to medium brown and medium to full-bodied. Barley wines are usually malty sweet, fruity, and estery, with medium to high bitterness levels. Hop aroma and taste can be anywhere from low to high. Expect to taste the alcohol. Low to medium diacetyl is acceptable.

OG/FG:	1.080–1.120+/1.018–1.030+
ABV:	8.0–12.0+
IBUs:	35–70
SRM:	8–22

Commercial examples: Young's Old Nick, England; Thomas Hardy's Ale, England

Beginner suggestions: Successful barley wines are big and bold beers. Use at least 9 pounds of extract to achieve the correct body and strength. Remember to aerate the wort sufficiently before pitching a British yeast strain, and to pitch enough healthy yeast to ferment the beer completely. Full fermentation should take two to three weeks. A couple weeks of aging wouldn't hurt, either.

British Brown Ale (13-b)

Brown ale is a close relative to pale ale. Aside from the obvious color difference, brown ales are also slightly maltier than the pale ales. Brown ales are also less aggressively hopped because the water you use for brewing traditional brown ale is chalky, and this hardness in the water tends to accentuate the hop's bitter qualities.

Brown ales are relatively low-gravity beers that yield low alcohol content after quick fermentations. You use chocolate malt to impart the brown color and chocolaty palate. Some brewers add small quantities of light molasses or brown sugar to lend other flavor and aroma nuances to the beer. The nose may also hint of fruit, nuts, and toffeelike aromas.

Flavor profile: Deep copper to brown. Hop flavor and aroma are low, with fruity esters lingering behind. Sweet and malty with hints of chocolate; low bitterness and diacetyl. Medium-bodied.

OG/FG:	1.040–1.052/1.008–1.013
ABV:	4.2–5.9
IBUs:	20–30
SRM:	12–22

Commercial examples: Samuel Smith Nut Brown Ale, England; Maxim Double Maxim, England

Beginner suggestions: Start with 5 pounds of amber-hopped malt extract and add 1 cup of dark brown sugar for added color and flavor complexity.

British Strong Ale (17-a)

Another stout style, rarer than most, is strongly associated with pre-Bolshevik Russia. Dark British beers found favor among the czarist rulers of Russia, particularly for their brand of stout. Unfortunately, the English-made stout didn't travel well to St. Petersburg and other points east. To compensate for the short shelf life of their beer, British brewers raised the gravity and increased the hop content. Sure enough, the Russian rulers deeply admired this complex high-alcohol brew. The style has since come to be known as Russian stout, imperial stout, or the combined Russian imperial stout.

Flavor profile: Dark copper to very black. High level of fruity esters. Hop bitterness flavor and aroma medium to high. Rich and complex maltiness with a chewy texture; roasty, fruity, and bittersweet. Full-bodied with evident alcohol strength.

OG/FG:	1.075–1.095+/1.018–1.030+
ABV:	8.0–12.0+
IBUs:	50–90+
SRM:	30–40+

Commercial examples: Samuel Smith's Imperial Stout, England; Courage Imperial Russian Stout, England

Beginner suggestions: Imperial stouts need a lot of fermentable material as well as a lot of dark grain complexity. Start with at least 9 pounds of extract, and try achieving the color and character of this style by using specialty grains (dark crystal malt, chocolate malt, black malt, and roasted barley). Brewer's licorice and unsulfured dark molasses can also add fermentable sugars and flavor complexity.

English Porter (13-c)

The name *porter* is borrowed from a group of people known to consume large quantities of this beer: the porters at London's Victoria Station. Originally, it didn't exist as a single style. The porters had a habit of ordering portions of several beers mixed into the same drinking glass. This concoction came to be known as *three threads* or *entire.* One enterprising brewer capitalized on this habit by marketing a beer that closely approximated this blend of brews, and he used the name *porter* to identify it.

The brown malt used to make porter beer was kilned over a wood fire, which gave the malt, as well as the resulting beer, a distinctive smoky flavor and aroma. Although porters are no longer brewed with wood-kilned malts, today's porters may still suggest a hint of smokiness in the nose or on the palate. Today, two basic styles of porter are available: brown and American. Generally speaking, American microbrewers favor the American style of porter, whereas brown porter remains the forte of the British brewers.

Brown porter is a meeker version of its big brother, American porter. Body and color are lighter, though still maintaining a minimized dark-grain flavor and hue. Both the malty sweetness and hop bitterness are downplayed, which lowers the resulting alcohol to between 4 and 6 percent and makes this brew a little closer to a *session beer* (a beer conducive to consumption in large volumes).

Flavor profile: Medium to dark brown. Fruity esters are acceptable, and hop flavor and aroma are nonexistent to medium. No roast barley or strong burnt character is expected. Low to medium malt sweetness, with medium hop bitterness and low diacetyl. Light- to medium-bodied.

OG/FG:	1.040–1.052/1.008–1.014
ABV:	4.0–5.4
IBUs:	18–25
SRM:	20–30

Commercial examples: Samuel Smith Taddy Porter, England; Fuller's London Porter, England

Beginner suggestions: Try producing the color and flavor in your porter by adding specialty grains (dark caramel, chocolate malt, and black malt) to your pale malt extract rather than just buying a dark malt extract — the result is more satisfying. Start with 6 to 7 pounds of extract to achieve the desired body and alcohol content.

Irish Red Ale (15-a)

Traditional Irish ales are easy-drinking but full-flavored, malt-accented brews. One of the first Irish brands to hit the American market was George Killian Lett's Irish Ale. Unfortunately, when the Coors Brewing Company bought the label and began to produce it in the United States, it lost most of its original character — in fact, it isn't even brewed as an ale anymore. Due to its popularity, though, numerous red beers are produced throughout the U.S. in an effort to capitalize on the success of Killian's.

Flavor profile: Irish red ales are amber-to-deep-copper/red in color (thus their name). This style's caramel malt flavor and sweetness sometimes has a buttered-toast or toffee quality. Irish ales often exhibit a light taste of roasted malt, which lends a characteristic dryness to the finish. And not a shamrock in sight . . .

OG/FG:	1.036–1.046/1.010–1.014
ABV:	3.8–5.0%
IBUs:	18–28
SRM:	9–14

Commercial examples: Smithwick's Irish Ale, Ireland; O'Hara's Irish Red Ale, Ireland

Beginner suggestions: You can use either pale extract or amber-hopped extract — both finish within the generous color range for this style. If you choose the pale extract, try getting a little *kettle caramelization* by vigorously boiling the wort an extra half hour or more. If you want your red ale less Irish and more American, add 1 ounce of your favorite American hop to the kettle in the last 10 minutes of the boil.

Irish Stout (15-b)

Stout is a hearty, top-fermented beer strongly associated with the British Isles and Ireland; it's known for its opaque-black appearance and roasty flavors. The world of beer boasts six different styles of stout.

The terms *stout,* as it applies to beer, was first attached to the porter style. A bigger-bodied, more-robust porter was aptly described as being a *stout porter.* Exactly when a clear distinction was made between stout porters and the separate stout style that brewers recognize today is uncertain. Stout appears to have come into its own in the early 1800s, following the invention of a device for roasting barley and creating black malts — two of the hallmark ingredients for making stout.

Guinness is probably the standard-bearer for the stout style throughout the world, but it's more correctly known as a classic dry stout, or Irish-style stout. The classic Irish-style dry stout is the lightest and driest of the stout styles, as well as the least alcoholic. The classic Irish-style dry stout is defined by the roastiness of the unmalted roasted barley and the charred flavor of the black malt in the recipe.

Flavor profile: Opaque black. No hop flavor or aroma. Roasted barley character is expected. Slight malt sweetness or a caramel malt character is okay. Medium to high hop bitterness with a slight acidity or sourness is possible. A very low diacetyl level is okay. Medium-bodied.

OG/FG:	1.036–1.044/1.007–1.011
ABV:	3.8–5.0
IBUs:	25–45
SRM:	25–40

Commercial examples: Guinness Stout, Ireland; Murphy's Stout, Ireland

Beginner suggestions: Try producing the color and flavor in your stout by using specialty grains (dark caramel, chocolate malt, black malt, roasted barley) rather than by buying a dark malt extract — the result is more satisfying.

Oatmeal Stout (16-b)

Stout is a hearty, top-fermented beer strongly associated with the British Isles and Ireland; it's known for its opaque-black appearance and roasty flavors. The world of beer boasts six different styles of stout.

The term *stout,* as it applies to beer, was first attached to the porter style. A bigger-bodied, more robust porter was aptly described as being a *stout porter.* Exactly when a clear distinction was made between stout porters and the separate stout style that brewers recognize today is uncertain. Stout appears to have come into its own in the early 1800s, following the invention of a device for roasting barley and creating black malts — two of the hallmark ingredients for making stout.

Oatmeal stout is very similar to the Irish/dry style, but with a notably smoother and denser mouthfeel. Oats in the grist add very little in the way of aroma or flavor; they are there mostly to fill out the feel of the beer on the palate.

Flavor profile: Opaque black. No hop flavor or aroma. Roasted barley character is expected. Slight malt sweetness or a caramel malt character is okay. Medium to high hop bitterness. A very low diacetyl level is okay. Medium bodied with smooth, silky mouthfeel.

OG/FG:	1.045–1.065/1.010–1.018
ABV:	4.2–5.9
IBUs:	25–40
SRM:	22–40

Commercial examples: Samuel Smith Oatmeal Stout, England; McAuslan St-Ambroise Oatmeal Stout, Canada

Beginner suggestions: Try producing the color and flavor in your stout by using specialty grains (dark caramel, chocolate malt, black malt, roasted barley) rather than by buying a dark malt extract — the result is more satisfying. Add a cup of flaked oats or the equivalent amount of regular oatmeal to your brewpot along with your other specialty grains.

Old Ale (17-b)

English strong ale was the standard drinking-man's beer in the 1600s and 1700s. Lack of refrigeration and clean storage conditions called for a beer of considerable gravity and strength to prevail against bacterial contamination. Because these beers were particularly robust, high hopping rates were necessary to offset the cloying nature of the malt. The resulting beer had natural hop-preservative resins and a high alcohol content to stave off any contamination that was likely to occur during the long aging process. This extended aging period is the reason these brews are called old ales.

Old ales are full-bodied brews with a nutty, grainy malt character balanced by a fair amount of hop bitterness. Vigorous fermentations give the beer a noticeable fruity, estery nose resulting in a robust, complex, and slightly *vinous* (wine-like) beer overall.

Flavor profile: Light to deep amber. Fruitiness and esters are high; hop flavor and aroma can be assertive. Medium- to full-bodied. Very malty, with a fair amount of diacetyl evident. Alcoholic strength is noticeable. Historical versions may even contain low levels of acidity.

OG/FG:	1.055–1.088/1.015–1.022
ABV:	5.5–9.0+
IBUs:	30–60+
SRM:	10–22+

Commercial examples: Gale's Prize Old Ale, England; Theakston's Old Peculier, England

Beginner suggestions: Old ales require a fair amount of fermentable material in the recipe — try starting with 7 pounds of amber extract. Long, warm fermentations produce an abundance of fruity and alcoholic aroma, flavor, and mouthfeel. Two to three ounces of English bittering hops are necessary to maintain flavor balance.

Weizenbier (10-a)

Weizenbier is a malty, spritzy ale made by replacing much of the barley used in regular beers with a large portion of wheat malt. These German-style wheat beers have unique fruity and phenolic aromas and flavors that result from the specific strains of yeast used to ferment them. German-style wheat beers are alternatively known as *Weizenbier* or *Weissbier*. Of these two designations, *Weizen* (meaning *wheat*) is more correct than *Weiss* (which means *white*); these beers are typically a rich, golden color.

A traditional German Weizenbier must use at least 50 percent malted wheat, with the rest of the grist being malted barley. Weizenbier clones made elsewhere use anywhere between 25 and 75 percent wheat malt, depending on the whims of the brewer. Traditional Weizenbiers also have a dose of yeast added at bottling time for a secondary fermentation in the bottle. This state is called *Hefe-weizen* (*yeast-wheat*). Homebrewed wheat beer, if bottle-conditioned (that is, primed with sugar), is automatically a Hefe-weizen. Commercially, filtered *kristalklar* (*crystal-clear*) Weizenbier is also widely available.

Flavor profile: Pale to golden. Very fruity and estery. Low hop flavor and aroma. Clove and banana aroma and flavor are evident; vanilla, nutmeg, smoke, and cinnamon-like phenolics are also acceptable. No diacetyl. Low bitterness levels accompany a mild sourness. Light- to medium-bodied and highly effervescent. This style may come packaged with or without yeast in the bottle (Hefe-weizen or *kristalklar*).

OG/FG: 1.044–1.053/1.008–1.014

ABV: 4.3–5.6

IBUs: 8–15

SRM: 2–6

Commercial examples: Schneider Weisse, Germany; Hacker-Pschorr Weisse, Germany

Beginner suggestions: You can easily make a wheat-flavored beer of sorts by using wheat malt extract. The traditional German-style Weizen, however, gets most of its character from the yeast. You can get the fruity, estery, clovey, spicy aromas and flavors typical of true Bavarian Weizenbier only by using true Weizen yeast strains.

Weizenbock (10-c)

As with other beer styles, you can find many variations on the wheat beer theme. One such variation is Weizenbock. Just as bock beer is a malty-rich beer with a moderately higher alcohol content than your average lager beer, Weizenbock is a malty-rich German wheat beer brewed to a higher strength and increased alcohol content. It's basically a Weizenbier that's been supercharged.

Flavor profile: Deep copper to brown. Low hop flavor and aroma, although banana, cloves, and other phenolics may be present. Roasted malt and chocolate flavors are evident but no diacetyl. Medium-bodied.

OG/FG:	1.044–1.056/1.010–1.014
ABV:	4.3–5.6
IBUs:	10–18
SRM:	14–23

Commercial example: Weihenstephaner Hefeweissbier Dunkel, Germany; Franziskaner Dunkel Hefe-Weiss, Germany

Beginner suggestions: You can easily copy this beer style by starting with 5 to 6 pounds of wheat malt extract; add to that 0.5 pounds of chocolate malt steeped and strained into the brewpot. Keep in mind that traditional German-style Weizenbier gets most of its character from the yeast. You can get the fruity, estery, clovey, spicy aromas and flavors typical of true Bavarian Weizenbier only by using true Weizen yeast strains.

IN THIS CHAPTER

» Exploring intermediate beer styles

» Brewing these beers on your own

» Making the brewing process easier with tips and suggestions

Chapter 18 Intermediate Recipes

This chapter provides recipes for a wide variety of beer styles, most of which require the additional ingredients, equipment, and processes that land them in the intermediate level of homebrewing.

You'll likely notice that all of them are ales for the simple fact that lagers are more difficult to produce at home (you'll see those in Chapter 19). There are at least four recipes in this chapter that could be rendered as lagers as well as ales: American wheat beer, smoked beer, fruit beer, and spiced beer.

Ales, by traditional definition, are beers fermented with top-fermenting yeast at warm (ambient) temperatures for relatively short periods of time. Ales are primarily associated with England and Ireland, but you can find them in a wide variety of styles in most brewing nations such as Australia, Belgium, Canada, and the United States.

Also note that, although I've compiled these recipes, I didn't create all of them and have little control over how much or how little information they provide.

American Barley Wine (22-c)

The term *barley wine* sounds more like something you make from grapes, and yet its name mentions a grain. What's up with that? Well, the name implies a beverage made from barley but that has the strength and character of wine; you soon see that the name is apropos.

American barley wine is an American take on the classic English style of old ale. With its huge body, almost-overwhelming malty flavor, and the kick of a mule, barley wine isn't for the weak-kneed. These complex and alcoholic brews pack a one-two punch of flavor and strength because of the high level of fermentable sugars, or *gravity*. Barley wine has more than twice the strength of a European pilsner. The resulting alcohol content is around 9 to 12 percent by volume. Needless to say, these potent potables aren't intended for summer consumption. In fact, brewers usually produce barley wine in limited quantities, often earmarked for holiday celebrations or as a winter tipple. And because of its alcoholic strength and high terminal gravities, you can store barley wine for future consumption.

The color range for barley wine is forgiving, usually starting out around copper and working its way into the deep ambers. The nose is pungent — an olfactory cornucopia of fruits and malt aromas, ethanol, and hop bouquet. Correctly balancing the bold, malty character of this style requires copious amounts of hop bittering, further intimidating the novice beer drinker. The finish is always long, complex, and warming in the throat.

Flavor profile: Copper to medium-brown and medium- to full-bodied. Barley wines are usually malty sweet, fruity, and estery, with medium to high bitterness levels. Hop aroma and taste can be anywhere from low to high. Expect to taste the alcohol. Low to medium diacetyl is acceptable.

OG/FG:	1.080–1.120+/1.016–1.030+
ABV:	8.0–12.0+
IBUs:	50 - 100
SRM:	9–18

Commercial examples: Sierra Nevada Bigfoot, California; Anchor Old Foghorn, California

Boobs Barley Wine

AWARD WON: 2ND PLACE, AHA NATIONALS

BREWER: CHUCK BOYCE

Malt extract:	12 pounds light malt extract
Specialty grain:	3 pounds Klages malt, 0.5 pounds dextrin malt, 0.5 pounds crystal malt
Bittering hops:	9 ounces Bullion (90 mins.)
Flavoring hops:	1.5 ounces Fuggles (15 mins.)
Finishing hops:	1.5 ounces Cascade (2 mins.)
Yeast:	Wyeast #1056
Primary:	4 weeks at 75° Fahrenheit
Secondary:	2 weeks at 65° Fahrenheit

Imperial Stout (20-c)

Another stout style, rarer than most, is strongly associated with pre-Bolshevik Russia. British brewers found favor among the czarist rulers of Russia, particularly for their brand of stout. Unfortunately, the English-made stout didn't travel well to St. Petersburg and other points east. To compensate for the short shelf-life of their beer, British brewers raised the gravity and increased the hop content. Sure enough, the Russian rulers deeply admired this complex high-alcohol brew. The style came to be known as Russian imperial stout, but now it's mostly known as just imperial stout.

The Americanized version is even more complex than the British antecedent: darker, richer, hoppier, and more highly alcoholic. This will get the Russkies' attention!

Flavor profile: Dark copper to very black. High level of fruity esters. Hop bitterness flavor and aroma medium to high. Rich and complex maltiness with a chewy texture; roasty, fruity, and bittersweet. Full-bodied with evident alcohol strength.

OG/FG:	1.075–1.115+/1.018–1.030+
ABV:	8.0–12.0+
IBUs:	50–90+
SRM:	30–40

Commercial examples: Bell's Expedition Stout, Michigan; North Coast Old Rasputin, California

Fountainhead Black Magic

AWARD WON: 1ST PLACE, AHA NATIONALS

BREWER: RANDE REED

Malt extract:	6.6 pounds Munton and Fison Old Ale kit, 5 pounds Munton and Fison light DME
Specialty grain:	12 ounces black patent malt, 12 ounces roasted barley, 12 ounces 40-L caramel malt
Bittering hops:	3 ounces Nugget (60 mins.)
Flavoring hops:	1 ounce Nugget (10 mins.)
Yeast:	Red Star Dry Champagne
Primary:	7 weeks at 70° Fahrenheit
Secondary:	6 weeks at 70° Fahrenheit

American IPA (21-a)

One particular substyle of English-style pale ale is known as *India pale ale*, or *IPA* for short. American IPA is a craft beer interpretation of this historical style, and it's essentially the style that put the American craft beer industry on the map (you can do a little bit of time traveling by simply trying Anchor Liberty Ale, considered by many to be the first-ever beer of its kind, brewed way back in 1975). Pretty soon it seemed like every craft brewer in the U.S. had a version of IPA on offer, often as its flagship brand.

The basic, simple differences between British IPAs and American IPAs are the malts, hops, and yeasts used (British ingredients vs. American ingredients). British IPAs tend to be fruitier, whereas American IPAs have cleaner fermentations and are more obviously hoppy.

Contrary to popular beer lore, IPA did not originate from shipments of beer being shipped to India from Britain, nor is oak character considered part and parcel of the style (though oaked IPAs are welcome in the wood-aged categories in competitions).

Flavor profile: A considerably hoppy and rather bitter ale that showcases American-grown hop varieties. Hop aroma is prominent, often smelling of pine and citrus fruit. Hop flavor is medium to high, and bitterness can be aggressive. Malt flavor is low to medium, often slightly grainy, and often with a toasty edge. Low fermentation characteristics; slight fruitiness can be expected, but diacetyl is not appropriate.

OG/FG: 1.056–1.070/1.008–1.014

ABV: 5.5–7.5

IBUs: 40–70

SRM: 6–14

Commercial example: Bell's Two-Hearted Ale, Michigan; Stone IPA, California

Exchequer India Pale Ale

BREWER: MARTY NACHEL

Malt extract:	6.6 pounds Northwestern extract
Specialty Grain:	1 pound 40-L crystal malt, ⅛ pound roast malt
Bittering hops:	1.5 ounces Centennial (60 mins.)
Finishing hops:	1 ounce Cascade (10 mins.)
Dry hop:	1 ounce Simcoe
Yeast:	Wyeast #1098
Misc. flavoring ingredients:	8 ounces malto-dextrin powder
Primary:	1 week at 65° Fahrenheit
Secondary:	2 weeks at 65° Fahrenheit

TYPICAL/UNUSUAL PROCEDURES USED: Add 1 ounce of Cascade hops and malto-dextrin powder to secondary fermenter.

American Pale Ale (18-b)

Americans have been brewing ale since the first wave of colonists reached the shores of the New World in the 1600s. Despite the onslaught of lager-brewing in the mid-1800s and the subsequent dominance of this country's beer market by bottom-fermenting breweries, American ale-brewing has persevered. With the recent upsurge in small-batch brewing, American ales have been leading the craft-brewing renaissance.

American-style ale is characterized by a copper color and medium maltiness. It's lighter in color and body compared to its English counterpart, but American pale ales are rather aggressively bittered with American-grown hop varieties from the Pacific Northwest.

Flavor profile: Pale to deep amber to copper. These beers offer medium hop flavor and aroma and are fruity and estery. Expect low to medium maltiness and high hop bitterness, with a bit of diacetyl and low caramel flavor. Medium-bodied.

OG/FG:	1.045–1.060/1.010–1.015
ABV:	4.5–6.2
IBUs:	30–50
SRM:	5–10

Commercial examples: Sierra Nevada Pale Ale, California; Great Lakes Burning River, Ohio

Give Me Liberty, or . . . Else

BREWER: MARTY NACHEL

Malt extract:	6 pounds Northwestern light
Specialty grain:	2 pounds 40-L crystal malt
Bittering hops:	1 ounce Northern Brewer (60 mins.)
Flavoring hops:	1 ounce Northern Brewer (30 mins.), 1 ounce Spalt (15 mins.)
Finishing hops:	1 ounce Cascade (5 mins.)
Dry hop:	1 ounce Cascade
Yeast:	Wyeast #2112
Primary:	7 days at 65° Fahrenheit
Secondary:	21 days at 65° Fahrenheit

American Wheat Beer (1-d)

American wheat beers, although their ingredient profile may mirror the traditional German-style Weizen, generally contain a lower percentage of wheat malt (15 to 50 percent) and are typically fermented with a simple top-fermenting (ale)

yeast. American wheat beers, therefore, lack the clovey phenolics, bubblegum, banana, and spicy flavors and aromatics of traditional German Weizenbiers.

Flavor profile: Golden to light amber. Low to medium fruitiness and esters; no phenolic character is evident. Malt and hop aroma and flavor are subdued; low to medium bitterness is expected. Low diacetyl is okay. Light- to medium-bodied.

OG/FG:	1.040–1.055/1.008–1.013
ABV:	4.0–5.5
IBUs:	15–30
SRM:	3–6

Commercial examples: Bell's Oberon, Michigan; Goose Island 312 Urban Wheat Ale, Illinois

How Wheat It Is!

AWARD WON: 2ND PLACE, CHICAGO BEER SOCIETY

BREWER: MARTY NACHEL

Malt extract:	6 pounds Northwestern wheat
Specialty grain:	½ pound 20-L crystal malt
Bittering hops:	2 ounces Hallertauer
Finishing hops:	0.5 ounces Hallertauer
Yeast:	Wyeast #1056
Primary:	5 days at 65° Fahrenheit
Secondary:	14 days at 65° Fahrenheit

Belgian Dubbel (26-b)

The word *Trappist*, which often precedes the name of this Belgian dubbel, doesn't so much denote a type of beer as it does a type of brewery. A Trappist beer is brewed at one of the fourteen or so Trappist abbey breweries that exist in the world. Any secular brewer who markets an imitation of one of these breweries' products must use the term *abbey beer* (also *Abdij in Flemish and Abt in French).*

Although the beers made by these Cistercian monks vary in style, they all feature high gravities, warm fermentations, top fermenting yeasts, and bottle-conditioning. Some of these monastic brewers add candi sugar to the brew during the boiling process, resulting in rather high-octane libations. The high fermentation temperatures produce a full range of fruity and estery aromas and flavors.

Some Trappist breweries produce ales in three graduated strengths. The mild single is typically just for the monks' personal consumption; the dark dubbel is a stronger version of the single; and the golden tripel is the most potent (which leads me to wonder what a home run would taste like). As you might expect, secular breweries also brew their own versions of these popular ales.

Because much of the Trappist beers' characters are a result of the yeast, brewers seeking to replicate the style correctly must obtain these strains. Homebrewers have easy access to these yeast strains through the larger and well-established yeast producing companies.

Flavor profile: Dark amber to brown. The aroma is a combination of sweet, malty, and nutty, with low levels of fruity esters in the background. Medium- to full-bodied, with mild bitterness and very low diacetyl.

OG/FG:	1.062–1.075/1.010–1.018
ABV:	6.0–7.6
IBUs:	15–25
SRM:	10–17

Commercial examples: Affligem Dubbel, Belgium; La Trappe Dubbel, Netherlands

Dubbel Trubbel

BREWER: MARTY NACHEL

Malt extract:	7 pounds liquid malt extract
Specialty grain:	1 pound Special "B" 221 L crystal malt, 0.5 pound Belgian CaraVienne malt, 0.5 pound biscuit malt
Bittering hops:	1 ounce Styrian Goldings (60 mins.)
Flavoring hops:	0.5 ounce Saaz (40 mins.)
Yeast:	Wyeast #1214
Misc. fermentable ingredients:	1 pound brown sugar
Primary:	7 days at 65° Fahrenheit
Secondary:	12 days at 55° Fahrenheit

Belgian IPA (21-b)

This beer style is relatively new and somewhat unique, tracing its genesis to the early 2000s. It's basically a cross between an IPA and a Belgian pale ale or tripel; it exudes the spiciness of Belgian yeast along with the aggressive bitterness of (mostly European) hops. American brewers arrived at the style simply by fermenting their IPAs with a traditional Belgian yeast, whereas Belgian brewers just hopped up their pale ales and tripels. The result is the best of both worlds — a complex fruity, spicy, golden beer with firm bittering and a dryish finish.

Flavor profile: Initial flavor is spicy and estery, with occasional banana and citrusy fruit flavors. Malt flavor is light and grainy-sweet. Bitterness is fairly high and may be accentuated by spicy yeast-derived flavors. The finish is generally medium-dry and carbonation levels tend to be on the high side.

OG/FG:	1.058–1.080 / 1.008–1.016
ABV:	6.2–9.5
IBUs:	50–100
SRM:	5–8

Commercial examples: Brasserie d'Achouffe Houblon Chouffe, Belgium; Poperings Hommel Bier, Belgium

Belgian Abbey

BREWER: NORTHWESTERN EXTRACT CO.

Malt extract:	9.3 pounds Northwestern Gold
Specialty grain:	10 ounces CaraMunich malt
Bittering hops:	2 ounces Mount Hood (60 mins.)
Finishing hops:	0.5 ounces Hersbrucker (5 mins.)
Yeast:	Wyeast #1098, Wyeast #1214
Primary:	2 weeks (temperature not given)
Secondary:	4 weeks (temperature not given)

TYPICAL/UNUSUAL PROCEDURES USED: Pitch the first yeast in the primary fermenter and the second yeast in the secondary fermenter.

Belgian Tripel (26-c)

The word *Trappist*, which often precedes the name of this Belgian tripel, doesn't so much denote a type of beer as it does a type of brewery. A Trappist beer is brewed at one of only fourteen Trappist breweries that exist in the world Any secular brewer who markets an imitation of one of these breweries' products must use the term *abbey beer* (also *Abdij, Abt*).

Although the beers made by these Cistercian monks vary in style, they all feature high gravities, warm fermentations, top fermenting yeasts, and bottle-conditioning. Some of these monastic brewers add candi sugar to the brew during the boiling process, resulting in rather high-octane libations. The high fermentation temperatures produce a full range of fruity and estery aromas and flavors.

Some Trappist breweries produce ales in three graduated strengths. The mild single is just for the monks' personal consumption; the dark dubbel is a stronger version of the single; and the golden tripel is the most potent. The elusive quadrupel is the darkest and rarest of them all. As you might expect, secular breweries also brew their own versions of these popular ales.

Because much of the Trappist beers' characters are a result of the yeast, brewers looking to replicate the style correctly must obtain these strains.

Flavor profile: Light, pale gold. Light malty and hoppy aroma. Banana esters and flavors are expected. The hop/malt balance is neutral, but the finish may be sweet. Medium to full body. Alcohol content is high but shouldn't be tasted. Spicy and phenolic flavors may be evident.

OG/FG:	1.075–1.085/1.008–1.014
ABV:	7.5–9.0
IBUs:	20–40
SRM:	4.5–7

Commercial examples: Westmalle Tripel, Belgium; Unibroue La Fin du Monde, Canada (this is a secular "abbey" version of this style)

Tripel Play

BREWER: MARTY NACHEL

Malt extract:	7 pounds pale liquid malt extract
Specialty grain:	0.5 pounds Belgian aromatic malt, 0.5 pounds Belgian CaraVienne malt
Bittering hops:	1 ounce Hallertau (60 mins.)
Flavoring hops:	0.5 ounces Saaz (40 mins.)
Yeast:	Wyeast #1214
Misc. fermentable ingredients:	0.5 pounds invert sugar, 0.5 pounds light honey
Fining agent/ clarifier:	1 teaspoon Irish moss
Primary:	7 days at 65° Fahrenheit
Secondary:	12 days at 55° Fahrenheit

TYPICAL/UNUSUAL PROCEDURES USED: See the sidebar "Making invert sugar syrup" in Chapter 8.

Black IPA (21-b)

Black IPAs are a variant of American IPA. According to sources, this beer style was first commercially produced in Vermont around 1990. It was later popularized in the Pacific Northwest (where it was known locally as *Cascadian dark ale*) and in Southern California starting in the early-mid 2000s. Black IPAs seemed to peak in popularity in the early 2010s before fading considerably.

Black IPAs offer the palate dryness, hop-forward balance, and flavor characteristics of an American IPA, but are darker in color. Dark malts add a gentle and supportive flavor, but not a strongly roasted or burnt character.

The balance and overall impression is of an American or double IPA with restrained roast similar to the type found in Schwarzbier. They are not as rich and roasty as the American stout and porter styles; instead, they have less body and increased smoothness and drinkability.

Flavor profile: Medium to high hop flavor, low to medium malt flavor, with restrained chocolate or coffee notes, but not burnt or ashy. The roasty notes should not clash with the hops. Light caramel or toffee may be experienced. Medium-high to very high bitterness. Dry to slightly off-dry finish, with a bitter but not harsh aftertaste.

OG/FG:	1.050–1.085/1.010–1.018
ABV:	5.5–9.0
IBUs:	50–90
SRM:	25–40

Commercial examples: 21st Amendment Back in Black, California; Stone Sublimely Self-Righteous Black IPA, California

Juxtaposed

BREWER: STEVE THANOS

Base grain:	9 pounds pale malt extract (LME), 2 pounds Munich malt extract (LME)
Specialty grain:	12 ounces chocolate wheat, 8 ounces Carafa Special III
Bittering hops:	1 ounce Columbus (60 mins.)
Flavoring hops:	1 ounce Citra (15 mins.), 1 ounce Citra (5 mins.), 3 ounces Citra (at flame-out, 0 mins.), 3 ounces Citra (dry hop 5 days)
Yeast:	Imperial Yeast Citrus A20
Water treatment:	2 teaspoons gypsum, 1 teaspoon calcium chloride
Primary:	3 weeks at 65° Fahrenheit

TYPICAL/UNUSUAL PROCEDURES USED: Perform a single step infusion mash at 154° Fahrenheit for 1 hour.

Dark Mild (13-a)

Dark mild is a darker, low-gravity, malt-focused British session ale readily suited to drinking in quantity. It is refreshing yet flavorful for its (low) strength, with a wide range of dark malt or dark sugar character.

Most are low-gravity session beers around 3.2 percent alcohol, although some versions may be made in the stronger (greater than 4 percent) range for export, festivals, seasonal, or special occasions. These are generally served on cask because session-strength bottled versions don't often travel well. A wide range of interpretations are possible.

Historically, the term *mild* simply described an un-aged beer, and could be used as an adjective to distinguish between aged or more highly hopped beers. Modern milds trace their roots to the weaker ales of the 1800s, which started to get darker in the 1880s, but it was only after World War I that they become dark brown. The term *mild* is currently somewhat out of favor with consumers, and many breweries no longer use it — or brew it.

Flavor profile: Generally, a malty beer, although possibly with a wide range of malt- and yeast-based flavors (e.g., malty, sweet, caramel, toffee, toast, nutty, chocolate, coffee, roast, fruit, licorice, plum, raisin) over a bready, biscuity, or toasty base. Can finish sweet to dry. Versions with darker malts may have a dry, roasted finish. Low to moderate bitterness, enough to provide some balance but not enough to overpower the malt in the balance. Moderate fruity esters and low hop flavor is typical.

OG/FG:	1.030–1.038/1.008–1.013
ABV:	3.0–3.8
IBUs:	10–25
SRM:	14–25

Commercial examples: Greene King XX Mild, England; Theakston Traditional Mild, England

Pointon's Proper English Mild

AWARD WON: SILVER MEDAL, 2012 GABF PRO AM

BREWER: SCOTT POINTON

Malt extract:	4.25 pounds light DME
Specialty grain:	9 ounces English crystal malt (65 L), 7 ounces English dark crystal malt (121 L), 4 ounces pale chocolate malt (215 L), 4 ounces of Carafoam malt (2 L), 1 ounce black patent malt (525 L)
Bittering hops:	1.5 ounces Fuggles (60 mins.)
Flavoring hops:	None
Finishing hops:	None
Yeast:	Wyeast #1318
Water treatment:	Use R/O water with no other treatment
Fining agent:	Whirlflock tablet
Primary:	1 week at 70° Fahrenheit
Secondary:	None

Dunkelweizen (10-b)

As with other beer styles, you can find many variations on the wheat-beer theme. One such variation is Dunkelweizen. Meaning *dark wheat*, this style is to regular Weizen what Munich Dunkel is to Munich Helles (see Chapter 19). Plainly stated, this style is just a Weizen beer that's darkened and imbued with a mild chocolatey-caramelly flavor by the use of lightly roasted crystal or Munich malts.

Flavor profile: Deep copper to brown. Low hop flavor and aroma, although banana, cloves, and other phenolics may be present. Roasted malt and chocolate flavors are evident but no diacetyl. Medium-bodied.

OG/FG:	1.044–1.057/1.008–1.014
ABV:	4.3–5.6
IBUs:	10–18
SRM:	14–23

Commercial example: Hopf Dunkle Weisse, Germany; Franziskaner Hefe-Weisse Dunkel, Germany

Slam Dunkel

BREWER: MARTY NACHEL

Malt extract:	6 pounds Northwestern wheat extract, 1 pound light DME
Specialty grain:	1 pound 20-L crystal malt, 0.5 pounds chocolate malt
Bittering hops:	1.5 ounces Northern Brewer (60 mins.)
Flavoring hops:	0.5 ounces Hallertauer (30 mins.)
Finishing hops:	0.5 ounces Hallertauer (5 mins.)
Yeast:	Wyeast #3068
Primary:	7 days at 60° Fahrenheit
Secondary:	14 days at 60° Fahrenheit

English IPA (12-c)

One particular substyle of English-style pale ale is known as India pale ale, or IPA for short. The beer ostensibly got its name from Britain's colonial presence in India during the 1700s and 1800s. The name *India pale ale* was first applied to this style of beer around 1830 when British brewer George Hodgson's IPA dominated the market.

The popularity of the style declined over time and the IPA style nearly disappeared altogether in the late twentieth century. The style experienced a resurgence in the 1980s when American craft brewers began brewing their well-hopped versions of the British base beer, and the rest, as they say, is history.

Flavor profile: Golden to deep amber. Very fruity and estery. Medium maltiness with moderate hop bitterness and low diacetyl. Hop flavor and aroma are medium to high. Alcoholic strength is often evident. Medium-bodied.

OG/FG:	1.050–1.070/1.010–1.015
ABV:	5.0–7.5
IBUs:	40–60
SRM:	6–14

Commercial examples: Samuel Smith India Ale, England; Fuller's India Pale Ale, England

Exchequer India Pale Ale

BREWER: MARTY NACHEL

Malt extract:	6.6 pounds Northwestern extract
Specialty grain:	1 pound 40-L crystal malt, ⅛ pound toasted malt
Bittering hops:	1.5 ounces Northern Brewers (60 mins.)
Finishing hops:	1 ounce Kent Goldings (10 mins.)
Dry hop:	1 ounce Fuggles
Yeast:	Wyeast #1098
Misc. flavoring ingredients:	8 ounces maltodextrin powder
Primary:	1 week at 65° Fahrenheit
Secondary:	2 weeks at 65° Fahrenheit

TYPICAL/UNUSUAL PROCEDURES USED: Add 1 ounce of Fuggles hops and maltodextrin powder to secondary fermenter.

Fruit Beer (29-a)

In recent years, fruited beer seems to have become all the rage in the U.S., but European brewers have been making beers with fruit in them for centuries (Belgian-style fruit lambic is one such example.) Today, however, spurred by consumer interest, virtually every beer style known to man comes with a fruit variation.

Homebrewers wanting to emulate their favorite fruit beer styles have the advantage of using fruit extracts and syrups rather than real fruit. These fruit flavors, easily found at well-stocked homebrew supply stores, run the gamut from cherry to blueberry to marionberry (hey, wasn't he the mayor of . . .?)

Keep in mind that "fruit beer" is not so much a beer style as it is a beer category; it's a convenient catch-all for any beer style made with fruit in it. Therefore, it's impossible to neatly sum up how a fruit beer should taste.

Flavor profile: Fruit beers often are made with an anything-goes attitude. In light of this approach, I have no way to accurately describe what you may expect from one of these beers.

OG/FG:	Refer to BJCP base style guidelines
ABV:	Refer to BJCP base style guidelines
IBUs:	Refer to BJCP base style guidelines
SRM:	Refer to BJCP base style guidelines

Commercial examples: Founders Rübæus, Michigan; New Glarus Wisconsin Belgian Red, Wisconsin

Cherry Ale

AWARD WON: 1ST PLACE, AHA NATIONALS

BREWER: DAVID G. HAMMAKER

Malt extract:	6 pounds English pale extract
Bittering hops:	0.5 ounces Bullion (45 mins.)
Finishing hops:	1 ounce Hallertauer (10 mins.)
Yeast:	Red Star Ale (dry)
Misc. flavoring ingredients:	10 pounds sweet cherries
Primary:	2 weeks at 60° Fahrenheit
Secondary:	10 weeks at 60° Fahrenheit

TYPICAL/UNUSUAL PROCEDURES USED: Pour the hot wort over the cherries in the fermenter; top off with cool water and add yeast.

Saison (25-b)

Saisons are a family of refreshing, highly attenuated, hoppy, and fairly bitter Belgian ales with a very dry finish and high carbonation, characterized by a fruity, spicy, sometimes phenolic fermentation profile, and the occasional use of spices for complexity. Several variations in strength and color exist.

This style generally describes the standard-strength pale version, followed by differences for variations in strength and color. Darker versions tend to have more malt character and less apparent hop bitterness, yielding a more balanced presentation. Stronger versions often have more malt flavor, richness, warmth, and body simply due to the higher gravity.

Sourness is totally optional, and if present it's at low to moderate levels, but a saison should not be both sour and bitter at the same time. The high attenuation may make the beer seem more bitter than the IBUs suggest. Pale versions are often more bitter and hoppy than darker versions. Yeast selection often drives the balance of fruity and spicy notes and can change the character significantly; this allows for a range of interpretations.

Saisons are often referred to as *farmhouse ales* in the U.S., but this term is not common in Europe where they are simply part of a larger grouping of artisanal ales. This particular artisanal ale is from Wallonia, the French-speaking part of Belgium. It was originally a "provision" beer — a lower-alcohol product so as to not debilitate farm and field workers — but tavern-strength products also existed. The best known modern saison, Saison Dupont, was first produced in the 1920s.

Flavor profile: A balance of fruity and spicy yeast, hoppy bitterness, and grainy malt with moderate to high bitterness, and a very dry finish. The fruity and spicy aspects are medium-low to medium-high, and hop flavor is low to medium, both with similar character as in the aroma. Malt is low to medium, with a soft, grainy palate. Very high attenuation, never with a sweet or heavy finish. Darker versions will have more malt character, including flavors from the darker malts. Stronger versions will have greater malt intensity and a light alcohol note.

OG/FG:	1.048–1.065/1.002–1.008
ABV:	3.5–5.0% (table-strength saison)
	5.0–7.0 (standard saison)
	7.0–9.5% (super-strength saison)
IBUs:	20–35
SRM:	5–14 (pale saison)
	15–22 (dark saison)

Commercial examples: Saison Dupont, Belgium; Saison de Pipaix, Belgium

Sunday Saison

AWARD WON: GOLD MEDAL 2014 BOSS CHICAGO CUP CHALLENGE

BREWER: SCOTT POINTON

Malt extract:	5 pounds extra light DME, 1 pound golden light LME, 1 pound wheat LME
Specialty grain:	1.5 pounds of cane sugar added with 30 minutes left in the boil
Bittering hops:	1.7 ounces Saaz (60 mins.)
Flavoring hops:	None
Finishing hops:	None
Yeast:	Wyeast #3724
Water treatment:	Use R/O water with no other treatment
Fining agent/ clarifier:	Whirlflock tablet
Primary:	Pitch yeast at 70° Fahrenheit and let it go for a few days (temp will climb into the mid to upper 70s). When fermentation activity starts to lag (around day 3 or 4) move the fermenter to a warmer place to get the fermentation temp up into the 80s. This will help avoid the dreaded Belgian saison yeast "stall." Allow primary fermentation to continue until the gravity is down to 1.010 or less.
Secondary:	None

Spiced, Herb, or Vegetable Beer (30-a)

Although you don't see many herb and spice beers on your local beer retailers' shelves, a few do exist. If homebrewers had their say, many more would be available. The herb-and-spice-beer category is one of the more popular among homebrewers because it presents an almost unlimited number of choices.

Herbs and spice beers may include lemongrass, ginger (what — you've never heard of ginger ale?), cumin, allspice, caraway, mace, pepper, cinnamon, nutmeg, and clove, among myriad others. Some *sage* advice: Take the *thyme* to peruse the spice section of your local supermarket — a *mint*-condition spiced brew may *curry* favor with the beer judges.

Vegetables in beer, on the other hand, are very few and far between — and, to my knowledge, no such thing as a vegetable extract is made for brewing — so you're pretty much limited to pumpkin, beets, and hot peppers here.

Flavor profile: Herb, spice, and vegetable beers are often made with an anything-goes approach. In light of this practice, I have no way to accurately describe what you may expect from one of these beers.

OG/FG:	Refer to BJCP base style guidelines
ABV:	Refer to BJCP base style guidelines
IBUs:	Refer to BJCP base style guidelines
SRM:	Refer to BJCP base style guidelines

Commercial examples: Left Hand Good JuJu, Colorado; Southern Tier Cinnamon Roll Imperial Ale, New York

Wassail While You Work

AWARD WON: 1ST PLACE, DUKES OF ALE SPRING THING

BREWER: MARTY NACHEL

Malt extract:	10 pounds Northwestern light
Specialty grain:	1 pound 40-L crystal malt
Bittering hops:	2 ounces Mount Hood (60 mins.)
Flavoring hops:	1 ounce Northern Brewer (30 mins.)
Finishing hops:	1 ounce Cascade (5 mins.)
Dry hop:	1 ounce Cascade
Yeast:	Pasteur Champagne (dry)
Misc. flavoring ingredients:	2 sticks of cinnamon, 1 teaspoon of cloves
Primary:	11 days at 60° Fahrenheit
Secondary:	25 days at 60° Fahrenheit

Smoked Beer (32-b)

The Franconian city of Bamberg, Germany, is famous for its *Bamberger Rauchbier* (*Bamberg smoke beer*). This style, although very popular in northern Bavaria, is rarely produced elsewhere in the world. Many beers are said to be acquired tastes, but Rauchbier takes that description to a whole new level.

A beer gets its smoked character as a brewer kilns his malt over a wood fire (typically beechwood, but sometimes alder, apple, or cherry) or even a peat fire. The grain retains this smokiness and imparts this quality in the beer as it's mashed. How smoky the resulting beer is depends on how long you leave the malt to smoke and how much of the grain bill consists of smoked malt. The smoked character of the beer varies from one brewer to the next but is often assertive and always noticeable.

But the use of smoked grains isn't limited to making Rauchbier. You can imbue any existing beer style with smoke aroma and flavor just by adding smoked malt to the recipe. The trick to making a good smoked beer, however, is achieving the perfect balance between the malt and the smoke. Porter is one style that seems to be a particularly good host for smoke character. Just remember to sip the beer and not inhale it.

Flavor profile: Dark amber to dark brown. The intensity of the smoke character may be medium to high. You should notice a balance between smokiness and the expected flavor characteristics of the base beer style. Smoky flavors may range from woody to somewhat bacon-like depending on the type of malts used. Peat-smoked malt can add an earthiness to your beer. The balance of underlying beer characteristics and smoke can vary, although the resulting blend should be somewhat balanced and enjoyable. Smoke can add some dryness to the finish.

OG/FG:	Refer to BJCP base beer style guidelines
ABV:	Refer to BJCP base beer style guidelines
IBUs:	Refer to BJCP base beer style guidelines
SRM:	Refer to BJCP base beer style guidelines

Commercial examples: Alaskan Smoked Porter, Alaska; Yazoo Brewing Sue, Tennessee

Smokey the Beer (Smoked Porter)

BREWER: MARTY NACHEL

Malt extract:	6 pounds Northwestern dark extract
Specialty grain:	1 pound 40-L crystal malt, 0.75 pounds chocolate malt, 1 to 2 pounds of quality smoked malt (depending on how much smoke character you want in your beer)
Bittering hops:	2 ounces Northern Brewer (60 mins.)
Flavoring hops:	1 ounce Fuggles (15 mins.)
Yeast:	Wyeast #1028
Primary:	6 days at 65° Fahrenheit
Secondary:	10 days at 65° Fahrenheit

Sweet Stout (16-a)

Sweet stout (alternatively known as London-style or cream stout) is the English counterpoint to the classic Irish-style dry stout. Although you find many similarities between the two, the principal difference is how you achieve their roasted character. The classic Irish-style dry stout is defined by the roastiness of the unmalted roasted barley and black malt, whereas the London-style sweet stout often uses chocolate malt in its place. With regards to the obvious contrast between these stouts' sweet and dry character, the sweet stout has a creamier texture, a slightly higher gravity, and sweetness across the palate resulting from the use of milk sugar (lactose), which beer yeast can't ferment. In some instances, this style is also referred to as milk stout or cream stout.

Flavor profile: Opaque black. No hop flavor or aroma. Sweet maltiness and caramel flavors are evident, and the roasted barley character is mild. Hop bitterness is low. Low diacetyl is okay. Medium- to full-bodied.

OG/FG:	1.044–1.060/1.012–1.024
ABV:	4.0–6.0
IBUs:	20–40
SRM:	30–40+

Commercial examples: Watney's Cream Stout, England; Left Hand Milk Stout, Colorado

Macke's Son Stout

AWARD WON: 1ST PLACE, B.O.S.S. 5TH ANNUAL HOMEBREW COMPETITION

BREWER: MARTY NACHEL

Malt extract:	6 pounds Northwestern light
Specialty grain:	1 pound roasted barley, 1 pound Belgian Special "B" 221-L crystal malt, 0.25 pounds black malt
Bittering hops:	2 ounces Northern Brewer
Flavoring hops:	1 ounce Fuggles
Yeast:	Wyeast #1084
Misc. fermentable ingredients:	12 ounces dark molasses
Misc. flavoring ingredients:	1 pound lactose powder
Primary:	7 days at 60° Fahrenheit
Secondary:	14 days at 65° Fahrenheit

Wee Heavy (17-c)

Strong Scotch ale is — surprise! — the Scottish equivalent of English old ale. The main differences are that strong scotch ales are less aggressively hopped, which contributes to this rounder, maltier character. Low levels of carbonation are also an important characteristic of the style and help maintain a certain softness on the palate.

Strong Scotch ale (or Scots ale) is known as a *wee heavy* and, like most Scottish ales, is categorized by a *Shilling designation*, which corresponds to the higher gravities of these ales. Strong Scotch ales usually start at around 90 Shilling and can go as high as 120 Shilling. Scotch ales are ordered by their Shilling designation in Highland pubs.

Strong Scotch ales share the same flavor characteristics as lighter Scottish ales but to an exaggerated degree. Strong Scotch ales are typically overwhelmingly malty — almost to the point of being cloyingly sweet — and the low hopping rates do little to cut the intense maltiness. Regrettably, the lack of protective hop resins in this beer style also tends to diminish its shelf-life, leaving only the alcohol to fend off the inevitable stale off flavors. Strong Scotch ale is often roused during the fermentation process to keep the yeast active. This practice results in relatively low final gravities and alcohol potentials as high as 8 percent by volume. The use of peat-smoked malt is one of the traits of the finest Scotch whiskies, one that's only occasionally shared between strong Scotch ale and Scotch whisky.

Flavor profile: Deep copper to dark brown. Hop flavor and aroma are very low. Overwhelmingly malty, but clean alcohol flavor balances the malt character. Hop bitterness is low, and diacetyl is medium to high. Full-bodied. Faint smoky character is okay.

OG/FG:	1.070–1.130/1.018–1.040
ABV:	6.5–10.0
IBUs:	17–35
SRM:	14–25

Commercial examples: Orkney Skull Splitter, Scotland; Traquair House Ale, Scotland

A Peek Under the Kilt Ale

AWARD WON: 1ST PLACE, AHA NATIONALS

BREWER: JIM CAMPBELL

Malt extract:	6 pounds light extract, 3.3 pounds amber extract, 1 pound light DME
Specialty grain:	2 pounds crystal malt, 0.5 pounds Munich malt, 0.5 pounds flaked barley, 0.5 pounds wheat malt, 0.25 pounds roasted barley
Bittering hops:	0.75 ounces Chinook (75 mins.), 1 ounce Hallertauer (75 mins.)
Flavoring hops:	1 ounce Cascade (30 mins.),1 ounce Kent Goldings (10 mins.)

Finishing hops:	1 ounce Cascade (5 mins.)
Yeast:	Wyeast #1056
Water treatment:	0.5 teaspoons gypsum, 0.5 teaspoons salt, 0.5 teaspoons ascorbic acid
Fining agent/ clarifier:	0.5 teaspoons Irish moss
Primary:	38 days at 65° Fahrenheit

Witbier (24-a)

This Belgian style of beer is now quite popular in the United States due to the popularity of the eponymous brand, Blue Moon. Because Belgium is a linguistically divided nation, a situation that can cause additional misunderstanding of this style of beer is the fact that in the French-speaking provinces, people call this brew *biere blanche*, and in the Flemish-speaking regions, the same beer is known as *witbier*. Both names refer to the white appearance of the beer. It's not actually white, of course, but it's very pale yellow and often cloudy with sediment, which helps create its white cast. Both the paleness and the cloudiness can be partly attributed to the high percentage (45 percent) of unmalted wheat that goes into the beer. The balance of the grist is pale barley malt.

This style comes from the Brabant town of Hoegaarden, which is known for its wheat-based beers. What sets witbier apart from the other wheat beers of the region is the inclusion of unconventional beer ingredients, such as the rind of the bitter Curaçao orange, the lemony coriander seed, and another secret spice believed to be grain of paradise (also known as alligator seed). The beer is generally hopped with the English Kent hop. After a relatively short and cool fermentation, the beer gets another dose of yeast before being bottled for additional conditioning.

Flavor profile: Hazy pale yellow. Hop flavor and aroma are desirable, but bitterness should be only low to medium. Low to medium fruity esters are typical. Low to medium body. Mild, sweet malt, and spicy character early, finishing on the dry side. Low diacetyl levels are okay.

OG/FG:	1.044–1.052/1.008–1.012
ABV:	4.5–5.5
IBUs:	8–20
SRM:	2–4

Commercial examples: Hoegaarden Witbier, Belgium; Unibroue Blanche de Chambly, Canada

Jealous Wit

BREWER: NORTHWESTERN EXTRACT CO.

Malt extract:	6.6 pounds Northwestern Weizen
Bittering hops:	2 ounces Cascades (5.5 AAU) (50 mins.)
Flavoring hops:	0.5 ounces Styrian Goldings (5.3 AAU) (20 mins.)
Finishing hops:	1 ounce Northern Brewer (7.5 AAU) (10 mins.)
Dry hop:	0.5 ounces Cascades
Yeast:	Wyeast #3944
Misc. fermentable ingredients:	3 pounds clove honey
Misc. flavoring ingredients:	0.5 ounces crushed coriander seed (in secondary fermenter), 0.25 ounces orange peel (in secondary fermenter)
Fining agent/ clarifier:	1.5 tablespoons Irish moss

» Brewing these beers on your own

» Making the brewing process easier with tips and suggestions

Chapter 19
BJCP Beer Style Guidelines and Advanced Recipes

This chapter provides recipes for a wide variety of beer styles, all of which require the additional ingredients, equipment and processes — specifically grain mashing — that means they are in the Advanced stage of homebrewing.

All of the lager beer styles that you didn't see in Chapters 17 and 18 can be found here, along with many of the more complex ale styles and one or two additional hybrid beers.

Lagers, by traditional definition, are beers fermented with bottom-fermenting yeast at cold temperatures for relatively long periods of time. Lagers are strongly associated with Germany and the Czech Republic, along with other brewing nations such as Australia, Canada, Japan, Mexico, and the United States.

Also note that, although I've compiled these recipes, I didn't create all of them and have little control over how much or how little information they provide.

American Lager (1-B)

The pale, American-style premium lager represents the most-produced beer style in the United States, as well as in other countries such as Australia, Canada, Japan, and Mexico that have followed in the footsteps of the American industrial brewers.

American-style lagers, despite their categorical name, are still rather one-dimensional beers compared to those made in Europe and elsewhere. The reasons for this lie largely in the cheaper ingredients used to make them and the treatment of beer in America as a beverage designed for mass consumption. American craft brewers, on the other hand, are producing premium lagers that are more deserving of the name.

Flavor profile: Very pale to golden. No fruitiness, esters, or diacetyl. Low malt aroma and flavor are okay. Low hop flavor or aroma is okay, but low to medium bitterness is expected. Effervescent. Light-bodied.

OG/FG:	1.040–1.050/1.004–1.010
ABV:	4.2–5.3
IBUs:	8–18
SRM:	2–3.5

Commercial examples: Budweiser, US; Miller High Life, US.

Butt-Scratcher

AWARD WON: 1ST PLACE, AHA NATIONALS

BREWER: STEVE DANIEL

Base grain:	4 pounds 2-row malt, 3 pounds 6-row malt
Specialty grain:	1 pound rice
Bittering hops:	1.5 ounces Hallertauer (60 mins.), 1 ounce Cascade (10 mins.)
Yeast:	Wyeast #2308
Primary:	21 days at 50° Fahrenheit
Secondary:	30 days at 32° Fahrenheit

Typical/unusual procedures used: Precook the rice prior to mash. Mash all grains at 151° Fahrenheit for 60 minutes.

Altbier (7-B)

The concept of a German ale has oxymoronic overtones. German brewers are generally recognized as the world leaders in the production of high-quality lager beers, so imagining them creating original ale styles may be difficult. Because neither single yeast-cell isolation nor artificial refrigeration was at anyone's disposal in the early days of brewing, brewers had to work with what they had: top-fermenting yeast strains. Thus, they created the German ale.

One of these ale styles is known as *Altbier.* The style is strongly associated with the city of Düsseldorf, although it also has lesser ties to Münster and Dortmund. The German word *alt,* contrary to popular belief, doesn't mean *ale* but rather *old,* a reference to Old World brewing styles. Modern-day Altbiers are fermented warm, as is common to ale styles, but they're aged cold, as are lagers. The Altbier profile is deep amber to dark brown in color. The hop blend is complex and can differ from one brewery to the next. German hop varieties are typically best, but American domestic varieties suffice.

Flavor profile: Medium to high maltiness. Medium to high bitterness. Very low in hop flavor with no hop aroma. Low fruitiness and esters. Light- to medium-bodied.

OG/FG:	1.044–1.052/1.008–1.014
ABV:	4.3–5.5
IBUs:	25–50
SRM:	9–17

Commercial examples: Pinkus Alt, Germany; Zum Uerige, Germany

League City Alt Part 3

AWARD WON: 1ST PLACE, AHA NATIONALS

BREWERS: STEVE AND CHRISTINA DANIEL

Base grain:	8 pounds 2-row malt, 2 pounds Munich malt
Specialty grain:	2 pounds crystal malt
Bittering hops:	0.75 ounce Perle (90 mins.)
Yeast:	Wyeast #2308
Primary:	3 weeks at 50° Fahrenheit
Secondary:	4 weeks at 32° Fahrenheit

TYPICAL/UNUSUAL PROCEDURES USED: Mash the grains for 1 hour at 152° Fahrenheit.

Belgian Dark Strong Ale (26-D)

As is true of other Belgian ale categories, the Belgian dark strong ale category functions as a catchall — in this case, for darker-colored high-gravity ales that don't fit in with any other Belgian styles. The most notable of the Belgian dark strong ales is the Trappist *quadrupel*, or *quad*, for short.

Flavor profile: Deep amber to coppery brown. Medium-bodied and fairly alcoholic. Low hop flavor and aroma belie the potential for high hop bitterness. Very malty but with an acidic edge.

OG/FG: 1.075–1.110/1.010–1.024

ABV: 8.0–12.0+

IBUs: 20–35

SRM: 12–22

Commercial examples: Abbaye de Rocs Grand Cru, Belgium; Chimay Grande Reserve, Belgium

Brune Dream

AWARD WON: 3RD PLACE, 2007 DAYTON BEERFEST

BREWER: TOM DENNIS

Base grain:	12 pounds pale malt
Specialty grain:	2 pounds Vienna malt, 1 pound Munich malt, 1 pound CaraMunich malt, ¾ pound CaraPils malt, ¼ pound biscuit malt, 1 ounce chocolate malt
Bittering hops:	2.5 ounces Hallertau (60 mins.)
Flavoring hops:	0.75 ounces Hallertau, (10 mins.)
Finishing hops:	0.75 ounces Hallertau, (3 mins.)
Yeast:	WLP 500
Misc. fermentable ingredients:	1 pound corn sugar (dextrose)
Primary:	2 weeks at 75° Fahrenheit
Secondary:	2 weeks at 70° Fahrenheit

TYPICAL/UNUSUAL PROCEDURES USED: Mash at 152° Fahrenheit for 60 minutes. Mash out at 170° Fahrenheit for 10 minutes. Sparge with 170° Fahrenheit water. Boil for 90 minutes.

Berliner Weisse (23-A)

Named for Germany's capitol city but dubbed the "Champagne of the North" by Napolean, Berliner Weisse is a beer style that is both popular and hard to find. It's popular in the United States and hard to find in its home country.

This pale, refreshing, bracingly acidic beer had been a regional specialty of Berlin that almost disappeared altogether. Although it's now made with regularity by craft brewers in the U.S., it's barely recognizable because of all the adjuncts and flavorings thrown in to mask its hallmark acidity. Yes, the Germans do offer a *schuss* (a shot) of *himbeer* (raspberry) or *waldmeister* (woodruff) syrup to soften the beer's acidic palate, but that choice is left to the imbiber; it's never pre-flavored with sugar or fruit.

Flavor profile: Doughy, bready, and sometimes grainy wheat flavor. Clean lactic sourness dominates the palate; a restrained lemony or tart apple fruitiness may be detected.

OG/FG:	1.028–1.032/1.003–1.006
ABV:	2.8–3.8
IBUs:	3–8
SRM:	2–3

Commercial examples: Berliner Kindl Weisse, Germany; Bayerischer Bahnhof Berliner Style Weisse, Germany

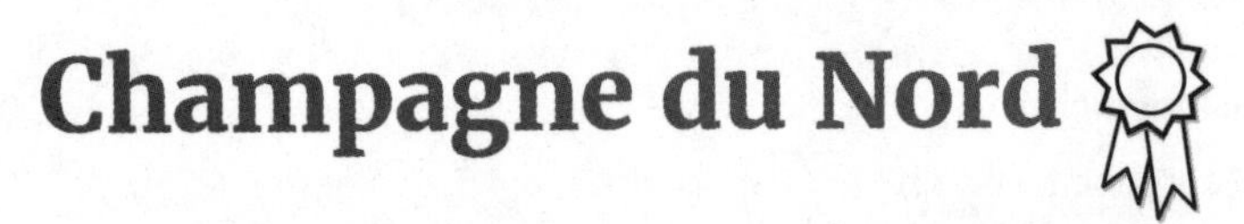

Champagne du Nord

AWARD WON: GOLD MEDAL BRAZILIAN NATIONAL HOMEBREW COMPETITION 2019

BREWER: DOUGLAS MERLO (BRAZIL)

Base grain:	3 pounds pilsner malt, 3 pounds wheat malt
Bittering hops:	2 ounces Hallertau Magnum 12 AA% (60 mins.)
Yeast:	Wyeast #1056 or US-05
Water treatment:	None needed

Primary: 2 days at 65°F, 8 days at 68°F

Secondary: 15 days at 34°F

TYPICAL/UNUSUAL PROCEDURES USED: Perform a single step infusion mash at 148° Fahrenheit for 1 hour. Add lactic acid one day before the bottling until the beer reaches a pH of 3.5

Bock (6-C)

The northern German city of Einbeck was the first center of commercial brewing in the 13th century. Beer from Einbeck became known as *beck beer* (no relation to Beck's beer). Beck beer was famous throughout the Hanseatic League of cities on the North Atlantic but completely unknown in the south of Germany. Beck beer's eventual introduction to the south took place several hundred years later, at the wedding of the Duke of Braunschweig to the daughter of a wealthy aristocrat from the south. The wedding took place in Bavaria in the early 1600s and was attended by nobility from distant states. The Bavarians embraced the beer style from the north and adopted it as the beer of choice in the state-commissioned Hofbrauhaus in Munich. The brew soon became known as *bock beer* — a corruption of *beck* in the Bavarian accent.

Bavarians like to downplay the Einbeck connection in favor of a local interpretation of the beer's origin. *Bock* means *billy goat,* which is the animal associated with the zodiacal sign of Capricorn that rules over the months of December and January, when brewers start making bock beer. Yet another version suggests that the male goat is a symbol of fertility synonymous with the spring season. One thing is for sure — bock beer is *not* what's cleaned out of the bottom of the vats once a year!

Traditional bock beer is a hearty bottom-fermented beer with a generously malty character and burnt toffee dark-grain flavors. It has a creamy mouthfeel and the finish is lengthy and malty sweet. Hop bitterness is subdued — it's just enough to cut the cloying character of the malt. The color can run the spectrum from a deep burnt orange to mahogany. The alcohol content is usually considerable; a true German bock beer must have a minimum alcohol content of 6.5 percent to be called a bock.

Flavor profile: Deep copper to dark brown. No hop aroma, fruitiness, or esters are evident. The malty-sweet character predominates in aroma and flavor, with some toasted chocolate-malt character. Low bitterness, low hop flavor, and low diacetyl are okay. Medium- to full-bodied.

OG/FG:	1.064–1.072/1.013–1.019
ABV:	6.3–7.2
IBUs:	20–27
SRM:	14–22

Commercial example: Spaten Bock, Germany; Einbecker Ur-Bock, Germany

Basically Bock

AWARD WON: 2ND PLACE, AHA NATIONALS

BREWER: PHIL RAHN

Base grain:	10 pounds Klages malt, 4 pounds Munich malt
Specialty grain:	2 pounds crystal malt, 6 ounces chocolate malt
Bittering hops:	1 ounce Perle (60 mins.), 1.5 ounces Hallertauer (40 mins.)
Finishing hops:	0.5 ounces Hallertauer (5 mins.)
Yeast:	Wyeast #2308
Primary:	2 months at 44° Fahrenheit
Secondary:	2 months at 65° Fahrenheit

TYPICAL/UNUSUAL PROCEDURES USED: Mash at 149° Fahrenheit for 2 hours.

Cream Ale (1-C)

Cream ale seems to be an American innovation. These beers are fermented at cold temperatures with either ale yeasts or blends of ale and lager yeasts.

The idea behind cream ale is to produce a pale beer of medium gravity, ferment it with ale yeasts, and age it cold like a lager beer. Although the original cream ales were produced this way, some brewers ferment newer versions with lager yeast or a mixture of ale and lager yeasts.

The cream part of the name has nothing to do with dairy products — presumably, the original brewers of cream ale wanted the name to suggest that this style has a creaminess about it. It doesn't.

Flavor profile: Very pale. Low fruitiness or esters are okay. Low hop flavor or aroma is also okay. Faintly sweet malt character offers a low to medium bitterness. Light-bodied and effervescent.

OG/FG:	1.042–1.055/1.006–1.012
ABV:	4.2–5.6
IBUs:	8–20
SRM:	2–5

Commercial examples: Genesee Cream Ale, New York; Little Kings Cream Ale, Ohio

Colby's Cream Ale

AWARD WON: 1ST PLACE, AHA NATIONALS

BREWER: RODNEY HOWARD

Base grain:	8.5 pounds pale malt
Specialty grain:	0.5 pounds Munich malt, 0.5 pounds flaked rice
Bittering hops:	0.33 ounces Eroica (60 mins.), 0.33 ounces Eroica (45 mins.)
Flavoring hops:	0.33 ounces Galena (30 mins.), 0.33 ounces Galena (15 mins.)
Finishing hops:	1 ounce Fuggles (5 mins.)

Dry hop:	1 ounce Tettnanger
Yeast:	Whitbread Lager (dry)
Primary:	4 weeks at 70° Fahrenheit
Secondary:	3 weeks at 45° Fahrenheit

TYPICAL/UNUSUAL PROCEDURES USED: Mash at 156° Fahrenheit for 45 minutes. After conversion, sparge with 172° Fahrenheit water.

Czech Dark Lager (3-D)

This rich, dark, malty beer from the Czech Republic sports a considerable mouthfeel without being heavy or cloying. It is the Czech version of a dark lager that straddles the Munich Dunkel and Schwarzbier styles, though richer and with more hop character than both.

The U Fleků brewery has been operating in Prague since 1499, and produces the best-known version of this style. Many small, new breweries in the Czech Republic are brewing this style.

Flavor profile: Deep, complex maltiness dominates this beer, abetted by caramel, toffee, toast, nuts, licorice, and dried fruits. Hop bitterness is moderate, but always accedes to the malt.

OG/FG:	1.044–1.060/1.013–1.017
ABV:	4.4–5.8
IBUs:	18–34
SRM:	17–35

Commercial examples: Budweiser Budvar Tmavý Ležák, Czech Republic; Pivovar Březnice Herold, Czech Republic.

Chubby Czecher

AWARD WON: GOLD MEDAL, 2018 BOSS CHICAGO CUP CHALLENGE

BREWER: SCOTT POINTON	
Malt extract:	7 pounds Munich LME
Specialty grain:	5 ounces Carafa II malt (425 L)
Bittering hops:	1.5 ounces Hallertau (60 mins.)
Flavoring hops:	1 ounce Hallertau (20 mins.)
Finishing hops:	None
Yeast:	Wyeast #2487 Hella Bock
Water treatment:	Use R/O water with no other treatment
Fining agent/ clarifier:	Whirlfloc tablet
Primary:	1 week at 50° Fahrenheit, then slowly raise temperature to 60° over 1 week, then lager at 38° for 2 weeks.
Secondary:	None

Czech Pilsner (3-B)

Pilsner beer developed in Plzen, Bohemia, in the mid-1800s. Today, pilsner is the world's most popular style of beer and, more than any other, is what most Americans think of if the subject turns to beer. Small wonder. Most major breweries in the world produce something akin to this style. Unfortunately, most pay little tribute to the original.

The original brand of pilsner beer — still the standard-bearer in the industry — hails from the town of Plzen, which is now part of the Czech Republic. The name of that brand — Pilsner Urquell — even makes note of the fact that it's the original; *Urquell* means "original source." The pilsner name (in all its many forms: *pils*, *pilsner*, *pilsener*, *plzensky*) derives from this Bohemian town, where the brewery was built in 1842. The golden-colored, bottom-fermented beer brewed there quickly became popular in Europe and, eventually, throughout the world.

The style is pale, malty, and well-hopped. The aroma has the unmistakable kiss of the Saaz hop from the Zatec region near Plzen. Caramel notes are often observed, as is a hint of diacetyl rounding out the sweetness and mouthfeel. One key ingredient in a real pilsner beer is the extremely soft water, similar to that pumped from the aquifers under the Urquell brewery.

Flavor profile: Pale to golden. No fruitiness or esters; low to medium hop flavor and aroma are expected. Low to medium maltiness is evident in aroma and flavor, with caramel notes in background. Medium to high bitterness with low diacetyl is okay. Light- to medium-bodied.

OG/FG:	1.044–1.056/1.044–1.060
ABV:	4.2–5.8
IBUs:	30–45
SRM:	3.5–6

Commercial examples: Pilsner Urquell, Czech Republic; Czechvar Pilsner, Czech Republic

Bitter Pill(s)

BREWER: MARTY NACHEL

Base grain:	8 poundspilsner malt
Specialty grain:	0.5 pound CaraVienne malt
Bittering hops:	1 ounce Saaz (60 mins.)
Flavoring hops:	0.5 ounces Saaz (45 mins.)
Finishing hops:	0.5 ounces Saaz (20 mins.)
Yeast:	Wyeast #2278
Fining agent/ clarifier:	1 teaspoon Irish moss
Primary:	6 days at 55° Fahrenheit
Secondary:	16 days at 45° Fahrenheit

TYPICAL/UNUSUAL PROCEDURES USED: Perform a protein rest at 128° Fahrenheit for 15 minutes; an intermediate rest at 145° Fahrenheit for 15 minutes; and a saccharification rest at 152° Fahrenheit for 60 minutes. Sparge with 168° Fahrenheit water.

Doppelbock (9-A)

Oddly enough, a religious order of Italian monks invented Doppelbock. The Order of St. Francis of Paula, cloistered high in the Bavarian Alps, developed this distinctive brew to sustain themselves through periods of fasting. They named this higher-alcohol double bock *Salvator,* in honor of the Savior; thus, Paulaner Salvator was born. In reverence to the original, all subsequent German Doppelbocks are given names that end in *-ator.* Most American microbrewers continue the tradition of using the *-ator* suffix, making Doppelbocks easy to spot on a beer list or menu.

Flavor profile: Amber to dark brown. Slight fruitiness and esters are expected but no hop aroma. The malty sweetness of this beer is evident in the aroma and flavor and may be intense. Low bitterness, low hop flavor, and low diacetyl are okay. High alcohol flavor may be present. Very full body.

OG/FG:	1.072–1.112/1.016–1.024
ABV:	7.0–10.0+
IBUs:	16–26
SRM:	6–25

Commercial examples: Paulaner Salvator, Germany; Augustiner Maximator, Germany

Scintillator

AWARD WON: 1ST PLACE, AHA NATIONALS

BREWER: STEVE DEMPSEY

Malt extract:	3.3 lbs. BME Munich Gold, 1 pound light DME
Base grain:	7 pounds Munich malt
Specialty grain:	2 pounds 20-L crystal malt
Bittering hops:	1.25 ounces Hallertauer (4.1 AAU)
Flavoring hops:	1 ounce Tettnanger (3.8 AAU)
Yeast:	Wyeast #2308

Water treatment:	0.33 teaspoon gypsum, 1.66 teaspoons calcium carbonate, 0.33 teaspoon Epsom salt, 0.5 teaspoon salt
Primary:	1 day at 65° Fahrenheit
Secondary:	21 days at 47° Fahrenheit
Tertiary:	21 days at 38° Fahrenheit

TYPICAL/UNUSUAL PROCEDURES USED: Mash at 156° Fahrenheit for 2 hours.

Double IPA (22-A)

Taking IPA to a whole 'nother level, this relatively recent American innovation reflects the trend of American craft brewers pushing the envelope to satisfy the need of hop lovers for increasingly intense products. Double IPAs are obviously bigger than a standard IPA in both alcohol strength and overall hop level (bittering and finish), though they don't quite approach the level of barley wine. The style of beer is definitely a showcase for hops, however. And because of the preponderance of hop character, a healthy malt base is also required.

Flavor profile: Golden amber to reddish copper; dry-hopped versions may be a bit hazy. Very fruity and estery. Medium maltiness with high hop bitterness and low diacetyl. Biscuity and toasty malt flavors may be experienced. Hop flavor and aroma are medium to high, accentuating the fruity, citrusy, and piney qualities of American hops. Alcoholic strength is often evident. Medium-bodied.

OG/FG:	1.065–1.085/1.008–1.018
ABV:	7.5–10.0+
IBUs:	60–100+
SRM:	8–14

Commercial example: Stone Ruination Double IPA, California; Pliny the Elder, California

Hannah's Ambrosia Imperial I.P.A.

AWARD WON: 1ST PLACE, NORTHWEST REGIONAL, 1ST ROUND AHA NATIONALS

BREWER: JOE FORMANEK

Base grain:	15 pounds Simpson's Maris Otter pale 2-row
Specialty grain:	2 pounds Cargill special pale malt, 1 pound Weyermann wheat, 0.5 pounds DMC aromatic malt, 0.5 pounds DMC biscuit malt, 0.5 pounds DMC CaraPils malt
Bittering hops:	4 ounces Centennial (60 mins.)
Flavoring hops:	2 ounces Centennial (10 mins.), 2 ounces Willamette (10 mins.), 2 ounces Cascade (10 mins.), 1 ounce homegrown hops (Cascade/liberty blend) (10 mins.)
Dry hop:	1 ounce Centennial, 1 ounce Willamette
Yeast:	WLP002 English Ale
Clarifier:	1 teaspoon Irish moss (rehydrated)
Water treatment:	Carbon-filtered tap water
Primary:	7 days at 65° Fahrenheit.
Secondary:	16 days at 65° Fahrenheit.

TYPICAL/UNUSUAL PROCEDURES USED: Perform a single infusion mash at 155° Fahrenheit for 45 minutes. Boil for 60 minutes.

German Pils (5-D)

A light-bodied, highly attenuated, golden-colored lager adapted from the original Czech pilsner to suit brewing conditions in Germany; first brewed in the 1870s. The term *pils* is often applied to this style to differentiate it from the Czech exemplar.

In its homeland, examples of the style tend to get drier and hoppier as you travel from south to north. But no matter where you are, this beer style is eminently suited to quaffing by the liter on a warm summer afternoon.

Flavor profile: Bready and crackery in the nose, lightly malty on the palate. Medium to high hop bitterness with the spiciness associated with the noble hop varieties grown in Germany — specifically Tettnang, Spalt, and Hallertau.

OG/FG:	1.044–1.050/1.008–1.013
ABV:	4.4–5.2
IBUs:	22–40
SRM:	2–4

Commercial examples: Bitburger Premium Pils, Germany; Trumer Pils, Austria

Hasselhoffing

BREWER: STEVE THANOS

Base grain:	9 pounds Pilsner malt
Bittering hops:	1 ounce Tettnang (60 mins.)
Flavoring hops:	1 ounce Tettnang (15 mins.), 1 ounce Tettnang (5 mins.)
Yeast:	Imperial Yeast Global L13
Water treatment:	2 teaspoon gypsum, 1 teaspoon calcium chloride
Primary:	3 weeks at 50° Fahrenheit and cold crash for 4 weeks at 36° Fahrenheit

TYPICAL/UNUSUAL PROCEDURES USED: Perform a single step infusion mash at 152° Fahrenheit for 1 hour.

Gose (23-G)

Gose, named for the central German town of Goslar, is more closely associated with Leipzig today. Though the style is documented to have been around as early as 1740, local production of Gose ceased completely in 1966.

Gose (pronounced with two syllables: GO-zuh) has the distinction of being the only beer style made with salt — along with coriander seed, which dovetails well with the beer's acidity.

Flavor profile: Light to moderate sourness. Light doughy, bready malt flavor. Lemony-citrusy flavor and tang. Background salinity should not be obvious or lingering. Dry, fully attenuated finish; refreshing.

OG/FG:	1.036–1.056/1.006–1.010
ABV:	4.2–4.8
IBUs:	5–12
SRM:	3–4

Commercial examples: Döllnitzer Ritterguts Gose, Germany; Bayerisch Bahnhof Leipziger Gose, Germany

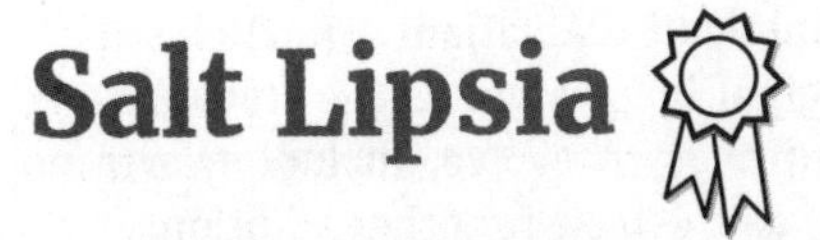

AWARD WON: SILVER MEDAL, SOUTH BRAZILIAN BEER COMPETITION

BREWER: DOUGLAS MERLO (BRAZIL)

Base grain:	5 pounds pilsner malt, 3.5 pounds wheat malt
Bittering hops:	3 ounces Hallertau Magnum 12 AA% (60 mins.)
Yeast:	Wyeast #1056 or US-05
Water treatment:	None needed
Primary:	2 days at 65°, F 8 days at 68°F
Secondary:	15 days at 34°F

TYPICAL/UNUSUAL PROCEDURES USED: Perform a single step infusion mash at 150° Fahrenheit for 1 hour. Add 1 oz. of table salt (sodium chloride) at the last 15 minutes of the boil. Add 1 oz. of crushed coriander seeds at flameout. Add lactic acid one day before the bottling until the beer reaches a pH of 3.5.

Hazy IPA (21-C)

Hazy IPA is an American IPA with intense fruit flavors and aromas, a soft body, and a smooth mouthfeel. It is often opaque with substantial haze (thus the name). The style features less perceived bitterness than traditional IPAs but is always massively hop-forward. It's for this lack of bittering that I contend that hazies are not true India pale ales.

The style is also known as *New England IPA* or *NEIPA*, and often referred to as *juicy IPA*, as well. An emphasis on late hopping, especially dry-hopping, with hops with tropical fruit qualities lends the juicy character for which this style is known.

The style's trademark haziness comes from dry-hopping, not suspended yeast, starch haze, or other techniques; hazy turbidity is to be expected, but unfortunately some hazies are rendered completely muddy or murky.

There are scant few beer styles that are uniquely American, but this is definitely one of them — it's also one of the most recent. It's known to have originated in the New England region of the U.S. as an American IPA variant. The Alchemist's Heady Topper beer is believed to be the original inspiration as the style grew in popularity during the 2010s. The style continues to evolve, including a trend towards lower bitterness and using the style as the base for other additions.

Flavor profile: High to very high fruity hop flavor; low to medium malt flavor. Low to medium perceived bitterness, often masked by the fuller body and soft, off-dry to medium finish. The hop character in the aftertaste should not be sharp or harsh. Should not be sweet, although high ester levels and lower bitterness may sometimes give that impression.

OG/FG: 1.060–1.085/1.010–1.015

ABV: 6.0–9.0

IBUs: 25–60

SRM: 3–7

Commercial examples: Hill Farmstead Susan, Vermont; Tree House Julius, Massachusetts

NEIPA for the Summer

BREWER: ERICK MARTELL

Base grain:	9 pounds US 2-row malt, 2 pounds UK Golden promise, 1 pound flaked wheat, 12 ounces flaked oats
Hops:	1.5 ounces Amarillo (10 mins.), 1.5 ounces Amarillo (0 mins), 1 ounce Citra (whirlpool), 1 ounce Galaxy (whirlpool), 1 ounce Mosaic (whirlpool), 2.5 ounces Citra (dry hop), 1 ounce Galaxy (dry hop), 1 ounce Mosaic (dry hop)
Yeast:	White Labs WLP095
Water treatment:	¼ tsp 10% phosphoric acid, ¾ tsp calcium chloride in the mash, ¼ tsp calcium sulfate in the mash
Primary:	2 weeks at 66° Fahrenheit
Secondary:	2 weeks at 60° Fahrenheit

TYPICAL/UNUSUAL PROCEDURES USED: Perform a single step infusion mash at 152° Fahrenheit for 1 hour. Boil for 75 minutes adding hops per recipe. Ferment at 64 F. for 3 weeks, and then secondary ferment for between 2 and 3 weeks.

Helles Bock (4-C)

German-style helles bock is a pale version of traditional bock. The profile is similar except for the omission of the chocolate grain, which in essence removes the chocolate flavors and most of the dark color. *Maibock*, a style brewed for consumption in the month of May (Mai), is basically a helles bock with a more pronounced hop character in the aroma and on the palate. Some brands are even dry-hopped for added bouquet.

Flavor profile: Pale to amber. No hop aroma, fruitiness, or esters. The malty, sweet character predominates in aroma and flavor. Unlike the traditional bock, it has no toasted chocolate-malt character. Low bitterness, low hop flavor, and low diacetyl are okay. Medium-bodied.

OG/FG:	1.064–1.072/1.011–1.018
ABV:	6.3–7.4
IBUs:	23–35
SRM:	6–9

Commercial examples: Einbecker Mai-Ur-Bock, Germany; Ayinger Maibock, Germany

Hella Good Maibock

BREWER: MARTY NACHEL

Base grain:	10 poundspilsner malt
Specialty grain:	0.5 pounds CaraVienne malt, 0.5 pounds CaraMunich
Bittering hops:	1 ounce Hallertau (60 mins.), 1 ounce Hallertau (40 mins.)
Flavoring hops:	0.5 ounces Hallertauer (20 mins.)
Yeast:	Wyeast #2206
Fining agent/ clarifier:	1 teaspoon Irish moss
Primary:	6 days at 60° Fahrenheit
Secondary:	14 days at 45° Fahrenheit

TYPICAL/UNUSUAL PROCEDURES USED: Perform a protein rest at 128° Fahrenheit for 15 minutes; an intermediate rest at 145° Fahrenheit for 15 minutes; and a saccharification rest at 152° Fahrenheit for 60 minutes. Sparge with 168° Fahrenheit water.

Kölsch (5-B)

This clean, crisp, delicately balanced beer has a fruity edge due to the ale yeast that is used for fermentation. Despite this, kölsch is traditionally lagered to give it its inherent drinkability.

Kölsch gets its name from the city of Köln (Cologne in the French tongue), and only those brewers that belong to the Köln Brewers Union may use the kölsch name because it is considered a protected appellation in Germany.

Kölsch is also one of a handful of beer styles that has its own beer glass style; the narrow, cylindrical *Stange* is made in a small range of volume sizes.

Flavor profile: Delicate malt flavor with almost imperceptible fruitiness; medium bitterness with dryness and crispness in the finish.

OG/FG:	1.044–1.050/1.007–1.011
ABV:	4.4–5.2
IBUs:	18–30
SRM:	3.5–5

Commercial examples: P.J. Früh Kölsch, Germany; Gaffel Kölsch, Germany

Innocent Betrayal

BREWER: STEVE THANOS

Base grain:	8.5 pounds pilsner malt, 1 pound Munich malt
Bittering hops:	14 ounces Magnum (60 mins.)
Flavoring hops:	14 ounces Magnum (5 mins.)
Yeast:	White Labs WLP029
Water treatment:	2 teaspoon gypsum, 1 teaspoon calcium chloride
Primary:	3 weeks at 68° Fahrenheit and cold crash for 4 weeks at 36° Fahrenheit

TYPICAL/UNUSUAL PROCEDURES USED: Perform a single step infusion mash at 154° Fahrenheit for 1 hour.

Märzen (6-A)

Märzen, Oktoberfest, and Vienna beers are pretty much of the same pedigree — they're all bottom-fermented, malty, and medium- to full-bodied.

Oktoberfest beer, as an individual style, is an offshoot of another, larger lager style known as Märzen or Märzenbier. This fairly heavy, malty style of beer is brewed in the spring and named for the month of March (*März*). It was often the last batch of beer brewed before the warm summer months, during which brewing was ill-advised (back before the invention of refrigeration, of course). This higher-gravity beer was then stored in alpine caves and consumed throughout the summer. Whatever beer was left in storage at harvest time, also at the beginning of the new brewing season, was hauled out and joyously consumed.

A party atmosphere was already present in the Oktoberfest celebration, but it took on a more reverent slant in 1810. In late September of that year, Bavaria's crown prince married Theresa Von Sachsen-Hildburghausen. This very public event just happened to coincide with the rollout of the excess Märzenbier. The good people of Munich so enjoyed the state celebration that they agreed to commemorate the nuptial feast and its pageantry on an annual basis. The breweries of Munich were certainly not against the idea — more than a million people attend the event every year, which takes place on the *Theresienwiese* (Theresa's meadow), named for the royal bride.

Today, Munich's Oktoberfest begins on a Saturday in mid-September with the Lord Mayor's proclamation *"O'zapft is!"* ("It's tapped!") as he taps the ceremonial first keg of beer. The festival then lasts 16 days and ends on the first Sunday in October.

Flavor profile: Amber to coppery orange. No fruitiness, esters, or diacetyl are evident. Low hop flavor and aroma are okay. The malty sweetness boasts of a toasty malt aroma and flavor. Low to medium bitterness is just enough to keep the malty character from becoming cloying. Medium-bodied.

OG/FG:	1.054–1.060/1.010–1.014
ABV:	5.6–6.3
IBUs:	18–24
SRM:	8–17

Commercial examples: Würzburger Oktoberfest, Germany; Capital Oktoberfest, Wisconsin

(Unnamed)

AWARD WON: 1ST PLACE, AHA NATIONALS

BREWERS: DENNIS AND CINDY ARVIDSON

Base grain:	5 pounds 2-row malt, 3 pounds Munich malt, 0.75 pounds home-roasted 2-row malt, 0.5 pounds wheat malt, 0.33 pounds Scottish malt
Bittering hops:	1 ounce Styrian Goldings (120 mins.), 1 ounce Saaz (120 mins.)
Yeast:	Wyeast #2308
Water treatment:	1 gram calcium chloride each in mash and sparge water
Primary:	40 days at 38° Fahrenheit
Secondary:	30 days at 38° Fahrenheit

TYPICAL/UNUSUAL PROCEDURES USED: Mash the grain at 156° Fahrenheit for 90 minutes.

Munich Dunkel (8-A)

What most drinkers know as German dark beer is basically a lager beer that has an additional roasted malt thrown in to add complexity to the aroma and palate. These dark versions of the Munich pale lager (*Münchner-style Helles*) style tend to be somewhat sweeter and only marginally heavier on the palate; most of this style's reputation as being heavy and strong is exaggerated. (Confusion reigns because any and every malt beverage with a color that remotely resembles the amber band in the color spectrum is now branded a dark beer.)

Ironically, *all* the original Munich-made beers were fairly dark until the introduction of helles lager earlier this century. Because of its widespread popularity, most Bavarian brewers began making helles lager, thus making the dunkel style even less popular.

Flavor profile: Copper to dark brown. No fruitiness or esters should be experienced. Nutty, roasty, chocolatey, and malty characteristics may be noticeable in the aroma and flavor. Low hop flavor and aroma are typical, as is medium bitterness. Low diacetyl is acceptable. Medium-bodied.

OG/FG:	1.048–1.056/1.010–1.016
ABV:	4.5–5.6
IBUs:	18–28
SRM:	17–28

Commercial examples: Hopf Dunkles, Germany; Ayinger Altbairisch Dunkel, Germany

AWARD WON: 1ST PLACE, AHA NATIONALS

BREWER: STU TALLMAN

Base grain:	7.5 pounds pale Lager malt, 2 pounds Munich malt, 2 pounds 40-L crystal malt
Bittering hops:	1.25 ounces Saaz (90 mins.)
Yeast:	Wyeast #2206
Primary:	21 days at 50° Fahrenheit
Secondary:	21 days at 37° Fahrenheit

TYPICAL/UNUSUAL PROCEDURES USED: Perform a three-step infusion mash.

Munich Helles (4-A)

German light lagers aren't low-calorie beers; they're just pale-colored. The original pale lager beer was brewed in Munich in 1928. In that year, the famous Paulaner Brewery introduced a *helles* (pale) lager, which was therefore known as *Münchner-style helles* or *Munich helles*. This style is meant to be an everyday libation, and it's quaffed by the liter throughout Bavaria.

Munich helles is pale yellow to brilliant gold in color and light- to medium-bodied. The accent is on the maltiness, with just enough hop bitterness extracted from noble hop varieties to balance the malt. The downplayed hop character is the principal difference between pale lager and pilsner and one to look out for in buying American microbrews.

Flavor profile: Pale to golden. No fruitiness or esters; hop flavor and aroma are okay. Medium malty sweetness. Low bitterness and no diacetyl are expected. Medium-bodied.

OG/FG:	1.044–1.048/1.006–1.012
ABV:	4.7–5.4
IBUs:	16–22
SRM:	3–5

Commercial examples: Spaten Münchner Hell, Germany; Augustiner-Bräu Lagerbier Hell, Germany

AWARD WON: 2ND PLACE, AHA NATIONALS

BREWER: DAVE MILLER

Base grain:	5.75 pounds 2-row Lager malt
Specialty grain:	1 pound CaraPils malt, 0.25 pounds Munich malt
Bittering hops:	1.75 ounces Hallertauer (75 mins.), 1.75 ounces Hallertauer (45 mins.)
Yeast:	Wyeast #2007
Water treatment:	Lactic acid (enough to acidify water to pH 5.7)
Primary:	3 weeks at 50° Fahrenheit
Secondary:	7 days at 50° Fahrenheit

TYPICAL/UNUSUAL PROCEDURES USED: Mash the grains with a protein rest for 30 minutes at 130° Fahrenheit and a starch rest for 60 minutes at 150° Fahrenheit; mash out for 5 minutes at 168° Fahrenheit. Sparge with 5 gallons of water at 165° Fahrenheit.

Classic Style Smoked Beer (32-A)

This category is intended for smoked versions of Classic Style beers, except if the Classic Style beer has smoke as an inherent part of its definition; of course, that beer should be entered in its base style, such as Rauchbier.

Rauchbier literally means *smoke beer* in German, and few styles are as polarizing as this one — you either love it or hate it. At its core, it's a beechwood-smoked, malty, amber German lager. The expected profile is of toasty-rich malt, restrained bitterness, clean fermentation, and a relatively dry finish is enhanced by a noticeable-to-intense smoke character.

Rauchbier is considered a historical specialty of the city of Bamberg, in the Franconian region of Bavaria in Germany. Although smoked beers certainly were made long ago, the origins of this specific style are unclear; they must have been developed after Märzen was created (Märzenbier is the base for this style).

But this category is not just about Rauchbier; brewers these days are starting to add smoke character to beer styles that previously had none (go figure!).

The smoke character and intensity in a given beer varies by maltster and brewery, so you have to expect some aroma and flavor variations in these styles when drinking — not all examples are highly smoked. In any case, there should be a well-balanced fusion of the malt and hops of the base beer style with a pleasant and agreeable smoke character.

Flavor profile: Different woods used to smoke malt result in unique flavor and aroma characteristics. Beechwood, other hardwoods such as oak, maple, mesquite, alder, pecan, apple, or cherry, or other fruitwoods may be used to smoke malts. These may often be evocative of smoked meats like bacon, ham, or sausage.

OG/FG: varies with BJCP base style guidelines

ABV: varies with BJCP base style guidelines

IBUs: varies with BJCP base style guidelines

SRM: varies with BJCP base style guidelines

Commercial examples: Aecht Schlenkerla Rauchbier Märzen, Germany; Brauerie Spezial Rauchbier Märzen, Germany

David's Smoke in the Water

BREWER: DAVID LEEDS

Base grain:	7 pounds Weyermann smoked malt, 2 pounds, 12 ounces Weyermann Munich light
Specialty grain:	4 ounces Weyermann Carafa II Special (de-husked)
Bittering hops:	2 ounces German Hallertau (first wort hop)
Yeast:	Wyeast 2308 Munich Lager
Water treatment:	None
Primary:	7 days at 52°F, then allow to warm for 7 more days, no warmer than 68°. On day 15, slowly lower temp to 42° before racking to secondary.
Secondary:	2 weeks minimum (4+ is ideal) at 33°

TYPICAL/UNUSUAL PROCEDURES USED: 1 hour mash @152° Fahrenheit. Sparge with 165° Fahrenheit water. One hour boil. Add one Whirlfloc tablet in the last 15 minutes.

If the smoke flavor is too intense, adjust to taste, substituting 2-row pale malt for up to 4.5 lbs. of the smoked malt.

Schwarzbier (8-B)

Schwarzbier literally means *black beer* in German. This dark German lager balances roasted yet smooth malt flavors with moderate hop bitterness. The lighter body, dryness, and lack of a harsh, burnt, or heavy aftertaste helps make this beer quite drinkable.

Although it's sometimes called a *black pils*, the beer is rarely as dark as black or as hop-forward and bitter as a pils. Likewise, this style has nothing in common with ales such as porter or stout; it has none of the roasty and charred character associated with those beers.

Schwarzbier is considered a regional specialty from Thuringia, Saxony, and Franconia in Germany. It has served as the inspiration for black lagers brewed in Japan. Somewhat ironically, its popularity grew after German reunification in 1990.

Flavor profile: Light to moderate malt flavor, which can have a clean, neutral character to a moderately rich, bread-malty quality. Light to moderate roasted malt flavors can give a bitter-chocolate palate. Medium-low to medium bitterness. Light to moderate spicy, floral, or herbal hop flavor. Clean lager character. Dry finish. Some residual sweetness is acceptable but not traditional.

OG/FG: 1.046–1.052/1.010–1.016

ABV: 4.4–5.4

IBUs: 20–35

SRM: 19–30

Commercial Examples: Köstritzer Schwarzbier, Germany; Kulmbacher Mönchshof Schwarzbier, Germany

Spirit of Stammtisch

BREWER: STEVE THANOS

Base grain:	8 pounds Vienna malt
Specialty grain:	8 ounces British crystal malt 45L, 8 ounces pale chocolate malt, 4 ounces Carafa II
Bittering hops:	1 ounce Magnum (60 mins.)
Flavoring hops:	1 ounce Tettnang (10 mins.)
Yeast:	Imperial Yeast Harvest L17
Water treatment:	1 teaspoon gypsum, 1 teaspoon calcium chloride
Primary:	3 weeks at 50° Fahrenheit and cold crash for 4 weeks at 36° Fahrenheit

TYPICAL/UNUSUAL PROCEDURES USED: Perform a single step infusion mash at 152° Fahrenheit for 1 hour.

Vienna Lager (7-A)

This moderate-strength continental amber lager has a soft, smooth maltiness and a balanced, moderate bitterness, yet finishing relatively dry. The malt flavor is clean, bready-rich, and somewhat toasty, with an elegant impression derived from quality base malts and process, not specialty malts or adjuncts. Unfortunately, many traditional examples have become sweeter and more adjunct-laden, now seeming more like international amber or dark lagers.

Developed by Austrian brewer Anton Dreher in Vienna in 1841, the style became popular in the mid-late 1800s. Some claim that the Vienna lager style was created in response to the introduction and popularity of the Märzenbier-based Oktoberfest style in neighboring Germany.

Vienna lager was eventually introduced to Mexico by Santiago Graf and other Austrian immigrant brewers in the late 1800s; the Negra Modelo and Dos Equis brands are said to be one of the only remaining examples of the style in Mexico, though they bear little resemblance to their exemplar.

Flavor profile: Soft, elegant malt complexity is in the forefront, with a firm enough hop bitterness to provide a balanced finish. The malt flavor tends towards a rich, toasty character, without significant caramel, biscuity, or roast flavors. Fairly dry, soft finish, with both rich malt and hop bitterness present in the aftertaste. Floral, spicy, or herbal hop flavor may be low to none. Clean fermentation profile.

OG/FG:	1.048–1.055/1.010–1.014
ABV:	4.7–5.5
IBUs:	18–30
SRM:	9–15

Proper Nomenclature

BREWER: STEVE THANOS

Base grain: 9 pounds Vienna malt

Specialty grain: 4 ounces pale chocolate malt

Bittering hops: 1 ounce Tettnang (60 mins.)

Flavoring hops: 0.5 ounces Tettnang (10 mins.)

Yeast: Imperial Yeast Ukel L28

Water treatment: 2 teaspoon gypsum, 1 teaspoon calcium chloride

Primary: 3 weeks at 50° Fahrenheit and cold crash for 4 weeks at 36° Fahrenheit

TYPICAL/UNUSUAL PROCEDURES USED: Perform a single step infusion mash at 154° Fahrenheit for 1 hour.

6 Alternative Brewing

IN THIS PART . . .

Learn how to make beer's sister beverage — cider.

Consider making a "wine" from honey (mead).

Explore your option to make hard seltzer at home.

Become a "green" brewer by practicing eco-friendly brewing practices.

Go gluten-free.

Join the thousands who are now barrel-aging and souring their beers at home.

» Cider-making recipes

Chapter 20
In-Cider Information

The art of homebrewing generally denotes brewing beer in one's home. However, this definition doesn't necessarily exclude the options to make other somewhat-similar fermented beverages, such as cider. It's probably safe to say most homebrewers never try their hand at making a cider, but they already have all the equipment they need, so why not present the information in case the occasion should arise? Well, here it is . . .

Exploring the Cider Option

Once the most popular beverage in America, hard cider is making a comeback of sorts, hot on the heels of the microbrewing revolution. In fact, some suggest that cider is now where craft brews were about 20 years ago and continues to grow in interest.

Hard cider, for the uninitiated, is a fermented beverage made from the juice of apples. (Regular, or *soft,* cider is unfermented and therefore contains no alcohol.) Hard cider is predominantly a British drink, although its traditions in the U.S. run deep. Its production may include optional ingredients such as white and brown sugars and various other fruits and spices, depending on the producer and the style.

Because of its combined acid and alcohol content, cider also has a shelf-life that often exceeds that of beer.

CIDER-BAR

The word *cider* appears to be a derivation of the Hebrew *shekar,* which means "strong drink." The recorded history of cider dates back to the first-century B.C. Roman soldiers under Julius Caesar, who discovered this drink while marching across the Kentish countryside in southern Britain and brought it back with them to Rome (introducing it to the rest of western Europe along the way). Following the Norman conquest of England in 1066, the consumption of cider increased immeasurably. (Being from the north of France, the Normans had no trouble appreciating this champagne-like beverage.) Under King Henry VIII, England made deliberate attempts to develop apple orchards for cider-making purposes. Cider production peaked in the 1700s, only to lose ground due to the increased taxation of cider in the 1800s.

In the United States, cider was the beverage of choice among the white Anglo-Saxon protestants who settled the original colonies, but its popularity diminished in the mid-1800s, following the arrival of millions of German and Eastern European immigrants whose preferred drink was beer. Cider lost out again to the nonalcoholic soft drinks introduced to the American populace at the turn of the century.

Comparing apples to apples

The cider-making industry uses a wide variety of apples. At their most basic level, apples fall roughly into two categories: *bittersweet* and *culinary.* Most of us are familiar with the culinary varieties, such as Granny Smith, Jonathan, Macintosh, and Golden Delicious, but few of us know of the wide variety of bittersweet apples that go by monikers such as Northern Spy, Kingston Black, Golden Russet, and Newton Pippen. The culinary varieties are the ones cooks use in apple pies or applesauce or that you just eat plain. The bittersweet apple varieties tend to have thicker skins and elevated tannin levels (which contribute the bitterness) and higher acid contents that make them less desirable for common consumption.

TECHNICAL STUFF

The natural sugars you find in apples are mostly mono- and disaccharides, which are both highly fermentable. The breakdown is approximately 75 percent fructose, 15 percent sucrose, and 10 percent glucose.

Most brand-name ciders are blends of the juices of different apple varieties, which create a wider spectrum of flavors. This blending also allows the cider producer to exercise more control over the cider flavor — especially if one or more of the apple crops experiences a bad growing season. And blending also results in a greater consistency in the finished product. The largest cider maker in the world (Bulmer, in England) uses 15 varieties of apples to produce the various brands it markets.

The key to making a good and enjoyable cider is to find the correct balance between the apple character (sweetness and flavor) and the natural acidity found in cider. Many people find the puckery tang of cider a little too assertive. If you count yourself among them, try adding a can of frozen apple concentrate to the mix to intensify the apple flavor, or add honey or juices of other flavorful fruits to cut through the acid levels in your cider.

TIP

Some cider makers even blend in a small percentage of pear juice, which is less acidic, thus reducing some of the cidery bite. A cider made from a majority of pear juice is rightly called a *perry.*

The quality of your cider depends greatly on your source of fermentable material — in this case, apples or apple juice. Because apple pressing is rather long and laborious, you could say it's best left to the hardcore cider makers; the juice route is more appealing to homebrewers.

Sorting cider styles

The antiquated Anglo style of cider, which originated in Britain, is generally more tannic and ale-like because of the cider makers' use of ale yeasts and bittersweet apples. (The greater use of bittersweet apples is what sets English ciders apart from North American ciders.) The Anglo style is also more costly because it requires longer fermentations. The newer Continental style, popular in the United States, is generally sweeter and more like sparkling wine.

And speaking of sparkling wine, you can render ciders and perries with various levels of carbonation from *still* (uncarbonated) to *sparkling* (highly carbonated). The level of mild carbonation in between still and sparkling is called *petillant,* which isn't to be confused with *petulant* (or *flatulent*, for that matter!)

According to competition guidelines set by the Beer Judge Certification Program, you can produce cider and perry in any of the following styles:

C1 Standard Cider and Perry

- C1A New World Cider
- C1B English Cider
- C1C French Cider
- C1D New World Perry
- C1E Traditional Perry
- C2 Specialty Cider and Perry

- C2A New England Cider
- C2B Cider with Other Fruit
- C2C Apple Wine
- C2D Ice Cider
- C2E Cider with Herbs and Spices
- C2F Specialty Cider and Perry

For additional details on cider and perry styles, check out this link: `https://www.bjcp.org/beer-styles/introduction-to-cider-guidelines/`.

Ciders of any style may also range from sweet to dry, depending on the types of apples you use, as well as the yeast strain you use to ferment the juice (see the list in Table 20-1). Furthermore, you may also serve cider *draft style*, which is pasteurized and filtered, or in the more natural *farmhouse style*, which is traditionally served unfiltered from a cask.

TABLE 20-1 **Sweetness Description List**

Sweetness	Description
Dry	This corresponds to a final specific gravity less than 1.002. There is no perception of sweetness.
Medium-dry	This corresponds to a final specific gravity of 1.002–1.004. There is a hint of sweetness but the cider is still perceived primarily as dry. Also known as semi-dry.
Medium	In the range between dry and sweet, corresponding to a final gravity of 1.004–1.009. Sweetness is now a notable component of the overall character.
Medium-sweet	Corresponding to a final gravity of 1.009–1.019. The cider is sweet but still refreshing. Also known as semi-sweet.
Sweet	Equivalent to a final gravity of over 1.019. The cider has the character of a dessert wine. It must not be cloying.

TIP

If you're looking for a few commercial ciders for comparison tasting, try the three most popular brands in the U.S.: Woodchuck, Angry Orchard, and Crispin. Two lesser-known brands, Ace and Original Sin, are worth seeking out. The leading non-U.S. brands include Magners, Woodpecker, Strongbow (from the U.K.), and Rekorderlig from Sweden.

Making Cider

Although the various cider style categories open to homebrewers at competitions are evidence of its acceptance and appeal, cider making is still catching on with homebrewers. This may be because cider's tart taste isn't to everyone's liking, but it may just be that many homebrewers are unaware of how easy cider is to make. Technically, only one ingredient is necessary to make cider: apples (or apple juice)! No water, no yeast — just the forbidden fruit.

Okay, I'm misleading you just a bit. Apples (and freshly squeezed apple juices), like grapes, *do* come complete with their own resident wild yeasts, but for better control over the cider-making process, I recommend you destroy these uninvited apple yeasts by heating the juice to at least 180° Fahrenheit, and then choosing and adding the proper yeasts. As far as water goes, apple juice naturally contains a high percentage of water and therefore doesn't require dilution.

Before you embark on your cider-making journey, be sure to check out the secondary fermentation procedures in Chapter 11. Cider making is very similar to beginner extract brewing (see Chapter 10) except for the secondary fermentation process.

Because the amount of apple juice you buy represents the finished batch size (remember, you're not diluting), you must heat all of your apple juice. This restriction means you either have to get a brewpot that can hold five gallons of liquid, or you have to heat your apple juice a couple gallons at a time until it's all heated. I don't recommend reducing your batch size because a lot of damaging airspace may be left in your primary and secondary fermenters that can cause oxidation problems later. The easy answer to this dilemma, if you choose to pursue small-batch brewing, is to simply buy smaller fermenters and carboys.

The first place to shop for apple juice is at your local grocer. Most large grocery stores carry at least a few different brands of apple juice and cider. But brand names aren't as important as product contents. Juice that's sugar-free and preservative-free is best.

Some serious cider makers prefer to buy their apple juice fresh from the local farmers' market or at roadside stands. This practice is fine, but keep in mind that this juice (which is often sold as soft cider) isn't pasteurized, and you need to stabilize it before you pitch yeast into it. You also need to use such juice quickly because unpasteurized and preservative-free apple juice soon begins fermenting on its own! I don't recommend boiling unfiltered apple juice; the easiest way to stop wild and unintentional fermentations is to mix sulfur dioxide in the juice, which you can do simply by adding one crushed Campden tablet to the *must*

(unfermented liquid). Winemakers use Campden tablets regularly, and most homebrew supply shops stock them.

If you boil unfiltered apple juice, a semipermanent haze forms in the liquid. *Fruit pectin* causes this discoloration, and after it sets (or *gels*), the only way to remove it is by filtration. (It doesn't affect the taste, however, and is hardly worth the effort of filtering out.)

You can greatly enhance cider (like some beer styles) with the addition of fruits or fruit flavors, some spices, or even some other fermentable sugars such as honey or brown sugar. Cider also benefits from long periods of aging (anywhere from a couple of months to several months), so adding some more complex flavorings to your cider is no big deal. You can add some of these directly to the brewpot, and you should add some to the secondary fermenter (see Chapter 8 for flavoring ideas and procedures).

Cider Considerations: Recipes

With the following cider recipes, you can produce an interesting libation appropriate for special occasions, competition, or just for sipping with friends. An added bonus is that you don't have to buy any extra equipment — your beer-brewing equipment is all you need.

REMEMBER

Although making cider is no more difficult than is brewing an extract beer, you should be familiar with secondary fermentation procedures before attempting these recipes (see Chapter 11). Because of this relative ease of brewing, I haven't broken these recipes out into beginner, intermediate, and advanced levels.

English Cider (C1B)

You make *English cider* without the addition of adjunct sugars or flavorings. In England, where the cider tradition began, Ale yeasts are preferable over champagne or other types; this use results in fruitier ciders with more residual sweetness. Traditional ciders should be light-bodied with a crisp apple flavor.

Rotten to the Corps

BREWER: DENNY LAKE

Apple Juice: 5 gallons (preservative-free)

Yeast: Nottingham dry Ale yeast

Nutrient: 2 ounces yeast nutrient

Primary: 8 days at 65° Fahrenheit

Secondary: 21 days at 65° Fahrenheit

TYPICAL/UNUSUAL PROCEDURES USED: Add priming sugar only at bottling for sparkling cider.

New England Cider (C2A)

New England cider is a very natural style, typically made with New England apples for relatively high acidity. Additives may include molasses, small amounts of honey, and raisins. Because of the addition of white and brown sugars, New England cider also sports elevated alcohol levels (7 to 13 percent). Medium- to full-bodied, New England cider offers a pronounced apple aroma and flavor, ending with a throat-warming finish.

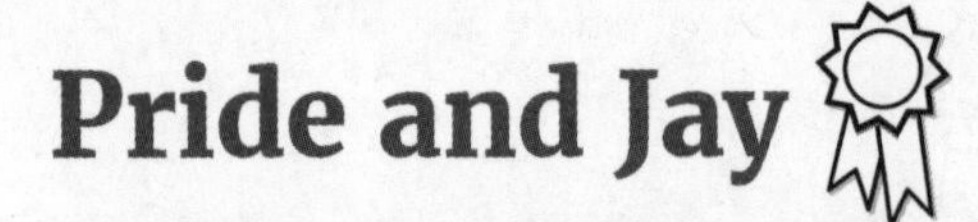

Pride and Jay

BREWER: JAY LUBINSKY

Apple Juice:	5 gallons (unpasteurized, preservative-free)
Yeast:	None added (spontaneously fermented)
Misc. fermentable ingredients:	5 cups granulated white cane sugar, 0.5 cup dark-brown sugar
Flavoring ingredients:	1.5 teaspoons grape tannin, 10 ounces raisins, 6 ounces oak chips
Primary:	10 days at 65° Fahrenheit
Secondary:	14 days at 65° Fahrenheit

TYPICAL/UNUSUAL PROCEDURES USED: Use apple juice immediately. Boil and cool 5 cups of white sugar with 5 cups of apple juice. Add sugar, juice, and tannin to rest of juice. Let ferment naturally. After fermentation subsides, add the raisins and let sit about 10 days or until fermentation subsides again. Transfer to the secondary fermenter. Boil the oak chips in a little water for 10 minutes; add to the cider. Let sit for a week or two, depending on desired oakiness. Bottle and age for 3 months.

Specialty Cider (C2F)

As in the Specialty Beer category, *specialty ciders* run all over the map — you may use any and all adjuncts and yeast (and you often do). At least 75 percent of the fermentable material should consist of apple juice.

Big Apple Punch

BREWER: PHILIP CURCIO

Apple Juice:	4.5 gallons
Yeast:	Pasteur Dry Champagne
Misc. fermentable ingredient:	1 pound light honey
Flavoring ingredient:	1 750-ml bottle of raspberry liqueur
Primary:	14 days at 65° Fahrenheit
Secondary:	30 days at 65° Fahrenheit

TYPICAL/UNUSUAL PROCEDURES USED: Heat the apple juice and honey together and cool; pitch the yeast. Add the raspberry liqueur to the secondary fermenter while racking the cider to the carboy.

» Mead-making recipes

Chapter 21
A Meading of the Minds

Although the product of homebrewing is usually beer, you can apply the same equipment and techniques to other tasty purposes as well — specifically, making mead. Many homebrewers never take a shot at making a mead, but in this chapter, I give you the lowdown on mead and its origins, as well as some recipes, in case you ever get the mead wanderlust.

Mulling Over the Mead Option

Mead is a simple fermented beverage made from honey and water; it's also one of the more natural and uncomplicated beverages known to man. Despite its simplicity, however, mead is intoxicatingly enjoyable — pun intended, of course — and when well made, it can rival the finest wines in the world.

Throughout the millennia, mead was believed to have curative, restorative, and aphrodisiac qualities; how's that for an uncomplicated beverage? The concept of a honeymoon derives from the ancient belief that drinking honey wine (mead) for one full moon (28 days) was a way to increase fertility among newlyweds.

THE MEADY MUSE

Mead is one of the most sublime beverages known to man, but it's most often referred to as the "nectar of the gods." Historically, mead has had strong ties to Norse Vikings, English kings, and Celtic roustabouts (and all the sacking and pillaging ascribed to them). Mead is often the subject of poetic, even lyrical verse, and it features prominently in ancient mythology and other classic literature such as the *Rig-Veda*, the *Odyssey, Beowulf,* the *Kalevala,* and the *Heimskringla* (Norse King Sagas). Pliny, Plutarch, Homer, Chaucer, Pepys, Shakespeare, Rabelais, and Washington Irving all mention it in their works as well. One notable work that doesn't mention mead is the Bible, presumably because of mead's close association with pagan gods.

The honey bunch: Appreciating honey

To understand and appreciate mead is to understand and appreciate honey. Mead is, after all, a simple dilution of honey in water fermented with yeast.

Bees, of course, produce honey. After the energetic honeybee collects nectar from flowers, it partially digests and regurgitates it in the form of honey. The bees store the honey in their hexagonal honeycombs, which are also made from bee excretions. (If that doesn't make you appreciate honey, nothing will!)

Honey is highly fermentable because it's mostly sugar. The quantities of natural sugars in honey vary from one variety to the next, but all honeys contain a mixture of fructose, glucose, and sucrose sugars. A small percentage of honey content is made up of unfermentable stuff such as aromatic oils, gums, resins, fats, acids, and the bees' digestive enzymes — yum! Taken as a whole, pure and natural honey is a healthy potion containing a handful of minerals such as iron, potassium, and phosphorus and vitamins A, B, C, and K. Unfortunately, the more processed the honey is, the fewer of these goodies you're likely to find in it.

TECHNICAL STUFF

The natural sugars you find in honey are mostly mono- and disaccharides, both highly fermentable — very similar to what you'd find in fruit juice. What are vastly different, however, are the flavor and viscosity of honey when compared to fruit juice.

Estimates reveal over a thousand different kinds of honey in the world, each with a different color and flavor (though these differences may be miniscule). Most commercially produced honeys are blends of various types, which tends to foster homogeneity among them. Lighter honeys such as clover, alfalfa, and wildflower are good for mead making because their flavor contribution is mild. Dark honeys, on the other hand, can be rather aggressive and even harsh-tasting. For meads with some taste complexity, pure *varietal*, or single-source, honey is highly desirable. Varietal honeys are those derived primarily from a single blossom. The downside is that most of the varietal types are also fairly scarce and, therefore, often more expensive.

Here are some varietal honeys that produce very tasty mead:

- Orange blossom
- Mesquite
- Fireweed
- Tupelo

Many brand-name meads are typically made from a homogenous blend of honeys, which pretty much guarantees consistency between batches. Those meads made from varietal honey usually broadcast that fact on their labels.

The honey-brew list: Mead styles

As previously mentioned, traditional mead is rather uncomplicated and pretty easy to make. Things start to get interesting when you use a single variety of honey or start adding various adjunct sugars, spices, and flavorings to your mead.

Just so you don't get lulled into a false sense of familiarity with this honey-based libation, brewers also divide mead into substyles. Fermenting plain honey and water produces traditional mead, but by simply adding other flavorings and fermentable sugars, you can produce different styles of mead. Here's a breakdown of mead substyles:

- *Braggot* is mead made with a portion of fermentable ingredients derived from malted grain. In other words, braggot is part beer. (This style is occasionally called *brackett*.)
- *Cyser* is mead to which you add apple juice. (I guess that would make it a cider-cyser.)
- *Hippocras* is a spiced *pyment* (a mead made with grape juice and spices).
- *Melomel* (also called *Mulsum*) is mead to which you add fruit juices other than apple or grape.
- *Metheglin* is mead to which you add herbs and spices. *Gruit* is the common term that refers to a mixture of herbs and spices used to flavor meads.
- *Morat* is mead to which you add mulberries.

» *Pyment* (also called *Clarré* by the French) is mead to which you add grape juice.

» *Rubamel* is mead fermented specifically with raspberries.

According to the Beer Judge Certification Program competition guidelines, brewers can make mead at home in any of the following styles:

» M1. Traditional Mead
  - M1A. Dry Mead
  - M1B. Semi-sweet Mead
  - M1C. Sweet Mead

» M2. Fruit Mead
  - M2A. Cyser
  - M2B. Pyment
  - M2C. Berry Mead
  - M2D. Stone Fruit Mead
  - M2E. Melomel

» M3. Spice Mead
  - M3A. Fruit and Spice Mead
  - M3B. Spice, Herb and Vegetable Mead

» M4. Specialty
  - M4A, Braggot
  - M4B. Historical Mead

    A Historical Mead is a historical or indigenous mead that doesn't fit into another subcategory, such as Ethiopian *tej* or Polish meads.

REMEMBER

All meads, regardless of style, should exhibit some, or all of these attributes:

» **Sweetness:** *Sweetness* simply refers to the amount of residual sugar in the mead; a mead may be *dry, semi-sweet,* or *sweet.* Sweet meads shouldn't be cloyingly sweet or have a raw, unfermented honey character. Sweetness is independent of strength; body is related to sweetness, but dry meads can still have some body. Dry meads don't have to be bone dry.

One of the keys to making a good and enjoyable mead is to achieve the correct balance between the honey (sweetness and flavor) and the acidity in the mead. Like brewers who use bitter hops to balance the natural grain sweetness of beer, mead makers need something to offset the cloying taste of syrupy sweet mead. You can add powdered or liquid acids, such as citric, malic, and tartaric acids, to mead for flavor balance and complexity. Well-stocked homebrew shops sell Acid Blend packets that contain this exact mix of citric, malic, and tartaric acids.

Occasionally, due to a low original gravity or overly aggressive yeasts, mead can come out much drier than you intended. If your mead turns out this way, you can always add a little more honey directly to the mead at bottling time to sweeten it up. To avoid the possibility of exploding bottles, however, you need to make sure all the yeast remaining in solution is 100 percent dead by using potassium sorbate (according to package directions) to prevent renewed fermentation. Obviously, this tip applies only to uncarbonated (*still*) meads (see the next bullet).

- **Carbonation:** A mead may be still, petillant, or sparkling. Still meads don't have to be totally flat — they can have some very light bubbles. *Petillant* meads are lightly sparkling and can have a moderate, noticeable amount of carbonation. *Sparkling* meads aren't gushing but may have a character ranging from mouth-filling to an impression akin to Champagne or soda pop. (Making a petillant or sparkling mead is a simple matter of adding additional fermentable sugar to the mead at bottling time. Check out Chapter 14 for more on bottling and carbonation.)
- **Strength:** A mead may be categorized as *hydromel, standard,* or *sack strength*. *Strength* refers to the alcohol content of the mead (and therefore to the amount of honey and fermentable ingredients used to make the mead). Stronger meads have a greater honey character and body (as well as alcohol content) than weaker meads, although this isn't a strict rule.
- **Honey variety:** Some types of honey have a strong varietal character that is likely to affect its aroma, flavor, color, and acidity. There are dozens to choose from; where and how to obtain them is the question. The National Honey Board maintains an awesome honey locator on their website: `www.honey.com`.
- **Specialty ingredients:** Different mead styles may include fruit or vegetables, herbs and spices, sugars, malt, etc. that provide a unique character. Many meads are aged in oak and oak character is acceptable in every mead style.

The vast majority of commercially made meads you encounter are likely middle-of-the-road meads: standard, semi-sweet, and still. Fortunately for the non-brewing consumer, commercial mead is growing in diversity and availability, but it depends greatly on your local purveyor of adult beverages.

MEAGER MEADS

Why isn't mead more popular and available today? Several factors have probably affected the decline of mead. One possibility is that wine simply overtook it in popularity; grapes are, and have always been, far more abundant than honey, and the scarcity of any commodity directly affects its price on the free market. As to why more commercial wineries don't produce mead, it's probably as simple as a lack of awareness and demand on the part of the consumer. And the amount of time required for the proper fermentation and aging of mead can be excruciatingly long (but worth every month). The leading source of mead in the United States today is the hobbyists (homebrewers and home winemakers) who make it in their kitchens and basements. Of the relatively few commercial meaderies in the United States, many of them are wineries that have ventured into the mead-making arena.

TIP

If you're looking for a few commercial meads for comparison tasting, try scouting out Schramm's mead, B. Nektar mead, White Winter mead, Redstone mead, Midwest Meadwerks, or Superstition mead.

Sweet Success: Making Magnificent Mead

Although homebrewing competitions have accepted mead with open arms (and categories), mead making is still not very common among homebrewers. This unpopularity may stem from the fact that mead is an acquired taste, but perhaps the main obstacle is that many homebrewers are unaware of how easy mead is to make. After all, all you really need to make mead is honey.

Okay, that statement is a bit deceptive. To make a *tasty* mead, you need to dilute the honey with water and pitch it with yeast, but these are minor points. Technically, unpasteurized honey may even spontaneously ferment if left in an unsealed container. I don't think it would taste very pleasant, though.

Choosing your honey

As you're shopping for honey, check out the honey aisle of your local grocery store. Most large grocery stores carry at least a few different brands of honey, but keep in mind the vast majority of commercial honeys are blended and homogenized — they're all virtually the same. You may want to travel that extra mile or spend that extra dollar to purchase a specialty or varietal honey from a specialty food store, a roadside food stand or farmers' market, or a local beekeeper.

WARNING

Some hardcore mead makers prefer to buy their honey closer to the source — at the local farmers' market or at roadside stands. Keep in mind that this honey often isn't pasteurized (or even filtered), and you need to stabilize it before you pitch yeast into it. The quickest way to kill unwanted wild yeast or bacteria is to mix sulfur dioxide into the *must* (unfermented honey and water dilution); you can do this by adding one crushed Campden tablet to the must. Winemakers and mead makers use Campden tablets regularly, and most homebrew supply shops stock them.

Boiling your honey to kill of any resident bacteria is also an option, but be careful: Boiling may also kill off a lot of the delicate aromatics of the honey, too. The best way to boil safely is to pour the honey into water that's already boiling and immediately turn off the heat. Stir well.

TIP

Sometimes raw honey begins to crystallize within its jar or container, which makes it difficult to pour out. I've found that microwaving the container for a few seconds causes the honey to quickly revert to its syrupy form.

Mead-iocre? Not! Fermenting your mead

The brewer has a fair amount of control over the fermentation process; some sweet mead yeasts aren't very alcohol-tolerant and cease fermenting before they've consumed all the available sugars. On the other hand, liquid culture dry mead yeasts or Champagne yeasts are very alcohol-tolerant and consume as much available sugar as they can. Given honey's high degree of fermentability and some yeast strains' alcohol tolerance, your mead could conceivably end up with a final gravity of 0.999 or lower, which is even less dense than water.

Most meads start with original gravities greater than 1.080 and ferment down to final gravities below 1.020. This level of attenuation results in alcohol levels above 9 percent, which is equivalent to most table wines. For the homebrewer, it takes about 12 pounds of honey in a 5-gallon batch to get to this starting gravity point, but it's not unheard of for mead makers to use as many as 15 to 18 pounds of honey in a 5-gallon batch. Figure on a dilution rate of 2½ to 3 pounds of honey per gallon of water to achieve the appropriate starting gravity.

At high original gravities, however, yeasts have a tough time staying motivated. It helps to make sure you've aerated the must before you pitch the proper amount of yeast. In order to keep fermentation moving along, you may need to rouse the yeast by agitating the fermenter or by racking the mead over to another vessel. Adding fresh, healthy yeast to a mead already in the secondary fermenter isn't out of the question, either.

Consider using a yeast nutrient to aid in fermentation. Yeast nutrient is a blend of vitamins, minerals, amino acids, nitrogen, zinc, and other trace elements designed to help wine and mead ferment completely.

Don't be surprised if your primary mead fermentations continue for two weeks to a month. Secondary fermentations typically last months rather than weeks. Three to six months is the norm, but nine to twelve months isn't out of the ordinary for extremely high gravity meads or those with lots of flavor components that benefit from aging and melding, such as bold fruit flavors or aggressive spices. Some mead makers who are fans of oak-aged white wines such as Chardonnay can throw toasted oak chips into the secondary fermenter as they rack the mead into it.

Before you dive headlong into mead making, take a look at the secondary fermentation procedures in Chapter 11. Check out Chapter 10 as well; mead making is very similar to beginner extract brewing except for the secondary fermentation process.

Finally, you're not just stuck with plain old honey-and-water meads; like a lot of beer styles, you can jazz up your mead by adding spices, fruits or fruit flavors, or even other fermentable sugars like brown sugar. Because mead benefits from long periods of aging (anywhere from a couple of months to several months), adding more complex flavorings to your mead is no problem: Chuck 'em in the brewpot or the secondary fermenter. (See Chapter 8 for flavoring ideas and procedures.)

PROGRESS REPORT: PROGRESSIVE MEAD

Another way (one that lives in legend as far as I know because no one I associate with has tried it) to make a high-gravity mead is called *progressive mead*. The idea is that you brew a mead of regular gravity and strength in a smaller batch size to leave room in your fermentation vessel. After the initial fermentation subsides, you boil more undiluted honey, cool it, and mix it with the existing mead as you rack it over to the secondary fermenter. Along with the fresh dose of honey, you may need more yeast and yeast nutrient, too.

Because it's progressive, you don't have to stop at a second helping of honey. As the legend goes, you can continue adding more honey in this fashion until you run out of space in your fermenter (or your yeasts die of alcohol toxicity).

I Mead a Drink: Mead Recipes

These mead recipes, like the cider recipes in Chapter 20, allow you to create a tasty, competition-worthy concoction perfect for special occasions (even if that occasion is Wednesday). As a bonus, you don't even need any new equipment; your beer-brewing gear is perfect.

Because mead brewing is pretty low-key, these recipes don't offer separate beginner, intermediate, and advanced levels. Be aware, however, that even after you've bottled your mead, it may not reach its peak flavor potential for another 2 to 6 months.

Traditional Mead (M1)

Traditional mead is one of the least-complicated meads to make. It's a simple mix of honey and water that you can ferment to various levels of sweetness. The following recipe (Lindisfarne Libation) is on the dry end of the sweetness scale.

Lindisfarne Libation

BREWER: MARTY NACHEL

Honey:	12 pounds wildflower (unpasteurized)
Yeast:	Pasteur Champagne (dry)
Nutrient:	2 ounces yeast nutrient
Primary:	16 days at 65° Fahrenheit
Secondary:	21 days at 65° Fahrenheit

TYPICAL/UNUSUAL PROCEDURES USED: Add the yeast nutrient to the must in primary fermenter.

Specialty Mead (M4)

Specialty mead is one that combines elements of two or more other mead categories, or one that simply doesn't fit the style description of any other mead category. These meads are often made with an "anything goes" attitude.

Winter Holiday Sweet Mead

1ST PLACE, FIRST ROUND, 2001 AHA NATIONALS

BREWER: TIM REITER

Honey:	14 pounds wildflower
Apple Juice:	4 gallons (unpasteurized, preservative-free), chilled
Yeast:	Red Star Cote des Blanc (dry)
Misc. fermentable ingredients:	2 pounds dark brown sugar
Flavoring ingredients:	0.5 ounce cinnamon stick
Clarifying agent:	3 teaspoons Sparkolloid
Primary:	10 days at 65° Fahrenheit
Secondary:	14 days at 65° Fahrenheit

TYPICAL/UNUSUAL PROCEDURES USED: Heat the honey, brown sugar, and cinnamon in 1 gallon of water in the brewpot. Cool with chilled apple juice and pitch rehydrated yeast. After primary fermentation is complete, stir in rehydrated Sparkolloid. Bottle or keg after 2 weeks.

Pyment (grape melomel) (M2B)

Pyments, or grape melomels, are perfect meads for wine lovers since these are made with a mixture of honey, water, and grape juice. The ingredient mixtures and the grape juice type are all up to the mead maker (you).

Concord Grape Sweet Mead 

3RD PLACE BEST-OF-SHOW, CHICAGO BEER SOCIETY SPOOKY BREW 2001

BREWER: TIM REITER

Honey:	15 pounds generic honey
Yeast:	Red Star Cotes de Blanc (dry) rehydrated
Misc. fermentable ingredient:	4 gallons Concord grape juice (preservative-free), chilled
Clarifying agent:	2 teaspoons Sparkolloid
Primary:	10 days at 65° Fahrenheit
Secondary:	14 days at 65° Fahrenheit

TYPICAL/UNUSUAL PROCEDURES USED: Heat 1 gallon of water to 150° Fahrenheit. Add the honey and stir frequently to dissolve. Pour the chilled grape juice from high above the fermenter so it splashes on the bottom of the fermenter and aerates thoroughly. Add the honey/water mixture similarly and stir vigorously. Pitch rehydrated yeast. After primary fermentation is complete, stir in rehydrated Sparkolloid. Bottle or keg after 2 weeks.

» Familiarizing yourself with seltzer ingredients

» Differentiating among seltzer flavorings

» Following the step-by-step process of making seltzer

Chapter 22
Hard Seltzers

In about the year 2019 or so, a quiet revolution began taking place. Supplanting sales of both import and domestic craft beer was the upstart libation, Hard Seltzer. From practically out of nowhere this fresh, clean, thirst-quenching potion presented in dozens of exciting new flavors created an unexpected booming new category of alcoholic beverage.

Initially, brewers of beer both large and small were quick to dismiss this parvenu. Unfortunately for them, however, not only were they losing ground in this game, they were losing time. Skyrocketing sales of hard seltzers across the board forced many brewers to quickly arrive at the conclusion *Beat 'em or join 'em*, and, as it turns out, there was no beating them. Rather than continue to watch market share slip away and lose revenue to the seltzer makers, many commercial brewers made the prudent business decision to join the fray.

Making Seltzer Hard is Easy?

When you realize how incredibly easy it is to make hard seltzer, it's not difficult to see why so many players got in the game. And now that you're a homebrewer in good standing, you're also in a position to ask the same question of yourself. Do you also want to exercise your option and ability to make hard seltzer at home?

Before moving on, let's take a closer look at hard seltzer and define what it is, exactly. From a flavor perspective, seltzers are typically described as being:

- Clean
- Flavorful
- Effervescent
- Refreshing

While those descriptors are the hallmarks of a good hard seltzer, also of great importance are these attributes:

- Minimal alcoholic bite
- No fermentation off-flavors
- Very low residual sweetness
- Brilliant clarity

It doesn't hurt that hard seltzer is also low in calories and good for those with gluten restrictions. One other benefit of making hard seltzer at home is that once it's packaged it's a highly stable product; it's able to last for a long time with little likelihood of oxidation or other off flavors.

Seltzer, by common definition, is simply carbonated water (also known as club soda or soda water). Hard seltzer, like hard cider, means that it contains alcohol. So, the product that has been popularized by brand names like White Claw and Truly are essentially made of carbonated water, sugar and flavorings (well, the sugar eventually becomes alcohol -but we'll talk about that later). That's pretty much it.

This relatively simple formula suggests that it's also quite easy to replicate at home -and it is. It only becomes slightly more difficult when it comes down to choosing the particular water, the particular sugar, the particular yeast and the particular flavorings. Yes, these simple things matter.

Spotlight on Ingredients

Before diving into the actual procedural aspect of making hard seltzer, I need to get just a bit "sciency" on you, first. I mention in the previous paragraph that you need "particular" kinds of ingredients to make your beverage, namely water, sugar, yeast and flavorings — so now I have to get into those particulars.

Water

All natural water sources come complete with their own in-built mineral composition (for more on this, please review Chapter 7: On the Waterfront). This includes your own municipal tap water, by the way. Unfortunately, some of those minerals don't play well with fermenting sugar and they can often result in some unpleasant off-flavors and aromas in the finished product (some folks describe this as a minerally white wine type flavor, or worse). Lastly, water sources that contain minerality might also cause your seltzer to be somewhat less than crystal clear; some minerals may create a yellowish off-color or even a haze in the finished product.

For this reason, I suggest that you start with mineral-neutral water such as distilled water or reverse osmosis (RO) water; these should be readily available by-the-gallon through your local grocer. Somewhat contradictorily, some (but not all) of those minerals are good for yeast nutrition and fermentation; what this means is that you'll will have to build back some of those minerals and nutrients later in the brewing process.

Sugar

The world is full of all different kinds of refined and unrefined sugars, but not all are appropriate for making hard seltzer. While the vast majority of us are familiar with cane sugar, which is called "sucrose" (also commonly referred to as "table" sugar), few are aware of the refined sugar derived from corn, which is known as "dextrose." This is the preferred type for making hard seltzer (for more on dextrose or corn sugar, refer to Chapter 8).

TECHNICAL STUFF

In order for yeast to fully consume liquefied sugars, the sugar must be completely broken down first. Dextrose breaks down and dissolves more completely than sucrose; therefore, yeast prefers dextrose over sucrose. This is what makes corn sugar more readily fermentable than cane sugar.

Yeast

Did I mention that hard seltzers contain alcohol? And did I mention alcohol is created by yeast during fermentation? And did I mention that there are scores of yeast strains out there? And did I mention that most yeast strains come with their own aroma and flavor profiles? This is why it's important to choose the right yeast to ferment your seltzer, those being the most aroma and flavor-neutral yeast possible. Below are some highly recommended yeast brands and strains:

- Safale US-05 American Ale Yeast
- Lalvin EC 1118 Dry Wine Yeast
- Omega Labs OYL 071 Lutra Kveik
- Red Star Premier Cuvee Champagne Yeast

Flavorings

The market is replete with all kinds of natural and artificial flavorings that appeal to your sense of taste, but it's not just about flavor. Some flavorings are in the form of syrups that contain sugar; others are in the form of extracts, which do not contain sugar. Most commercial seltzer makers choose to use extracts primarily for consistency, but it shouldn't go without noting that extracts don't add carbs or calories.

Also note the use of the words *natural* and *artificial*. The more natural a product is, the more natural it will likely taste. *Artificial*, on the other hand, is an adjective that describes flavor that does not taste natural. Get it?

TIP

Although the easiest way to flavor a neutral hard seltzer base is by adding unfermentable flavorings and organic acids to the carbonated base wash, another simple way to make variants from a single batch of neutral base wash is to add flavored syrups as it's being served. This is a great way to experiment with a wide assortment of different syrups and flavorings.

Flavorings can take the form of purees, liquid drops, powders, crystals and who knows what else. For pure ease of use, hard seltzer makers find it hard to ignore products like Amoretti Beverage Infusions, which are sold through homebrew supply stores (among many other locations), or SodaStream Flavor Drops, which is widely available at major retail stores throughout the U.S.

TIP

Another sensible — but not inexpensive — option for flavoring your hard seltzer while simultaneously priming it, is fruit liqueurs (avoid cream liqueurs). Flavored liqueurs contain high levels of sugar that would sufficiently carbonate your seltzer; a 750ml bottle contains enough sugar to carbonate a 5-gallon batch. More importantly, liqueurs are made with high quality, rich and consistent flavor and aroma. And, yes, this will also boost the alcohol content a smidge.

To get the purest, most flavorful, most authentic fruit flavor, it makes sense to simply use whole fruits. But this comes with its own challenges, too. First of all, you can say goodbye to a clear seltzer; using fining agents (like chitosan or gelatin) or filtration will strip away some of those authentic flavors you're trying to imbue in the first place. Second, you'll need to sanitize the fruit in a neutral distilled spirit like grain alcohol or vodka to make sure resident bacteria doesn't spoil your seltzer. Third, you're going to have to juice the fruit (and strain the pulp, if any) before adding it to your wash. Is it all worth it? Only you can answer that.

WARNING

A word of caution regarding any flavoring you use, regardless of brand or medium — follow instructions closely and taste as you go. It's very easy to overdo it: "If a little is good, a lot is better" is faulty logic.

So, What About All Those Minerals and Nutrients?

It's a good thing you asked — and I'll try to keep this simple. Like humans, yeasts need proper nutrition to do what they were designed to do, namely, ferment sugar into alcohol and carbon dioxide. When yeast ferments grape juice (fructose) into wine, or grain sugar (maltose) into beer, it's getting all the important minerals and nutrients it needs to finish the job sufficiently. However, when yeast is only being fed corn sugar and water, its diet is terribly lacking and it will very likely have a problem completing the task of fermenting all that processed sugar into alcohol and CO_2.

In order to help the yeast along, it's highly recommended that you add the minerals and nutrients that yeast like and need, to the sugar and water mixture. Specifically, yeast like to dine on stuff like:

- Magnesium sulfate (aka, Epsom salt)
- Magnesium chloride
- Sodium bicarbonate (aka, baking soda)
- Diammonium phosphate

Fortunately, you don't need to be a chemist or go to your local apothecary to buy all these things separately. Homebrew supply outlets — both brick-and-mortar and online — sell premixed packages of these minerals and nutrients. You'll find them with catchy names like Fermaid O Yeast Nutrient (the "O" stands for organic), Go Ferm Protect or Yeastex 82. Be forewarned, though; most of these premixes are proprietary, so exact ingredients and quantities of each are rarely divulged.

TECHNICAL STUFF

While contemplating which nutrient pack to buy and use, you're likely to see references to "FAN"; this is short for Free Amino Nitrogen. FAN helps yeasts strengthen their cell walls and prepare for the process of converting simple sugar to CO_2 and alcohol.

One last comment about making sure your yeast is happy and healthy: You need to feed them more than once to get the job done well. This means you'll need to add these nutrients to the fermenter up to three times within the one-week span of fermentation. You'll see these called out in the timeline below.

The Bottom Line

The bottom line on making a good seltzer is to use the right water, sugar and yeast that will produce the most neutral-smelling and tasting base liquid — essentially an intentionally bland drink. Once you've achieved this, then you can start adding the best-tasting flavors that won't have to compete with the wash for your palate's attention.

For the purpose of this chapter on seltzers, the word used to describe the fermented liquid before it has been flavored is *wash*.

TECHNICAL STUFF

The word *wash* is used in the liquor industry to refer to the fermented liquid before it's distilled. Obviously, your seltzer is not destined to be distilled, but contrary to the words *must* in the wine industry and *wort* in the brewing industry, wash describes a liquid that is already fermented.

Step-by-Step: How to Make Hard Seltzer

Before starting the brewing process, you'll want to make sure you have the following equipment on hand to make the neutral base/wash:

- Brewpot and lid
- Stirring spoon
- Sanitized fermenter and lid
- Airlock (and rubber stopper, if needed)

Before starting the brewing process, you'll want to make sure you have the following ingredients for the neutral base/wash on hand (flavorings are added later):

- 5.5 gallons water — distilled or reverse osmosis (RO)
- 6 pounds dextrose (corn sugar)
- Minerals and nutrient packet of your choice (three packets for three separate additions)
- The yeast brand and type of your choice (they are all packaged in amounts appropriate to properly ferment your beverage)

Without further abrew, here is the list of steps you'll have to take to make your first batch of hard seltzer.

1. **Add a minimum of 2 gallons of water to your brewpot (the rest will be added after the boil). Bring to a boil.**
2. **Add all of the dextrose to the boiling water, stirring it in as you pour. Dissolve all sugar until the liquid is again clear. Continue boiling for another 15 minutes.**
3. **Cool the liquid to below 80° F. This can be done with cold sink baths or with an immersion chiller (see Chapter 2).**
4. **Pour the cooled liquid into your sanitized fermenter. Top up with the remainder of the 5.5 gallons of water that didn't go into your brewpot.**

REMEMBER

Though it's not entirely necessary, if you're working with a hydrometer to track your hard seltzer's fermentation, this is the point at which you would take an original gravity reading. . .and it should be around 1.040 or so. For a review of hydrometer readings, see chapter 10, Beginner Brewing Directions.

5. **Add the yeast and the first nutrient addition. Simply pour it or sprinkle it on top of the liquid.**
6. **Cover your fermenter and affix the airlock (and stopper, if needed). Set fermenter aside in a cool, dark location in your home. Fermentation should begin within about 12 hours.**
7. **Add the second nutrient addition about 36 to 48 hours after pitching the yeast. Do not stir in.**
8. **Add the third nutrient addition when you see the fermentation activity is starting to wane, or about 72 hours into fermentation. Do not stir in.**

9. **When fermentation is complete (5 to 7 days after pitching the yeast), cool the wash down as cold as possible to encourage the yeast to settle out of solution. This aids in making the finished product clear.**

REMEMBER

Again, if you're working with a hydrometer to track your hard seltzer's fermentation, this is the point at which you would take a final gravity reading . . . and it should now be around 1.000, or even lower. This means the sugar was 100 percent consumed by the yeast and there should be no residual sweetness.

TIP

Though it's not absolutely necessary, if you are a stickler for crystal clear seltzer, then you can use products like chitosan (this is made from shellfish, so be aware of allergies) or unflavored gelatin to help you achieve that clarity. Use according to package directions.

10. **After 24 hours at the coolest temperature possible, siphon transfer the wash to a sanitized secondary vessel, leaving all the yeast sediment behind. It's important not to move or jostle the fermenter during this process so you don't stir up any of the yeast sediment. For this process you need:**

    - Sanitized glass carboy or bottling bucket
    - Sanitized racking cane
    - Sanitized transfer tubing

TECHNICAL STUFF

Commercially-produced seltzers are typically clarified by filtration and/or the use of centrifuges, but these processes and pieces of equipment are beyond the pocketbooks of most homebrewers. Gravity and sedimentation are the next best thing.

11. **When the wash has been transferred to your secondary vessel, this is where all flavorings are added.**

    If you plan to bottle your hard seltzer, this is the point in time at which you would also prime the wash with additional dextrose; this small additional dose of corn sugar is what will be converted to carbon dioxide within the sealed bottle, thereby carbonating your beverage.

12. **Commence bottling your seltzer. You can review priming and bottling steps in Chapter 14.**

13. **After allowing the requisite two weeks for the remaining yeast to consume the priming sugar and carbonate your beverage, your bottled seltzer should be ready to drink. Be sure to chill it down first.**

    If you have the equipment to serve your beverage on draught (see Chapter 16, "Keggling: Bottling's Big Brother"), then no further ingredients or processes are necessary, other than transferring your seltzer to your keg and carbonating it. What are you waiting for?

» Not chilling your beer

» Brewing organically

Chapter 23

Going Green: Being an Eco-Friendly Homebrewer

With all the talk these days of greenhouse gasses, carbon emissions, ozone holes, and melting glaciers, the concept of green products and practices are gaining steam (which isn't necessarily a green energy source). *Green* (for those of you who may have just awakened from a coma) generally refers to anything that's ecologically or earth-friendly. And it's not just car manufacturers who are becoming earth-conscious; even the international brewing industry is turning green, so to speak, and homebrewers everywhere are also doing their little part. This chapter takes a look at those products and practices that juxtapose the concepts of brew and green. Solar-powered brew kettle, anyone?

Brewing Green Beer: It's Not Just for St. Patrick's Day Any More

Very few people begin homebrewing out of necessity because commercial beer is readily accessible to just about everyone everywhere. But rather than simply buy a product out of convenience, these brewers make the conscious choice to spend their money, time, and effort on a pastime that isn't inherently easy or convenient. Now, with this same dedication and conviction, many homebrewers are making the choice to spend additional money, time, and effort to pursue the same hobby with the added challenges of brewing in a way that many consider socially conscious. Ecologically friendly brewing isn't necessarily cheaper or easier, but, on the other hand, some aspects of eco-friendliness can actually conserve resources — including your money.

Using the oft-repeated mantra of "Reduce, Reuse, Recycle" as a starting point, homebrewers have different avenues on which to begin their walk toward eco-friendliness. Ultimately, each individual brewer has to decide which of these practices is workable within his or her own circumstances. The following sections provide some ideas to get you started in your quest to become a green brewer.

Reduce

The first step in brewing green is reducing your usage of anything that's not eco-friendly. Here are some ways to make brewhouse reductions:

- **Your energy usage:** Gas heat is typically more economical to use than electrical heat and typically costs energy companies less to produce. Wherever possible, consider brewing with propane gas on high-BTU so-called turkey-cooker burners.

  WARNING

  Always allow for proper ventilation when using high-BTU propane burners. These are best used outdoors, away from flammable structures.

- **Your energy needs:** *Jacketing* (insulating) metal mash tuns, sparging vessels, and brewpots conserves heat. Not only will you save energy, but you'll also likely attain higher temperatures more quickly and sustain them longer.
- **Your usage of non-organic brewing ingredients:** Non-organic farming adds tons of toxic chemicals to the earth's soil and water each year. See the "Organically Speaking" section later in this chapter for more on organic issues.

  TIP

  Try growing your own organic hops at home. See Chapter 30 for more details on this process.

GREEN WITH ENVY

Commercial breweries are leading the way within the industry by employing green practices specific to their operations. Not only are these methods helping the breweries' bottom lines, but they're also gaining positive attention from local governments and the media. Some inspirational examples:

- The Mad River Brewing Company received an award from its hometown of Blue Lake, California, for reducing its solid wastes by a whopping 97 percent.
- The Sierra Nevada Brewing Company of Chico, California, was honored by then-Governor Arnold Schwarzenegger and awarded a $2.4-million rebate by the local gas and electric company for installing an energy-efficient power plant that lightened the load on the municipal power grid while significantly reducing air emissions.
- In 2003, Brooklyn Brewery in Brooklyn, New York, was the first business in New York City to operate on 100 percent wind-generated electricity.
- The New Belgium Brewery in Fort Collins, Colorado, following its own mission statement of "Ethical and Environmental Responsibility," has won several awards for its dedication to environmental ethics. The employee-owned brewery produces 100 percent of its own energy through the use of wind turbines and a unique *cogeneration* process by which bacteria produce methane gas. (A couple of beers and a bowl of chili usually work for me.)
- In Australia, the Foster's brewing conglomerate is adopting a new brewing technology that produces energy via brewery waste products. Called a *Microbial Fuel Cell,* this device feeds on organic substances like sugar, starch, and alcohol found in brewery wastewater, which it then turns into Watts and stores in a battery that can power various electrical components within the brewery. In addition to creating energy, the technology also leaves clean water and non-polluting carbon dioxide as by-products.

- **Your reliance on cleansers and sanitizers that aren't environmentally friendly:** You can't always avoid using environmentally *un*friendly cleansers and sanitizers, but reducing their use helps.

TIP

Two highly recommended environmentally friendly products are B-Brite, which is a no rinse, non-toxic all-purpose cleanser, and biodegradable Five Star PBW (Powdered Brewery Wash).

- **Your electricity usage:** If you use a refrigerator exclusively for your homebrew, you can save a considerable amount of energy by investing in a temperature controller (see Chapter 31). Most refrigerators maintain a temperature range of 30° to 40° Fahrenheit. If you raise the temperature just 10 degrees, you can save enough each month on electricity to pay for one batch of beer each year! And if you have a home kegging system, a refrigerator tap can also help save energy. By dispensing your brews from outside the refrigerator, you don't have to open the door as frequently, which significantly cuts down on the amount of energy needed to keep your brews cold.

Reuse

Another way to brew green is to reuse as much as you can to avoid contributing more waste to the environment. Here are some things you can reuse in your home brewery:

- **Your cleaning and sanitizing solutions:** It's not unreasonable to keep and reuse cleaning and sanitizing solutions that are only lightly used. Consider disposing of them only after several uses; it won't affect their power.

  TIP

  I know one conservative homebrewer who cleans all ten of his beer kegs one at a time by pouring the same sanitizing solution from one to the next over a period of a few hours.

- **Your cooling water:** This can be the water you use to cool your brewpot in the sink or the water that flows through your wort chiller. Think of both sources as usable water for cleaning dishes, for watering house plants, for mopping floors, for filling the dog's water bowl — whatever! The water that flows from wort chillers isn't only drinkable; it's also already heated. Consider pointing the chiller outflow hose into a clothes washing machine, or just use it to clean your home brewery when you're done brewing.

  WARNING

  The water that emerges from a chiller immersed in a pot of just-boiled wort may initially be as hot as 160° to 180° Fahrenheit. So let it cool a bit before you give Sparky a bath.

- **Your yeast:** It reproduces by itself, for Pete's sake! As I discuss in Chapter 30, you can re-propagate your yeast and keep a yeast bank in your fridge.

Recycle

Another way to brew green is to recycle as much as you can to reduce your contribution to the world's landfills. Here are some things in your home brewery that you can recycle:

- **Your plastic and glass:** When plastic equipment is no longer suitable for brewing or when beer bottles or carboys break, don't just throw them in the garbage. Both are likely recyclable, which means they won't add unwanted and unnecessary volume to a garbage dump somewhere.

TIP

When I decide that a large volume plastic vessel is no longer usable for brewing, I demote it to serving as a holding tank for reusable sanitizing solution. This practice guarantees that I always have some at the ready for that last-minute sanitizing of something I may have overlooked.

- **Your grain:** If you're a gardener, grain makes an excellent addition to compost piles. If you know anyone who owns any barnyard animals, spent grain is also a great food source for horses, cows, pigs, and so on. And you can always make high-fiber homemade bread with spent brewing grains.

No-Chill Brewing

Taking the "Reduce" example another step further, here's a new approach to being an eco-friendly brewer.

I remember when I first started brewing at home. One of the hardest things to accomplish was cooling down the brewpot filled with just-boiled wort. I used to do multiple sink baths, where you place the brewpot in a stopped-up sink and run the coldest possible water around it to cool it off. It seemed to take forever and ran a lot of good clean water down the drain.

Then came wort chillers which sped up the process immeasurably . . . but also ran a lot of perfectly good water down the drain.

Now, after years of believing that quick chilling was absolutely necessary for making good beer, along came some eco-minded Australian homebrewers showing us how wrong we can be.

Just as necessity has been the mother of other inventions, the need to conserve water in Australia and other drought-stricken locations made no-chill brewing a new, acceptable technique. Knowing just how much water was being wasted on the beer chilling process, Aussie homebrewers have found success by just racking the hot wort into a sanitized container and allowing it to cool down naturally to yeast pitching temperature.

The key to making no-chill brewing work is to use a food grade HDPE (high density polyethylene) fermenter.

Never, ever pour hot wort into a carboy or any other glass vessel. You run the risk of injury from severe burns or broken glass.

But be aware there are four possible downsides for your brew here:

- Carefully rack the hot wort into the fermenter; try to minimize contact with air (*hot side aeration*); otherwise your beer may pick up oxygen that will cause it to go stale more quickly.
- Something called DMS (dimethyl sulfide) may get trapped in your beer, giving it a creamed-corn or cooked-corn aroma and flavor. But assuming your wort underwent a good rolling boil, most DMS should have been driven out of the beer at this point.
- When you use the no-chill method, your wort will remain at hop isomerization temps for a lot longer than normal (175° F (79° C) and above). No-chill brewers counteract this by postponing each hop addition by about 20 minutes. Failing to adjust hopping schedules has a tendency to leave the resulting beer with grassy hop flavor and excess bitterness.

  No-chill brewing seems to favor beer styles that are more malt-forward. Highly hopped beers, such as IPAs, don't seem to readily pass the taste test.
- There won't be the usual "cold break" (proteins clump up and drop out of solution) you get when you chill your beer, so the end result will likely be a cloudier beer. This can be counteracted with typical clarification techniques.

On the plus side, you can save water and time each time you brew a beer, and you save money by not having to buy a wort chiller. Good on ya, mate!

Organically Speaking

Brewing organic beer is really not as difficult as you may think, especially with the rapidly spreading interest in organic foods and ingredients. Organically grown ingredients for beer making are slowly but surely trickling down from the commercial brewing sources to homebrew supply shops. Rest assured, as the interest in organic beer grows, so too will the availability of organic ingredients.

Keep in mind, though, that you won't find any real financial incentive for brewing organic beer. This is but one of many steps toward becoming a green brewer; the real incentive to brew organically is rooted in the deep satisfaction of knowing that you're not placing an added burden on the environment. A commitment to sustainable agriculture and the environment is what brewing organic beer is really all about.

And, in case you're concerned, the process of brewing organic beer is no different from brewing regular beer; you're simply switching from non-organic ingredients to organic ingredients. The only caveat to this generalization is that if you're serious about maintaining high organic standards, organic ingredients and beer should never come in contact with any piece of equipment that you previously used to store, brew, or ferment non-organic ingredients and beer unless you first thoroughly cleaned and sanitized it to remove traces of all the verboten pesticides and fertilizers.

Why use organic ingredients?

The following are some important — and somewhat opinionated — considerations about organic brewing:

- **Brewing organically allows you to brew better beer.** Beer made with organic ingredients tends to be much clearer without requiring chemicals or fining agents, which in turn results in a cleaner taste.

TECHNICAL STUFF

  On average, organic malts have a lower protein content, which results in reduced haze problems in your finished beer. Also, organic malts leave no chemical deposits that may interfere with fermentation.

- **Brewing organically can contribute to your overall health and well-being.** By using organic ingredients, you can avoid consuming the often-toxic chemicals farmers and food processing companies use.
- **Brewing organically contributes to a better world.** Organic farming reduces erosion, soil nutrient depletion, water shortages, and pollution by not using chemicals to fertilize crops or to fight pests and diseases. Per acre, organic farming also provides more agricultural jobs than conventional farming.

By using organically grown ingredients to make your beer, you're automatically improving its purity. You're also supporting the organic farming industry, which contributes to the amount of land farmed in a sustainable and chemical-free way.

Beware of the urban myth that organic beers are less likely to produce hangovers due to their lack of chemicals — not true! Now where'd I put the aspirin?

Tracking the trend

The recent movement toward organic farming and the production of organically grown foods is well documented. Domestic sales of organic food and drink soared to new highs in 2020, jumping to over $60 billion, according to the 2021 Organic Industry Survey released by the Organic Trade Association (OTA).

It seems natural, then, that beer would also follow the trend — and it has. According to OTA data, organic beer sales went up 3.4 percent between 2017 and 2018 (the latest sales figures available) and even the world's largest brewer, AB InBev, has entered the market with its own organic beer label.

The modern organic beer movement traces its roots to Brauerei Pinkus-Müller in Münster, Germany, where the first all-organic beer was brewed in 1979 as the result of the brewer's disappointment in the declining quality of conventional malt at the time. He found organic malt to be a superior substitute, and the brewery switched to all-organic brewing a little over a decade later. Germany alone now boasts about 30 organic breweries. Pinkus-Müller's organic beers eventually influenced brewmasters abroad. In 1997, the USDA established the National Organic Program, which opened the door for Morgan Wolaver to found the first all-organic brewing company, Wolaver's Organic Ales, in Santa Cruz, California (alas, no longer in business).

The worldwide brewing industry is making huge strides on the organic beer sector, but American commercial brewers are lagging a bit behind. Perhaps more brewers in the U.S. would make organic beers today if it weren't for the many challenges they face. For example, the organic certification process can be expensive and burdensome, and some of the raw ingredients can be difficult to secure in bulk. It can also be expensive to maintain separate equipment for organic brewing. Luckily, most homebrewers have an easier time of it (for starters, you don't have to be certified). But if you're more interested in drinking organic beer than making it, check out the nearby "Perhaps you'd like to peruse our list of non-toxic beers?" sidebar.

Certifiably nuts: Determining what's really organic

Simply put, the United States Department of Agriculture (USDA) standards for organic beer are the same as those for organic foods: Ingredients must be grown without toxic pesticides or synthetic fertilizers in soil free from chemicals for at least three years, and bioengineered ingredients are a no-no. Keep in mind this organic certification process is kind of a work in progress. USDA regulations are likely to continue changing and modifying in the future.

TECHNICAL STUFF

Bioengineered ingredients are common in food production, including bioengineered corn that may appear in the brewing industry. The certified-organic label is a guarantee that the product doesn't contain bioengineered ingredients, in case you are trying to avoid foods with bioengineered ingredients.

PERHAPS YOU'D LIKE TO PERUSE OUR LIST OF NON-TOXIC BEERS?

Beer	Brewery	Country
Michelob Pure Gold	Anheuser-Busch	USA
Crosspath Organic Golden Ale	Allagash	USA
Fresh Cut Dry Hopped Pilsner	Peak Organic	USA
Laurelwood Free Range Red Ale	Hopworks	USA
Foret	DuPont	Belgium
Golden Promise	Caledonian	UK
Organic Chocolate Stout	Samuel Smith	UK
Jade	Benifontaine	France
Pinkus Alt	Pinkus-Müller	Germany

I should add that this description is *over*-simply put. Although this may all sound pretty straightforward, the specifics regarding how organically grown ingredients affect brewing processes and exactly how to define organic ingredients make this topic anything but simple. Check out the "It's not organic till the USDA signs" sidebar for all the boring details.

According to the United States Department of Agriculture (USDA), there are three levels of certifications for multi-ingredients products, such as beer. These include:

- **100-Percent Organic:** A beer brewed from all organic ingredients. For this kind of a beer, you can be sure that there are no pesticides or inorganic fertilizers used, and the end product is free from chemicals.
- **Organic:** Any beer labeled organic contains 95 percent organic ingredients. In such a case, the brewery would not find organic ingredients for the remaining five percent. On both organic and 100-percent organic beers, you might see the USDA organic seal.
- **Made with Organics:** These beers feature 70 percent organic ingredients. Most of these beers do not have the USDA organic seal. In most cases, breweries use either organic hops or malt, and all the other ingredients are not organic. Organic malt is the easiest to find, and most of the "Made with Organics" beers feature only malt and hops as the organic ingredients.

IT'S NOT ORGANIC TILL THE USDA SIGNS

In order for a beer to qualify for organic certification, the USDA requires that 95 percent of the ingredients used be organic. In other words, it must contain 95 percent organic ingredients, with the other 5 percent being non-organic ingredients on the USDA National List, provided that organic equivalents aren't commercially available in sufficient quantity. Are you still with me?

Currently, the National List only contains five items: corn starch, water-extracted gums, kelp, unbleached lecithin, and pectin. Besides hops, there are an additional 38 ingredients currently under consideration for inclusion on the National List.

This is how the USDA breaks down its organic certifications according to product composition:

- A raw or processed agricultural product sold, labeled, or represented as "100 percent organic" must contain, by weight or fluid volume, 100 percent organically produced ingredients.
- A raw or processed agricultural product sold, labeled, or represented as "organic" must contain, by weight or fluid volume, not less than 95 percent organically produced raw or processed agricultural products. Any remaining product ingredients must be organically produced, unless not commercially available in organic form, or must be nonagricultural substances or non-organically produced agricultural products produced consistent with the National List.
- Multi-ingredient agricultural products sold, labeled, or represented as "made with organic (specified ingredients or food group[s])" must contain, by weight or fluid volume, at least 70 percent organically produced ingredients produced and handled in accordance with USDA organic specifications.

Thirsty yet? Read your labels carefully . . .

Unless you've memorized the entire list of the USDA's organic certifications, what you read on product labels ranges from vague at best to outright confusing at worst. The four basic building blocks of beer are grain (typically malted barley), hops, yeast, and water, and the following sections tell you what you need to know about selecting organic versions of each.

Water

In terms of volume, water makes up about 95 percent of beer. Assuming you've got average filtered water, you don't have to worry about organic issues with it (and water isn't considered an ingredient by the USDA anyway).

Grain

Next up is the grain. Malted barley is the primary source of beer flavor and character, followed by wheat, corn, rice, oats, rye, and so on. All of these grains — malted or unmalted — now grow both organically and non-organically, so obviously, you need to be careful in choosing the grain you use to make organic beer. And in addition to the standard organic regulations against pesticides, herbicides, and fertilizers, watch out for grains tainted with GMOs.

To keep this stuff out of your beer, the best place to start brewing organic beer is with organic malt. Many brewers consider organic grain difficult to work with when compared to non-organic grain. Non-organic malt is easy to handle because of the uniformity in the barley kernels, and, unfortunately, uniformity falls victim to organic practices. Other than this disadvantage, you can substitute organic malts pound-for-pound in your favorite recipes. One big plus is that organic malts have a slightly higher conversion rate than conventional malts, so you can consider reducing the amount of organic grain in your recipe by 1 or 2 percent. Specialty malts are pretty much interchangeable.

The heading of organic malt also encompasses extracts produced with organic ingredients. As of now, only one organic malt extract is available to homebrewers. Fortunately, it's a pale, unhopped extract, which gives you a lot of leeway in your recipe formulation.

For homebrewers and beer lovers who may have grain-related food allergies, you can also find a small variety of gluten-free grains available, including buckwheat, millet, and quinoa. See Chapter 24 for more on gluten-free brewing.

Hops

Hops constitute the next-largest percentage of brewing ingredients, but their certification, status, and viability are currently in a state of flux (I think that's near Rhode Island). Yes, you can get organically grown hops, but not in great quantities; hops are subject to a variety of diseases and other growth-related problems. Quite a bit of confusion also surrounds the need for organic hops in the first place. Most small organic brewers insist on using them to make their products 100 percent organic, or at least to make their beers USDA Organic Certified (95 percent organic ingredients). Larger breweries argue that because hops constitute less than 5 percent of the total ingredient profile of their beers, beers brewed with non-organic hops still qualify for organic certification. And the debate rages on . . .

Hops are notoriously difficult to grow organically because they're subject to many diseases such as wilt, mildew, and hop mites. (See Chapter 5 for more on hops.) This is why no large-scale commercial hop grower in the United States has taken the risky leap to organic hop production. Currently, most of the few organic hop varieties available in the U.S. are imported from New Zealand, Germany, and the U.K. Of course, this scarcity affects the brewers' bottom lines as well; imported organic hops are 20 to 30 percent more expensive than conventional domestic hops.

Yeast

Finally, yeast is the last puzzle piece. Yeast itself is organic, but the liquid medium in which you propagate it will have an effect on its organic certification. If the grain-based wort was produced from non-organically grown grain, the yeast is considered non-organic. Eco-friendly homebrewers can also get specially packaged yeast; ask your homebrew supplier about their selection of organic yeast.

Adjuncts

Those brewers who like to use adjunct sugars in their beers can rest assured their interests are being looked after as well. In addition to organic rice syrup, brewers may also find cane sugar, corn sugar, and maltodextrin in the organic market.

WARNING

The USDA has recently developed a program to label foods that contain bioengineered ingredients to help allow consumers to identify foods containing bioengineered ingredients, and, for those concerned about their consumption, to avoid them. However, be aware that corn is one of the most bioengineered crops; to completely avoid GMOs, use a substitute for corn sugar such as malt extract or organic cane sugar.

More-intrepid brewers can also find a wide variety of organically grown herbs and spices. If you can't get these from your favorite homebrew supplier, your average organic food store probably stocks them.

» Dealing with gluten intolerance

» Brewing gluten-free beer

Chapter 24
Gluten-Free Brewing

Imagine going the rest of your life without beer; what a depressing thought! Unfortunately, some very real physical conditions make beer consumption difficult for many people. Luckily, beer made without gluten-filled products provides a glimmer of hope for these folks. For sufferers of gluten intolerance, brewing their own beer at home presents an opportunity to continue enjoying their favorite beverage without the risks normally associated with their condition.

Honestly speaking, beers made from gluten-free grains aren't likely to match regular beer for taste and quality. But to someone facing a lifetime beer-drinking restriction (gasp!), gluten-free beer is like manna from Heaven — made without gluten, of course. This chapter is all about brewing these gluten-free beers at home. Don't worry: The processes are largely the same; you just have to be more careful about the ingredients you choose.

Getting to Know Gluten

As I detail in Chapter 4, brewers have used many different grains to brew beer over the millennia. Barley is the most popular because of its many positive attributes and contributions toward making good beer. Wheat runs a close second in grain preference, distantly followed by rye. The problem with these grains — at least for people who suffer from *celiac disease*—is they all contain gluten.

MORE ABOUT CELIAC DISEASE

Celiac Disease is also known as *gluten-sensitive enteropathy, gluten intolerance,* or *celiac sprue.* Gluten intolerance is an auto-immune response some people's bodies have to gluten; this reaction damages the lining of the small intestine. The result is that nutrients quickly pass through the small intestine instead of being absorbed. Estimates show that 1 in every 133 people in the United States may be affected by this chronic, inherited disease that can ultimately lead to malnutrition if not treated. The disease is permanent, and damage to the small intestine will occur every time a sufferer consumes gluten, even if he or she doesn't experience any symptoms.

Gluten, which is a combination of the proteins *gliadin* and *glutenin*, is responsible for triggering an autoimmune reaction in the small intestines of people with celiac disease. That reaction can be very debilitating, causing the sufferer great discomfort and possibly long-term disruption to the function of their small intestine. This means they don't get the nutrients they need out of their food and may experience a range of other health issues as well. The only treatment available to people with gluten intolerance is a lifelong avoidance of products that contain gluten. That means no regular beer in their diets. (Check out the "More about celiac disease" sidebar for more information.)

TECHNICAL STUFF

Gluten helps make bread dough very elastic (so the yeast can make it rise) and gives the bread its characteristic chewiness. As a component of barley, wheat, and rye, gluten gives beer a thickness and chewiness as well.

In response to the growing demand for gluten-free beers in the commercial market, several breweries around the world introduce new gluten-free products each year (see the nearby "No disputin' gluten-free beers" sidebar for a list). England even hosts an international gluten-free beer festival each year.

Here's how they decide whether a beer is truly gluten-free or not:

- **Dedicated gluten-free:** The beer is brewed in a 100 percent dedicated gluten-free facility, which means no gluten product ever enters the brewery. This is the safest option for those with celiac disease.
- **Gluten-free:** The beer is brewed with gluten-free ingredients and is safe for celiacs to consume.
- **Gluten-reduced:** The beer is brewed with gluten, but the gluten content is reduced using an enzyme that breaks the gluten down. These beers contain trace amounts of gluten and may not be safe for celiacs to consume.

NO DISPUTIN' GLUTEN-FREE BEERS

Most of these brewers use 100 percent gluten-free ingredients and processes in the production of their beers. However, some of the filtering processes used by these breweries simply render gluten undetectable — which would result in a *low*-gluten, not gluten-*free*, beer. Unless a beer is totally gluten-free, celiac sufferers have no assurance that it's completely safe for them to drink. Buyer and imbiber beware!

Beer	Brewery	Country
New Grist	Lakefront	U.S.
Shakparo Ale	Sprecher	U.S.
Bard's Gold	Bard's Tale	U.S.
Redbridge	Anheuser-Busch	U.S.
Pale Ale, Lager	Omission	U.S.
Porter	Aurochs	U.S.
Green's Discovery Amber Ale	DeProef	Belgium
G-Free Pilsner	St. Peter's	U.K.
Pale Ale	Glutenberg	Canada
Mongozo Buckwheat White	Mongozo Beers	Belgium
Daura	Damm S.A.	Spain

WARNING

Look for an ingredient listing of grains that don't contain gluten; these types of beers contain less than 20 parts per million (ppm) of gluten.

From Intolerant to Tolerable: Brewing Gluten-Free Beer at Home

Let me set the record straight here: Gluten-free beers don't taste exactly like regular beers. Compared to regular brewing, the ingredients available for gluten-free beer are limited, so you have to use your imagination when formulating your gluten-free beer recipes. I address this topic in greater detail a bit later.

Readying your equipment

One of the first considerations for the at-home brewer is making sure their equipment doesn't cause cross-contamination. In other words, if you've previously brewed regular beer in the equipment, you need to redouble your cleaning efforts. This includes everything from your grain mill (if you brew all-grain) to your brewpot, your fermenters, your transfer hoses, your bottles, and every piece of equipment in between. Don't take chances here; even the minutest traces of gluten can make a celiac sufferer ill. See Chapter 3 for details on proper cleaning and sanitation practices.

Substituting safe ingredients

The next consideration is where to obtain the appropriate ingredients for brewing gluten-free beer. Start with the easiest parts: Neither water nor hops play any part in gluten-free brewing, so don't worry about these ingredients. Just brew with what's readily available. The main ingredient concern is the fermentable grain or starch you plan to substitute for the glutinous barley or wheat you use to brew typical beers.

The following list spells out the prohibited grains (and their derivatives) that celiac sufferers need to avoid:

- Barley or malted barley
- Malt or malt flavoring
- Malt vinegar
- Rye
- Wheat (including durum, semolina, kamut, and spelt)
- Triticale (sometimes used in brewing)

Although sorghum and buckwheat are the most commonly substituted gluten-free grains (check out the "Sorghum and buckwheat" sidebar), you have plenty of options when you're looking for safe grains and starches:

- Sorghum
- Buckwheat
- Rice

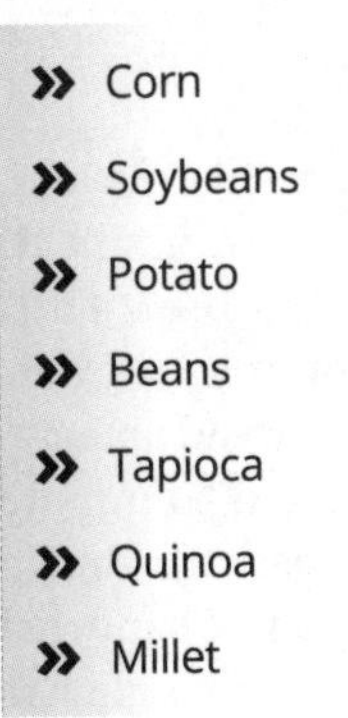

- Corn
- Soybeans
- Potato
- Beans
- Tapioca
- Quinoa
- Millet

Note: Although consuming uncontaminated oats in moderation (1 cooked cup a day) is considered safe for the average celiac sufferer, health professionals are concerned that most oats may be cross-contaminated with glutinous grains.

The following sections suggest other safe ingredient substitutes.

Extract-ly what you need

Fortunately for the extract brewer, a couple of products on the market make life easier for the celiac sufferer. At least one major maltster in the U.S. markets white sorghum syrup. Pound-for-pound, this syrup is equivalent to regular malt extract, and you can use it in the same way. Be sure to read labels, however; in at least one of these products, processors add simple sugars (white cane sugar, honey) during production. This added sugar creates a more-fermentable beer, which typically results in a drier beer.

This point is where your imagination kicks in. In order to keep your beer sweet and flavorful, consider adding flavorings, adjuncts, herbs, and spices to keep it interesting. Try using corn or rice syrup, molasses, treacle, brown sugar, or fruit juices and the like to make your gluten-free brew unique.

SORGHUM AND BUCKWHEAT

Sorghum is a valuable food source in its native northeast Africa. It's a vigorously growing grass that tolerates the African climate very well, which makes it a common ingredient in African beer. Buckwheat, which traces its roots (no pun intended) to central and western China, is actually an herb. Its nuts are milled, separating the edible interior (called *groats*) from its outer husk. The groats are then roasted and used as a grain. Buckwheat blossoms are also full of nectar, which makes them popular on beekeeping farms. Hmmm, now I'm thinking mead . . .

Gluten-free but flavorful

Yet another way to enhance your beer with grain-like flavors without any concern about gluten is to roast your buckwheat or sorghum. If you like roasty-toasty flavors in your beer or you want to make your brew a little darker, consider roasting some raw sorghum or buckwheat grain in your oven and steeping it in your wort as you would a specialty malt. Simply spread about a pound of grain on a pizza tin (or similar apparatus) and roast for 10 to 30 minutes at 350° Fahrenheit (depending on the degree of toastiness you desire). You can use this roasted grain immediately or store it refrigerated in a sealable sandwich bag. You can use anywhere between a 1/4 pound and a full pound in a single batch for more complex beer flavor and overall character.

WARNING

Depending on your source of gluten-free grains, be aware that some grains may be sold as seed and not intended for human consumption. This seed may be treated with junk you don't want to be drinking in your beer later on.

Brewing gluten-free beers from all grain

For you all-grain brewers who want to try your hands at making gluten-free beer, listen up . . . er, uh, read carefully. This undertaking has a degree of difficulty above and beyond brewing regular all-grain beers. The first consideration here is finding the right grains in sufficient quantity at a reasonable price. You also have to make sure they're the malted variety. As always, start with your local purveyor of homebrew supplies. If your favorite homebrew shop doesn't stock them, you should be able to find many gluten-free grains in better supermarkets or health-food stores. If not, try searching for them online. Finding the right grains can be somewhat expensive but well worth the price and effort for someone who can't drink beer otherwise.

As always, when making beer from all grain you must first mash your grain. One of the main challenges in mashing gluten-free grains is that they're low in *diastatic power.* In other words, they lack the requisite enzymes for conversion. (Check out Chapter 12 for more on mashing procedures.) You might want to consider adding amylase enzyme to your mash water — about 1 teaspoon per 5 gallons of water. (See Chapter 11 for more information about enzymes.)

Another issue with gluten-free grains is that many of them — including sorghum — are huskless. This deficiency means you need to add about 1/2 pound of rice hulls to your mash in order to lauter and sparge efficiently.

If you choose to forego mashing and attempt to gelatinize your gluten-free grains, be aware that the gelatinization temperature of the starches in most gluten-free grains is higher than that of regular brewing grains. With sorghum, corn, and rice, the gelatinization temperature is about 180° Fahrenheit, but these grains contain fewer required enzymes to convert the starches to soluble sugars. Adding an amylase enzyme preparation (about 1 teaspoon per 5 gallons of water) is helpful in this regard.

Armed with this knowledge, formulating a recipe for gluten-free beer is no different from any other regular beer. Simply substitute your favorite gluten-free grain for barley or wheat. For yeast suggestions, check out the next section.

Last, but not yeast

The last of the four principal beer ingredients is yeast. Yeast by itself isn't harmful to people with celiac disease. Therefore, you can use dry yeast to ferment any gluten-free beer as long as you rehydrate it in plain water (with no malt products). What is harmful to celiac sufferers is the liquid medium in which commercial yeast is propagated; the base solution of this medium is typically wort derived from malted barley.

So, if you make a liquid yeast starter at home, it must be gluten-free, too. If you use a normal yeast strain, you need to plate out the yeast on a petri dish or slant and then propagate the culture from a single yeast colony by using molasses or sorghum syrup as your culture media. As always, you must carry out all these processes in a very sterile environment.

» Aging your beer in or on wood

» Understanding the many ways of souring beer

» Making your beer acidic

Chapter 25
Barrel Aging and Souring Beer

Digging deep into brewing history, you'll find that the use of wooden barrels has been around for centuries. Barrels replaced clay pots and amphorae a millennia ago in Europe, and in that time they've been used to ferment beer, age it, and transport it, as well as to serve beer directly from the wooden vessels.

That was until post-Prohibition (1930s) when vessels made of metals — such as stainless steel and aluminum — and eventually food grade plastics, replaced the oaken vessels. These far more durable kegs relegated the old leaky barrels to the scrap heap of brewing history. Or so it was thought.

Within the last half century, however, some American brewers decided to re-visit the idea of aging beer in wood, including the Ballantine Brewing Company (originally of Newark, New Jersey, now owned by Pabst). They were certainly ahead of their time when they introduced their oak-aged Ballantine IPA in the late 1970s, a beer that to this day I consider perspective-changing. (See Figure 25-1.)

A couple decades later, Larry Bell, owner of Bell's brewery in Kalamazoo, Michigan, was doing some barrel-aging experimentation of his own, though he never fully capitalized on the venture. The key detail in both of these instances is that the barrels being used were raw oak; they had never been used to age any beverage other than beer.

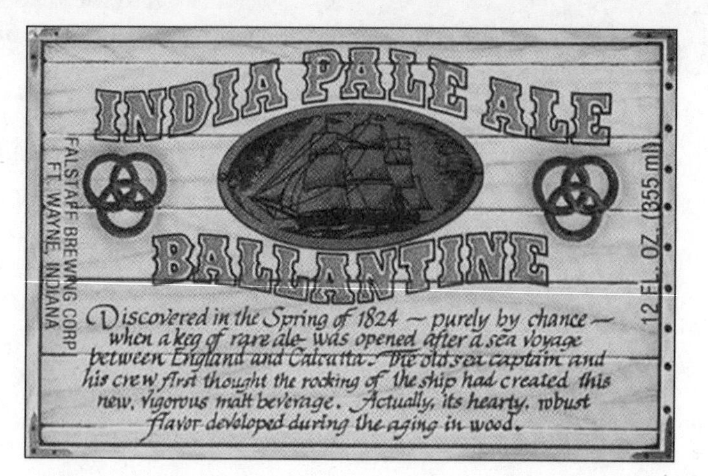

FIGURE 25-1: Ballantine's oak-aged IPA.

The current trend towards aging beer in oaken barrels that previously contained other fermented or distilled liquids has only been around for a bit longer than a quarter century. In fact, it can be traced to a specific year and a specific brewery.

In 1995, Goose Island Head Brewer Greg Hall was planning a special 1,000th batch of beer brewed at the Chicago brewery founded by his father, John Hall, just seven years earlier. The beer was to be a big and brawny imperial stout with an alcohol content to match. Hall, who was a fan of Kentucky bourbon, conceived the idea of aging his commemorative beer in barrels used by one of his favorite distilleries, Jim Beam. The resulting beer, branded Bourbon County stout, was a groundbreaking success, and, despite thinking that he might never brew that beer again, Hall's BBC is still the standard-bearer for Bourbon barrel-aged beers today. It's also ascribed with having inspired many other variations on this barrel-aging theme.

Barrel-Aging Beginnings

Although Greg Hall and Goose Island Beer Company are credited with introducing the world to the pleasures of barrel-aged beer, it's not only possible, but probable, that local homebrewers actually led the experimentation of aging beer in and on wood. A handful of Chicago area homebrew clubs are known to have toyed with barrel aging a year or three in advance of Hall's memorable creation.

I can attest to my own experimentation in this field as early as 1988, though it came about in a rather different way. In those days, old wine and whiskey barrel halves were sold at home centers and plant nurseries as decorative flower planters. While prepping a couple of these for my wife's prized petunias, I drilled through the head of the half barrel with a 1-inch spade bit to allow for ample water drainage. As the bit bored through, heating up the wood, the intoxicating aromas of oak and red wine met my nostrils, and I was instantly entranced! Recalling the old Ballantine IPA, I knew immediately I needed to gather the fragrant wood shavings and store them away them for my next beer experiment.

Soon thereafter I brewed a Belgian dubbel that was to destined to become one of the best beers I would ever make. After a cursory primary fermentation, I racked the beer into my wood shaving-bedded carboy and allowed it to take a nice month-long nap. Though the wait seemed interminable, it was worth every day and hour. The fruity flavors of the dubbel were a seamless match for the red wine notes, and the sweetness of the base beer was perfectly balanced against the dry tannins from the oak. Not only was that beer heavenly to sip and savor at home, it also fared well in competition, winning 1st and 2nd place ribbons in the same contest in consecutive years!

Old World barrel usage and New World barrel usage

Quickly reviewing the first two sections of this chapter, I need to clarify a couple of things before moving forward. The first thing is what I call "Old World" barrel usage vs. "New World" barrel usage. The wooden beer barrels that I mentioned that had been in use going back a millennia ago (the "Old World"), were typically pitch-lined.

Pitch is another term for sap from pine trees or other coniferous trees, and this pitch served two primary purposes. First, it helped to seal the barrel by filling in cracks and holes between the barrel staves where beer might have otherwise leaked out. Second, the pitch formed a thin barrier between the liquid and the wood, thus keeping any extraneous flavors — both good and bad — from seeping into the beer.

Now, in the "New World" method of keeping beer in barrels, the wood-based flavors are considered desirable; thus, the barrels now being used are not only not pitch-lined, but they are most often acquired from wineries and distilleries where the barrels formerly stored wine and distilled products. The added flavors of the wines and distillates are what give these New World barrel-aged beers their esteemed character.

In wood vs. on wood

The second thing I need to clarify is the difference between "in wood" and "on wood." The story about Goose Island aging that commemorative beer in an oak barrel is an obvious example of a beer aged *in* wood (the beer is literally in the barrel). The vignette about racking my Belgian dubbel onto a bed of wood shavings in my carboy is a straightforward example of a beer being aged *on* wood. Homebrewers will have to assess their home brewery situation before deciding to go all-in or all-on.

It's fair to say that not all homebrewers will be able to age their beer in barrels, and there are a few perfectly legitimate reasons for this:

- The unavailability of the desired barrel (size and/or type)
- The prohibitive cost of obtaining a barrel (in excess of $100, plus shipping)
- Lack of storage space in the home brewery
- Depending on batch size, an insufficient amount of beer to fill a full-size barrel

TIP

If you're a member of a homebrew club, you can do like many others have: Pool your resources. As few as a half-dozen brewers making 5 gallon batches each can fill a 30-gallon barrel.

Even if any of the preceding reasons describe your situation, there's no reason to despair. There are still multiple ways you can imbue your beer with those incredibly wonderful aromas and flavors of a true barrel-aged beer. Besides, it's much cheaper, easier, and quicker to add wood to a beer-filled vessel than the other way around.

At the homebrewing level, there are many options for you to consider. You can add wood shavings directly to your carboy, just as I did. Homebrew supply shops sell oak in a variety of forms, including rough wood chips, smooth and uniform cubes, infusion spirals of varying sizes, and more. (See Figure 25-2.)

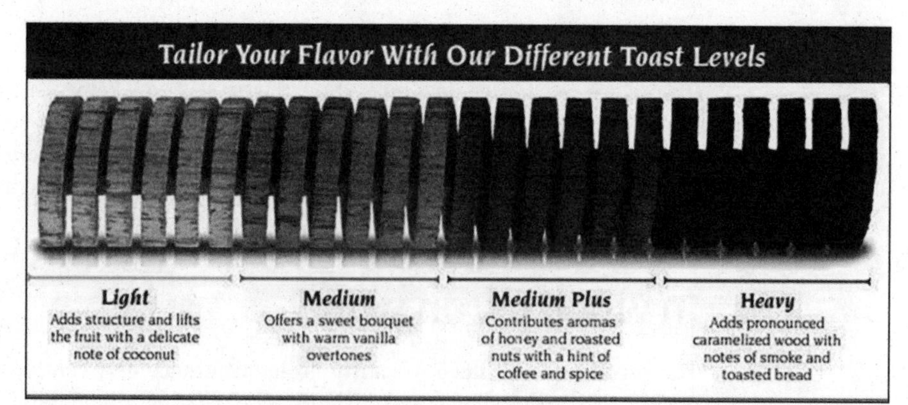

FIGURE 25-2: Oak infusion spirals showing various toast levels.

While shopping for these oak products, you may notice that you're given your choice in the "toast" level of the product. Just as bourbon barrels are toasted (charred) on their insides, oak products are also toasted to varying degrees — usually light, medium, and heavy. What level of toast you choose will have an effect on the color, aroma, and flavor of your beer, so it's best to stick with light toast for paler beers and darker toast for darker beers. These products are typically sold in quantities appropriate to batch sizes.

What is missing when you buy these products, though, is the flavor of the barrel, that is, the taste of the wine or the distilled liquor that you might want to infuse into your beer. This means you'll have to soak your chips, cubes, or spirals in your favorite alcohol beverage before adding them to your secondary vessel. I suggest allowing them to soak for at least one week prior to adding them to the beer. This also has the added benefit of sanitizing the wood prior to adding it to your beer.

American mega-brewer Anheuser-Busch likes to tout the fact that its Budweiser beer is "beechwood aged." What this means is that small rough planks of beechwood are added to the aging vessel "*which enhances fermentation creating a crisper, more sparkling carbonation while imparting smoothness to the characteristic taste of Budweiser*," according to the A-B website. It should be noted that because the same wood planks are regularly rinsed and reused, this method does not leave any residual wood flavor in the beer.

Oak Is Oak-kay

So, what is it about oak wood, in particular, that makes it perfect for making barrels and for aging a variety of beverages? It's been long established that oak is the species of preference for barrel-making for the following reasons:

- Oak is durable.
- Oak is less porous than many other wood species.
- Oak imbues beer (and wine and whiskey) with pleasant and desirable flavors.
- Oak is abundant in Europe and North America (where the majority of the world's wines, whiskies, and beers happen to be made).

American white oak is considered more robust than European white oak, which, unless you are a bourbon maker, is not necessarily a good thing. French *Limosin* oak is considered top-of-the-line by winemakers.

Old Barrel Flavors Create New Beer Flavors

The fact that the first-ever commercial example of a barrel aged beer was bourbon flavored was, more-or-less, happenstance. Because American bourbon makers can only use a barrel once before discarding it, it means that there was always an overabundance of old bourbon barrels and bourbon makers practically gave them away.

Due to the great interest in barrel-aged beers today, though, the demand for old bourbon barrels has skyrocketed — and so has the price. But where some brewers saw roadblocks, others saw opportunity. They simply turned their attention to other barrel-aged distillates, including, especially, wine.

Now beers are also aged in a huge variety of barrels that once contained these alcoholic beverages:

- Whiskey
- Scotch
- Rum
- Tequila
- Gin
- Sherry
- Red and white wine
- Fortified wine (port, Madeira)
- Distilled wine (brandy, cognac)

Heck, there are even beers that have been aged in old Tabasco sauce barrels. Now that's a hot shot!

TECHNICAL STUFF

The Dogfish Head brewery is known for making boundary-pushing beers; among them is one that was aged in unusual wood from South America. Palo Santo Marron is a brown ale aged in the exotic palo santo wood from Paraguay. *Palo santo* means *holy tree*, and its wood has been used in South American wine-making communities.

Over a Barrel

Given the potentially huge number of flavor combinations among beer styles and barrel flavors, it's a good idea to take a closer look at the variables involved in barrel aging.

I recommend starting with determining what type of barrel will be used; you need to know what you're working with (bourbon, red wine, tequila, and so on).

Next, you need to decide on a base beer style. Will you be brewing a porter, a stout, a Belgian quad? Some beer styles just naturally work better with certain barrel flavors than others. Lighter, paler beers are a better match for white wine, gin, and tequila barrel flavors, whereas dark beers have a greater affinity for bourbon, scotch, whiskey, and red wine.

Do you plan to do any blending or will you be leaving it "straight" (unblended)? Of course, in order to do any blending you need more than one barrel source — though it need not be a different barrel type. It's just as possible to blend a beer between two bourbon barrels, for instance, as it is to blend between a bourbon barrel and a gin barrel.

TECHNICAL STUFF

"Blending" is an important technique used by brewers of barrel-aged beers (and sour beers) to soften the rough edges of some beers, while brightening the flavors of others. Older beers can soften the bold and brash flavors of a younger beer, whereas a younger beer can liven up an older, mellowed beer.

The Boston Beer Company takes barrel blending to a new level with its 50-plus proof Utopias beer. Ever since 2007, every Utopias release has spent time in both aging barrels and finishing barrels, sometimes as many as three different brands and beverage types mixed together to create the finished blend.

Oxidation and Bacteria

As if choosing barrel types and pairing beer styles was not enough for brewers to think about, they also have to take into consideration the level of oxidation that occurs while the beer is aging over longer periods of time.

As beer ages in wooden barrels, the staves of the barrel absorb a portion of the beer, and a further amount may evaporate over time, which can leave a void. Some brewers may top-up their barrels with more beer to fill that void; other brewers may fill the void by blanketing the beer with a layer of carbon dioxide gas.

Still other brewers may choose to allow their beer to age and develop totally naturally and not do anything about the void in the barrel. The process of allowing minute amounts of air to seep through the wood is a very slow, controlled oxidation, which leads to a depth of flavor that can't be gained any other way.

With long-term aging in mind, brewers can't always set a packaging date on the calendar ahead of time. More often than not, the beer decides when it's ready.

Barrel-aged and wood-aged beers need to be tasted periodically to assess their flavor progression. This process can take weeks, months, or even years.

Regarding bacteria, the staves of a wooden barrel are a perfect place for them to hide out. Beer-souring microbes make a home in the wood, and once they are there, they're hard to get rid of. I'll have more to say about these bugs in "Souring Beer," later in this chapter.

Good vs. Evil?

While the beer is quietly slumbering away within the barrel, it is slowly but measurably disappearing. Like all liquids exposed to air, a portion of the beer naturally evaporates over time. This portion is referred to as *angel's share*. And because the barrel wood is somewhat porous, another portion of the beer is absorbed by the wood. This portion is called *devil's cut*. Between good and evil, as much as 25 percent of the beer may be lost over time. It's one of the reasons why barrel-aged beer is often expensive to buy.

Extraction in Action

This absorption of the beer by the wood, by the way, is called *extraction*, and it's a very natural and efficient way of flavoring the beer with the character of the barrel. Over time, whether it's from season-to-season or just day-to-night, the ambient temperatures where the barrel is stored may fluctuate up and down. In warm temperatures, the barrel imperceptibly expands, allowing beer to be absorbed into the wood. As the temperature cools, the barrel contracts, forcing much of the beer back inside the barrel. In doing so, the flavors hidden within the barrel wood are extracted from it, imbuing the beer with the wonderful flavors of the oak and of the beverage previously stored within the barrel.

Even though there's plenty of science in barrel-aging beer, it will always be more of an art form. There are so many variables and so many options that each beer produced can be a work of liquid art on its own. It takes time and it takes patience, but the rewards can be flavorful beyond measure.

Souring Beer

The first time I tasted what is generically called a sour beer today was at a beer tasting with British beer expert Michael Jackson in Boulder, Colorado, in 1986. The beer in question was Rodenbach Grand Cru, assuredly a world-class example of a Flanders red ale. Although it was not the first time I'd tasted an acidic beer, it was definitely the first time I tasted a beer that was soured on purpose!

Sour beers have been a part of brewing reality throughout the millennia, but typically, acid flavor in beer was considered undesirable. It usually meant something went wrong; unwelcome microbes ruined the beer. In fact, before the advent of artificial refrigeration brewers often ceased brewing during the warm summer months because beer spoilage was so common.

And yet, perusing beer style guidelines we can find quite a few different beers for which acidic flavor profiles are common. And, in fact, the generic sour beer category is currently one of the fastest growing segments in the craft beer market.

I say "generic" sour beer category because it's rarely acknowledged outside the brewing community that the various acidic beer styles in existence get their brisk flavor and character in very different ways. They all seem to get lumped together in a singular category when, in fact, they are very different from one another. I address this in greater detail later in this chapter.

Meanwhile, here's a reminder that there are three ways beer can go sour in a brewery — not all of them are good.

- **Unintentionally:** Beer that went bad as a result of a mistake at the brewery; poor beer handling or poorly maintained equipment caused the beer to go "off."
- **Intentionally:** Beer that is made according to a sour style; the recipe is specifically designed to produce a sour-tasting beer.
- **Anticipated:** Beer that is acidified as a matter of barrel microbes' predicted influence on the finished beer; the actual outcome cannot be known in advance.

REMEMBER

Just to clarify: Not all barrel-aged beers are soured and not all sour beers are barrel-aged.

Acidic Does Not Always Equal Sour

Another way that the category of so-called sour beers is misunderstood is that the acid levels in these beers differ from very low to quite high, and their resulting sour perception mirrors this.

At the low end of the sour spectrum the acidity might be described simply as *tart*. From there, the acidity level would step up to *tangy*, then *puckery*, then, ultimately, *vinegary*. Here are some examples of foods that would fit these descriptors:

- Tart: Greek yogurt, cranberries
- Tangy: Barbecue sauce, raspberries
- Puckery: Pickles, sauerkraut
- Vinegary: Worcestershire sauce, vinaigrette

I think it's fair to say that there's a notable acidic difference between Greek yogurt and vinaigrette dressing . . . and so it is with beer styles.

Simple Sours vs. Complex Sours

To help understand the world of acidic beers, it helps to break them down into two easy-to-comprehend categories: simple sour beers and complex sour beers.

It can be said that simple sour beers are generally

- German in origin
- Produced in days to weeks
- Soured with lactic acid (considered a clean-tasting acidity)
- Typically fermented and aged in stainless-steel vessels
- Beers whose acidity levels range from tart to tangy

Simple sours of German origin would include:

- Gose
- Berliner Weisse
- Lichtenhainer

It can be said that complex sour beers are generally

- Belgian in origin
- Produced in months to years
- Soured with multiple microbes
- Fermented or aged in wooden vessels
- Beers whose acidity levels range from tangy to vinegary

Complex sour beers of Belgian origin would include:

- Lambic
- Gueuze (this is a blend of different ages of lambic)
- Flanders red ale
- *Oud bruin* (a.k.a. Flanders brown ale)

The "Bugs" in Sour Beer

So how do brewers sour their beers? Well, creating acidic flavor in beer is done with different ingredients as well as with different processes. Sometimes it's done very intentionally and sometimes it occurs very naturally.

To start with, it's important to familiarize yourself with the various bacteria that are responsible for acidifying beer (see Figure 25-3). Among the most common are

- ***Lactobacillus:*** If you've ever inadvertently taken a swig of milk that's gone bad, you've already experienced the taste of *Lactobacillus*. *Lacto*, for short, is a milk-souring bacteria that also affects beer and is most common in German-style sour beers.

» ***Pediococcus:*** *Pediococcus* is a bacteria that is commonly found in spontaneously fermented beers as well as in barrel-soured beers. *Pedio*, for short, is anaerobic, which means it can survive in oxygen-free environments, including beer. Unlike *Lactobacillus*, Pedio's acidity is rather less clean-tasting and can even be a bit funky; it's very often found in most Belgian sour beer styles. *Pediococcus* can also be blamed for creating buttery tasting diacetyl in beer and in poorly sanitized beer equipment.

» ***Acetobacter:*** If you've ever tasted malt vinegar, you know what *Acetobacter* can do to beer. Among the beer-souring bugs, *Acetobacter*, or *Aceto* for short, is the most damaging. No beer style should ever be as sharply acidic as straight vinegar, but certain Belgian styles, such as lambic and Flanders red ales, can certainly display light vinegary notes as part of its flavor profile.

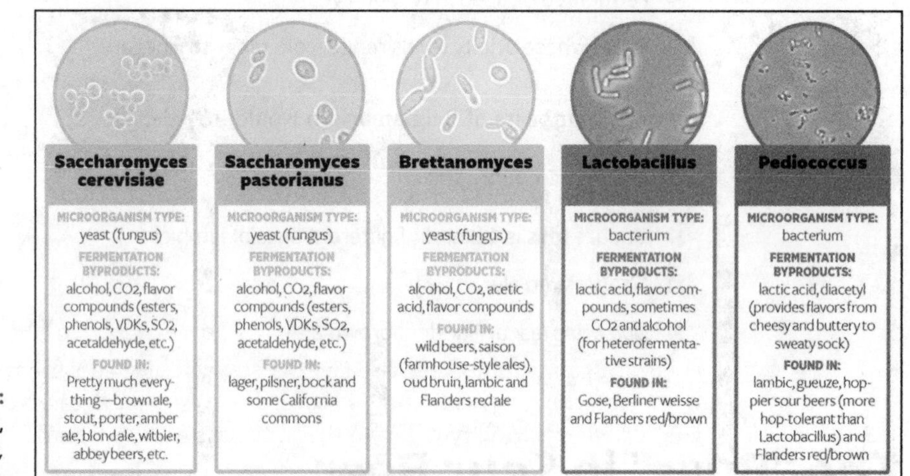

FIGURE 25-3: Beer yeast, *Brettanomyces*, and bacteria.

Beer Souring Processes

There are also several ways to acidify your beer — without even including those done by mistake. You can acidify your beer at various stages throughout its production beginning as early as the day you mash the grain. These stages can be divided into three easy-to remember categories:

» Pre-fermentation

» Fermentation

» Post-fermentation

Pre-fermentation

Acidifying your beer pre-fermentation includes

- Sour mashing
- Kettle souring

Both of these processes are fairly easy to do — and that goes a long way towards explaining why there is a profusion of sour beers in the craft beer industry. These types of beer can be made quickly and cheaply.

Sour mashing is simple because the *Lactobacillus* needed for acidification is already present on the grain. All you have to do is allow a small portion of raw malt to steep in your mash for 12 to 48 hours to allow the *Lactobacillus* to acidify the mash before continuing with your typical mashing and brewing procedures.

It's very important to work with a pH meter (see Chapter 31) to keep your mash acidity in check. The typical range for acidic beers is about 3.6 to 3.8 for medium sour and 3.2 to 3.5 for aggressively sour beers.

The beauty of sour mashing is that all of the Lacto bacteria is killed off during the boiling phase, leaving all that wonderful acidity in the wort intact.

Simple sour mashing

Following is a simple list of sequential steps needed to perform a simple sour mashing technique. Acidifying your beer doesn't get much easier than this. Unless you're kettle souring (you'll find that info in the next section).

1. **Mash as usual. Run through your regular mash schedule to convert the grain starches to sugar. Be sure to mash out (raise the temperature to 170°F to kill off the enzymes). The high temperature should also kill any bad bacteria.**
2. **Drop the mash temperature to 115-120°F (46-49°C).**
3. **Inoculate the mash with a specific *Lactobacillus* culture or simply toss in a handful of un-milled grain (take advantage of the Lacto that's naturally present on the grain). If you opt for the culture, it's a good idea to make a starter like you would with yeast before you stir it in so the bacteria can establish itself and choke off any competition from other bacteria.**

4. **Protect your mash from oxygen and other bacteria. Purge the top of your mash tun with CO_2 and then press a layer of plastic wrap into the mash, making sure that there are no bubbles. Don't forget to cover the mash tun.**
5. **Hold the mash temperature at 115-120°F (46-49°C) and wait. This is the hardest part. It helps to use electric blankets or heating pads to accomplish this.**
6. **Give the mash at least 8 to 12 hours before checking the level of sourness. Use your pH meter to see if you're in the target 3.6–3.8 range. Most likely, you'll need to give it more time if you're brewing a more assertively sour beer.**
7. **Once the mash pH is the proper range, continue with sparging as you normally would. Finish the brewing process as with any other beer.**

Simple kettle souring

Kettle souring beer is a bit different, but it's even easier. Your job is to lower the pH of your wort to the desired level, and the simplest way to do this is by adding food-grade lactic acid directly to the wort in the kettle.

Because lactic acid is available through homebrew suppliers, you can simply buy it and add measured doses of it directly to your brew kettle to achieve the desired pH level. This is typically done with an eye dropper.

REMEMBER

When adding lactic acid directly to your brew, make sure it's to the full volume of beer (5 gallons, 10 gallons, and so on), not just what's in the brew kettle. Otherwise, your pH readings and the sourness level itself will be way off.

Adding lactic acid directly to the wort also has other benefits. First and foremost, it reduces the chance of other infections from happening. Acidification of the wort to a pH of 4.5 or lower is very effective at staving off other unwanted bacterial strains, thus helping to avoid microbial contamination.

Second, lactic acid can be added to the beer after fermentation is over, allowing you to expertly dial in the amount of sourness needed. It's a win-win situation.

REMEMBER

Sour mashing and kettle souring are fine for making a standard Gose, Berliner Weisse or Lichtenhainer beers, but using these processes falls far short of producing any of the traditional Belgian sour beer styles. For those styles, much more complexity is required. Unfortunately, some craft brewers fail to acknowledge this distinction.

Fermentation

Acidifying your beer during fermentation means

- Pitching known beer-souring microbes such as *Lactobacillus, Pediococcus*, and *Acetobacter*.
- Using "spontaneous fermentation" to inoculate your wort

Spontaneous fermentation is a very Old World method of allowing wild airborne yeast and bacteria to initiate fermentation without any help from the brewer. Because wild yeast and bacteria are very different depending on where in the world you are, this method of fermentation can be a real crap shoot.

Here are some yeast brands and strains that can help you create your favorite sour beer styles:

- White Labs WLP655 Belgian Sour Mix
- Wyeast 3763 Roeselare Blend
- Omega OYL 605
- Wildbrew Philly Sour

Post-fermentation

Acidifying your beer post-fermentation means

- Pitching known beer-souring microbes into your beer following fermentation with "normal" (*Saccharomyces*) beer yeast.
- Aging your beer in barrels or foeders whose wood is known to harbor the "bugs" listed previously in this chapter.

A foeder (pronounced FOO-*der*) is a large, oak vessel used for fermenting and aging wine and beer.

TIP

WARNING

HAVE YOU MET BRETT?

Speaking of wild yeast, there is one class of wild yeast known colloquially as *Brett*. This is short for *Brettanomyces*, and its presence in beer is welcomed by some and loathed by others.

Brettanomyces means *British fungus*, which is a reference to the fact that it was British brewers who first identified this critter in beer. Brett is known to have many different species, each with its own unique character. Some of the most common species found in beer are

- *Bruxellensis*
- *Clausenii*
- *Delbruckii*
- *Lambicus*

Generally speaking, Brett imparts a "wild" character to beer, which is often described as barnyard, wet dog, or horse blanket aroma (did I mention that Brett was not universally appreciated?). Brett also has a very drying effect on the palate.

Brettanomyces is also mistakenly believed to sour beer. Yes, Brett does produce minute quantities of acid, but never enough to give the perception that a beer is sour. The fact that Brett is often found in the company of bacteria like Lacto, Pedio, and Aceto is probably why it gets wrongly blamed — or credited, depending on your partiality — for souring beer.

If you'd like to get an idea of what a Brett beer tastes like, seek out a bottle of Orval from the Trappist monastery in Belgium; it's considered a world classic.

Various Brett yeast strains can be bought through all of the usual yeast suppliers and homebrew supply outlets. It's can also be found in prepackaged yeast and bacteria blends designed to make classic beer styles such as lambic or Flanders red ale.

Be forewarned — when Brett entrenches itself in your brewery equipment, it's very hard to get rid of it. Sometimes it's easier to just buy new equipment than to try to kill off the pesky and persistent microbe.

7 Putting Your Brew to the Test

IN THIS PART . . .

Figure out what to do with your beer after it's been packaged (besides drinking it).

Find out how good your beer is by way of proper evaluation.

Learn how to identify problems with your beer and how to correct them.

Enter your beer into competitions to get judges' feedback and maybe even win prizes!

» Pouring and drinking your brew

» Choosing beer glassware

» Washing and storing your glasses

Chapter 26 Storing and Pouring

Beer drinkers don't typically have to face the prospect of storing large quantities of beer for long periods of time, but you're a homebrewer now, and the rules are different. With each batch of brew you make, you produce the equivalent of slightly more than two cases of bottled beer. And this stuff isn't just any beer; it's homemade, it's unpasteurized, and it's technically alive. (Remember: Some yeast is still at work in each bottle.) This kind of beer requires — and deserves — a little more attention. How you store and pour your homebrew can make a world of difference in how it tastes. In this chapter, I give you the lowdown on the proper storage of your homebrew, as well as some pouring techniques and tips for glass selection. I also discuss the pros and cons of different glass-cleaning methods.

Storing Your Suds

Average commercial-beer drinkers don't need to concern themselves with the correct storing of beer because they usually purchase and consume it within a couple of days (if not hours). For homebrewers, however, this issue is worthy of attention; after all, they've put a lot of time and effort into their finished product.

REMEMBER

The term *finished product* (when used in conjunction with homebrew) is actually a misnomer. As long as live yeast is in the bottle, the beer is never really a finished product — it continues to change over time.

How do I store it?

Unlike wine bottles, homebrew bottles don't need to be stored horizontally. Wine is stored this way to keep the cork from going dry — which is not a problem with bottle caps. Actually, keeping your beer bottles standing upright minimizes the beer's contact with any oxygen that has also been sealed in the bottle with the beer.

What's most important about storing your homebrew is making sure the beer is in a location in your home that's cool and dark, because both heat and light can destroy beer flavor.

Where do I store it?

For the first two weeks after you bottle your brew, you want to store it in a cool (50+° Fahrenheit), dark location while it silently *conditions* (clarifies and carbonates). Back away from the fridge — it's too cold for this brief conditioning phase. Your brew eventually becomes clearer, and the carbonation level gradually increases. To satisfy your curiosity, you may want to open a bottle every couple of days during this time to keep tabs on your beer's progress. Or you can simply give a bottle a little jiggle and see whether bubbles emerge from the beer.

After you've conditioned your brew to your liking, you need to store it in the coolest and darkest place possible (without freezing it) to stunt the yeast activity within the bottle and to protect it from those elements that will cause your beer to deteriorate, such as heat and light.

Your best storage bet is an alpine cave, but a spare fridge or cool, dark spot in your basement is sufficient. I realize that not everyone has the luxury of a spare refrigerator or even a basement, so, forgoing these possibilities, a crude beer cellar is better than nothing at all — consider using a ground-level interior closet, a crawl space, or even an abandoned root cellar. Hey, if you've got little to work with, you need to be flexible. And the closer you can get to serving temperature (42 to 48° Fahrenheit), the better.

REMEMBER

The two most important criteria for this beer cellar are that it be cool and that it be dark. You want to factor in accessibility at some point; what good is an effective beer cellar if it effectively keeps you from easily getting a beer?

WARNING

You *don't* want to use a garage for storing your beer. Garages, unless thermostatically controlled, experience wide temperature fluctuations on a daily basis, and they usually get way too hot or way too cold (depending on your geographic location and the time of year). But a spare fridge in your garage, well, now you're talking!

How long do I store it?

By and large, you want to consume homebrewed beer fresh, typically within three months of bottling. However, a handful of beer styles not only stand up well to storage but actually improve with short-to-long-term aging. The styles that fit this category are all high-gravity beers: barley wines, strong ales, imperial stouts, Doppelbocks, some of the Belgian Trappist styles, and especially meads. Although many beers are still good after several months, even the hardiest beers are likely to give in to oxidation over an extended period of time, particularly if improper technique was used during the bottling process (see Chapter 14 for tips on bottling).

Pouring Procedures

The simple act of serving a beer doesn't need to be done with a flourish, but it does go a bit beyond drinking beer straight out of the bottle. This fact is especially true when serving homebrewed beer.

Correct presentation of any beer automatically includes glassware or even plastic ware (as long as it's clean). Appearances aside, the underlying concept here is that, by pouring out the beer, you release much of the pent-up carbonation. This frothing effervescence creates the beer's head, releases the brew's aromatic bouquet, and lessens its carbonic bite.

TIP

Speaking of aromatic bouquet, less gas trapped in the liquid means less gas trapped in your intestinal tract.

Out of the bottle . . .

With homebrew, most people — even most homebrewers — prefer to leave the yeast dregs in the bottle. (These can taste pretty nasty.) Mastering this pouring technique requires patience, timing, and a steady hand — especially if you're pouring your beer into more than one glass. Not to belabor the point, but careful pouring has a lot less to do with clear beer than it does with clear air — live yeast continues the fermentation process within your digestive system, which often results in excess, um, flatulence. Be aware that jostling your bottles of homebrew causes the yeast sediment to cloud up the beer. Either handle the bottles gently or allow the yeast to resettle to the bottom of the bottles.

REMEMBER

Absolutely nothing is wrong with drinking the yeast sediment, which is actually high in the water-soluble B-complex vitamins — unless you have something against bloating and gas. Apparently, this is not a problem for fans of Hefeweizen, which is traditionally served *mit Hefe*, or with the yeast.

Of course, you don't have to worry about clean pouring if you choose to filter your homebrew. (See Chapter 31 for more about filtering.)

TIP

The best way to pour a beer is to start by tilting your glass on a 45-degree angle. Just plop it right down the side of the glass, and starting with a glass large enough to hold the full contents of the bottle really helps. A huge head forms immediately, so you may want to slow the pour or tilt the glass back up to a 90-degree angle as the beer nears the top. You also want to be a little less aggressive when pouring wheat beers or any brew that includes wheat malt as a heading agent, as well as any homebrew that's getting on in age. A true head is at least 1 inch thick, or two fingers in depth.

One of the finer points of beer presentation that too many drinkers often overlook is the correct serving temperature. Most beers are served much too cold for serious appreciation. The average refrigerator is set to keep things chilled to around 38° to 40° Fahrenheit. I can think of at least three reasons not to serve your beer this cold:

- The colder the beer, the less carbonation it releases and the smaller the head.
- The less carbonation a beer releases, the less aroma it gives off.
- These temperatures numb the palate to the point that it can't discern many of the beer's flavor nuances (which explains why American mass-market beers are best served just above the freezing mark).

Although you must make a little extra effort and plan ahead to serve beers at their correct temperatures, the rewards are great. Drinking beer at the correct temperature enables you to smell and taste all that the beer has to offer. Serve most Lagers between 42° and 48° Fahrenheit and most ales between 46° and 52° Fahrenheit. Authentic stouts can be served as warm as 55° Fahrenheit, which is *British cellar temperature*. Most high-gravity barley wines and strong ales are best lightly chilled or at room temperature, like a snifter of brandy.

TIP

To save time as you clean and sanitize your bottles for your next brew, always rinse each bottle thoroughly after you empty it and then store it upside down. If you drink your homebrew from a keg, always clean and rinse the keg thoroughly after it's empty, too. See Chapter 16 for keg cleaning instructions.

. . . and into the glass

Stylish beer glassware serves primarily as a commercial product enhancement. Beyond visuals, however, the various shapes and sizes of beer glasses play an even more meaningful role. Specialized beer glassware enhances the aromas of the beer — for example, glasses that are deep or that curve inward toward the top are very effective in capturing and concentrating a beer's aromas.

The act of pouring beer into a glass (known as *decanting*) also enables carbonation to escape from the beer and lets the beer warm a bit if you've served it too cold. Decanting also allows you to pour a clearer beer if you're not partial to the yeast sediment in a homebrewed beer.

In the realm of tradition, many beer styles actually have a glassware style dedicated to them. A pilsner beer, for example, belongs in any of the many tall, stemmed, pilsner-style glasses. A stout, on the other hand, is perfectly at home in a simple pint glass. The nice thing about beer glassware, however, is that you're not bound by any hard-and-fast rules.

General rules on beer glassware suggest that simple beers can be served in simple glasses; well-aged and expensive beers deserve the regal treatment. Figure 26-1 shows you several different types of beer glasses; the following list helps you decide what to put in them:

- Aromatic Trappist ales and Belgian fruit beers for thin, stemmed glasses
- Rich and spirituous barley wines, old ales, and imperial stouts for small, brandy-snifter-type glasses (or even cordials)
- Aromatic beers such as witbier for wide-bowled glasses
- Light, spritzy, and aromatic beers for tall, narrow glasses
- Wheat beers for thick glasses (which help keep the beer cooler longer)
- Strong beers for deep, tulip-shaped glasses

The following list demystifies a few of the many specific glass styles that you may encounter anywhere today, as well as their suggested uses:

- **Beer flute:** This slim and dainty glass with a stem and base can be used for pilsners and similar beers; however, it's meant for beers that emulate wines, such as Belgian fruit beers. Flutes emphasize the aromatics of beer.
- **Dimpled pint mug:** This glass used to be the standard drinking vessel in British pubs. It has slowly and quietly given way to the straight-sided pint glass, which is easier to store on crowded pub shelves. Wherever you may find it, the pint mug is well suited to English ales and bitters.

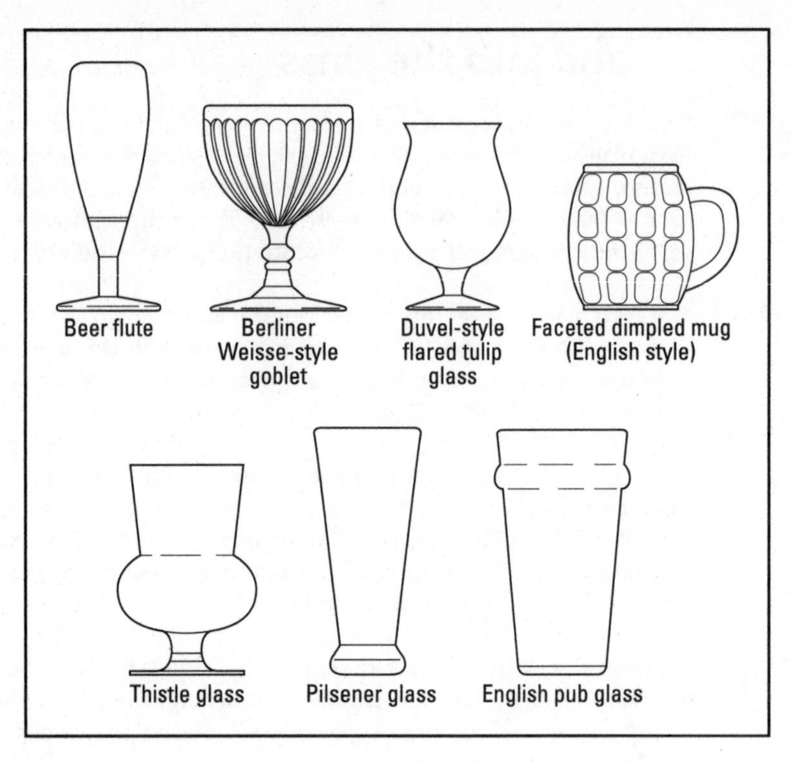

FIGURE 26-1: A wide range of beer glasses lets you choose the right one for your beer style.

- **Goblet:** Used almost exclusively for Berliner-style Weissbiers, this glass has a chalice-like appearance, with a wide, shallow bowl and a heavy stem and foot. This shape discourages excessive head formation; additionally, the drinker's nose fits inside the glass's mouth, which enhances the aromatic experience.
- **Pilsner:** Pilsner glasses come in a variety of styles. The more elegant ones are tall, footed, wafer-thin glasses that hold 10 or 12 ounces. The more common versions are usually either hourglass-shaped or tumblers that are slightly flared at the top. These ordinary pilsner glasses hold between 8 and 12 ounces and were designed specifically for pilsner beers.
- **Pint glass:** The pint glass is probably the most pedestrian and interchangeable beer glass. The standard *shaker* (so called because bartenders like to use this glass for shaking mixed cocktails) pint glass is a thick glass that tapers outward toward the top and holds 16 ounces of beer. (Before you say "duh!" read on.) You can also find an *imperial pint glass* that holds 20 ounces of beer, but it's not common in the U.S. This style of pint glass is perfect for any style of beer.

  Pint glasses of both sizes can be found with *sleeves* — bulges near the top of the glass that protect its lip from nicking if the glass tips over. The sleeve also enables you to stack the glasses one inside the other without them becoming wedged. Another style of pint glass is a slightly curvaceous version of the standard pint called a *pub glass.*

- **Thistle:** Thistle glasses help intensify a beer's aroma. The silhouette of the thistle glass is exactly what the name implies: It resembles a thistle flower. Drinkers use this uniquely-shaped glass almost exclusively for strong Scottish ales. (The thistle is the symbol of the Scottish crown.) However, this affectation is attributed to the Belgians, who developed a fondness for this style of beer after Scottish soldiers stationed in Belgium during World War I brought their strong Scottish ale with them.
- **Tulip:** Tulip-shaped glasses are very effective in capturing the aromatic qualities of beer. The tulip glass also closely resembles its name; these bulbous glasses often have a flared opening to enable the drinker to sip the beer and the foam at the same time, creating a creamy mouthfeel. Many drinkers favor tulip glasses for strong Belgian beers.
- **Weizenbier glass:** The Weizenbier is a tall, shapely, wide-rimmed glass that holds at least 18 ounces. It's ideal for holding a half liter of wheat beer (and the beer's towering head).

So do you need to run out and buy a dozen different sets of beer glassware to consume correctly? Not at all. Beer drinking should be enjoyable, and a great part of that enjoyment is comfort. Choose a beer-glass style that's comfortable to use and then enjoy using it — often. I recommend having a set of 16-ounce pub style pint glasses on hand, as well as a set of more elegant tulip glasses to show off your proud brews.

Dirty Deeds: Cleaning Beer Glassware

After you've made your choice in glassware, commit yourself to keeping the glasses clean. No matter which beer goes in which glass, one thing is for sure — keeping your beer glassware absolutely free of dust, oily fingerprints, lipstick, and soapy residue is crucial. All these potential contaminants can have a detrimental effect on the beer.

WARNING

The phrase *beer clean* describes a particular level of cleanliness. This term isn't just lip service — beer glasses need to be spotlessly clean in order to present the beer in its best light. The beer betrays any shortcomings in the cleansing and rinsing practices.

Even though a glass looks clean, it may not be. As you're rinsing, look at how the water drains off the glass. If the water sheets off the glass, the glass is beer clean;

if the water breaks up, streaks, or spots, the glass is still dirty. When pouring, check for bubbles that appear on the bottom or sides of the glass below the head — these indicate invisible soap residue, grease, or dust. (Cracks and chips also attract bubbles.) Soap residues and dust in a glass can cause a beer to go flat quickly, and any fats or grease can break down and destroy the surface of the head.

The most reliable way to check for a beer-clean glass is to pour a beer into the glass, allowing a good head to form. After the beer stands for a few minutes, the head should remain firm and compact. If you didn't properly clean the glass, the foam breaks up, leaving large fish-eye bubbles.

Depending on your level of seriousness, you can clean beer glassware in a number of ways. The best thing to do is to rinse your beer glasses thoroughly in hot water right after you use them. This may seem a bit compulsive, but it's very effective at keeping your glasses residue-free. Some drinkers are so averse to cleaning their beer glasses in soapy water that a hot-water rinse is as far as they want to go.

Check out both sides to this argument: One camp says that household dishwashing soaps are scented and can be hard to rinse off. The other camp (the one I belong to) says that if you use very small amounts of unscented dishwashing liquids and follow up immediately with a hot water rinse, you don't do any damage.

I can give you a better (and more compulsive) way to clean your glasses. Draw a sink full of hot water and add a couple of heaping tablespoons of baking soda. Use a clean dishcloth to reach the deepest recesses of the glass. Pay particular attention to the rim, making sure that you remove any lipstick or lip balm. The dishwasher itself can't do a better job.

Finally, be wary of running your glasses through the dishwasher. Food particles don't always rinse and drain out of the dishwasher after each cycle, and they could end up in your beer. Regardless of how you choose to clean your glasses, always follow with a good hot rinse and then air-dry them in a dish drainer.

Never towel-dry beer glasses. The towel can leave traces of soap, body oil, and especially lint on the glasses.

At the professional or commercial level, where governmental regulations apply, health departments require chemical sanitizers or sterilizers, including products made with *trisodium phosphate* (TSP). Commercial establishments generally use a glass-cleaning compound that's odorless, sudsless, non-fat based, and free-rinsing.

Storing Your Steins

The storing of your glassware is just as important as its cleaning. A poor storage location can make your cleaning efforts all for naught. Make sure you store air-dried glasses away from unpleasant odors, grease, or smoke coming from restrooms, kitchens, or ashtrays. If possible, store the glasses upside down in a breakfront, credenza, or similar, relatively dust-free environment.

TIP

Don't store glassware in the freezer. The glasses can pick up odors from food in the freezer, and frozen glasses are uncomfortable to hold. (They also leave a nasty water ring wherever you set them down.) Your homebrew deserves better.

» Evaluating beer objectively and subjectively

» Speaking homebrew-ese

Chapter 27
You Can't Judge a Bock by Its Cover: Evaluating Beer

Drinking beer shouldn't be a one-dimensional experience, although it can be if you let it. Consuming beer or wine (or even food, for that matter) is an activity that you need to approach as a full-sensory experience. The more of your senses you involve, the more you remember of the experience (positive or otherwise).

If you cook a barbecued steak for dinner, you don't just see the meat cooking on the grill; you also hear the sizzling of its juices, and you smell its tantalizing aromas wafting through the air. As you taste the steak, you not only savor the flavor, but you also describe the steak in a tactile manner — saying that it's moist and tender or dry and tough as leather (especially if you eat at my house).

Now transfer these mental notes to tasting beer. This chapter tells you how.

Because of all the senses and nuances involved in evaluating beer, a special beer lingo has evolved to help describe the entire beer experience. (Notice that I didn't say beer-*drinking* experience — the beer experience involves more than simply tasting!) I cover these special kinds of words later in this chapter.

Tuning In to Your Beer

As you pour a beer into a glass, listen to the splashing of the liquid and the fizzing of the escaping carbonation. See the fine bubbles race upward through the liquid, only to get lost in a blanket of dense foam. Watch the head rise and swell up over the lip of the glass. Breathe in the full bouquet of aromas emanating from the beer. Taste the many flavors of the malt, hops, and other ingredients. Feel the viscosity of the beer and the prickly effervescence of the carbonation on your tongue and palate. Even after you swallow, you can continue to discern the various flavors and textures of the departed beer.

When you find that you give each beer you drink this kind of attention, congratulations are in order: You've made the first step in the painless transition from plain old beer drinker to beer evaluator. This change in outlook means that you're tuning in to your beer; you're no longer just drinking it — you're *experiencing* it. As a homebrewer, this experience is a useful tool. The more you pay attention to the beers you drink, the better you become at picking up different aromas, flavors, and sensations. Your finely tuned sensory organs can then help you fine-tune your own homebrew.

Most beer drinkers find themselves simply enchanted by beer. Recognizing and identifying the beer's attributes helps you understand the basis for your enchantment. However, like most human objects of desire, beer can also have some negative traits in addition to the good ones. Rating a friend or lover according to a checklist is rather callous, but evaluating a beer by this method is not only acceptable, I highly recommend it.

Evaluating One Sense at a Time

You want to get all or as many of your senses as possible involved in the beer experience. Your sight, naturally, is the first sense to transmit an image of the beer to your brain. However, because the aromatics of the beer are very *volatile* (meaning that they're fleeting), you need to give your nose the opportunity to register the olfactory data first. Your sense of smell can also become desensitized as it becomes accustomed to the smell wafting from your glass, so taking the opportunity to appreciate a beer's fragrance at first contact is very important. After you give your sense of smell its turn, you can take a visual snapshot of the beer; follow this visual by taking in the taste and aftertaste, and then take time for reflection. In correct order, the sequential steps to experiencing beer are as follows:

1. Smell
2. Look
3. Taste
4. Aftertaste
5. Reflect

The following sections explore each of these experiences in more detail.

The nose knows

The fact that your nose is located above your mouth is no fluke of nature. A quick look anywhere in the animal kingdom confirms this statement. The strategic location of the nose enables you to detect questionable odors emanating from potentially digestible items before you eat or drink them. This nasal early-warning system safeguards man and beast alike from unknowingly ingesting anything that may be detrimental to their health.

Nothing about beer should have you fearing for your health and well-being (shameless overconsumption notwithstanding), but whether you need it as a warning system or not, your ability to smell is of great importance as you drink. A huge part of your ability to taste is directly connected to the olfactory functions. Even as you taste beer, you also smell it in the *retronasal passage* at the back of the throat. Flavor relies on aroma, and the human nose can detect thousands of aromas. Overlooking this fundamental aspect of the beer-evaluation process would be negligent.

Alcoholic-beverage evaluators discuss the aromatic properties of their respective drinks by using the word *nose.* Nose, appropriately enough, is also the word they use to describe the total olfactory experience, which includes aroma *and* bouquet. (To distinguish between these terms, think of *aroma* as if it were a sound and *bouquet* as the volume level or intensity of that sound.) Beer connoisseurs also use the word *nose* interchangeably as a noun and verb: "He nosed his beer studiously," or "She commented on the beer's pungent nose."

So what kinds of aromas can you as beer evaluators expect to encounter? You face both positives and negatives. The positives are those smells that you expect to find in a correctly made beer of a particular style, and the negatives are odors that indicate flaws in the beer. Somewhere in between are the aromas that you don't expect to find that don't necessarily indicate problems. These smells are aromas that don't belong to the style of beer you're evaluating — they aren't necessarily bad, but stylistically speaking, they're incorrect.

REMEMBER

Each beer style comes with its own aroma and flavor profile; the following sections offer only general parameters.

Positive aromas

Positive aromas result from the fermentation process and accentuate or underline the main ingredients in the beer. The following list describes several of these aromas:

- The first (and usually most obvious) aroma you encounter is the *malt character* of the beer. This aroma can run from perfumy-sweet to rich and caramelly, depending on the beer style. Ales tend toward fruity and occasionally buttery (or butterscotchy) aromas that you can trace to warm fermentations and certain yeast strains. Depending on how dark the beer is, roasty, toasty, or chocolatey aromas may also emanate from the specialty grains you added to the beer during brewing.
- The second most obvious aroma you may encounter (depending on the beer style) is the *hop character* of the beer. This aroma, of course, depends on hops: What variety and quantity of hops the brewer used, when she added the hops to the boiling beer, and whether she added aromatic hops to the beer during the secondary fermentation phase. (See the discussion on dry hopping in Chapter 11.) Common descriptors for these hop aromas are herbal, spicy, grassy, floral, piney, citrusy, and occasionally tropical fruit (as well as Sleepy, Grumpy, and Doc). You may very well get a whiff of the hops even before you smell the malt — it all boils down to the individual beer style and recipe.
- Positive aromas that directly result from the fermentation process may include fruity esters, *diacetyl* (a buttery smell) in small quantities, and nuttiness. You may even detect alcohol in the beer's nose.

REMEMBER

After you home in on the particular aromas in the beer, try to gauge their intensities. Although lots of beer styles feature many of the same aromatics, the different components vary in intensity.

Negative aromas

Negative aromas may include plastic-like and cooked-vegetable odors, rotten eggs, skunkiness, paint-thinner, olives or pickles, and wet dog, among other scents. (Makes ya kinda thirsty, doesn't it?) I detail the possible causes of each of the preceding aromas in Chapter 28.

You can inadvertently create negative aromas (and flavors) in any one of the following four ways:

- You may have used flawed ingredients to make the beer. Stale hops or moldy grain may inadvertently find their way into a brewpot now and again. (As the brewer, you need to exercise strict quality control over your ingredients.)
- You may be guilty of procedural mistakes — for example, steeping the grain at too high a temperature, oversparging the mash, or fermenting at too high a temperature.
- Wild fermentations by rogue bacteria or wild yeast may contaminate a batch anytime between cooldown of the wort and bottling (or canning or kegging) the beer.
- The way in which you store your bottled, canned or kegged beer may affect the beer's aroma (as well as the length of time you age it). See Chapter 26 for more on proper storage techniques.

TIP

Make sure you carefully follow all the directions in sanitizing, brewing, and storing your beer to help ensure that your homebrew has positive aroma and bouquet — and flavor, of course!

Seeing is beer-lieving

Sight is the most trusted sense you have. Experts in such matters say that you base 75 percent of your perception of the world on sight; maybe that's why many beer drinkers fall into the trap of making hasty judgments of beer based on what they see. In terms of beer evaluation, the eyes may not lie, but they can only tell half-truths. A beer that looks dark, rich, strong, and roasty may be just plain dark. And what can your eyes tell you about taste or smell? Nothing — and that's the point: Your eyes can tell you only about the beer's appearance, and nothing else.

What should you look for in a beer? You can discern three things about a particular beer by using your eyes:

- **Color:** The colors that make up the various styles run the spectrum from pale straw to golden, amber, copper, orange, red, brown, and black — and everything in between. No one color is necessarily better than the other; each is the result of stylistic differences.

- **Clarity:** Many beer drinkers obsess over clear beer. If their Old Frothy isn't crystal clear, they refuse to drink it. With homebrew, however, even perfectly aged and clarified beer may again become cloudy if it's not handled correctly; you don't need to do much to disturb the yeast sediment on the bottom of the bottle.

  Commercial beer is crystal clear only because of filtering equipment and techniques developed in the 19th century. Most brews throughout history have been anywhere from hazy to murky. The source of this turbidity was the organic ingredients used in the beer-making process — especially the yeast. The particulate matter that clouded the beer was also what helped make the beer the nutritious drink that it was (and still is). And now with the rise in interest in NEIPAs (New England India pale ales), haze is the new craze! Due to this phenomenon, consumers of craft beer are far less concerned about the clarity of their beer.
- **Head retention:** Head retention can tell a short story about the beer in hand. All beers should be able to form and keep a head; the latter is as important as the former. The head should form quickly and be very tightly knit. The head may also take on a "rocky" appearance if sufficient proteins (from the grain) are present. If a brew can't form a proper head, it may have any one of a number of problems. (See Chapter 28 for more information on these problems.)

In good taste

Here's where I get down to the basics of beer consumption. Regardless of how a beer looks and smells, if it doesn't taste good, it hasn't fulfilled its obligation. Before delving into this subjective topic, take a closer look at the primary tasting receptor in the human body: the tongue.

TECHNICAL STUFF

The five principal tastes that the tongue differentiates are bitter, salty, sour, sweet, and *umami*, a Japanese word meaning *savory*. As shown in Figure 27-1, taste receptors are located across the tongue, but some areas are more sensitive to certain tastes than others. Notice that the tip of the tongue is the least-sensitive area. Flavor receptors are also located at the back and on the roof of the mouth, independent of the tongue.

Two tastes for the price of one

Beer tasting should be delineated between the first taste sensation experienced by the tip of the tongue (*foretaste*) and the *midtaste* or *true taste*, in which the beer displays its taste attractions completely. (The aftertaste I address separately in the following section.) The foretaste and midtaste should blend together mildly and harmoniously so as not to discourage further drinking.

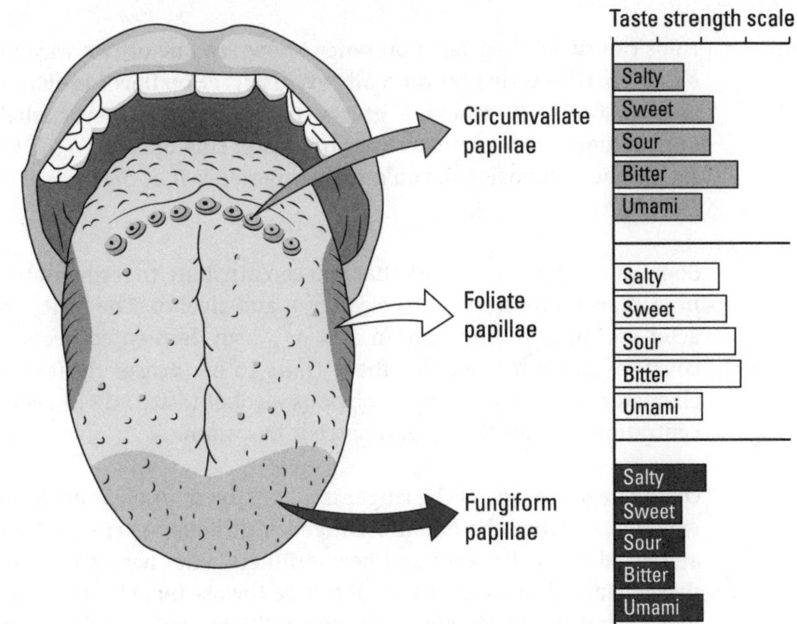

FIGURE 27-1: A taste strength map of the human tongue.

As is true of the aroma, the foretaste is of the sweet malt — this time, the result of the tongue's sweet-sensing region up front. With most adjunct-laden brews (those made with a lot of rice or corn), the sweetness is delicate and perfumy and only vaguely tastes of true malt flavor, mainly because of the lightening effect of the adjunct grain used. The fewer adjuncts you use, the more the rich, caramelly maltiness of the barley shows through. (See Chapter 8 for more information on brewing with adjuncts.)

As you use more specialty grains in brewing — roasted ones in particular — the beer's flavor becomes more *layered,* or complex. With the exception of crystal malt, these specialty grains rarely add sweetness — only the flavors of the individual grain. These specialty malts create a mosaic of toasty, roasty, nutty, toffee, and coffeelike flavors that meld into the finished brew. A lot of these flavors register in the middle and at the back of the tongue. Some of the more highly roasted malts add a dry, astringent taste that the tongue perceives as being bitter, much like strong or stale coffee, or grape tannin in wine. Certain beers may exhibit a slight tartness that you detect between the midtaste and the aftertaste.

Normally, sour flavors constitute a flaw in beer, but in several Belgian beers and at least two German beers, sourness is actually a prerequisite for the style. For the sake of a general rule, certain ales may have some sourness; lagers, however, definitely should not. Generally speaking, *lactic* sourness (which is more of a mild tartness) is preferable over *acetic* sourness (which is vinegary) unless you specifically intend the latter.

Hops can make their taste presence known in one of two ways: *Hop flavor* or *hop bitterness.* (The terms are mutually exclusive.) Hop flavor is distinctive and usually tastes a lot like its aroma — grassy, piney, floral, citrusy, herbal, cheesy, and so on; you normally experience it at midtaste. Hop bitterness, on the other hand, is rather one-dimensional; you mostly experience it at the back of the tongue and in the aftertaste.

Some of the positive flavors that you can attribute to fermentation include fruitiness, diacetyl (buttery, butterscotchy), and alcohol. The fruity and buttery character you usually find only in ales or warm-fermented beers. Brewers usually consider lagers that exhibit these traits to be incorrectly fermented and out of character. You should find an obvious alcohol taste only in beers that have concentrations higher than 7 or 8 percent by volume.

On the negative side of the ledger is a long list of unpleasant flavors that you may experience. From the harsh astringency of boiled grain to the rubbery taste of autolyzed yeast, brewers and beer drinkers alike need to be on the lookout for these palate-destroyers. Other defective flavors include cidery aldehydes, medicinal phenolics, bloody metallics, "poopy" enterics, and dozens of equally unappetizing tastes. (See the section "Relaying the Results: Homebrew Lingo, Jargon, and Vernacular," later in this chapter.)

After you home in on the various flavors, try to gauge their intensity. Most beer styles share common flavors, but the intensity of each fluctuates according to style.

Aftertaste can be a good thing!

The *aftertaste,* also called the *finish,* is one of the most important and enjoyable aspects of the beer-drinking experience, one that chiefly affects the decision whether to take another drink. American commercial beer drinkers had been brainwashed into believing that beer was not supposed to have an aftertaste and that beers that do are bad. What a shame! Imagine dining on succulent (and expensive) Maine lobster tail dipped in pure, drawn butter, only to have the flavor disappear from your mouth the second you swallow. That short flavor memory is what aftertaste is all about.

Many facets of the beer (including its faults) become more obvious in the aftertaste. The aftertaste is where you want to evaluate the various taste components of the beer, especially their harmony and balance.

REMEMBER

Certain beer styles strive to accentuate malt over hops and vice versa, but no one ingredient should completely dominate the other.

The aftertaste is a good time to assess the *body* and tactile quality of the beer. In beverage evaluation, body refers to the weighty feel or thickness of a product. A light beer you describe as light-bodied; an India pale ale you may describe as medium-bodied; and a Doppelbock you describe as full-bodied. Other, more colorful descriptors, such as *wimpy, thin, voluptuous, massive,* and *robust* are more effective at getting the point across.

The tactile aspect of beverage evaluation is called *mouthfeel.* You don't want to confuse taste and mouthfeel with one another — *taste* you interpret by way of the taste buds, and *mouthfeel* is the sensory experience of the whole inside of the mouth and throat. (That is, you don't taste cold; you feel it.) A light lager beer you may describe as effervescent and watery, and a stout you may describe as soft and chewy.

TECHNICAL STUFF

Astringency runs a fine line between taste and mouthfeel — and between hops and grain, for that matter. *Astringency* is like the mouthfeel of a grape skin (recognized as tannin in wine) or of strong tea. Hops contribute bitterness to the beer. Grain can also contribute its own bitterness in the form of *astringents.* This astringency straddles the fence between the "husky" flavor of the grain and a harsh, dry, or powdery mouthfeel. Very often, people who experience grain astringency wrongly attribute that experience to the hops. The key to distinguishing between hop bitterness and grain astringency is two-sided: You usually experience hop bittering farther back on the tongue, and grain astringency tends to affect the roof of the mouth (the soft palate) more than hop bitterness does.

You also experience alcohol most keenly in the aftertaste, not just in terms of flavor but in its warming sensation in the throat. This sensation can run from solventy heat to menthol-like cooling. As is the case with brandy or cognac, the alcohol sensation is one of the understated pleasures of a high-octane brew.

From Observations to Reflections

The *reflection* is essentially your overall impression of the beer. The difference here is that you made (or should have made) all the previous assessments objectively. Reflection is the time to take into account all those objective observations and then form a subjective opinion about the beer. Here's where you do your accounting and weigh all the checks and balances. If you're judging the beer according to a particular beer style, you need to evaluate it according to style guidelines rather than by personal preferences. If, however, you're judging strictly by matter of personal taste, you can simply go with a thumbs up or a thumbs down.

Here, again, the budding homebrewer faces another choice: objective versus subjective analysis. Not a difficult choice, not a life-changing one, but one to challenge your enthusiasm and your commitment to increasing your brewing expertise. Are you satisfied with the back-patting of your beer-guzzling buddies, or are you interested in getting legitimate and unbiased feedback on your brews? If you are, I suggest that you check out Chapter 29 for the lowdown on homebrew competitions.

Relaying the Results: Homebrew Lingo, Jargon, and Vernacular

If you're like most other homebrewers, after you're comfortably established in your new hobby you want to seek out and interact with your fellow enthusiasts — those who share your passion for brewing. The exchange of information on any specific subject generally requires a common language, and, just your luck, beer evaluation also has such a language. This little-known patois is absolutely necessary for professionals within the industry as a quality-control vocabulary, as well as for professionals outside the industry who evaluate brewers' products. Homebrewers also have a vested interest in this language.

One of the best illustrations of the beer vocabulary is the internationally recognized Beer Flavor Wheel developed by a gent named Dr. Morton Meilgaard, who headed up a group of technologists from the American Society of Brewing Chemists. On Dr. Meilgaard's wheel are 14 major categories covering every aspect of beer evaluation (see Figure 27-2). Notice that, although you can register taste in 7 of these categories, you can register aroma in 12 of them; the only two categories that your nose can't detect are salty and bitter.

These 14 categories further break down into 44 first-tier terms (terms such as *bitter*, *salty*, and *fruity*). Not listed here (for reasons of simplicity) are more than 80 second-tier terms and hundreds of comments, synonyms, and definitions that provide an in-depth (read: *professional*) understanding of correct beer evaluations.

REMEMBER

Notice that some of the descriptors for aroma and flavor can be considered both good and bad — these run according to stylistic parameters. Musty aromas and flavors, for example, are acceptable in some bottle-conditioned ales but are wholly inappropriate for a German lager.

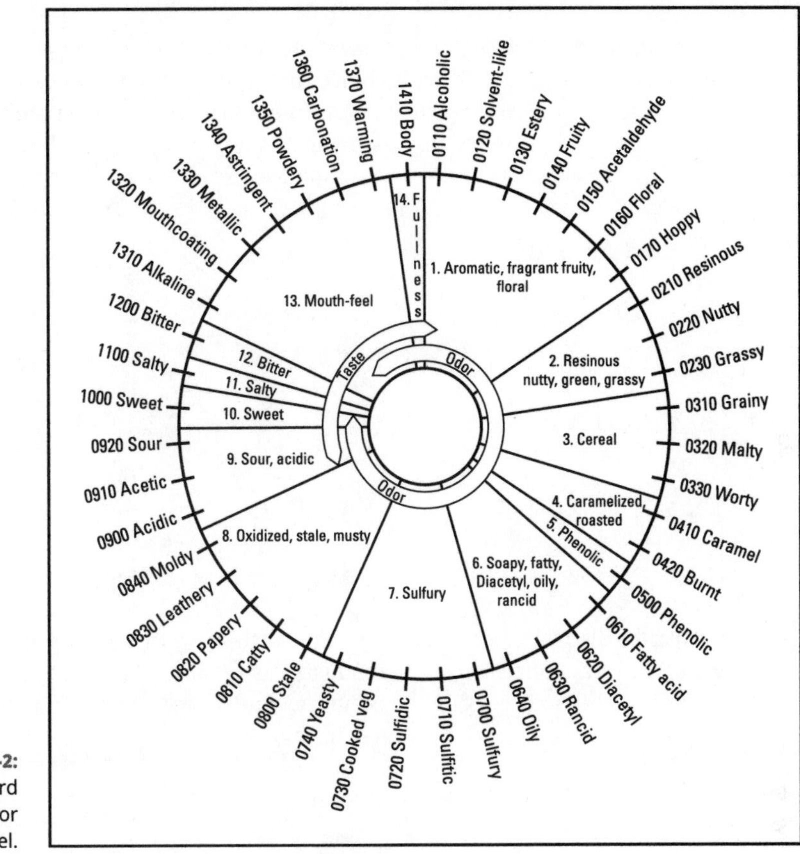

FIGURE 27-2: The Meilgaard Beer Flavor Wheel.

Reinventing the Wheel

As good and useful as the Beer Flavor Wheel has been for the past 50 years, it has now been improved upon by the Beer Flavor Map. Where the flavor wheel did its part in helping identify various aromas and tastes, the Beer Flavor Map expands on those descriptors and then goes at least one step better by also addressing descriptors for mouthfeel, too.

You can check out the Beer Flavor Map here: `https://www.draughtlab.com/flavormaps`.

- » **Solving flavoring problems**
- » **Correcting aroma woes**
- » **Resolving appearance issues**

Chapter 28
Troubleshooting

Just as everyone is a beginner once, everyone is also likely to make a mistake at least once. Making mistakes is actually an inevitable part of the homebrewing process; the key is to figure out what the problem is and then not repeat it. Identifying these goof-ups is the first step on the road to both quality and consistency in homebrewing.

Occasionally, adverse things happen to homebrewed beer that are difficult to understand and even more difficult to describe; the purpose of this chapter is to help you troubleshoot — in standard homebrew lingo — any problems that may occur during your homebrewing adventures. You may even want to read this chapter prior to brewing a batch just to reacquaint yourself with the many pitfalls of homebrewing as well as ready yourself with an appropriate reaction to any problem that may arise.

Fermentation Lamentations

Like naive and optimistic young parents, homebrewers sometimes have unrealistic visions of how perfect everything will be and often take for granted that things will happen exactly as expected. One good example is adding yeast to sweet, sugary wort. Many brewers assume the yeast hungrily consumes whatever they feed it, finishes eating at an appropriate time, and then takes its scheduled nap. Then reality strikes. Reality, in this case, is represented by the following list of fermentation problems.

Fermentation problems occur quite frequently — sometimes your fermentation gets off to a slow start, and sometimes it never wants to stop. The following sections describe what you should do if you ever face one of these situations.

No fermentation

Your fermentation never started? First, make sure it actually hasn't. Judging fermentation by the bubbles (or lack thereof) coming out of the airlock can sometimes be deceiving. Look at the beer (if it's in a glass fermenter) or peek through the airlock hole in the lid (if it's in a plastic fermenter). Do you see any foam or a ring of brownish scum around the fermenter? If so, the beer is fermenting or has fermented. Confirm this by using your hydrometer to check the gravity. The beer is typically done fermenting if the final gravity is ⅓ to ¼ of the original gravity. For example: A 1.045 beer ferments down to 1.015 to 1.012 or below. If after 24 to 48 hours fermentation has truly not begun — or you're just not sure — try adding more yeast.

Situations like this one give you good reason to keep a packet of dry yeast in the fridge for emergencies.

Be mindful of sanitary practices; how or when the beer ferments doesn't mean a thing if you contaminate the whole batch in the process. (See Chapter 3 for more advice on sanitation.)

If fermentation still hasn't begun after you add more yeast, you may have made one of the following mistakes:

- **You didn't rinse the sanitizer from the fermenter.** Sanitizer residue can kill yeast, too.
- **You put the fermenter in a place that's too cold.** Leave it at 64 to 72° Fahrenheit for ales.
- **You used old or dead yeast.** The yeast contained in ingredient kits is often so old that it's useless — always buy fresh yeast that has been kept refrigerated.
- **You rehydrated the yeast improperly by using water that was too hot (more than 110° Fahrenheit).** Also, don't leave the yeast in the rehydration water too long; 30 minutes is plenty.

- **You used good yeast but shocked it with sudden changes in temperature or by adding it to wort that was too cold (under 70° Fahrenheit) or too hot (over 110° Fahrenheit).**
- **You didn't use enough yeast.** Pitch 10 to 15 grams of dry yeast, or use one package of ready-to-pitch liquid yeast per 5 gallons of beer. (See Chapter 6 for more information on RTP yeast.)

REMEMBER

Slow-starting or stuck fermentations usually mean under-pitching of yeast, underaerated wort, or both. To correct these problems in the future, pitch a larger volume of yeast and make sure you properly aerate the wort before pitching.

TIP

High-gravity worts (those with a specific gravity of 1.056 or higher) need even more yeast and aeration for proper fermentation.

Stuck fermentation

What if the fermentation started well but seems to have become stuck? Again, looks can be deceiving — use your hydrometer to find out whether your fermentation is actually stuck or simply finished! Remember that you want the final hydrometer reading to be ⅓ to ¼ of the original gravity.

If the gravity is below 1.020, your brew has probably fermented out as much as it's going to. But it also depends on what your starting gravity was; yeasts typically ferment 75 to 80 percent of the available sugars in the wort. Some recipes also contain lots of unfermentable sugars.

If the fermentation is truly stuck and the wort still has a high gravity reading, do one (or more) of the following to help restart the fermentation process:

- **Add more fresh yeast or a different strain of yeast.**
- **Try to rouse the yeast with a sanitized spoon or by gently agitating the fermenter.** Mix the yeast off the bottom to wake it up and get it to start fermenting again. Try to do this without aerating the beer.
- **If all else fails, bottle, can, or keg the beer (kegging being the safest of the three options).** If you're bottling the beer, cut back the priming sugar to less than ½ cup to reduce the chance of exploding bottles. Chapters 14, 15, and 16 have more information about bottling, canning and kegging.

TIP

If the batch's alcohol level is above 7 percent, the yeast may have reached its limit for alcohol tolerance. Try adding a yeast with higher alcohol tolerance, like Kveik yeast or champagne yeast. (Champagne yeast also ferments cleanly, with no off flavors.)

Never-ending fermentation

If you have a beer that has been fermenting in the primary fermenter for more than 14 days, consider these possibilities:

- **Is the temperature too low?** (60° Fahrenheit for ales and 40° Fahrenheit for lagers may be too low.) Ale yeast works very slowly at these temperatures (if at all); try warming the beer up to get it to finish fermenting. You can do this by moving the fermenter to a warmer location in your home.
- **Are you making a lager?** Lagers typically take 10 to 14 days to ferment at proper temperatures (see the preceding bullet).
- **Do you have a wild yeast or bacterial contamination?** Rogue yeasts and bacteria are capable of fermenting sugars that pure beer yeast can't, so fermentation can appear to go on forever. If your beer actively ferments for over three weeks, it's probably contaminated, and your brew may be doomed. Smell and taste the beer and decide for yourself whether to keep it or toss it.
- **Did you rack into your secondary fermenter too soon?** If you're using a two-stage fermentation system, you may have racked the beer into the secondary fermenter too early. Never rack beer until vigorous fermentation is done (which usually takes a minimum of five days). By racking to a secondary vessel too early, you remove the beer from most of the yeast. What little yeast is left has to carry on the rest of the fermentation duties. Racking later is generally better than racking sooner. Try adding more yeast. See Chapter 11 for more on secondary fermentation.

In Bad Taste: Off Flavors and Aromas

Flavor is a complex combination of smell and taste. Sometimes, it can be difficult to tell whether the strange character of your beer is due to something you taste or smell. Pinpointing these flavors is the first step to fixing problems in your brew.

In the following sections, I give you a rundown of some common flavor and aroma defects, with possible causes and remedies (and Chapter 27 includes more evaluative information). Also check out the quick-reference troubleshooting tables at the end of this section.

Butter/butterscotch flavors

Buttery or butterscotchy flavors indicate the presence of a compound called *diacetyl.* Diacetyl occurs naturally in most warm fermentations but also dissipates naturally throughout the course of a proper fermentation cycle. Very obvious diacetyl flavor may indicate other problems, such as extremely warm fermentation temperatures, unhealthy yeast, underoxygenated wort, or bacterial contamination.

TIP

Homebrewers can reduce diacetyl levels in their beer by allowing a *diacetyl rest* at the end of primary fermentation. Yeast can reduce diacetyl levels in beer; the key is to not rack the beer over to a secondary fermenter for 2 to 3 days after initial fermentation has subsided to allow the yeast time to rid the beer of the diacetyl.

Many beer styles in the ale family — especially those from Britain — can exhibit noticeable diacetyl flavors. The presence of diacetyl in any lager beer, however, indicates a flaw.

TIP

It's sometimes difficult to distinguish between the caramelly flavors created by various malts (after all, caramel is made by heating butter and sugar) and the buttery flavor derived from diacetyl. Novice judges beware!

Sour/tart flavors

Sourness in the average beer is usually a sure sign of a bacterial contamination. These bacteria can produce lactic acid or acetic acid (found in vinegar), and these acids can range from the mild tartness of grapefruit to the mouth-puckering tanginess of lemons.

A common bacteria that creates lactic acid is *Lactobacillus,* whereas a common bacteria that creates acetic acid is *Acetobacter.*

You can easily prevent beer spoilage by increasing your cleaning and sanitizing efforts. Be especially suspicious of any scratched plastic equipment that may be harboring bacteria; you may need to replace that equipment. Also, be careful when handling grain around sanitized equipment — grain dust harbors bacteria that can travel airborne for long distances. All bacteria tend to multiply faster than yeast; this speed means if bacteria are present in your yeast cultures, they can increase dramatically every time you repitch the yeast. In this case, replace your yeast culture.

REMEMBER

In several beer styles — mostly Belgian styles — sour flavors aren't only acceptable, they're expected. Even the most famous stout in the world (Guinness) originally underwent a mild lactic fermentation (brewers sour a small portion of the beer and then blend it back into the rest of the batch).

Medicinal/plastic/smoky flavors

These flavors comprise part of a class of compounds called *phenols.* Phenolic flavors can come from wild yeast. The best cure is to improve your sanitation procedures and/or to replace your yeast culture.

Before knocking yourself out trying to eliminate *all* phenolic flavors, be aware that some beer styles actually include phenolics as part of their taste and aromatic profiles. These styles include Bavarian Weizenbier, some Belgian ales, and most smoked beers.

TIP

Chlorine can also give rise to these flavors, forming what are called *chlorophenols.* Always use dechlorinated water (preboiled or carbon-filtered), and be sure that you thoroughly rinse any bleach off of your equipment after sanitizing.

WARNING

Polyphenols can give your beer a husky, tannic bite. These can emanate from misuse of grain during the mashing and sparging procedures.

Papery/cardboard/sherry-like flavors (oxidation)

All beer will eventually go stale, but oxidation will speed up that process. That's why it's important not to aerate finished beer during the bottling process. (See Chapter 14 for bottling procedures.) Oxygen in finished beer is where these flavors come from. Remember the following:

- **Be careful when siphoning.** To avoid splashing or foaming, stir priming solution very carefully.
- **Don't aerate hot wort, either.** The oxygen comes back to haunt you later. (Aerate cooled wort only at pitching time.)
- **If you keg, use CO_2 to purge all vessels of oxygen.**
- **If you top-up fermenters with water, use boiled and cooled water.** This process removes oxygen from the water.
- **Fill bottles to the highest reasonable level.** This process minimizes air contact with the beer. Shoot for 1 inch from the bottle opening.

TIP

Oxygen-absorbing caps are available for bottles if you want to pay the higher cost. For all the good that these caps do, they aren't a cure for sloppy beer/wort handling.

Dry/puckering mouthfeel (astringency)

Sometimes, you may experience a dry, puckering sensation (similar to chewing on a red grape skin) in your beer's finish; you typically feel this on the back sides of the tongue and on the back of the roof of your mouth. This *astringency* is caused by compounds called tannins.

The most common cause of astringency is improper handling of grains (see bulleted list below). If you're not careful, tannins can be extracted from the grains and washed into the wort.

The following steps can help you keep the tannin extraction from malt husks to a minimum:

- **When milling malt, don't overcrack the grain.** Fine husk particles can easily get into the wort.
- **Don't oversparge grains.** By the time you extract the last bit of sugar, you've also extracted a good amount of tannins. Limit sparging to 2 quarts of water per pound of grain.
- **Don't use sparge water over 168° Fahrenheit.** Exceeding this temperature extracts tannins in large quantities.
- **Try to acidify your sparge water (less than 7.0 pH).** Alkaline pH (greater than 7.0) can also extract tannins from grains. You can also add gypsum to the sparge water to keep the mash pH and wort pH low. (The best pH for sparge water is between 5.0 and 6.0.)

Harshness/hotness

Occasionally, a beer may taste harsh or have a mouthfeel that's best described as *hot*. Many factors can cause a harsh tasting beer.

- **Excessive hopping rates can create a bitter harshness in your beer.**
- **Beers made with hard or chalky water can taste harsh.** See Chapter 7 for more on dealing with hard water.
- **High fermentation temperatures can produce *fusel alcohol*, which creates a hot, solvent-like sensation.** Try not to exceed a fermentation temperature of about 75° Fahrenheit, unless the specific yeast being used is known to perform better at higher temps, such as Kviek yeast.
- **Overcarbonated beers can have an unpleasant, prickly harshness on the palate.** Contaminated and overprimed beers are usually excessively carbonated.

Metallic flavor

Sometimes a metallic taste in your brew is the result of oxidation, but you can typically trace it back to iron utensils or equipment. Try to use copper or stainless-steel vessels for boiling. If you use enamelware pots, make sure that the ceramic surfaces aren't chipped. Also, if you can taste iron in your water, you can taste it in your beer. If this is the case, you need to consider buying bottled water for brewing.

Skunk aroma

Skunky smelling beer is the unfortunate result of storing beer in direct light for extended periods of time. Sunlight has the most detrimental effect, but fluorescent and incandescent light can also destroy beer aroma. Beer that smells skunky is referred to as *lightstruck*.

TIP

Skunks are not native to Britain and none are thought to be living in the wild there, so the concept of "skunky" aroma is lost on most British people. In Britain, beer that has been lightstruck is called *catty*.

Sulfury odors

Certain sulfury (hydrogen sulfide) odors can emanate from yeast and can smell like rotten eggs, burned matches, rubber, and so on. The source is usually yeast that's breaking down (a process called *autolysis*). The key to keeping these odors from occurring is to rack your beer promptly after primary fermentation. Most lager yeasts also naturally produce these odors; changing yeast strains or (in the case of lagers) proper aging can sometimes correct the problem.

Vegetal flavors and aromas

Occasionally, you may taste or smell a cornlike character in your beer. This quality comes from a compound called *dimethyl sulfide* or *DMS*.

DMS comes from the malt or, more specifically, the heating or boiling of the wort. Pale malts also produce more DMS than darker malts. Typically, DMS is driven off in the steam of the boil, but after you turn the heat off, DMS can still creep up in the wort. If you cool your wort too slowly, you trap large quantities of DMS in the beer. So the best preventative measure is to cool your wort as quickly as possible to keep DMS at a minimum. And never cover your brewpot, lest you trap DMS in your brew.

REMEMBER

One important point is that some DMS is part of the flavor profile of lager beers due to the fact that lager malts produce larger amounts of DMS. Although you can expect some DMS in lagers, you certainly don't need to purposely create it. If you use lager malts, you still have plenty of DMS in your beer.

Certain bacteria also create DMS. When this happens, very large amounts of DMS are typically present. These bacteria can also produce other flavors and odors that are reminiscent of vegetables, such as cooked cauliflower and broccoli. To minimize these off flavors, cool the wort and pitch the yeast as soon as possible.

Flavor and Aroma Therapy Quick References

So your beer stinks, huh? Well, if you're speaking literally rather than figuratively, the following table is for you. If your beer doesn't smell quite right, the problem can be any number of things. For this reason, Table 28-1 gives you some symptoms, the corresponding beer lingo, and then (most important) some possible sources of the problem.

If your brew tastes odd (or even *bad*), check out Table 28-2 for help discerning the most common off flavors, their correct names, and their possible sources.

TABLE 28-1 Beer Aroma Troubleshooting List

If Your Beer Smells Like	The Proper Term Is	The Source May Be
Adhesive bandages	Phenolic	Bacterial contamination; residue from a sanitizing agent (Note: This odor is expected of certain beer styles)
Apple cider	Acetaldehyde	Refined sugar in the recipe or bacterial contamination
Baby diapers	Enteric	Bacterial contamination; "wild" yeast fermentation
Banana	Banana esters	Certain ale yeast strains, particularly Bavarian Weizenbier and Belgian strong ales
Barnyard	Enteric	Bacterial contamination; "wild" yeast fermentation
Bubblegum	Bubblegum	Certain ale yeast strains, particularly Belgian strong ales and Bavarian Weizenbier
Butter/butterscotch	Diacetyl	Bacteria; certain yeast strains; warm fermentation; short aging

(continued)

TABLE 28-1 *(continued)*

If Your Beer Smells Like	The Proper Term Is	The Source May Be
Cardboard or paper	Oxidized	Contact with air; old, stale beer
Cauliflower or cooked cabbage	Vegetal	Bacterial contamination
Cloves	Phenolic	Certain yeast strains, such as those in Bavarian Weizenbier
Cooked corn	DMS (dimethyl sulfide)	Poor grain quality; bacterial contamination
Cooking sherry	Oxidized	Contact with air; long and warm fermentation
Green apple	Acetaldehyde	Refined sugar in the recipe; bacterial contamination
Leather	Oxidized	Contact with air; old, stale beer
Indelible marker	Phenolic	Bacterial contamination; residue of sanitizing agent
Matches (burnt) or sulfur	Hydrogen sulfide	Natural by-product of fermentation that's normally flushed out with the production of carbon dioxide
Mold	Moldy	Sanitation problem; leaking package seal
Nail polish remover	Solvent-like	Esters produced during high-temperature fermentations
Olives (green or black) or pickles	Acetic	*Acetobacter* contamination
Paint thinner	Solvent-like	Fusel alcohols produced during high-temperature fermentations
Rotten eggs	Hydrogen sulfide	Natural by-product of fermentation that's normally flushed out with the production of carbon dioxide
Rubber	Hydrogen sulfide	Yeast autolysis
Skunk	Lightstruck	Damage from light
Smoke	Phenolic	Use of dark or smoked grains that evoke this aroma
Soap	Soapy	Residue from sanitizing agents
Vinyl upholstery	Phenolic	Bacterial contamination; residue from sanitizing agents
Wet dog	Musty	Bacterial contamination; lengthy aging of bottle-conditioned beer; "wild" yeast fermentation

TABLE 28-2 Beer Taste Troubleshooting List

If Your Beer Tastes Like	The Proper Term Is	The Source May Be
Blood	Metallic	Iron in water supply; contact with metals
Butter/butterscotch	Diacetyl	Certain yeast strains; warm fermentations
Cardboard	Oxidized	Contact with air; old, stale beer
Cauliflower or cooked cabbage	Vegetal	Bacterial contamination
Chalk	Astringent	Overfermentation; misuse of grain
Cooked corn	DMS (dimethyl sulfide)	Poor grain quality; bacterial contamination
Cooking sherry	Oxidized	Contact with air; long, warm fermentation
Green apple	Acetaldehyde	Use of refined sugar; bacterial contamination
Harsh	Astringent	High hop bitterness; misuse of grain.
Olives or pickles	Acetic	*Acetobacter* contamination
Powdery	Astringent	Lack of sweetness; grain astringency
Salt	Salty	Use of brewing salts, especially sodium chloride and magnesium sulfate
Smoke	Phenolic	Use of dark or smoked grains that evoke this flavor
Soap	Soapy	Residue of sanitizing agents
Sour milk	Lactic	Lactic fermentation (which is intentional in some beer styles such as Berliner Weisse)
Sulfur	Hydrogen sulfide	Natural by-product of fermentation; can also be attributed to certain grains such as 6-row pale malt
Tin can, coins	Metallic	Iron in water supply; contact with metals

Conditioning and Appearance Problems

Once your beer is done fermenting, you need to condition it. *Conditioning* is an added aging process during which the beer is naturally clarified and recarbonated. As simple as the process seems, things don't always work out the way they should. The appearance of your beer may mean a lot to you, and color and clarity can influence how drinkers perceive it. This section addresses problems that may occur with the conditioning and appearance of your brew.

Flat out of gas

What if your beer is flat? If you can still feel the CO_2 bubbles on your tongue, but the beer just isn't holding a head, your beer isn't the problem — the dirty glass is. See Chapter 26 for more on proper glass-cleaning techniques.

If you can't even feel the carbonation, check these potential problems:

- **Did you condition the beer enough?** Typically, your beer needs at least two weeks to carbonate properly in the bottle or can. Lagers take even longer because of the cold storage. After you bottle your beer, be sure to keep the bottles or cans at 66° to 70° Fahrenheit for two weeks for proper conditioning. Don't store your beer cold until after this conditioning period is over.
- **Did you prime the beer with the proper amount of corn sugar?** Always use ½ to ¾ cup of corn sugar per 5 gallons of beer (but never more). And be sure that you thoroughly mix the priming sugar solution into the wort — pour the dextrose and water mixture into the bottling bucket before you drain the beer into it.
- **Did you thoroughly rinse your equipment?** Make sure you rinse all the equipment of sanitizer residue. Any residue can shock or kill the yeast necessary to carbonate the beer.
- **Did you tightly seal your bottles?** Prior to bottling, check all your bottles and caps for cracks, chips, or imperfections. These flaws let CO_2 escape from the bottles. Improperly seated caps can also be the culprit. If you can your beer, is your crimper properly crimping the lids?

Thar she blows! Overcarbonated beers

Got beer that foams and gushes? Again, check the priming rate. (See Chapter 14 for more on priming.) Also, be sure that your beer has fully fermented before you bottle it. Any residual unfermented sugar left in the beer causes your brew to become overcarbonated.

Another cause of overcarbonation can be contamination. Certain wild yeasts and bacteria consume sugars that beer yeast can't. This occurrence produces copious amounts of CO_2. The excess carbonation comes out of solution quickly and produces gushing. Remember to sanitize bottles, caps, and so on, and always boil your priming solutions. Do the same for cans and can lids.

In a haze: Cloudy beers

The average beer drinker is accustomed to crystal-clear, filtered beers. If your beer tastes good but has a haze, don't worry about it — most of the time the haze does not affect the flavor. Some beers, like unfiltered wheat beers, are cloudy by nature.

Eventually, most haze (especially yeast) settles out if given enough time. However, if you really need clear beer, you can try some clarifying products. Check out Chapter 9 to find out more about clarifying and fining agents.

Chill haze is a phenomenon caused by chilling your beer. A clear beer at room temperature becomes hazy when refrigerated. The haze doesn't affect the flavor and eventually settles out on its own. The beer also clears up if you allow it to warm up again.

With the introduction of the relatively new NEIPA (New England India pale ale) style, beer clarity is no longer an expectation or a given. These beers, often referred to as *juicy* or *hazy*, can often be cloudy to the point of opaque!

WARNING

Like anything else, fining agents have their drawbacks. Any time you remove something you want to get rid of (yeast, haze), you can also inadvertently remove something you don't want to get rid of (body, head retention). Be careful about improper use or overuse of finings.

Poor head, bad body

Do you need better body and head retention in your beers? Dextrins and proteins in your beer are responsible for a great body and a head to go with it (and who doesn't want that?). If you don't use any grains in your beer, you need to. Incorporating ½ to 1 pound of crystal malt or CaraPils malt (per 5-gallon batch) into your wort helps. (See Chapter 4 for more information about malts.) Adding flavorless malto-dextrin powder to your wort also works like a charm (use 4 to 8 ounces per 5 gallons).

» Becoming a beer judge

Chapter 29

Homebrew Competitions

Just as amateur chefs and bakers compete in chili cook-offs and pie bake-offs, homebrew competitions provide a competitive platform for people who like to make beer. Back in 1985, a dozen such competitions may have been held across the country, attracting a couple hundred entries; now a couple hundred competitions attract thousands of entries every year. These competitions are held at the local, regional, and national level and offer awards of varying sizes to the winners.

Because homebrew competitions had so much at stake, the American Homebrewers Association (AHA) in Boulder, Colorado, in conjunction with the Home Wine and Beer Trade Association (HWBTA), saw the need to establish the Beer Judge Certification Program (BJCP) to standardize judging and scoring procedures. (For more information regarding the BJCP and how to become a beer judge, check out the section "Becoming a Barrister of Beer" later in this chapter.) After establishing the BJCP, the AHA created a sanctioning program that guaranteed uniform rules and operations at all AHA sanctioned events.

Since I first joined the BJCP in 1986 (one of the first 70 people in North America and the first in the state of Illinois to do so), things have changed considerably. The BJCP is now its own entity being run by its own board of directors with elected representatives from around the country. And speaking of which, there are now BJCP chapters in many countries around the world, too.

Today, the homebrewing community leans heavily on the BJCP to conduct judge testing and to oversee certification, as well as to regularly update the all-important beer style guidelines, by which competitive homebrewers compare their brews to established standards. BJCP judges also use these guidelines to evaluate homebrews submitted to the many competitions that take place with regularity.

In this chapter, I give you the lowdown on BJCP-sanctioned beer competitions, including how they're run and how you can enter. If simply entering isn't enough involvement for you, I also cover how you can become a BJCP-certified beer judge.

What's Involved in Homebrewing Competitions?

The general format for a BJCP-sanctioned event goes something like this: The event's sponsor picks a calendar date far in advance of the competition, both for positioning purposes (so that it doesn't coincide with any other competitions) and for advertising purposes (to enable homebrewers to plan their entries ahead of time and to make sure that enough judges can attend). A homebrew club (or several clubs together) usually sponsors the event, but retail and online vendors— and especially homebrew suppliers— may also sponsor such an event. The sponsor must also reserve a location at which to hold the competition and actively solicit donations toward prizes.

Closer to the day of the event, the sponsor contacts qualified judges and coaxes and cajoles them into attending. (Judges only occasionally receive any compensation for their participation; usually a complimentary hotel room or a small travel stipend.) Meanwhile, word of the event spreads to potential competitors primarily via direct email, social media, and word-of-mouth. Customarily, all competitors must submit their entries at least one week in advance of the event so that the beer has time to settle and the competition committee can correctly register all entries. After the competition committee logs in the brews by beer style and category, they store the entries in cool conditions until the event.

The typical BJCP-sanctioned event may have as many as 28 major classifications and another 50 subcategories open to entries. The major classifications include beer, cider, mead, and even sake. If the competition committee doesn't receive enough entries to fill a certain category, it pairs those entries with other, similar categories and instructs the judges to judge them separately according to style — for example, the judges would judge German-style pilsners and Bohemian-style pilsners together in the same grouping but differently according to the established guidelines for their individual style.

How are the entries judged?

On the day of the event — or the first day, in the case of larger, multi-day competitions — the sponsor readies the location, assembles the panel of judges, and hands out judging assignments. *Stewards* — people who help the competition run smoothly (often beer judge trainees) — make sure that all judges have the correct judging forms and score sheets, appropriate writing implements, drinking water, and something to cleanse the palate between beers (usually French bread or unsalted crackers).

The standard BJCP scoring format uses a 50-point system. The aroma scores 0 to 12 points; the appearance, 0 to 3; the flavor, 0 to 20; the body, 0 to 5; and the overall impression, 0 to 10. The score sheet also addresses beer quality according to "Stylistic Accuracy, Technical Merit, and Intangibles" with check boxes (see Figure 29-1).

The competition committee pairs the event's judges according to their stylistic preferences and/or level of knowledge. (If a judge has no experience with Australian aboriginal ale, for example, that judge has no business judging that category.) No fewer than two judges ever judge a brew together.

After tasting the brew and writing their remarks on the score sheet, the judges usually discuss the beer's attributes together. Although judges are at liberty to disagree with one another on the finer points, their scores should always reflect a shared opinion of the beer within a 5-point margin. (A huge disparity in scores indicates a bias or fundamental lack of knowledge on the part of one or both judges.) The brewers always receive these score sheets shortly after the event.

In the name of fairness and objectivity, only the competition committee members, who are responsible for registering and logging in the entries, know the identities of the individual brewers. Judges aren't privy to any information that divulges the brewers' identities.

After all the beer categories are judged and the score sheets tabulated, the best beer from each category goes on to the Best-of-Show round. The competition committee hand-picks the most senior and experienced judges (from a pool of those who don't have a brew competing for the Best of Show) to adjudicate the beers at this level; they are usually National rank and higher. Judges use no score sheets; they choose the two or three beers that best represent their respective categories by process of elimination. The final three beers left standing receive first-, second-, and third-place honors, based on the judges' evaluations. (Some competitions may choose up to four or five Best-of-Show beers.)

Beer Judge

BEER SCORESHEET

http://www.bjcp.org
AHA/BJCP Sanctioned Competition Program
http://www.homebrewersassociation.org

Judge Name (print) ______________________

Judge BJCP ID ______________________

Judge Email ______________________

Use Avery label # 5160

BJCP Rank or Status:

☐ Apprentice ☐ Recognized ☐ Certified
☐ National ☐ Master ☐ Grand Master ___
☐ Honorary Master ☐ Honorary GM ☐ Mead Judge
☐ Provisional Judge ☐ Rank Pending ☐ Cider Judge

Non-BJCP Qualifications:

☐ Professional Brewer ☐ Beer Sommelier ☐ GABF/WBC
☐ Certified Cicerone ☐ Adv. Cicerone ☐ Master Cicerone
☐ Sensory Training ☐ Other ______________

Descriptor Definitions (Mark all that apply):

☐ **Acetaldehyde** – Green apple-like aroma and flavor.

☐ **Alcoholic** – The aroma, flavor, and warming effect of ethanol and higher alcohols. Sometimes described as *hot*.

☐ **Astringent** – Puckering, lingering harshness and/or dryness in the finish/aftertaste; harsh graininess; huskiness.

☐ **Diacetyl** – Artificial butter, butterscotch, or toffee aroma and flavor. Sometimes perceived as a slickness on the tongue.

☐ **DMS (dimethyl sulfide)** – At low levels a sweet, cooked or canned corn-like aroma and flavor.

☐ **Estery** – Aroma and/or flavor of any ester (fruits, fruit flavorings, or roses).

☐ **Grassy** – Aroma/flavor of fresh-cut grass or green leaves.

☐ **Light-Struck** – Similar to the aroma of a skunk.

☐ **Metallic** – Tinny, coiny, copper, iron, or blood-like flavor.

☐ **Musty** – Stale, musty, or moldy aromas/flavors.

☐ **Oxidized** – Any one or combination of stale, winy/vinous, cardboard, papery, or sherry-like aromas and flavors.

☐ **Phenolic** – Spicy (clove, pepper), smoky, plastic, plastic adhesive strip, and/or medicinal (chlorophenolic).

☐ **Solvent** – Aromas and flavors of higher alcohols (fusel alcohols). Similar to acetone or lacquer thinner aromas.

☐ **Sour/Acidic** – Tartness in aroma and flavor. Can be sharp and clean (lactic acid), or vinegar-like (acetic acid).

☐ **Sulfur** – The aroma of rotten eggs or burning matches.

☐ **Vegetal** – Cooked, canned, or rotten vegetable aroma and flavor (cabbage, onion, celery, asparagus, etc.)

☐ **Yeasty** – A bready, sulfury or yeast-like aroma or flavor.

Category # ______ **Subcategory (a-f)** ______ **Entry #** ______

Subcategory (spell out) ______________________

Special Ingredients: ______________________

Bottle Inspection: ☐ Appropriate size, cap, fill level, label removal, etc.

Comments ______________________

Aroma (as appropriate for style) ______/12
Comment on malt, hops, esters, and other aromatics

Appearance (as appropriate for style) ______/ 3
Comment on color, clarity, and head (retention, color, and texture)

Flavor (as appropriate for style) ______/20
Comment on malt, hops, fermentation characteristics, balance, finish/aftertaste, and other flavor characteristics

Mouthfeel (as appropriate for style) ______/ 5
Comment on body, carbonation, warmth, creaminess, astringency, and other palate sensations

Overall Impression ______/10
Comment on overall drinking pleasure associated with entry, give suggestions for improvement

Total ______/50

SCORING GUIDE

Outstanding	(45 - 50):	World-class example of style.
Excellent	(38 - 44):	Exemplifies style well, requires minor fine-tuning.
Very Good	(30 - 37):	Generally within style parameters, some minor flaws.
Good	(21 - 29):	Misses the mark on style and/or minor flaws.
Fair	(14 - 20):	Off flavors/aromas or major style deficiencies. Unpleasant.
Problematic	(00 - 13):	Major off flavors and aromas dominate. Hard to drink.

Stylistic Accuracy
Classic Example ☐ ☐ ☐ ☐ ☐ **Not to Style**
Technical Merit
Flawless ☐ ☐ ☐ ☐ ☐ **Significant Flaws**
Intangibles
Wonderful ☐ ☐ ☐ ☐ ☐ **Lifeless**

BJCP Beer Scoresheet Copyright © 2017 Beer Judge Certification Program rev. 170612
Please send any comments to Comp_Director@BJCP.org

FIGURE 29-1: Standard BJCP scoresheet.

The prizes at homebrewing competitions nowadays are nothing to sneeze at. Generally speaking, the larger the competition is, the more valuable the prizes are. The national competitions, especially the one hosted by the BJCP, are exceptionally generous, thanks to the donations that large breweries and allied businesses worldwide make.

ABOUT THE AHA AND THE BJCP

When the Beer Judge Certification Program was launched back in 1985, it was under the aegis of the American Homebrewers Association, itself an offshoot of the Association of Brewers in Boulder, Colorado. Since then, the BJCP has become its own entity, completely disassociated with the AHA.

All the competition rules, guidelines and beer styles used in this book follow those provided by the BJCP (`www.bjcp.org`). All manner of information about the BJCP can be found on their website. Keep in mind that the BJCP is an all-volunteer organization; therefore, there are no office numbers to call with questions or complaints, and the website is tended to on a "when we can get to it" basis. Contact, when necessary, is limited to Regional Representatives' email addresses and other Directory links listed on the website.

Meanwhile, the AHA is still alive and well and still an offshoot of the updated Brewers Association, a 501(c)6 not-for-profit organization, dedicated to promoting the community of homebrewers and empowering homebrewers to make the best beer in the world. Since 1978, the AHA has worked to educate people worldwide about the coolest hobby there is — homebrewing!

`https://www.homebrewersassociation.org/`

Email: `info@brewersassociation.org`

Phone: 1.303.447.0816 ext. 2

Toll Free: 1.888.822.6273 ext. 2

Although dozens of BJCP-sanctioned competitions take place locally and regionally each year, it's the National Homebrew Competition (NHC) that gets everyone's attention. The judging of this largest single-site competition (over 5,000 entries in 2021) takes place in conjunction with Homebrew Con, an annual gathering of homebrewers that is hosted by the American Homebrewers Association in a different U.S. city each year.

How do I enter a homebrew competition, and what are the rules?

To enter a homebrew competition, you first need to find out where and when the competitions take place. You can find this information at various locations on the

Internet. The standard eligibility requirement is simple: The beer must be genuine homebrewed beer made *in the home.* Beyond this standard rule, individual competitions may set the entry requirements and rules and regulations, including those described in the following list:

- **Competition entry fee:** The entry fee is a nominal amount to help defray the costs of hosting competitions. In addition to prizes (which may or may not be donations), competition committees must find a location for the event, which often comes at a price; they must provide food for the judges and stewards (who don't receive payment for their services); and they must cover the costs for mailings in advance of the event and again for mailings of score sheets and prizes after the event. Entry fees generally run from $10 per entry up to $15 per entry, depending on the event. Most events also give price breaks to brewers who submit more than, say, four or five entries.
- **Bottle and can size limits:** These limits are to keep all entries somewhat uniform. Typical bottle size requirements are from 12 to 16 ounces (in green or brown glass). If sponsors didn't impose limits on submission size, storage or refrigeration problems could result. Unusually sized or odd-shaped bottles can also compromise brewer anonymity. Acceptable can sizes are typically 12 and 16 ounces, too.
- **Number of bottles/cans per entry:** Most competitions require two bottles or cans per entry: One is for the first round of judging; if a particular beer takes first place in its category, it moves on to the Best-of-Show round, at which point the judges sample a fresh sample.
- **Category and classification:** The BJCP keeps a composite listing of some 20-odd major beer styles and their taste profiles, along with a multitude of lesser substyles. (See the recipe chapters in this book for more on these profiles.) These standards are respected throughout the homebrewing community. All BJCP-sanctioned events use BJCP beer style guidelines for judging purposes, but each event reserves the right to pick and choose which categories to judge at each event — make sure that you read the competition category rules carefully.
- **Entry deadline:** As I mention in the section "What's Involved in Homebrewing Competitions?" earlier in this chapter, the customary deadline is one week before the competition to give participants time for registration and cataloging, as well as to provide time for the beer to settle. Each competition committee, however, has the right to set a deadline as it sees fit.

How do I send my beer?

Anyone familiar with the U.S. postal laws knows that sending alcoholic beverages through the mail is illegal. Some package shipping services, however, deliver homebrewed beer to a designated location "for analysis only." (Like the U.S. Postal Service, these companies also make international deliveries.) Only once in many years of shipping homebrew this way was I ever questioned about the contents of my parcel or its purpose. Just make sure you pack the bottles and cans well, using wadded newspaper or Styrofoam packing peanuts. Line the inside of the box with a plastic bag and place the bottles or cans and packing material inside the liner. Some competitions recommend double-boxing for extra protection.

If you don't mind spending a couple extra bucks to safeguard your brews in transit, there is a company called Spirited Shipper that specializes in making high-quality cardboard shipping containers with glass bottles in mind.

REMEMBER

Make sure that you fill out all the necessary forms and attach them to bottles and cans, where appropriate — and don't forget to include the entry fee!

TIP

Many homebrewers who live close to the competition location drop off their brews at the designated location and save themselves the shipping costs.

HOW'S MY BREWING?

Sending your homebrewed beer to a sanctioned competition can be a very gratifying aspect of homebrewing. Beyond winning nice ribbons, medals, beer ingredients, and miscellaneous prizes, however, competitions offer homebrewers clear and objective evaluations of their beers by competent and knowledgeable beer judges. For each brew that you send to a sanctioned competition, you're guaranteed to receive all the judges' score sheets in return. These score sheets go beyond assigning a simple numerical score to your brew; because of their training, BJCP judges offer intelligent and coherent feedback on your beer. Although some of what they say about your brew may be guesswork, the judges' comments may also point out important negative attributes in your beer and in your brewing technique that may help you improve not only your beer but also your enjoyment of homebrewing. This information alone is often worth the entry fee.

The Best of the Best

If you are a type-A brewing personality or if you just love the thrill of competition, there are still two more ways to get in on the winnings. ***Bear in mind, both of these virtual competitions are dependent on your being successful in previous competitions; let's call them "pre-requisite" winnings.*** You don't have to submit any physical entries, just your scoresheets from a previous competition at which you won first place.

Both of these competitions maintain online leaderboards that can be easily viewed and monitored on their respective websites.

Master Championship of Amateur Brewing

The Master's Championship of Amateur Brewing (MCAB) is a biannual national championship competition for homebrewers. Brewers qualify for the annual MCAB championship event by placing first in any MCAB-recognized category of an independent homebrew competition that has been selected as a qualifying event for that year.

Because each qualifier is a qualifying event first place winner, the competition is very strong. Known as the "champions' championship," awards are given to the first three places in each category, as well as Grand Master and Grand Champion awards for best of show and most medal points, respectively.

Master Homebrewer Program

The Master Homebrewer Program is a nonprofit organization established to promote the mastery of amateur brewing. The objectives of the program are to recognize brewers for their excellence in the production of high-quality beer, mead, and cider; to promote the hobby of homebrewing by incentivizing brewers to stretch their breadth of knowledge across all styles; to act symbiotically with the BJCP; to encourage participation in competition; and to establish a quick and easy means of identifying experts in the field of homebrewing.

Becoming a Barrister of Beer

So you think you want to become a beer judge? You think that the job sounds like an easy gig? You think you'd get to drink a lot of free beer? The answer to the first question may be "Yes," but the answer to the second two is "No!" — conditionally speaking, of course. You do reach a point where the good aspects of the job far outweigh the bad, but becoming a certified beer judge is no cakewalk. If you think you're qualified just because you drink beer, think again.

What it takes to become a beer judge

Becoming good at judging beer takes time, practice, experience, perseverance, and a genuine desire to excel at the task. The following list describes in detail what developing these characteristics requires:

- **Time:** No one becomes an expert at anything overnight. Just because you've been drinking Old Foamy for years (since you were legally old enough, of course) doesn't qualify you for anything but a loyal-customer award and a rebate coupon. You need to spend time taste-testing and absorbing all the style parameters of various beers. The more you read, taste, and practice, the quicker you develop the skills you need to be a good beer judge. (Depending on your level of dedication, you can achieve judgeship within a year.)
- **Practice:** Even good and experienced judges need to practice beer judging. You must put your evaluation skills to the test regularly to stay sharp and in tune. You don't need to practice just at actual competitions either; regular evaluation of your own homebrews or store-bought beer accomplishes the same goal.
- **Experience:** A good beer judge has a deep and profound knowledge of beer styles and has personally tasted hundreds of different brands from different countries and breweries in a quest for this experience. And although you can conceivably become a beer judge without being a homebrewer, you'd miss a fundamental part of what the game is all about. Every certified beer judge I know is a homebrewer.
- **Perseverance:** Beer-judging opportunities don't always come to you. Some travel and a significant contribution of personal time are imperative to progress within the system. No one pays you for this honor, and no one reimburses you 100 percent for your expenses. And, according to my IRS audit, beer judging is still not a tax-deductible expense!
- **Genuine desire:** If you can't drink barley wine (a rich, thick, alcoholic ale) for three hours before lunch, if you can't stomach beer from 9 a.m. till 5 p.m., if you can't handle tasting brews for two or maybe even three days straight, you may want to take up stamp collecting instead of beer judging. And by the way, you get no guarantees that everything you judge is gonna taste good!

I can never forget one particular national competition during which a table of judges had to evaluate a garlic beer. That stuff was so potent they had to open the windows before judging could continue!

Your enthusiasm is undiminished? Your resolve unflagging? Good; you may find a place in the Beer Judge Certification Program. And because this program is the only one of its kind in the United States, you have no alternative choices if you really want to become a beer judge through an accredited organization.

TIP

Becoming a BJCP certified beer judge and progressing upward through the ranks can lead to bigger and better things. Due to their growth and popularity, large commercial competitions such as the Great American Beer Festival and the World Beer Cup are inviting greater numbers of BJCP judges to join the ranks of professional judges at these events. Likewise at international competitions that use BJCP rules, regulations, and beer style guidelines.

Advancing to supreme quart justice

The BJC Program was established in 1985 to educate already-knowledgeable people in correct procedural judging techniques and to standardize scoring methods. After a judge candidate proves her knowledge and ability by passing an entrance exam at a certain level, she may progress through the program by earning experience points for judging, stewarding, and organizing competitions. The number of points she receives depends on what position (organizer, judge, steward) she holds in a competition and how large the competition is (as measured by the number of entries). As she accumulates experience points, she can advance to the next level (assuming that she achieves a minimum exam score for that next level). I describe these levels in the following list:

- **Recognized judge:** This level requires a minimum test score of 60 percent. No judging experience points are needed to start at this level.
- **Certified judge:** This level requires a minimum test score of 70 percent and at least 5 experience points.
- **National judge:** This level requires a minimum test score of 80 percent and at least 20 experience points.
- **Master judge:** This level requires a minimum test score of 90 percent and at least 40 experience points.
- **Grand master judge:** This level requires a minimum test score of 90 percent, at least 100 experience points, and an additional point total based on special services performed on behalf of the BJCP.

Note: Retaking the test to achieve a higher score isn't only allowed — it's encouraged!

In addition to these official ranks, there are other terms used to describe judges who are not officially in the BJCP:

- **Apprentice judge** is a temporary rank used to describe someone who has taken but not passed a judging exam. The judge has two years to pass the same judging exam or become an Affiliated member, a special type of Inactive judge. Apprentice judges are not full members of the BJCP.
- **Provisional judge** is a term used to describe someone who has passed one of the BJCP online entrance exams; it is not a BJCP rank. This status is temporary; those passing an online qualifier exam have one year in which to pass a judging exam.
- **Non-BJCP judge** is the proper term to describe a person who has not taken a BJCP exam but who judges in competitions. This is not an official BJCP rank, but this description is used on the BJCP scoresheets.

There are also two honorary ranks — *honorary master judge and honorary grand master judge.* These positions are temporary designations bestowed by the BJCP on certain persons widely known for their judging skills and mastery of the craft who may not have fulfilled the official requirements of that level. British beer writer Michael Jackson was one such person given this honorific.

Last but not least, there are yet two more BJCP judge positions specific to judging cider and mead:

- **Cider judge** is awarded to someone who has taken and passed the Cider Judging Exam. If the judge has not passed the Beer Judge Exam, cider judge is a rank; otherwise, it is an endorsement.
- **Mead judge** is awarded to someone who has taken and passed the Mead Judging Exam. If the judge has not passed the Beer Judge Exam, mead judge is a rank; otherwise, it is an endorsement.

Anyone interested in becoming a BJCP certified judge must start by taking an online Beer Entrance Exam. The B.E. Exam is a qualifier for the Beer Judging Exam. A prospective beer judge must pass the Beer Entrance Exam as the first step to gaining certification. After a prospective beer judge takes and passes the B.E. Exam online, then they have to sign up for the Beer Judging Exam, which is an in-person beer tasting assessment.

Keep in mind none of this free. (How do you think the organization pays for administrative costs?) Taking the Beer Entrance Exam online costs $10; taking the Beer Judging Exam will set you back 40 bucks — but at least you get to taste beer!

SCORING AND EVALUATING BEER

From a professional-standards perspective, you must judge beer, like wine, according to its style. To judge a hearty vintage cabernet sauvignon against a field of young and fruity Beaujolais wines wouldn't be at all fair. Likewise, you can't compare a bock beer to a group of brown ales. You must judge each wine and each beer on its own merits and against wines and beers of like style. This type of judging is standard procedure in the various amateur and commercial beer competitions that take place across the United States, including the widely acclaimed Great American Beer Festival and the World Beer Cup.

For a person to critically evaluate beer this way, a reasonable understanding of beer styles and an ability to be fair and objective is integral to the process. Anyone who takes upon himself the task of evaluating beers should do so with at least a modicum of respect for the beer and a maximum of responsibility for the personal critique. The correct evaluation of beer requires the taster to follow certain rules of fairness. A clean palate is essential to a valid taste assessment of beer. (Judging beer immediately after eating raw onions or garlic chip dip, for example, is a definite no-no.) But you also want to avoid judging beer on an empty stomach (to lessen the possibility of inebriation).

Yet another problem inherent to taste evaluations that involve any product containing alcohol is the fact that alcohol itself deadens the various sensory systems of the human body — especially the palate. Thus, palate fatigue becomes a problem. *Palate fatigue* is what occurs if you taste too many beers, especially of like style, one after the other. It's also the main reason why wine tasters spit out the wine instead of swallowing it. Beer tasters, on the other hand, are just too appreciative to waste a good thing by following that example.

The BJCP administers the Beer Judging Exam throughout the country on many dates throughout each year. The frequency is determined by the number of requests for the exam in a given region and the availability of qualified proctors. (Proctoring these exams is one way higher-ranked judges can earn their service points.) For more and updated information, check out the Beer Judge Certification Program at `https://www.bjcp.org`.

8 The Part of Tens

IN THIS PART . . .

Get more hands-on by making your own do-it-yourself brewing projects.

Check out all the handy new gadgets and gizmos available to make your beer better, quicker, and easier.

Get your frequently asked questions answered here.

Chapter 30

Ten (or So) Ways to D.I.G.I.B.I.Y. (Do It, Grow It, Build It Yourself)

Homebrewers who are really into their hobby inevitably continue to discover more and experiment more, simultaneously expanding their horizons and their own control over their craft. This chapter is for those intrepid individuals who intend to immerse themselves deeply in new homebrewing techniques, as well as for the rest of you who just have lots of idle hours on your hands.

Banking Yeast

Yeast is the logical first choice for advanced involvement in the control over your beer's ingredients. *Yeast banking, ranching,* or *farming* — call the procedure what you want — is all about culturing your own pure yeast strains and keeping them on hand for future use in your home brewery. The basic idea behind yeast banking is that you keep several pure, live yeast cultures — in bulk quantity — on hand for inoculating your future brews. In short, if you bank your own yeast, you have the type of yeast you want when you want it and in sufficient quantities for pitching into your new brew.

REMEMBER

As is true of homebrewing itself, you can do your yeast banking on various levels. At the frugal end, you can use mason jars and cheap wine carafes for storing yeast. At the extravagant end, expensive glass beakers and flasks lend a high-tech look to your unfinished basement. The way you decide to go all depends on your approach.

WARNING

Before moving on, remember that sanitizing techniques either make or break your foray into yeast banking. If you aren't willing and able to practice absolutely *aseptic* (pristinely sanitary) yeast-handling techniques, maybe you should just throw the towel in now. (See Chapter 3 for more on proper sanitation procedures.)

Preparing to open your own bank

When starting up your yeast bank, you should keep it simple. The average homebrewer probably doesn't use more than a half-dozen different strains in a year's time. For each strain you intend to bank, you need the following equipment:

- At least one holding tank (for example, a mason jar, wine carafe, or glass flask). Call this slurry the *mother culture.* As you continue to propagate the yeast, you need more vessels.
- A rubber stopper to fit the holding tank (and any other vessels you add later).
- An airlock (for each vessel). See Chapter 2 for a discussion of airlocks.

Additional items you need on hand include isopropyl alcohol and sterile cotton balls for sanitizing yeast-handling equipment (butane lighters also come in handy to sterilize, or *flame,* the openings of beer-bottle holding tanks); dry malt extract to feed the yeast; pure clean water (the same as you brew with); and the yeasts! Although your goal is self-sufficiency, you still need to start with pure yeast cultures from a reliable yeast supplier.

TIP

Consider using self-stick labels to identify each strain if you're banking more than one. One yeast strain doesn't look a whole lot different from another, and confusion may undermine your efforts.

Creating yeast

Follow the directions in Chapter 12 for making a yeast starter culture, because that's basically what you're doing. The difference is that after the yeast completes its mini-fermentation in its holding tank, you can either repeat the procedure in a larger vessel (such as a half-gallon apple-cider jug) with more wort, or you can subdivide the yeast into several vessels of the same size. Using one large vessel is cheaper and easier than using several smaller ones, but the risk of contamination is lower if you separate the mixture into several vessels and open them one at a time rather than reopen the large one every time you need to pitch a brew. Regardless of how you store them, keep all your yeast cultures refrigerated until you need them.

TIP

As you're boiling the wort you intend to use as yeast food, make a larger batch and store the excess sterile wort in sanitized and capped beer bottles for future use. (Keep these bottles refrigerated, too.)

Handling Grain

Grain handling is an area of homebrewing into which very few homebrewers venture — and probably smartly so, because grain growing and malting procedures require vast amounts of land, equipment, capital, and expertise. This task, therefore, is best left to the farmers and maltsters who can provide you with high-quality product much more quickly and cheaply than you can possibly produce yourself.

You can, however, manipulate your grains in some small (and very tasty) ways. Roasting and smoking are a couple of the methods that can give you more control over your brew.

Roast-a-rama

Why would you want to roast your own grains? Again, it's a control issue (or lack of a social life). Roasted grains give your beer complexity by imbuing it with various toasty, roasty, and nutty flavors (which isn't to say that you can't just buy these same grains at the local homebrew supplier).

To roast your own grains, start with a couple of pounds of *unground* pale malt (ale or lager malt is fine) and follow these steps:

1. **Preheat the oven to 350° Fahrenheit.**
2. **Spread the grain out thinly on a cookie sheet or a pizza tin.**
3. **Place the grain tin on the highest oven rack, set a timer, and watch the grain closely.**

At increments of ten minutes or so, your grain should progress through a spectrum of gold, amber, copper, and brown colors. (The exact timing of these changes depends greatly on individual oven efficiency.) You need to monitor the color-to-taste relationship by periodically (and very carefully) tasting the grain as it's roasting.

You're always better off underroasting your grain than overroasting it. Take good notes regarding your procedures and use them as guidelines for the next time around.

If the grain is moist as it goes into the oven, the roasting enhances its aroma development. You can moisten the grain by briefly wetting it with a plant mister and allowing it to absorb the moisture for about an hour prior to roasting.

After you've roasted the grain to your satisfaction, allow it to cool sufficiently, put it into a sealed plastic bag, and leave it alone to mellow over a week's time before brewing with it.

Smoke 'em if you got 'em

Instead of just roasting your grains in an oven, you can opt to smoke them on a grill. You can imbue your grain (and beer) with a variety of smoky aromas and flavors by burning various types of wood in a barbecue grill or meat smoker. Put your malt (the same type of grain I describe in the preceding section) on something that enables the smoke to waft up through the grain.

One cost-effective smoking method is to buy some disposable aluminum roasting or pizza tins and poke holes in their bottoms; *do not* allow flames to touch these tins — they're designed for use in low-flame and low-heat applications and can melt in an instant. If you want to get a little more sophisticated, buy an all-steel strainer (no plastic handles or flammable parts) with a flat bottom. You probably don't want to use this utensil for anything else but smoking grain.

How long you smoke your grain depends on how much grain you're smoking, the intensity of the fire, the intensity of the smoke, and your tolerance for smoky grain. You need at least a half-hour to imbue the grain with some smoky character. After the grain has cooled, you're best off allowing it to mellow for about a week before using it; keep it stored in a plastic self-sealing bag.

Some wood choices you can use for smoking grain include alder, apple, beech, hickory, maple, pear, pecan, and oak; each variety brings its own qualities to the fire. Alder, for example, gives malt a sweet, delicate woodiness, and pecan is more pungent, intense, and spicy. Don't forget that you can use spicy mesquite chips or peat for that sharp creosote character found in some Scotch whiskies.

Di-vine Intervention: Growing Hops

Although only a minority of homebrewers grow hops, hop-growing certainly does have its advocates.

Homebrewers not only benefit from the bounty of the commercial hop-processing trade, but they can also now take advantage of the much smaller but equally satisfying glut of hop rhizomes. (A *rhizome* is a root cutting — the easiest way to start a new hop plant.) You can purchase hop rhizomes through many homebrew suppliers, although they're usually available only very early in the growing season. (That's late Fe*brew*ary through early April, of course.)

Here we grow!

You can successfully grow hops just about anywhere between the 40th and 50th parallels north and south of the equator. As long as the hops receive plenty of moisture and ample sunlight, they can thrive.

You need to plant the rhizomes at least a couple weeks after the winter thaw, in a hole about 6 inches deep (and similar in diameter) within a small mound of dirt. Cover the root cutting with loamy soil and pack tightly. Make sure that the location of the plant drains well because molds are quick to attack hop leaves. If you plant two or more hop varieties, space them at 2-yard intervals. (That's 3-foot spaces, not your neighbors' yards.) Because hops are climbing vines, you need to rig up a trellis or a network of stakes and twine that fans out from each hop plant. (Locate the stake close to the hop root.) Any rig lower than 8 feet high is hardly worth the effort, because hops can easily grow to greater than 20 feet high. (This lofty stature can present a challenge to the homebrewer at harvest time.)

As the hop shoots begin to emerge in late March or early April, clip all but the four healthiest bines. (For some odd reason, hop vines are called *bines.* Why? Who knows? Maybe the brewer who named them had too much of his own brew or was a lousy speller.) This clipping concentrates the plant's energies. As they grow upward on their own, they start to droop under their own weight — this point is when you need to train them on the twine. Wrap the plants loosely around the twine in a clockwise direction, coming up the twine (unless you live in the Southern Hemisphere, in which case you want to train them in a counterclockwise direction coming up). This positioning is important because the bines follow the sun from east to west every day as they grow. During peak growing season, healthy hop plants can grow as much as a foot each day.

TIP

To ensure a good, healthy plant and an abundant harvest, I always treat my hop plants to a biweekly application of water-soluble, all-purpose plant food for the first couple of weeks of the growing season.

Pick a hop, any hop

Harvest season begins sometime in August and may continue into October, depending on climatic conditions. As the hop flowers grow in size, sporadically check the development of the *lupulin glands.* You can find these glands by gently pulling the soft, leafy petals back against the stem; the yellow lupulin glands are at the base of each petal near the stem. As the season wears on, the hop flowers puff up slightly and the lupulin glands begin to swell. (Of course, how much is a swell if you're talking about something the size of a pinhead?)

WARNING

If the hops begin to burn in the sun or turn brown, you'd best pick them soon. If you allow the hops to deteriorate, you lose the freshness edge of growing your own hops.

Not all the hops mature at the same pace; you need to pick on several different occasions before the season ends. Checking the plant once a week should be fine unless the weather is particularly hot, cool, wet, or dry. If you pick on a regular weekly schedule, you usually have your hop-drying device emptied just in time for the next batch of freshly picked hops.

Drying and storing your hops

Each time you pick some hops, you need to dry them before storing them. Air-drying is fine, but how long this process takes depends on the humidity levels in the air. I usually dry my hops for a week to make sure that they're as dry as possible.

TIP

My hop-drying rig couldn't be any simpler. I use two same-sized window screens held tightly together with long bungee cords. Just spread the hops out evenly across one screen, then place the second screen over the hops and bind them together. If you don't have bungee cords, duct tape does the trick.

The dried hops should feel light and crumbly in your hands; in fact, the individual leaves may fall off the stem easily. Store them in self-sealing zipper-type sandwich bags (in the size of your choice). Attach self-stick labels to each bag, noting the variety (if you grow more than one) and the date you picked the hops. (You can also just mark the bag with a grease pencil.) You may want to weigh each bag, although quantity isn't really important until brewing day. Store all your hops in your freezer to keep them as long as possible.

Building Brewing Equipment

This section explains ways for you to take control of your brewing process by making your own equipment rather than buying it, thus enabling you to take more personal control over your spending processes as well.

Chillin' out: Immersion wort chillers

An *immersion wort chiller* is a very effective piece of equipment that's relatively easy and not incredibly expensive to make yourself (refer to Figure 12-2 earlier in the book). The basic idea behind the immersion wort chiller is to cool down your wort quickly (without subjecting your brew to contamination) so that you can pitch your yeast and start fermentation as soon as possible.

Start with a coil of copper tubing purchased at your local hardware store. This tubing should have a minimum inside diameter of 3/8 inches and be at least 25 feet long. The longer and wider the tubing is, the more effective it is, but I don't recommend exceeding 1/2 inch in diameter or 40 feet in length. (And this extreme size is necessary only for full wort boils — see Chapter 12 for more information on that process.) The circumference of the coil itself should be about two-thirds the diameter of your brewpot, and the coil height should equal the height of your brewpot. (You can fashion the coil's dimensions yourself by simply constricting or expanding the coil by hand.) Along with this tubing, you also need a regular garden hose (with a threaded end you can attach to a faucet) you can cut up into shorter pieces. To make bends in the copper tubing without kinking it, use an inexpensive manual spring-type tubing bender (available at most hardware stores). Make sure that you buy a couple expansion clamps for the hose connections.

By working with only the first and last foot or two of each end of the copper tubing, you leave the majority of the coil intact. With the copper coil standing on end, bend the top end of the tubing straight up from the coil and add a 90-degree outward bend. To this end, attach a section of garden hosing (with the threaded faucet attachment here) and tighten the two sections together by using a clamp. With the coil still standing on end, pull the bottom end of the tubing up through the middle of the coil to the same height as the first end and give it a 90-degree outward bend. To this bottom end, attach another length of garden hose and tighten the two together by using a clamp. Just rinse the chiller off, hook it up to a faucet, and, voilà! You're good to go.

Tuns of fun: Lauter tun

A lauter tun is absolutely necessary for effective sparging of all-grain brews. Making your own is simple. Typically, all you need are two 5-gallon plastic buckets, one of which must have a spigot. If you have a bottling bucket from your beginner homebrewing days, you're halfway home. Buy a second food-grade plastic (HDPE) bucket that fits into your bottling bucket. Using a 1/8-inch drill bit, cover the entire bottom of the second bucket with holes 1/4 inch apart. After you finish, make sure that you remove all plastic burrs inside the bucket and out.

By placing the second bucket inside your bottling bucket, you've got an effective straining system that enables you to draw off the wort through the spigot while the grain is held back (which is the fundamental concept behind the lauter tun); see Figure 30-1. One important consideration in setting up your double-bucket lauter tun: You need to keep the bottoms of the inside and outside buckets less than 2 inches apart. A larger space messes with the flow of wort through the grain bed and may also aerate the hot wort and contribute to oxidation problems down the line.

Another slightly more difficult way of making a larger-capacity lauter tun is by using a plastic cooler — the type people use for picnicking or camping. You can use both the rectangular ice-chest design and the upright circular types. I recommend a 10-gallon minimum capacity. The idea is to build a small manifold out of half-inch copper tubing (with the help of 90-degree elbows and T connectors) that rests on the bottom of the coolers and draws off the wort through the cooler's drain hole.

FIGURE 30-1: Assembling your own lauter tun.

For the rectangular cooler, you must connect and feed a series of four or five long parallel tubes into a short perpendicular tube at the drain end of the cooler. This end tube must then connect to a spigot or stopcock on the outside of the cooler for flow control. For the circular cooler, the best design is the shape of an X, with one leg connecting directly through the drain hole to the stopcock or spigot on the outside of the cooler.

TIP

If you need to seal the opening where the copper tubing exits the cooler, use the silicone caulk you typically use for bathroom applications. The silicone doesn't harm your beer.

For the tubing to drain correctly and channel the wort to the opening in the cooler, you must first slit or cross-cut the copper tubing with a hacksaw. You need to make several cuts about halfway through the tubing (you're not trying to cut pieces off) about every half inch or so apart. You also need to cap the open ends of the tubing so that no grain escapes with the wort. After you complete the slit-cutting, make sure you brush and rinse off any copper burrs. (Try wet-sanding with emery cloth.) Position the manifold tubes in the cooler with the slots facing downward.

TIP

You don't need to solder the parts together; copper fittings are normally snug enough to maintain connections. And by not making the connections permanent, you can more easily disassemble the manifold for cleaning purposes.

Pot o' plenty: Large-volume brewpot

Instead of buying a huge and expensive stock pot from a restaurant supply outlet, do what hundreds of homebrewers do — fashion one out of a real beer keg. This approach works well for several reasons:

- Beer kegs are stainless steel, just like brewpots.
- Buying a used beer keg is much cheaper than buying an equivalent-sized stock pot.
- The most common American beer keg (half-barrel) has a capacity of 15.5 gallons, which is more than enough for a full batch of homebrew. Even 50- and 30-liter European beer kegs are roomy enough.

The beer kegs that work best are the straight-sided Sanke kegs. The advantages to the Sanke keg are that no bung hole is cut in the side of the keg and it has built-in handles at the rim. Because Miller and Anheuser-Busch use these kegs extensively, you should have no difficulty finding them. After you get your hands on one, you need to find someone who does stainless steel welding. (If you're not in the trade, avoid doing the work yourself.) Stainless steel is a very hard metal, requiring specialized saw blades and drill bits. Make sure that someone trained in TIG (*tungsten inert gas*) *welding*, also known as *heliarc welding*, does the work for you; you can't weld stainless steel with regular mild-steel material. Unless you have good connections with people in the trade, you're going to fork over between $25 and $50 an hour for this kind of work. Fortunately, the work you need done doesn't entail much (and it's still cheaper than buying a new brewpot). You need to have your welder saw off and grind down the lid of the keg (at least to the point that it's no longer capable of ripping human flesh), and you want to have him or her attach a spigot near the bottom of the keg.

Cold feat: Lagering cellar

To brew authentic Lager beers, you need the capability to *lager* your beer, which means you need to store it in a cold environment for relatively long periods of time. Not many homebrewers have the means to do this because lagering requires time, space, energy, and money — four things that aren't always in great supply at the amateur level.

If you don't already have one, consider investing in a dedicated beer fridge. Because most refrigerators are designed to keep foods very cool (cooler than a lagering cellar should be), you need to buy one more item that enables the fridge to warm up a bit: an external thermostat. This *fermostat* controls the interior temperature of your beer fridge by shutting the refrigerator off at the temperature you designate. You can purchase this device through most homebrew suppliers and can hook it up in a matter of minutes. Again, effective lagering temperatures should remain fairly constant between 40 and 50° Fahrenheit, depending on the beer style.

Another way to capitalize on this concept is to build an enlarged beer cellar that includes removing the door of a refrigerator and attaching a large wooden box (complete with a utility or access door) in its place. Crafted of heavy plywood sheathing and lined with thick, durable insulating material such as Styrofoam, this box offers a two- or threefold increase in the fridge's capacity with very little increase in electrical usage. How big you make this box depends on your needs and space constraints. Let your imagination run wild!

Cold feat, Part II: Keezer

Similar to the lagering cellar described above, the keezer is getting to be a must-have among brewers who make — and drink — lots of beer at home. Keezers are like having your own draught beer cooler at your disposal, but it's bigger, better, and more functional than your average single-keg, single-tap kegerator.

Keezer is short for *keg freezer* because it starts with a chest freezer that is configured to keep multiple kegs of homebrew ready to pour and enjoy. Although the primary purpose of building a keezer is to have your finished beer on tap for your quaffing convenience, keezers can also function as a thermostatically-controlled lagering cellar for your carboys and miscellaneous fermentation vessels.

Do a Google search on "images of keezers" and you'll see there are as many different ways to trick out a keezer as there are people brewing their own beer at home. That's one of the beauties of making a keezer; you can personalize it in dozens of different ways. But to explain the entire freezer-to-keezer conversion process is far beyond the mission of this chapter. Suffice to say that there are many websites dedicated to explaining the step-by-step conversion process, as well as online homebrew equipment suppliers that sell conversion kits that include all the various taps, shanks, hoses, drip trays, thermostats, gas manifolds, and regulators needed to get the job done.

You don't want to be the last one on your block to have one.

Chapter 31

Ten (or So) Gizmos That Can Make Your Brewing Better and Easier

In the ever-expanding world of homebrewing, hundreds — perhaps thousands — of people are trying to build a better mousetrap (although what good a mousetrap is to a homebrewer, I may never know). Someone is always coming up with new and better ways to make beer at home. Tremendous changes have taken place in the almost three decades I've been brewing my own beer, and, undoubtedly, more fascinating and time-saving inventions are sure to appear in the future.

This chapter gives you an idea of the types of items available to make your brewing easier and more convenient. These gadgets aren't absolutely necessary for making good beer, and a few of them can put a real dent in your pocketbook. Whether you decide to buy them is just a question of how far you want to go with your hobby. You can purchase most — if not all — of these thingies through your favorite homebrew supplier.

Digital Thermometer and pH Meter

If you're practicing mashing techniques, you're already well aware of the need for thermometers and pH testing papers. Investing in digital equipment just makes the job a little bit easier and a lot more accurate. An appropriate digital thermometer costs anywhere between $15 and $40, and the pH meter will set you back $50 to $100.

Wort Aeration System

This system is a very effective way of aerating your wort to create a better environment for yeast respiration cycles. A pump sends ordinary air through a sterile filter and delivers it to the beer by way of a *beer stone* that diffuses oxygen into the beer. (This device isn't unlike the aerators that fish tanks use.) You can also find fully contained wort aeration systems that include a small canister of 99.9 percent pure compressed oxygen and an easy-to-sanitize stainless-steel diffusion stone. A wort aeration system will run you $40 to $70.

Auto Siphon

A couple of different kinds of auto siphons are available, but they mostly vary only by length and diameter. These gizmos help eliminate the risk of contamination and start siphon flows quickly and easily during racking and bottling procedures. You can expect to pay somewhere between $13 and $30 for an auto siphon.

Counterpressure Bottle Filler

This device allows homebrewers who keg their beer to transfer the beer into glass bottles without losing the beer's carbonation. This capability is important to kegging brewers who want to send bottles of their beer to competitions or to those who filter their homebrew. (See the following section for more information on the beer filter.) The bottle filler itself will cost you $70 to $100, but remember that it also requires a CO_2 system (tanks, gauges, hoses, fittings), which will increase your total cost. See Chapter 14 for more information on bottling; check out Chapter 29 for more on entering homebrew competitions.

Beer Filter

Beer filters do exactly what they say they do: They remove yeast and particulate matter, creating a clearer beer. To filter homebrew, however, you must force the liquid through the filter under pressure, which requires a CO_2 system and a minimum of two pressure vessels such as soda kegs. If you filter all the yeast from the beer, however, bottle-priming by using corn sugar is no longer an option, and you may need to artificially carbonate your beer. Homebrewers have a choice between the *plate* type of filter (about $50) and the *cartridge* type ($70). I vote for the more-convenient cartridge type. Remember that because this gadget requires a CO_2 system, the cost of whichever option you choose will go up. See Chapter 14 for more on bottling.

Germicidal Lamp

This hand-held germ eliminator is portable and battery-powered, and it can kill 99.9 percent of surface bacteria with a 10-second exposure. It's great for use as a dry sanitizer for all kinds of brewing and non-brewing equipment and will set you back $25 to $30.

Wort Transfer Pump

These electrical/mechanical devices take racking to a whole new level by eliminating the need to siphon. These pumps can be magnetic, diaphragm, or peristaltic, but they all do the same thing: make your life easier. Making your life richer may be another story: You'll need to plunk down $130 to $200+ for one of these babies. ***Note:*** Like all electrical devices used with or near liquids, always plug these pumps into a GFI- (ground fault interrupter) protected outlet.

Refractometer

Using a refractometer is the quick and easy way to measure the sugar content of any liquid such as unfermented wort (beer) or must (mead or wine). To convert degrees Brix (the refractometer's measuring scale) to specific gravity, multiply the Brix reading by .004 and add a whole number 1 (example: a Brix reading of 10 equals 1.040). Expect to pay between $50 and $160 for a refractometer.

Mashing Sparge Arm

This self-powered rotating sparge arm produces an evenly distributed, rainlike spray that doesn't bore holes in the mash. This sparger is made of brass and comes complete with a handy holding bracket. It's available in various diameters to fit various sparging vessels and costs between $35 and $150.

Counter-flow Wort Chiller

At first glance, you may think that this piece of equipment is redundant. Unlike the immersion-type wort chiller mentioned in Chapter 2, however, the *counter-flow* wort chiller is a quicker and more efficient means of cooling hot wort. Cold water in an outer hose flows in an opposite direction from the hot wort flowing within the inner copper tubing. This product runs anywhere from $80 to $300.

Stir Plate

As mentioned in the previous chapter, some brewers like to harvest and bank their own yeast strains to use in future brews (and save some money doing so). One item in particular that would be of value to these yeast ranchers is a quality *stir plate*. A stir plate is a motorized thingy that allows you to stir your yeast while keeping everything sanitary; it's done with the magic of magnetism.

Stir plates utilize magnetic attraction to create a vortex inside a container of wort — typically a flask, keeping the yeast in suspension and providing oxygen — which are both crucial to healthy yeast cell growth and replication. You can find a wide variety of these in the market, running anywhere from about $50 to $150, depending on their size and quality.

Hop Spider

The hop spider is a stainless steel mesh hop filter that hangs from the rim of your brew kettle. You can toss all your kettle hops directly into the hop spider without having to worry about whirlpooling or straining your hot wort in order to remove the organic hop remains. These can be found in different sizes with different price tags, from $16 to $40.

Tilt Hydrometer

One of the coolest things now available to the homebrewer is the Tilt hydrometer. This free-floating gizmo is a dual-purpose hydrometer and thermometer that works with Bluetooth technology. It allows you continuous real-time monitoring of your brew on your smartphone or device. Using the Tilt hydrometer means you never have to open your fermenter to measure your beer's gravity or temperature again.

But wait — there's more! You can even monitor multiple batches of beer by using Tilt hydrometers of different colors (each color has its own digital code). Coolness has a price, though; expect to fork over about $130 for each Tilt hydrometer you buy.

BREWING SOFTWARE

Nineteenth-century brewing and twenty-first-century technology are on a collision course. The result? Computer software and phone apps for homebrewers.

At the risk of sounding like a brewing bumpkin, not only do I not own brewing software, I probably wouldn't know what to do with it if I had it. I'd been formulating my own beer recipes (some of which I include in Part 5 of this book) for several years prior to the introduction of brewing software. I didn't need it then, and I don't need it now. You, however, may find it all very fascinating and useful.

Because this material represents a stretch of the technological turnpike that I don't travel, here's a passing glance at some of the many brewing software choices and phone apps that exist out there. These come with a wide variety of tools, charts, calculators and other elements important to planning your brewing recipes, as well as a wide variety of pricing. Time to do your homework.

- **Pro Mash:** `http://promash.com/`
- **BrewWizard:** `https://www.brew-wizard.com/`
- **BeerSmith 2:** `http://beersmith.com`
- **Brewers Friend:** `http://www.brewersfriend.com/`

(continued)

(continued)

- **BrewFather:** https://brewfather.app/?via=karl
- **BrewTarget:** http://www.brewtarget.org/
- **Brew Toad:** https://www.brewtoad.com/
- **Mr. Malty:** https://www.mrmalty.com/calc/calc.html
- **BrewPal:** http://www.djpsoftware.com/brewpal/
- **Beer Tools Pro:** https://www.beertools.com/
- **Beer Alchemy:** https://www.beeralchemyapp.com/
- **Brew Guru:** https://www.homebrewersassociation.org/brew-guru/

Chapter 32

Just the FAQs: Ten (or So) Frequently Asked Questions

People unfamiliar with the art and craft of homebrewing always seem to have the same questions. Here's a sampling of their oft-repeated queries, along with my answers to them.

How Much Is Taking Up Homebrewing Going to Cost?

At the beginner level, the minimum amount of equipment you need to brew beer correctly is going to run you in the vicinity of $100. This setup is relatively bare-bones in nature, but it's enough to get you up and running. Eventually, you want to acquire more and better equipment as you become more familiar and comfortable with the processes and procedures. (I know some homebrewers who've spent in excess of $1,000 on their home breweries.) You can comfortably get in the game for under $200.

How Much Does the Average Batch of Beer Cost?

The typical batch of homebrewed beer is 5 gallons, or 53.3 12-ounce bottles of beer. At the beginner level, the ingredients for a typical batch of malt extract-based beer run about $35 for a relatively simple pale ale, and up to $70 for a well-hopped, higher-alcohol-content beer style. The amount you actually pay fluctuates because of many factors, including where you shop for your ingredients (don't forget shipping charges for mail order), whether you buy top- or bottom-of-the-line ingredients, and the style of beer you like to brew. Big-bodied, alcoholic beers require more fermentable ingredients than do light-bodied, watery beers. (Barley wines can cost as much as 100 percent more to make than pale ales.)

And because extract brewers pay a premium for the convenience of using processed malt syrups, efficient all-grain brewers can produce beer more cheaply.

Where Can I Buy Homebrewing Supplies?

Local brick-and-mortar homebrew supply shops, unfortunately, are not as commonplace as they once were. But you may have heard of this little thing called the Internet? I understand quite a few online sites out there are just waiting for you to click and order your supplies A simple Google search on "Homebrew Supplies" should get you pointed in the right direction.

How Long Does Making a Batch of Homebrew Take?

At the beginner level, the actual hands-on part of the brewing process takes only about two hours, including setup and cleanup. On the day you bottle your beer, schedule at least three hours, including setup and cleanup.

At the extreme short end of the process, you can conceivably drink your beer within three weeks of brewing it, but most experienced homebrewers like their beers to age and mellow for as long as four to six weeks. Initial fermentation needs to last at least five to seven days. A maturation period in the fermenter lasts at least a week, maybe two. After you bottle, can, or keg your beer, you want to set aside another two weeks for the beer to carbonate and clarify correctly.

But don't be lulled into a false sense of instant gratification, some beers can take considerably longer depending on their style and strength.

Is Homebrewed Beer Better Than Commercially Made Beer?

Is it automatically better? No. Is it generally better? Not necessarily. Does the potential exist to make homebrew that's better than commercially made beer? Very emphatically, YES! It's been my experience that homebrewers have the ability to make some of the best beer in the world, if they're committed enough to try. I know because I've made some great beers and I've had the pleasure of tasting many truly outstanding world-class beers at homebrewing competitions (one of the perks of being a beer judge).

How Do You Carbonate Homebrew?

One of the natural functions of yeasts during fermentation is to produce carbon dioxide. After the initial phase of fermentation is complete, you can prime your beer by using a small (but exact) measure of highly fermentable sugar as you bottle or can it. The yeast cells that remain in the solution feed on these sugars and create the appropriate level of CO_2 carbonation within the sealed bottle or can. Check out Chapter 14 for more bottling information.

If you keg your beer (see Chapter 16), you can "force-carbonate" your beer in as little as 24 to 48 hours.

How Do I Add Alcohol to Homebrew?

You don't need to add alcohol to homebrew because the yeast naturally produces the alcohol during fermentation. Yeast cells feed on the natural malt sugars in the liquid, producing ethyl alcohol and carbon dioxide in return.

Can I Distill Homebrew into Whiskey?

Yes and no. Yes, distilling homebrew is technically feasible, but no, distilling any alcoholic beverage in a private residence is not at all legal in the United States — anytime or anywhere (unless, of course, you've registered your still with the appropriate governmental agencies).

Can I Sell Homebrew?

Not legally (in the United States). Attempting to sell an untaxed, unregulated alcoholic beverage is a violation of several state and federal laws — just ask Al Capone. Unless you want the FBI knocking on your door, I don't recommend it.

Why Shouldn't I Age Beer in the Plastic Primary Fermenter?

You have two good reasons not to age beer in a plastic primary fermenter. First, the beer would sit on all the yeast sediment and protein fallout from the fermented beer and would eventually pick up off flavors. Second, even HDPE (high-density polyethylene) food-grade plastic is permeable by oxygen molecules over a long period of time; glass and stainless steel, however, are completely impermeable.

Do I Have to Worry About Things Blowing Up in My House?

Tales of explosions while homebrewing are mostly old wives' tales. Any explosions that may occur while making beer at home are usually nothing more than excess carbon dioxide being vented from enclosed vessels such as fermenters, carboys, and bottles. The worst thing about these eruptions is the mess they leave for you to clean up.

Can I Turn My Homebrewing Hobby into a Business?

Absolutely! Just ask the hundreds (thousands?) of homebrewers who turned their passion into profit. Some of the best and most popular craft breweries in the industry today started out as a homebrewer's dream. Just remember that being successful is about much more than just making good beer. Blood, sweat, and tears (and money) are just as integral to the business as grain, hops, yeast, and water.

Index

A

B

C

D

E

F

G

H

M

N

O

P

Q

R

S

T

U

V

W

Y

Z

About the Author

Marty Nachel began brewing beer at home in 1985, shortly after finding out it was legal to do so. But once he got into the hobby he made up for lost time.

In the ensuing years, he also found other related hobbies, like beer judging, beer writing, and educating others about beer.

He became a beer judge through the Beer Judge Certification starting in 1986, and is still an active judge 37 years later. It's hard not to be when you're invited to participate in competitions as grand and prestigious as the Great American Beer Festival, World Beer Cup, Festival of Barrel Aged Beers, Copa Cervezas de America in South America, and African Beer Cup.

Marty started freelance writing in 1987 with an article published in *All About Beer* magazine. Scores of newsletters and articles later, he wrote his first book, *Beer Across America*, closely followed by his second book *Beer For Dummies* (now in its 2nd edition). Articles penned by Marty still occasionally appear in various print and online publications.

As a beer educator, Marty has always felt strongly about sharing the knowledge and experience he has gained throughout the years. He has been a freelance educator for several years, teaching about beer and brewing at local bars and breweries. When College of DuPage (Glen Ellyn, Illinois) was about to launch its Business of Craft Beer certificate program, Marty was invited to join the advisory board for the program to help create the curriculum, and he was later tapped to teach the prerequisite courses that led into the dual tracks in the program.

When time allows, Marty and his wife, Patti, plan their vacations to include brewery tours, which now number over 500 on four continents.

Dedication

Were it not for my wife, Patti, and the 47 years she has dedicated to her career, I would not know the pleasure of writing about beer for a living. Nor would I know the enjoyment of brewing beer at home without her forbearance (it helps that she enjoys my beer, too).

Though she and our two children reaped secondary benefits from our professional/domestic arrangement, no one has benefitted more from it than I. Thank you, Dear, from the bottom of my pint glass.

Author's Acknowledgments

My sincere thanks to all the people at John Wiley & Sons for creating this unique opportunity. I would especially like to thank acquisitions editors Zoe Slaughter and Audrey Lee for their part in making this all happen, as well as for giving me the proper focus throughout this project. A big thanks also to our editorial program coordinator Erin Calligan Mooney who helped re-secure all of the permissions for the recipes that appear in this book. Finally, heartfelt thanks to the composition services crew for all their behind-the-scenes help and effort. I owe you all a round of my best brew!

Most importantly, I would like to thank Christopher Morris, who served as both copy editor and project editor for this book. His diligence, focus, and incredible attention to detail created a comfortable and confident working relationship that made the writing and editing of this book much easier and more enjoyable.

Once again, I would like to thank my agent and book producer Steve Ettlinger for his boundless energy and enthusiasm while working on *Beer For Dummies*, a project which subsequently paved the way for this book. I am indebted to him for his vision, guidance, professionalism, and infinite good humor.

A huge thank you to Ed Bove, the "Education Czar" for the Brewers Of South Suburbia, who was instrumental in helping me brainstorm topics for an all-new, updated table of contents for *HFD3e*. Eternal gratitude and respect to Steve Kamp and Dick Van Dyke, my co-founders of the Brewers Of South Suburbia, who have now supported and guided B.O.S.S. for over 30 years.

Thanks again to Mike Pezan, a dedicated homebrewer who turned professional brewer. His technical know-how pumped life into the advanced chapters of this book and his sense of humor helped infuse these otherwise dry subjects with much needed levity.

Speaking of technical know-how, many thanks to Dr. Joe Formanek, our technical editor. Dr. Formanek (also known as "Dr. Longshot" for winning that Sam Adams-sponsored competition) is well respected in homebrewing circles, especially in the Midwest, where he continues to win scores of awards for his incredibly tasty homebrew. One of Joe's award-winning beer recipes can be found in the recipe section of this book.

Thanks also to Scott Pointon, Steve Thanos, Doug Merlo, David Leeds, and Erick Martell, who graciously responded to my call for some last-minute beer recipes — I think you'll really like the award-winning brews they provided.

Too numerous to mention by name are the many gifted homebrewers in the Chicago Beer Society, the Urban Knaves of Grain, and the Brewers Of South Suburbia (B.O.S.S.), whose talents inspired me to take up homebrewing in the first place and who continue to impress me with their brews even more every year. Through this book, may their enthusiasm infect you all . . .

Publisher's Acknowledgments

Acquisitions Editor: Audrey Lee
Project Editor: Christopher Morris
Copy Editor: Christopher Morris
Technical Editor: Joe Formanek
Production Editor: Mohammed Zafar Ali
Cover Image: © Ana Maria Serrano/Getty Images